# Tough Times in Rough Places

# TOUGH TIMES IN ROUGH PLACES

*Personal Narratives of*
*Adventure, Death and Survival*
*on the Western Frontier*

Edited by

## Neil B. Carmony and
## David E. Brown

THE UNIVERSITY OF UTAH PRESS

*Salt Lake City*

Printed on acid-free paper

06 05 04 03 02 01
5 4 3 2 1

ISBN 0-87480-700-X

# TABLE OF CONTENTS

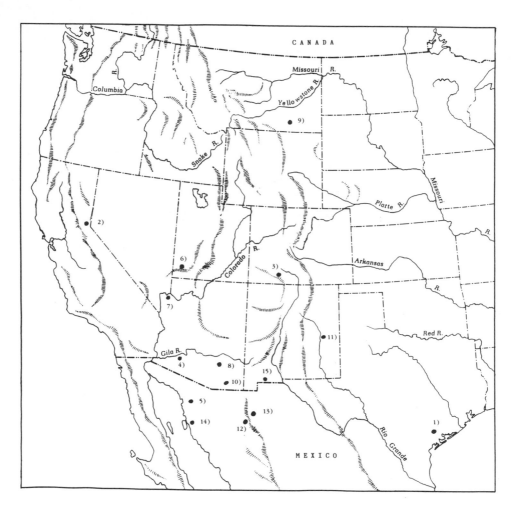

## "Tough Times in Rough Places"

| | | | | |
|---|---|---|---|---|
| 1. Duval | 4. Oatman | 7. White | 10. Earp | 13. Naegle |
| 2. Murphy | 5. Evans | 8. Oury | 11. Garrett | 14. Hoffman |
| 3. McGehee | 6. Lee | 9. Godfrey | 12. Maus | 15. Tompkins |

# INTRODUCTION

**No aspect of American history has so fired our imagination** as has the "winning" of the West. The exploration of a vast, rugged new country, the battles with wild animals and hostile people, and the land's eventual settlement by risk-taking pioneers are the stuff of lore and legend. And while any personal memory of the American frontier has long been quieted, its heros and villains continue to act out their adventures and morality plays in countless magazines, books, films, and television programs. Not surprisingly, most of these accounts involve human suffering and death and record how some exceptional individuals survived disaster at the hands of man and nature. Stories of the more notorious happenings are told and retold; details surrounding the most often told episodes are examined and re-examined. We never, it seems, get enough. Such events are, after all, our heritage.

Prowling around a now subdued West, we occassionally come upon an historical marker commemorating the site of some memorable incident. Some of these memorials, such as Custer National Battlefield, cover hundreds of acres and are visited by thousands of tourists; others, like the site of the attack on the Oatman family, are marked only by a forlorn cairn of rocks or a bronze plaque. Still others, such as the site of Old Camp Grant in Arizona, have only an old, greening cartridge case to remind us that something special happened there. Almost never does the visitor learn the full story, the true story, of what occurred and why. What information is gleaned is left to someone's vaguely remembered page in a history book and subsequent speculation around the campfire.

Curious to know more about some of the most discussed events, we have searched the written record in an attempt to find the people who participated in them. Thus it was that we came upon a number of firsthand accounts by the participants. Their stories not only tell what happened, but often give valuable insights into how and why such a tragedy occurred. Moreover, we found that some of these stories are remarkably well told, with an immediacy and authenticity that only a participant can pass along. Not a few of them communicate a horror that fiction could never conceive. Truth, after all, is almost always more powerful than what we can imagine.

To share our discoveries, we have gathered together fifteen renditions of some of the West's most gripping episodes for retelling in one volume. Not mere history lessons, each account is a harrowing adventure experienced by someone who was there. The tale-bearers run the full gamut of Western players -- mountainmen, soldiers of fortune, cavalry officers, immigrants, frontier women, prospectors, Mormon pioneers, and lawmen -- adventurers all. Many of the incidents are well known and involve famous names -- the Donner

Party, Geronimo, Old Bill Williams, John C. Frémont, General George Custer, Billy the Kid, Wyatt Earp and Pancho Villa. Other events and characters are more obscure -- the Crabb massacre, the odyessy of James White, the saga of Hyrum Naegle, and the desert ordeal of Jack Hoffman. All we believe depict the West as it really was, with elements of adventure and romance linked inevitably with the physical toughness and rough, harsh living inherent in frontier life. All, we think you will agree, are compelling reading.

The time frame of these adventures parallels the beginning and end of the Western frontier -- the period from 1835 until World War I. Locations stretch from Texas to California, and range from Montana southward to the Mexican border states of Sonora and Chihuahua. Adversaries include freezing ice and snow, heat and thirst, wild rivers, grizzly bears, vengeful armies, warring Indians, hate-filled mobs, religous zealots, and desperados. Some of the stories are uplifting, illustrating the resilience and ingenuity of the human spirit; others are decidedly sad, depressing, even horrific, showing how cruel and depraved mankind can be, with or without the veneer of civilization. Of such stuff is the West's mythology made.

We have kept our editorial commentary to a minimum. A headnote to each account introduces the players and sets the scene. Where appropriate, we have clarified particular points in the narrative, and told the reader what happened afterward. No attempt is made to dissect the particulars of the teller's story, or to present a detailed historical analysis. Nor do we make a moral judgement as to who was right and who was wrong. That the reader can determine for him- or herself.

A word of caution. Because these are personal observations, not all aspects of the events are covered. The teller, after all, can only speak to what he or she experienced. That the participant was emotionally involved, and not totally objective, is also a given. Some of the accounts, while honestly told, are undoubtedly self-serving. No one is going to purposely place his kin in a bad light or heap blame upon himself. Also, some of these accounts were originally published years after the event, and time may have colored the writer's memory or opinion.

Neill B. Carmony
David E. Brown

2

# EAST OF THE ALAMO: MASSACRE AT GOLIAD
## (1835-36)

## John C. Duval

**Editors' Note:** The great state of Texas honors many heroic figures from its past, including savvy Indian fighters, intrepid lawmen, and pioneer cattle barons. But the most beloved Lone Star heroes are those men and women who organized and defended the Texas Republic in the war for independence from Mexico. Stephen F. Austin and Sam Houston have large cities named after them, and a special reverence is bestowed upon those men who fought to the death during the seige of the Alamo at San Antonio.

When a general revolt against Mexican rule by American settlers broke out in the autumn of 1835, the few Mexican troops stationed in Texas found themselves outnumbered and outgunned. To crush the insurrection and punish its instigators, Mexican president and dictator, General Antonio López de Santa Anna, marched north from Mexico City with a force of 5,000 troops. Crossing the Rio Grande near Laredo on February 16, 1836, Santa Anna proceeded on to San Antonio where the rebellious Texans took refuge in the Alamo, an old mission building and compound, which they converted into a make-shift fort. On March 6, after unsuccessfully negotiating for the Texans' surrender, the Alamo was taken by storm. Although a few women and children were spared, all 182 of the male defenders were killed, including the Alamo's commander, Colonel William Travis, and frontiersmen Jim Bowie and Davy Crockett. The Mexican losses were enormous -- more than 1,000 killed.

What is less well known is that, a few days later, a brigade of 400 Americans under the command of Colonel James Fannin found themselves in a similar predicament near the town of Goliad, about ninety miles southeast of San Antonio. Here the volunteers were surrounded by a force of 1,400 Mexican troops under General José Urrea, who had crossed into Texas from Matamoros while Santa Anna was engaged at the Alamo. Seeing the hopelessness of their position, Fannin surrendered his command of mostly green troops on March 20, 1836. After spending a week under guard in Goliad, the prisoners were marched out of town on Palm Sunday and ruthlessly massacred by Urrea's soldiers. Only about thirty of Fannin's men managed to escape the slaughter.

One of those who did escape during the confusion of the killing was twenty-year-old John C. Duval from Bardstown, Kentucky. Caught up in the fervor for Texas independence, John's older brother, Burr, had organized a company of Kentucky volunteers to aid the Texans in their quest. Upon their arrival on the Texas coast the company was assigned to serve in Fannin's brigade. Like most of his comrades, Burr Duval was killed at Goliad, leaving his brother to tell the chilling tale of the volunteers' fate.

5

After his miraculous escape, John Duval returned to the United States. In the 1840's, however, he went back to Texas and lived there until his death in 1897. He served for a brief time in the Texas Rangers and became a good friend of the legendary ranger known as Bigfoot Wallace, eventually writing a book about him, the *Adventures of Bigfoot Wallace*. Duval first published the story of his Goliad massacre experiences in the 1860's in a series of articles in *Burke's Weekly* magazine. These articles, along with other stories written by Duval, were later collected and published in book form in 1892 under the title *Early Times in Texas*. "East of the Alamo" is extracted from that book.

The Texans had their revenge. A month after the Goliad massacre, a force of 800 outraged *Tejanos* led by Sam Houston surprised Santa Anna and 1,300 troops on the Plain of San Jacinto near present-day Houston. Within minutes the Mexican soldiers were routed, the vengeful Texans hot on their heels yelling "Remember the Alamo!" and "Remember Goliad!" Roughly half of the Mexicans were killed, the others captured. Santa Anna himself was taken prisoner. Totally demoralized by the capture of their leader, the remaining Mexican troops in Texas retreated south across the Rio Grande, leaving Texas as an independent republic until 1845 when it joined the United States. After his defeat at San Jacinto, Santa Anna spent several months in custody. He was then allowed to return to Mexico after promising to never again make war on Texas.

~ ~ ~ ~ ~

**In 1835 the people of Texas,** or rather the settlers from the "States," determined to throw off the Mexican yoke, and resist to the last extremity any further encroachment upon their liberties. At that time, with the exception of Mexicans and Indians, there was probably not more than twenty thousand people in the colonies, and although the Mexican government for several years previously had shown a disposition to ignore the rights and privileges guaranteed them under the Constitution of 1824, I hardly think the colonists with their limited means and numbers would have ventured to rebel against its authority, if they had not counted largely on getting all the aid they should need to carry out the revolution successfully, from their friends and brethren in the United States. In this expectation they were not disappointed. Many young men, from almost every state in the Union, armed and equipped at their own expense, hastened to the assistance of the colonists, as soon as the standard of rebellion was raised.

A volunteer company was organized for this purpose in my native village, and although I was scarcely old enough to bear arms, I resolved to join it. But it was no aspiration for "military fame" that induced me to do so. One of the frequent visitors at my father's house was an old friend of his, who had been in Texas and traveled over a considerable portion of it, and who subsequently held a position in the cabinet of the first president. He was enthusiastic in his praise of the country, and insensibly an ardent longing sprang up in my bosom to see for myself the "broad prairies," the beautiful streams and vast herds of buffalo and wild horses of which he had so often given me glowing descriptions. By joining this company I thought an opportunity would be afforded me of gratifying it which perhaps might never again offer itself, and so, in spite of the opposition of relatives and friends, my name was added to the muster roll.

I purchased a good Kentucky rifle (with the use of which I was already well acquainted), shot pouch, powder horn, tomahawk, and butcher knife, and thus equipped, with my knapsack on my shoulders, I fell into ranks, and amid the waving of handerchiefs and the cheering of bystanders I bid adieu to my native village and started for the "promised land" of Texas.

It was the latter part of November [1835] when we left [Bardstown, Kentucky] and though not very cold, the snow was some three or four inches deep on the ground, which retarded our march so much that we only made about twenty miles by sunset, when we halted for the night in a grove near the margin of a stream that empties into the famous "Salt River." We cleared away the snow from under the trees, built up log heaps for fires, and after eating our supper of hot coffee, hard tack and fried middling, for which our tramp had given us excellent appetites, we spread our blankets upon the fallen leaves and turned in for the night.

The next morning we were on the road by sunrise, and about dusk, after a toilsome and fatiguing march through the slush and mud (for a thaw had set in), we reached the city of Louisville and took up our quarters at the Galt House. The next day we purchased a supply of provisions -- enough to last us for the voyage -- and went on board of a steamer bound for New Orleans.

The fifth day, we reached New Orleans, fortunately just in time to secure a passage on a schooner that was to sail the next day for Velasco, a small port at the mouth of the Brazos River.

In the evening we embarked with all our goods and chattels on the schooner, and having made fast to a tow-boat, in company with two ships and a bark, we were soon under way, and bade farewell to the "Crescent City," and its forests of masts and tapering spires quickly faded away in the distance.

The Mississippi empties into the gulf by three mouths and about 10 o'clock the day after we had left New Orleans, we entered the one called the "Southwest Pass," and an hour or so afterwards we had crossed the "bar" and were rolling and tossing upon the blue waves of the gulf of Mexico. The line was cast off from the tow-boat, sails hoisted and soon we were scudding along before a fair wind in the direction of the distant shores of Texas. For a long way out we noticed that the blue waters of the gulf refused to "fraternize" with the vast muddy stream continually pouring in from the mouths of the Mississippi.

In a few hours we lost sight of the low shores of Louisiana, and nothing was to be seen but the sky and the apparently interminable waste of blue water. Our schooner was a small one, and with more than fifty passengers on board, it can easily be imagined we were packed rather too closely together for comfort. For my share of the sleeping accomodations, I appropriated a large coil of chain cable, in the hollow of which by doubling up after the fashion of a jack knife, I managed to snooze pretty comfortably at night.

On the morning of the seventh day after leaving Southwest Pass, the shores of Texas were dimly descernible from the masthead, looking like a long low cloud on the western horizon.

The country in the immediate vicinity of Velasco [Texas] is low, and back of it a dead level prairie extended as far as the eye could reach; consequently I must confess I was not much pleased with the first view of the "promised land." Velasco was a miserable little village consisting of two stores and a hotel, so called, and five or six grog shops, dignified with the name of "saloons." Opposite to it, on the south bank of the river was the rival city of Quintana, containing about the same number of shanties and a mixed population of Yankees, Mexicans and Indians.

We landed upon the Quintana side and pitched our camp upon the beach, adjoining the camps of several other companies that had arrived a few days previously. Here we remained two weeks or more, and as we were liberally supplied with rations by the patriotic firm of McKinney and Williams, and game and fish were to be had in abundance, we "fared sumptuously" every day. In hunting and fishing, making tents, cleaning our guns, and preparing in other ways for our anticipated campaign, our time passed pleasantly enough.

Whilst at this place our company was formally mustered into service of the embryo Republic of Texas. It was left optional with us to enlist for twelve months or for "during the war," and we unanimously chose the latter upon the principle of "in for a penny, in for a pound," or as Davy Crockett would have said, we resolved to "go the whole hog or none."

One day whilst we were encamped at Quintana we had quite an exciting scene, which bade fair for a time to initiate us into the realities of actual warfare. Two vessels were seen in the offing, one of them evidently in hot pursuit of the other. As soon as they had approached near enough to be distinctly seen through a glass, it was asserted by several who claimed to know, that the smaller vessel was the Invincible, a schooner recently purchased by Texas, and the larger one in pursuit was the Bravo, a noted Mexican privateer. In this opinion we were confirmed, as a sharp cannonading began between the two vessels. Our company was at once ordered on board of a small steamer lying in the mouth of the Brazos, with instructions to hasten to the assistance of the Invincible with as little delay as possible. We quickly got up steam, and notwithstanding the violence of the breakers on the bar, which on two occasions broke entirely over our little steamer, we were soon alongside the foremost vessel, which proved to be as we had supposed, the Texas schooner, Invincible. By this time the other vessel had approached near enough to be recognized as the Brutus, lately purchased also for the Texas navy, and after the interchange of some signals the firing ceased. Each vessel, it seems, had mistaken the other for the Bravo, and hence the pursuit of the Brutus, and the attempt of the Invincible to escape, as she had only a sailing crew on board; and we were compelled to return to camp without having had an opportunity of "fleshing our maiden swords."

A few days afterwards, our company was ordered to take up our quarters on board the Invincible, to serve as a kind of marine corps for her protection until a regular crew could be enlisted. Whilst on board of her, in the hope of meeting the Bravo, we took a cruise along the coast as far as the east end of Galveston Island.

After an unsuccessful cruise in search of the Bravo, we returned to Quintana, and pitched our tents again upon our old camping ground.

A day or so after our return to Quintana, the officer in command of the Invincible was instructed to take our company on board and to sail immediately for Copano, on Aransas Bay, where we were to disembark and march from thence to Goliad. It was rumored that a considerable force had already been concentrated at that point, under the command of Col. J. W. Fannin, destined for the invasion of the border states of Mexico, and of course we surmised that our company would form a part of the invading army.

We set sail about dark, with a brisk norther springing up, and by daylight the next morning we were in sight of Aransas Pass, which we shortly entered without difficulty, and cast anchor in a secure harbor behind the southwest point of Matagorda Island.

We remained on the island several days, passing the time very pleasantly hunting and fishing, and gathering oysters which were abundant in the bay, and then we embarked on board of a small vessel for Copano, which at that time was the principal port of South Texas. In a few hours we reached the port, and landing, we pitched our tents on the bluff just back of it. Here we found a company of Texas Rangers who had been on the frontier service for six months, during all of which time they had not seen a morsel of bread. They had subsisted solely upon beef and the game they killed. We gave them a part of the hard tack we had brought with us, and though wormeaten and musty, they devoured it with as keen a relish as if it had been the greatest delicacy.

Although they had had no bread for so long a time, they were healthy and in "good order."

From Copano (which consisted mainly of a warehouse and large tank of fresh water) we took up the line of march for Refugio, distant about twenty miles. It is situated on a little stream called Mission River, near the bank of which we pitched our tents, just before sunset. Refugio at that time contained about two dozen adobe huts (inhabited by a mixed population of Irish and Mexicans), and an old, dilapidated church, built, I was told, the same year that Philadelphia was founded.

The next morning we continued our march for Goliad, about thirty miles distant, but as we got a late start, we only made twenty miles or so by sunset, and pitched our camp near a pool of fresh water, under the shelter of some spreading live oak trees.

Early the next morning we took the road for Goliad again, and in the course of three or four hours we came in sight of the dome of the old Mission. Not long afterwards we entered the town and took up our quarters in an empty stone building near the old church. Here we found about four hundred men under the command of Colonel J. W. Fannin, the force with which it was designed to invade the border states of Mexico.

Goliad, at the time we arrived there, contained a population of about two thousand Mexicans who were *professedly* friendly to the Texans, but who afterwards, when Santa Anna invaded the country, proved to be their most vindictive foes. I must, however, make an exception in favor of the "Senoritas," who generally preferred the blue-eyed, fair complexioned young Saxons to their copper-colored beaux.

Goliad is situated on the south side of the San Antonio River, about forty miles above its mouth, and ninety-five miles below the city of San Antonio.

The lands around the place are rich and productive, and the locality (though we did not find it so) is a healthy one. Thousands of fat beeves roamed the prairies in its vicinity, and as corn could be had in abundance upon the neighboring ranches, we were well supplied with provisions. Besides, when the Texans took possession of the place, several months previous to our arrival, a large amount of sugar and coffee was found in the Mexican commissary department, which, of course, we did not scruple to appropriate to our own use.

In order to render his little force as effective as possible, when the time for action should come, Colonel Fannin ordered daily drills, which were my detestation and from which I invariably absented myself whenever I had a pretext for doing so. I greatly preferred hunting deer in the prairies and attending the "fandangos" or dances that took place daily and nightly in one part of the town or the other.

Not long after our arrival at Goliad the soubriquet of Mustangs or Wild Horses was acquired by our company from the following incident:

M---., our second lieutenant, was a man of great physical powers, but withal one of the most peaceful and most genial men when not under the influence of liquor. But occasionally he would get on a "spree" and then he was as wild as a "March hare" and perfectly uncontrollable. The Mexicans seemed to know him and to fear him, also, and when he was on one of his "benders" they would retreat into their houses as soon as they saw him and shut their doors. This proceeding, of course, was calculated to irritate M---., and he would forthwith kick the door from its hinges. On a certain occasion he battered down the doors of half a dozen houses in one street, and from that time the Mexicans called him the "Mustang" and finally the name was applied to the company.

Some time after our arrival at Goliad, information was obtained from some friendly Mexicans that General Santa Anna was preparing to enter Texas at the head of a large army; consequently all idea of invading Mexico, was abandoned, and we set to work to render the fortifications around the old missions as defensible as possible. We strengthened the walls in many places, built several new bastions on which artillery was placed in such a way as to command all the roads leading into the town.

Every day we were drilled by our officers for three hours in the morning and two in the afternoon, which, as I have said before was a great bore to me, as I would have preferred passing the time in hunting and fishing. We also deepened the trenches around the walls, and dug a ditch from the fort to the river, and covered it with plank and earth, so that we might obtain a supply of water, if besieged, without being exposed to the fire of the enemy. We were well supplied with artillery and ammunition for the same, and also with small arms, and had beef, sugar and coffee enough to last us for two months -- but very little bread.

Some time in February, a Mexican from the Rio Grande arrived at Goliad who informed Col. Fannin that Santa Anna had already or would shortly cross the river into Texas with a large army which would advance in two divisions, one towards Goliad and the other towards the city of San Antonio. Some days afterwards, two or three Texans came in from San Patricio, bringing the news that Capt. Grant and some twenty-five or thirty men stationed at that place, had been surprised by a force of Mexican guerrillas and all of them massacred. About this time also a courier from Refugio came in who stated to Col. Fannin that he had been sent by the people of that place, to ask for a detachment of men to escort them to Goliad, as they were daily expecting an attack from the guerrillas.

In compliance with this request, Col. Fannin sent Capt. King and his company (about thirty-five men) to act as escort for those families who desired to leave. When Capt. King and his men reached Refugio, they were attacked on the outskirts of the town by a large force of

Mexican cavalry, and being hard pressed they retreated into the old mission, a strong stone building, at that time encompassed by walls. There they defended themselves successfully, and kept the Mexicans at bay until their artillery came up, when they opened fire upon it with two field pieces which soon breached the walls, and the place was then taken by storm. Capt. King and some seven or eight of his men (the only survivors of the bloody conflict), were captured and led out to a post oak grove north of town, where they were tied to trees and shot.

About this time a courier arrived bringing a dispatch from Gen. Houston to Col. Fannin, and it was rumored in camp that the purport of this dispatch was "that Col. Fannin should evacuate Goliad and fall back without delay towards the settlements on the Colorado." But as to the truth of this I cannot speak positively. At any rate Col. Fannin showed no disposition to obey the order if he received it -- on the contrary, hearing nothing from Capt. King, although he had sent out three scouts at different times to obtain information of his movements, all of whom were captured and killed, he despatched Maj. Ward with the Georgia Battalion (about one hundred and fifty strong) to his assistance. They were attacked before they reached Refugio by a large force of Mexican cavalry. They made a gallant defense for some time against the vastly superior numbers of the enemy, but at length their ammunition was exhausted and they were compelled to retreat to the timber on the river, where they were surrounded by the Mexican cavalry, and most of them finally captured.

This division of our small force in the face of an enemy so greatly our superior in numbers, was, in my opinion, a fatal error on the part of Col. Fannin.

Hearing nothing either from Capt. King or Major Ward, and satisfied from information obtained by our scouts that a large force of Mexicans was in the vicinity of Goliad, Col. Fannin and his officers held a council of war in which it was determined to evacuate the place and fall back as rapidly as possible towards Victoria on the Guadalupe river. The same day, I believe, or the next after this council of war was held, a courier came in from San Antonio bringing a dispatch, as I was informed, from Col. Travis, to the effect "that he was surrounded in the Alamo by Santa Anna's army, and requesting Col. Fannin to come to his relief without delay."

Rations for five days and as much ammunition as each man could conveniently carry were immediately issued, and our whole force, including a small artillery company with two or three field pieces, started for San Antonio, crossing the river at the ford a half mile or so above town. After crossing the river and marching a short distance on the San Antonio road, a halt was made and our officers held a consultation, the result of which (I suppose) was the conclusion that we could not reach San Antonio in time to be of any assistance to Col.

Travis. At any rate we were marched back to Goliad, recrossing the river at the lower ford.

A few hours after we had got back to our old quarters, a detachment of Mexican cavalry, probably eighty or a hundred strong, showed themselves at a short distance from the fort apparently bantering us to come out and give them a fight. Col. Horton, who had joined us a few days previously with twenty-five mounted men, went out to meet them, but when he charged them they fled precipitately, and we saw them no more that day.

That evening preparations were made to abandon the place; to that end we spiked our heaviest pieces of artillery, buried some in trenches, reserving several field pieces, two or three howitzers and a mortar to take with us on our retreat. We also dismantled the fort as much as possible, burnt the wooden buildings in the immediate vicinity and destroyed all the ammunition and provisions for which we had no means of transportation.

The next morning we bade a final farewell, as we supposed, to Goliad, and marched out on the road to Victoria. We had nine small pieces of ordnance and one mortar, all drawn by oxen as were our baggage wagons. Our whole force comprised about two hundred and fifty men, besides a small company of artillery and twenty-five mounted men under Col. Horton.

We crossed the San Antonio River at the ford below town, and a short distance beyond Menahecila Creek we entered the large prairie extending to the timber on the Coletto, a distance of eight or nine miles. When we had approached within two and a half or three miles of the point where the road we were traveling entered the timber (though it was somewhat nearer to the left) a halt was ordered and the oxen were unyoked from guns and wagons, and turned out to graze. What induced Col. Fannin to halt at this place in the open prairie, I cannot say, for by going two and a half miles further, we would have reached the Coletto Creek, where there was an abundance of water and where we would have had the protection of timber in the event of being attacked. I understood at the time that several of Col. Fannin's officers urged him strongly to continue the march until we reached the creek, as it was certain that a large body of Mexican troops were somewhere in the vicinity; but however this may be, Col. Fannin was not to be turned from his purpose, and the halt was made.

## The Battle of Coletto Creek

At length after a halt of perhaps an hour and a half on the prairie, and just as we were about to resume our march for the Coletto, a long dark line was seen to detach itself from the timber behind us, and

13

another at the same time from the timber to our left. Some one near me exclaimed, "Here come the Mexicans!" and in fact, in a little while, we perceived that these dark lines were men on horseback, moving rapidly towards us. As they continued to approach, they lengthened out their columns, evidently for the purpose of surrounding us, and in doing so displayed their numbers to the greatest advantage. I thought there were at least *ten thousand* (having never before seen a large cavalry force), but in reality there were about a thousand besides several hundred infantry (mostly Carise Indians).

In the meantime we were reformed into a "hollow square" with lines three deep, in order to repel the charge of the cavalry, which we expected would soon be made upon us. Our artillery was placed at the four angles of the square, and our wagons and oxen inside. Our vanguard under Col. Horton, had gone a mile or so ahead of us, and the first intimation they had of the approach of the enemy was hearing the fire of our artillery when the fight began. They galloped back as rapidly as possible to regain our lines, but the Mexicans had occupied the road before they came up and they were compelled to retreat. The Mexicans pursued them beyond the Coletto, but as they were well mounted they made their escape.

The loss of these mounted men was a most unfortunate one for us. Had they been with us that night after we had driven off the Mexicans, we would have had means of transportation for our wounded, and could easily have made our retreat to the Coletto.

When the Mexicans had approached to within half a mile of our lines they formed into three columns, one remaining stationary, the other two moving to our right and left, but still keeping at about the same distance from us. Whilst they were carrying out this maneuver, our artillery opened upon them with some effect, for now and then we could see a round shot plough through their dense ranks. When the two moving columns, the one on the right and the one on the left were opposite to each other, they suddenly changed front and the three columns with trumpets braying and pennons flying, charged upon us simultaneously from three directions.

When within three or four hundred yards of our lines our artillery opened upon them with grape and cannister shot, with deadly effect, -- but still their advance was unchecked until their foremost ranks were in actual contact in some places with the bayonets of our men. But the fire at close quarters from our muskets and rifles was so rapid and destructive, that before long they fell back in confusion, leaving the ground covered in places with horses and dead men.

Capt. D----'s company of Kentucky riflemen and one or two small detachments from other companies formed one side of our "square," and in addition to our rifles, each man in the front rank was furnished with a musket and a bayonet to repel the charge of cavalry. Besides my rifle

14

and musket I had slung across my shoulders an "escopeta," a short light "blunderbuss" used by the Mexican cavalry, which I had carried all day in expectation of a fight, and which was heavily charged with forty "blue whistlers" and powder in proportion. It was my intention only to fire it when in a very "tight place," for I was well aware it was nearly as dangerous *behind* it as before. In the charge made by the Mexican cavalry they nearly succeeded in breaking our lines at several places, and certainly they would have done so had we not taken the precaution of arming all in the front rank with the bayonet and musket. At one time it was almost a hand to hand fight between the cavalry and our front rank, but the two files in the rear poured such a continuous fire upon the advancing columns, that, as I have said, they were finally driven back in disorder. It was during this charge and when the Mexican cavalry on our side of the square were within a few feet of us, that I concluded that I had got into that "tight place" and that it was time to let off the "scopet" I carried. I did so, and immediately I went heels over head through both ranks behind me. One or two came to my assistance supposing no doubt I was shot (in truth I thought for a moment myself that a two ounce bullet had struck me) but I soon rose to my feet and took my place in the line again just as the cavalry began to fall back. Now, I don't assert that it was the forty "blue whistlers" I had sent among them from my "scopet" that caused them to retreat in confusion. I merely mention the fact that they did fall back very soon after I had let off the blunderbuss among them. My shoulder was black and blue from the recoil for a month afterwards. When I took my place in the line again, I never looked for my "scopet," but contented myself while the fight lasted with my rifle.

The Mexicans had no doubt supposed they would be able to break our lines at the first charge, and were evidently much disconcerted by their failure to do so; for although they reformed their broken columns and made two more attempts to charge us, they were driven back as soon as they came within close range of our small arms.

When they were satisfied that it was impossible for them to break our lines, the cavalry dismounted and surrounding us in open order, they commenced a "fusilade" upon us with their muskets and escopetas, but being very poor marksmen, most of their bullets passed harmlessly over our heads. Besides, this was a game at which we could play also, and for every man killed or wounded on our side I am confident that two or three Mexicans fell before the deadly fire from our rifles. But there were with the Mexicans probably a hundred or so Carise Indians, who were much more daring, and withal better marksmen. They boldly advanced to the front, and taking advantage of every little inequality of the ground and every bunch of grass that could afford them particular cover, they would crawl up closely and fire upon us, and now and then the discharge of their long single barrel shot guns was followed by the fall of some one in our ranks. Four of them had crawled up behind some bunches of tall grass within eighty yards of us, from whence they delivered their fire with telling effect. Capt. D-----who was using a heavy Kentucky rifle, and was known to be one of the best marksmen in his company, was requested to silence these Indians. He took a position near a gun carriage, and whenever one of the Indians showed his head above the tall grass it was perforated with an ounce rifle ball, and after four shots they were seen no more. At the moment he fired the last shot Capt. D---- had one of the fingers of his right hand taken off by a musket ball. When the Mexicans quit the field, we examined the locality where these Indians had secreted themselves, and found the four lying closely together, each one with a bullet hole through his head.

At the commencement of the fight a little incident of a somewhat ludicrous character occurred. We had some five or six Mexican prisoners (the couriers of the old padre, captured at Carlos' Ranch). These we had placed within the square, when the fight began, for safe keeping, and in an incredibly short time, with picks and shovels, they dug a trench deep enough to "hole" themselves, where they lay "perdue" and completely protected from bullets. I for one, however, didn't blame them, as they were non-combatants, and besides to tell the truth when bullets were singing like mad hornets around me, and men were struck down near me, I had a great inclination to "hole up" myself and draw it in after me.

The fight continued in a desultory kind of way until near sunset, when we made a sortie upon the dismounted cavalry, and they hastily remounted and fell back to the timber to our left, where, as soon as it was dark, a long line of fires indicated the position of their encampment.

The night was anything but rest for us, for anticipating a renewal of the fight the next morning, all hands were set to work digging entrenchments and throwing up embankments, and at this we labored unceasingly till nearly daylight. We dug four trenches enclosing a square large enough to contain our whole force, throwing the earth on the outside on which we placed our baggage and everything else available, that might help to protect us from the bullets of the enemy.

Before we began this work, however, Col. Fannin made a short speech to the men, in which he told them "that in his opinion, the only way of extricating themselves from the difficulty they were in, was to retreat after dark to the timber on the Coletto, and cut their way through the enemy's lines should they attempt to oppose the movement." He told them there was no doubt they would be able to do this, as the enemy had evidently been greatly demoralized by the complete failure of the attack they had made upon us. He said, moreover, that the necessity for a speedy retreat was the more urgent, as it was more than probable that the Mexicans would be heavily reinforced during the night. He concluded by saying that if a majority were in favor of retreating, preparations would be made to leave as soon as it was dark enough to conceal our movements from the enemy. But we had about seventy men wounded (most of them badly) and as almost every one had some friend or relative among them, after a short consultation upon the subject, it was unanimously determined not to abandon our wounded men, but to remain with them and share their fate, whatever it might be.

Our loss in the Coletto fight was ten killed and about seventy wounded (Col. Fannin among the latter), and most of them badly, owing to the size of the balls thrown by the Mexican escopetas, and the shotguns of the Indians. The number of our casualities was extremely small considering the force of the enemy, and the duration of the fight, which began about three o'clock and lasted till nearly sunset. I can only account for it by the fact that the Mexicans were very poor marksmen, and that their powder was of a very inferior quality. There was scarcely a man in the whole command who had not been struck by one or more spent balls, which, in place of mere bruises would have inflicted dangerous or fatal wounds if the powder used by the Mexicans had been better.

I can never forget how slowly the hours of that dismal night passed by. The distressing cries of our wounded men begging for water when there was not a drop to give them, were continually ringing in my ears. Even those who were not wounded, but were compelled to work all night in the trenches, suffered exceedingly with thirst. Even after we had fortified our position as well as we could, we had but little hopes of being able to defend ourselves, should the Mexicans as we apprehended, receive reinforcements during the night, for we had but one or two rounds of ammunition left for the cannon, and what remained for the small arms was not sufficient for a protracted struggle.

Some time during the night it was ascertained that three of our men (whose names I have forgotten) had deserted, and shortly afterwards as a volley of musketry was heard between us and the timber on the Coletto, they were no doubt discovered and shot by the Mexican patrol.

Daylight at last appeared, and before the sun had risen we saw that the Mexican forces were all in motion, and evidently preparing to make another attack upon us. When fairly out of the timber, we soon discovered that they had been heavily reinforced during the night. In fact, as we subsequently learned from the Mexicans themselves, a detachment of seven hundred and fifty cavalry and an artillery company had joined them shortly after their retreat to the timber. In the fight of the previous day they had no cannon.

They moved down upon us in four divisions, and when within five or six hundred yards, they unlimbered their field pieces (two brass nine pounders) and opened fire upon us. We did not return their fire, because as I have said, we had only one or two rounds of ammunition left for our cannon, and the distance was too great for small arms. Their shot, however, all went over us, and besides, the breast works we had thrown up would have protected us, even if their guns had been better aimed. We expected momentarily that the cavalry would charge us, but after firing several rounds from their nine pounders, an officer accompanied by a soldier bearing a white flag, rode out towards us, and by signs gave us to understand that he desired a "parley." Major Wallace and several other officers went out and met him about half way between our "fort" and the Mexican lines. The substance of the Mexican officer's communication (as I understood it at the time) was to the effect that "Gen. Urrea, the commander of the Mexican forces, being anxious to avoid the useless shedding of blood (seeing we were now completely in his power), would guarantee to Col. Fannin and his men, on his word of honor as an officer and a gentleman, that we would be leniently dealt with, provided we surrendered at *discretion*, without further attempt at hopeless resistance." When this message was delivered to Col. Fannin, he sent word back to the officer "to say to Gen. Urrea, it was a waste of time to discuss the subject of surrendering at *discretion* -- that he would fight as long as there was a man left to fire a gun before he would surrender on such terms."

A little while afterwards the Mexicans again made a show of attacking us, but just as we were expecting them to charge, Gen. Urrea himself rode out in front of his lines accompanied by several of his officers and the soldier with the "white flag." Col. Fannin and Major Wallace went out to meet them, and the terms of capitulation were finally agreed upon, the most important of which was, that we should be held as prisoners of war until exchanged, or liberated on our parole of honor not to engage in the war again -- at the option of the Mexican commander in chief. There were minor articles included in it, such as that our side arms should be retained, etc.

When the terms of capitulation had been fully decided upon, Gen. Urrea and his secretary and the interpreter came into our lines with Col. Fannin, where it was reduced to writing, and an English translation given to Col. Fannin which was read to our men.

I have said nothing as yet of the Mexican loss in the fight and I cannot do so with any certainty, of my own knowledge; but there is no doubt it was much greater than ours. They told us after we had surrendered that we had killed and wounded several hundred.

After our surrender we were marched back to Goliad, escorted by a large detachment of cavalry, and there confined within the wall surrounding the old mission.

### Prisoners of War at Goliad

A day or so after our return as prisoners to Goliad, Maj. Ward and his battalion, or rather those who survived the engagement they had with the Mexicans, near Refugio, were brought in and confined with us, within the walls enclosing the old mission; and also a company of about eighty men under the command of Maj. Miller, who had been surprised and captured at Copano just after they had landed from their vessel. These men were also confined with us, but kept separate from the rest, and to distinguish them each had a white cloth tied around one of his arms. At the time, I had no idea why this was done, but subsequently I learned the reason.

The morning of the sixth day after our return to Goliad, whether the Mexicans suspected we intended to rise upon the guard, or whether they merely wished to render our situation as uncomfortable as possible, I know not, but at any rate from that time we were confined in the old mission, where we were so crowded we had hardly room to lie down at night. Our rations too, about that time, had been reduced to five ounces of fresh beef a day, which we had to cook in the best way we could and eat without salt.

Although, thus closely confined and half starved, no personal indignity was ever offered to us to my knowledge, except on two occassions. Once a Mexican soldier pricked one of the our men with a bayonet, because he did not walk quite fast enough to suit him, whereupon he turned and knocked the Mexican down with his fist. I fully expected to see him roughly handled for this "overt act," but the officer in command of the guard, who saw the affair, came up to him and patting him on the shoulder, told him he was "muy bravo," and that he had served the soldier exactly right. At another time one of our men was complaining to the officer of the guard of the ration issued to him, who ordered one of the soldiers to collect a quantity of bones and other offal lying around, and throwing them on the ground before the man, said, "There, eat as much as you want -- good enough for Gringos and heretics."

On the morning of the 27th of March, a Mexican officer came to us and ordered us to get ready for a march. He told us we were to be liberated on "parole," and that arangements had been made to send us to New Orleans on board of vessels then at Copano. This you may be sure, was joyful news to us, and we lost no time in making preparations to leave our uncomfortable quarters. When all was ready we were formed into three divisions and marched out under a strong guard. As we passed by some Mexican women who were standing near the main entrance to the fort, I heard them say "pobrecitos" (poor fellows), but the incident at the time made but little impression on my mind.

19

One of our divisions was taken down the road leading to the lower ford of the river, one upon the road to San Patricio, and the division to which my company was attached, along the road leading to San Antonio. A strong guard accompanied us, marching in double files on both sides of our column. It occurred to me that this division of our men into three squads, and marching us off in three directions, was rather a singular maneuver, but still I had no suspicion of the the foul play intended us. When about half a mile above town, a halt was made and the guard on the side next the river filed around to the opposite side. Hardly had this manuever been executed, when I heard heavy firing of musketry in the directions taken by the other two divisions. Some one near me exclaimed, "Boys, they are going to shoot us!" and at the same instant I heard the clicking of musket locks all along the Mexican line. I turned to look, and as I did so, the Mexicans fired upon us, killing probably one hundred out of one hundred and fifty men in the division. We were in double file and I was in the rear rank. The man in front of me was shot dead, and in falling he knocked me down. I did not get up for a moment, and when I rose to my feet, I found that the whole Mexican line had charged over me, and were in hot pursuit of those who had not been shot and who were fleeing towards the river about five hundred yards distant. I followed on after them, for I knew that escape in any other direction (all open prairie) would be impossible, and I had nearly reached the river before it became necessary to make my way through the Mexican line ahead. As I did so, one of the soldiers charged upon me with his bayonet (his gun I suppose being empty). As he drew his musket back to make a lunge at me, one of our men coming from another direction, ran between us, and the bayonet was driven through his body. The blow was given with such force, that in falling, the man probably wrenched or twisted the bayonet in such a way as to prevent the Mexican from withdrawing it immediately. I saw him put his foot upon the man, and make an ineffectual attempt to extricate the bayonet from his body, but one look satisfied me, as I was somewhat in a hurry just then, and I hastened to the bank of the river and plunged in. The river at that point was deep and swift, but not wide, and being a good swimmer, I soon gained the opposite bank, untouched by any of the bullets that were pattering in the water around my head. But here I met with an unexpected difficulty. The bank on that side was so steep I found it was impossible to climb it, and I continued to swim down the river until I came to where a grape vine hung from the bough of a leaning tree nearly to the surface of the water. This I caught hold of and was climbing up it hand over hand, sailor fashion, when a Mexican on the opposite bank fired at me with his escopeta, and with so true an aim, that he cut the vine in two just above my head, and down I came into the water again. I then swam on about a hundred yards further, when I came to a place where the bank was not quite so steep, and with some difficulty I managed to clamber up.

The river on the north side was bordered by timber several hundred yards in width, through which I quickly passed and I was just about to leave it and strike out into the open prairie, when I discovered a party of lancers nearly in front of me, sitting on their horses, and evidently stationed there to intercept any one who should attempt to escape in that direction. I halted at once under cover of the timber, through which I could see the lancers in the open prairie, but which hid me entirely from their view.

Whilst I was thus waiting and undecided as to the best course to pursue under the circumstances, I saw a young man by the name of Holliday, one of my own messmates, passing through the timber above me in a course that would have taken him out at the point directly opposite to which the lancers were stationed. I called to him as loudly as I dared and fortunately, being on the "qui vive," he heard me, and stopped far enough within the timber to prevent the lancers from discovering him. I then pulled off a fur cap I had on, and beckoned to him with it. This finally drew his attention to me, and as soon as he saw me he came to where I was standing, from whence, without being visible to them, the lancers could be plainly seen.

A few moments afterwards we were joined by a young man by the name of Brown, from Georgia, who had just swam the river, and had accidentally stumbled on the place where Holliday and I were holding a "council of war" as to what was the best course to pursue. Holliday, although a brave man, was very much excited, and had lost to some extent his presence of mind, for he proposed we should leave the timber at once and take the chances of evading the lancers we saw on the prairie. I reasoned with him on the folly of such a proceeding, and told him it would be impossible for us to escape in the open prairie from a dozen men on horseback. "But," said Holliday, "the Mexicans are crossing the river behind us, and they will soon be here." "That may be," I replied, "but they are not here yet, and in the mean time something may turn up to favor our escape." Brown took the same view of the case I did, and Holliday's wild proposition to banter a dozen mounted men for a race on the open prairie was "laid upon the table."

Whilst we were debating this (to us) momentous question, some four or five of our men passed out of the timber before we saw them, into the open prairie, and when they discovered the lancers it was too late. The lancers charged upon them at once, speared them to death, and then dismounting robbed them of such things as they had upon their persons. From where we stood the whole proceeding was plainly visible to us, and as may be imagined, it was not calculated to encourage any hopes we might have had of making our escape. However, after the lancers had plundered the men they had just murdered, they remounted, and in a few moments set off in a rapid gallop down the river to where it is probable they had discovered other fugitives coming out of the timber. We at once seized the opportunity thus afforded us to leave the strip of timber which we knew could give us shelter but for a few moments longer, and started out, taking advantage of a shallow ravine which partially hid us from view. We had scarcely gone two hundred yards from the timber, when we saw the lancers gallop back to take up their position at the same place they had previously occupied. Strange to say, however, they never observed us, although we were in plain view of them for more than a quarter of a mile, without a single brush or tree to screen us.

We traveled about five or six miles and stopped in a thick grove to rest ourselves, where we stayed until night. All day long we heard at intervals irregular discharges of musketry in the distance, indicating, as we supposed, where fugitives from the massacre were overtaken and shot by the pursuing parties of Mexicans.

As the undergrowth was pretty dense in the grove where we had stopped, we concluded the chances of being picked up by one of these pursuing parties would be greater if we traveled on than if we remained where we were, and we determined to "lie by" until night. In talking the matter over and reflecting upon the many narrow risks we had run in making our escape, we came to the conclusion that in all probability we were the only survivors of the hundreds who had that morning been led out to slaughter; although in fact as we subsequently learned, twenty-five or thirty of our men eventually reached the settlements on the Brazos. Drs. Shackleford and Barnard, our surgeons, were saved from the massacre to attend upon Mexicans wounded in the fight on the Coletto, and when their forces retreated from Goliad after the battle of San Jacinto these were taken to San Antonio, where they were ultimately liberated. Our own wounded men, or rather those of them that survived up to the time of the massacre, were carried out into the open square of the fort, and there cruelly butchered by the guard. Capt. Miller and his men were saved, because, as I was subsequently informed, they had been captured soon after they landed from their vessel, without any arms, and of course without making any resistance.

Col. Fannin, who was confined to his quarters by a wound he had received at the fight on the Coletto, soon after the massacre of his men, was notified to prepare for immediate execution. He merely observed that he was ready then, as he had no desire to live after the cold-blooded, cowardly murder of his men. He was thereupon taken out to the square by a guard, where he was seated on a bench, and his eyes blindfolded. A moment before the order to "fire" was given, I was told (though I cannot vouch for the truth of the statement) he drew a fine gold watch from his pocket, and handing it to the officer in command of the guard, requested him as a last favor to order his men to shoot him in the breast and not the head. The officer took the watch, and immediately ordered the guard to fire at his head. Col. Fannin fell dead and his body was thrown into one of the ravines near the fort. Thus died as brave a son of Georgia as ever came from that noble old State.

# ACROSS THE PLAINS TO THE SIERRA NEVADA
## WITH THE DONNER PARTY
### (1846-47)

## Virginia Reed Murphy

**Editors' Note:** Of all the tales of hardship endured by pioneer families, easily the most famous is that of the California-bound Donner Party. Their terrible ordeal while snowbound in the Sierra Nevada during the winter of 1846-47 is unmatched for horror and human suffering.

The nucleus of the Donner Party consisted of three prosperous farming families from Illinois: George Donner, age 62, his wife Tamsen, 45, and their five children, ages three to 14; Jacob Donner (George's brother), 65, his wife Elizabeth, 45, and their seven children, also aged three to 14; and James F. Reed, 46, his wife Margaret, 32, and their four children, aged three to 13. Margaret Reed's oldest daughter, Virginia, was from a previous marriage. Although James Reed was Virginia's stepfather, she was devoted to him. Both George and Jacob Donner had also been married before, but none of their grown children joined the expedition. Seven young men had been hired as teamsters, and the Reeds brought along a young woman who worked for the family as a domestic, and her brother. Also accompanying the party was Margaret Reed's 75-year-old invalid mother. In mid-April, 1846, thirty-one people set off from Springfield, Illinois, for the trailhead at Independence, Missouri.

All three families were *very* well off. Their nine wagons were of the best quality available and loaded with expensive household goods. James Reed had brought an impressive selection of French wines and brandies, and the women had packed silk dresses and sterling silverware. Each family had thousands of dollars in cash with which to buy land in California. The question arises, then, why would successful, well-established, middle-aged people pull up stakes and head across an unknown wilderness with young children in tow? To most of us, a move to Philadelphia or Boston to enjoy the comforts of city life would have been more reasonable. But the Donners and the Reeds were risk-takers, and even before the discovery of gold in 1848, the lure of California was strong.

The first emigrant wagon train had crossed the plains to the West Coast in 1841. Each year thereafter a few more parties set out for Oregon and California. By the time the Donner party headed West, several hundred people a year were making the trek. An important promoter of these early emigrations was Lansford W. Hastings, who had made the overland journey in 1842 and had become California's first great publicist. Hastings' book, *The Emigrants' Guide to Oregon and California,* was the pioneer's "Bible," and the members of the Donner Party were well acquainted with it. Unfortunately, while well-meaning, most of the book's information was vague and of little practical use to travelers.

On May 3rd, the Donner Party headed west across the prairie from Independence. The group had by now grown to more than a hundred people and more would join the train along the way. Virginia Reed, thirteen years old when the trip began, would write of the Donner Party's ordeals forty-five years later. In her account, published in *Century Magazine* in 1891 and reprinted here, she described the crossing of the Great Plains with all the youthful enthusiasm she must have felt, when, as a girl, she embarked on the adventure of her life. Indeed, for the first three months the trip went smoothly, and the plains were crossed with no great difficulty.

As the train approached Fort Bridger in southwestern Wyoming, a rider met the emigrants with an open letter from Lansford Hastings addressed to "all California emigrants now on the road." In his letter, Hastings urged all California-bound travelers to take a new route he had just explored and named "The Hastings Cut-Off." Unlike the established trail that proceeded north of the Great Salt Lake and the Great Salt Desert, Hastings route headed southwest from Fort Bridger and swung around the south end of the lake. The "Cut-Off" then crossed the middle of the desert before joining the old trail along the Humboldt River in Nevada. Hastings proudly announced that his discovery would cut three hundred miles off of the journey and save much valuable time. This self-proclaimed expert on western travel was himself just a few days ahead, guiding a train on his new route.

On reaching Fort Bridger, the emigrants were in a quandary as to which trail to take. James Reed, anxious to get to California as quickly as possible, was sold on the Hastings route; others wanted to stick to the established road. Finally, the Reeds, the Donners, and several other families, eighty-seven people in all, headed out on the new cut-off, leaving the rest of the party to take the Fort Hall road. It was now the last day of July.

Things turned sour almost immediately. The new trail led across the incredibly rugged Wasatch range where the emigrants got lost. Soon they were hacking their way through dense woods and forcing their way down boulder-clogged canyons. It took them three weeks to go thirty-five miles. Weary and worn out, the party did not emerge from the Wasatch Mountains until August 27. Instead of gaining time, they had fallen behind schedule.

The wagon train now skirted the south end of the lake and entered the desert. Told that the worst of the Great Salt Desert would take two days to cross, the emigrants learned that this waterless stretch took six grueling days to traverse. Dead oxen and abandoned wagons littered the trail. Never a tight-knit group, the party became totally demoralized. Cursing Hastings with every step, the members turned on each other out of fear and frustration. Finally, with supplies low, they struck the main road along the Humboldt -- now a nearly-dry creek.

The going was still arduous, however, and tempers continued to flare. James Reed got into a fight with a young teamster named John Snyder who hit Reed with the butt of his bullwhip; Reed responded by thrusting his hunting knife into Snyder's chest, killing him. The young man was well liked, and a crisis developed. Some wanted to lynch Reed on the spot. Instead, a meeting was held, and it was decided to banish him from the company. His family would be allowed to stay with the train, but Reed was forced to travel ahead on a saddle horse.

With food running out and oxen flagging, the exhausted emigrants slowly began the long pull toward the summit of the Sierra Nevada. It was now woefully late in the year -- all of the other trains had by now crossed over to the other side. By the time that the Donner Party's advance wagons reached Truckee Lake (now Donner Lake) at 6,000 feet elevation, it had begun to snow. Although the pass was only another three miles up the trail, it was another 1,100 feet higher in elevation. All attempts to cross were frustrated by snowstorms of incredible fury and maddening duration.

A small log cabin at the lake provided some refuge, and the emigrants hastily built two more. The Donners, straggling behind, were about six miles back on the trail when the snow caught them. They built some crude lean-tos, and like the rest of the party, settled down to await either an improvement in the weather or rescue. Among those present at the upper camp by the lake were the Reeds, Breens, Murphys, Eddys, Kesebergs, and the Graveses. In all, eighty-three people were stranded. It was the end of October and spring would be a long time coming.

We will let Virginia Reed tell the story of that terrible winter in the mountains. But contrary to what one might expect, her recollections are not all bitter ones. Her grandmother had died far back on the plains, but otherwise her family survived intact. James Reed, unencumbered by wagons and gear, had crossed over to California before the passes had been closed by snow and feverishly worked to rescue the party. Like her stepfather, her mother, eight-year-old sister Martha ("Patty"), and two brothers, James Jr. (five) and Thomas (three) lived to enjoy their new home in California. Nor did any of her family experience the horror of eating human flesh as was reported for some members of the party. By contrast, four of the Donner children died in the Sierras and those who survived were orphaned. About half of the marooned party succumbed in the twenty-foot-deep snows from cold and starvation.

The Reeds eventually settled near in the Santa Clara Valley and prospered. All of the children lived to maturity. Mrs. Reed, never in strong health, died in 1861. James Reed died in 1874 at the age of seventy-four.

~ ~ ~ ~ ~

**I was a child when we started to California,** yet I remember the journey well and I have cause to remember it, as our little band of emigrants who drove out of Springfield, Illinois, that spring morning of 1846 have since been known in history as the "Ill-fated Donner Party" of "Martyr Pioneers." My father, James F. Reed, was the originator of the party, and the Donner brothers, George and Jacob, who lived just a little way out of Springfield, decided to join him.

All the previous winter we were preparing for the journey and right here let me say that we suffered vastly more from fear of the Indians before starting than we did on the plains; at least this was my case. In the long winter evenings Grandma Keyes used to tell me Indian stories. She had an aunt who had been taken prisoner by the savages in the early settlement of Virginia and Kentucky and had remained a captive in their hands five years before she made her escape. I was fond of these stories and evening after evening would go into grandma's room, sitting with my back close against the wall so that no warrior could slip behind me with a tomahawk. I would coax her to tell me more about her aunt, and would sit listening to the recital of the fearful deeds of the savages, until it seemed to me that everything in the room, from the high old-fashioned bedposts down even to the shovel and tongs in the chimney corner, was transformed into the dusky tribe in paint and feathers, all ready for the war dance. So when I was told that we were going to California and would have to pass through a region peopled by Indians, you can imagine how I felt.

Our wagons, or the "Reed wagons," as they were called, were all made to order and I can say without fear of contradiction that nothing like our family wagon every started across the plains, It was what might be called a two-story wagon or "Pioneer palace car," attached to a regular immigrant train. My mother, though a young woman, was not strong and had been in delicate health for many years, yet when sorrows and dangers came upon her she was the bravest of the brave. Grandma Keyes, who was seventy-five years of age, was an invalid, confined to her bed. Her sons in Springfield, Gersham and James W. Keyes, tried to dissuade her from the long and fatiguing journey, but in vain; she would not be parted from my mother, who was her only daughter. So the car in which she was to ride was planned to give comfort. The entrance was on the side, like that of an old-fashioned stage coach, and one stepped into a small room, as it were, in the center of the wagon. At the right and left were spring seats of a Concord coach. In this little room was placed a tiny sheet-iron stove, whose pipe, running through the top of the wagon, was prevented by a circle of tin from setting fire to the canvas cover. A board about a foot wide extended over the wheels on either side of the full length of the wagon, thus forming the foundation for a large and roomy second story in which were placed our beds. Under the spring seats were compartments in which were stored many articles useful for the journey, such as a well filled work basket and a full assortment of medicines, with lint and bandages for dressing wounds. Our clothing was packed -- not in Saratoga trunks -- but in strong canvas bags plainly marked. Some of mama's young friends added a looking-glass, hung directly opposite the door, in order, as they said, that my mother might not forget to keep her good looks, and strange to say, when we had to leave this wagon, standing like a monument on the Salt Lake desert, the glass was still unbroken. I have often thought how pleased the Indians must have been when they found this mirror which gave them back the picture of their own dusky faces.

We had two wagons loaded with provisions. Everything in that line was bought that could be thought of. My father started with supplies enough to last us through the first winter in California, had we made the journey in the usual time of six months. Knowing that books were always scarce in a new country, we also took a good library of standard works. We even took a cooking stove which never had had a fire in it, and was destined never to have, as we cachéd it in the desert. Certainly no family ever started across the plains with more provisions or a better outfit for the journey; and yet we reached California almost destitute and nearly out of clothing.

The family wagon was drawn by four yoke of oxen, large Durham steers at the wheel. The other wagons were drawn by three yoke each. We had saddle horses and cows, and last but not least my pony. He was a beauty and his name was Billy. I can scarcely remember when I was taught to sit a horse. I only know that when a child of seven I was the proud owner of a pony and used to go riding with papa. That was the chief pleasure to which I looked forward in crossing the plains, to ride my pony every day. But a day came when I had no pony to ride, the poor little fellow gave out. He could not endure the hardships of ceaseless travel. When I was forced to part with him I cried until I was ill, and sat in the back of the wagon watching him become smaller and smaller as we drove on, until I could see him no more.

Never can I forget the morning when we bade farewell to kindred and friends. The Donners were there, having driven in the evening before with their families, so that we might get an early start. Grandma Keyes was carried out of the house and placed in the wagon on a large feather bed, propped up with pillows. Her sons implored her to remain and end her days with them, but she could not be separated from her only daughter. We were surrounded by loved ones, and there stood all my little schoolmates who had come to kiss me good-by. My father with tears in his eyes tried to smile as one friend after another grasped his hand in a last farewell. Mama was overcome with grief. At last we were all in the wagons, the drivers cracked their whips, the oxen moved slowly forward and the long journey had begun.

Could we have looked into the future and have seen the misery before us, these lines would never have been written. But we were full of hope and did not dream of sorrow. I can now see our little caravan of ten or twelve wagons as we drove out of old Springfield, my little black-eyed sister Patty sitting upon the bed, holding up the wagon cover so that Grandma might have a last look at her old home.

That was the 14th day of April, 1846. Our party numbered thirty-one, and consisted chiefly of three families, the other members being young men, some of whom came as drivers. The Donner family were George and Tamsen Donner and their five children, and Jacob and Elizabeth Donner and their seven children. Our family numbered nine, not counting three drivers -- my father and mother, James Frazier and Margaret W. Reed, Grandma Keyes, my little sister Patty (now Mrs. Frank Lewis, of Capitola), and two little brothers, James F. Reed, Jr., and Thomas K. Reed, Eliza Williams and her brother Baylis, and lastly myself. Eliza had been a domestic in our family for many years, and was anxious to see California.

Many friends camped with us the first night out and my uncles traveled on for several days before bidding us a final farewell. It seemed strange to be riding in ox-teams, and we children were afraid of the oxen, thinking they could go wherever they pleased as they had no bridles. Milt Elliott, a knight of the whip, drove our family wagon and let us out. He had worked for years in my father's large saw-mill on the Sangamon River. The first bridge we came to, Milt had to stop the wagon and I remember that I called to him to be sure to make the oxen hit the bridge, and not to forget that grandma was in the wagon. How he laughed at the idea of the oxen missing the bridge! I soon found that Milt, with his "whoa," "haw," and "gee," could make the oxen do just as he pleased.

Nothing of much interest happened until we reached what is now Kansas. The first Indians we met were the Caws, who kept the ferry, and had to take us over the Caw River. I watched them closely, hardly daring to draw my breath, and feeling sure they would sink the boat in the middle of the stream, and was very thankful when I found they were not like grandma's Indians. Every morning, when the wagons were ready to start, papa and I would jump on our horses, and go ahead to pick out a camping-ground. In our party were many who rode on horseback, but mama seldom did; she preferred the wagon, and did not like to leave grandma, although Patty took upon herself this charge, and could hardly be persuaded to leave grandma's side. Our little home was so comfortable, that mama could sit reading and chatting with the little ones, and almost forget that she was really crossing the plains.

Grandma Keyes improved in health and spirits every day until we came to the Big Blue River, which was so swollen that we could not cross, but had to lie by and make rafts on which to take the wagons over. As soon as we stopped traveling, grandma began to fail, and on the 29th day of May she died. It seemed hard to bury her in the wilderness, and travel on, and we were afraid that the Indians would destroy her grave, but her death here, before our troubles began, was providential, and nowhere on the whole road could we have found so beautiful a resting place. By this time many emigrants had joined our company, and all turned out to assist at the funeral. A coffin was hewn out of a cottonwood tree, and John Denton, a young man from Springfield, found a large gray stone on which he carved with deep letters the name of "Sarah Keyes; born in Virginia," giving age and date of birth. She was buried under the shade of an oak, the slab being placed at the foot of the grave, on which were planted wild flowers growing in the sod. A minister in our party, the Rev. J. A. Cornwall, tried to give words of comfort as we stood about this lonely grave. Strange to say, that grave has never been disturbed; the wilderness blossomed into the city of Manhattan, Kansas, and we have been told that the city cemetery surrounds the grave of Sarah Keyes.

As the river remained high and there was no prospect of fording it, the men went to work cutting down trees, hollowing out logs and making rafts on which to take the wagons over. These logs, about twenty-five feet in length, were united by cross timbers, forming rafts, which were firmly lashed to stakes driven into the bank. Ropes were attached to both ends, by which the rafts were pulled back and forth across the river. The banks of this stream being steep, our heavily laden wagons had to be let down carefully with ropes, so that the wheels might run into the hollowed logs. This was no easy task when you take into consideration that in these wagons were women and children, who could cross the rapid river in no other way. Finally the dangerous work was accomplished and we resumed our journey.

The road at first was rough and led through a timbered country, but after striking the great valley of the Platte the road was good and the country beautiful. Stretching out before us as far as the eye could reach was a valley as green as emerald, dotted here and there with flowers of every imaginable color, and through this valley flowed the grand old Platte, a wide, rapid, shallow stream. Our company now numbered about forty wagons, and, for a time, we were commanded by Col. William H. Russell, then by George Donner. Exercise in the open air under bright skies, and freedom from peril combined to make this part of our journey an ideal pleasure trip. How I enjoyed riding my pony, galloping over the plain, gathering wild flowers! At night the young folks would gather about the camp fire chatting merrily, and often a song would be heard, or some clever dancer would give us a barn-door jig on the hind gate of a wagon.

Traveling up the smooth valley of the Platte, we passed Court House Rock, Chimney Rock and Scott's Bluffs, and made from fifteen to twenty miles a day, shortening or lengthening the distance in order to secure a good camping ground. At night when we drove into camp, our wagons were placed so as to form a circle or corral, into which our cattle were driven, after grazing, to prevent the Indians from stealing them, the camp fires and tents being on the outside. There were many expert riflemen in the party and we never lacked for game. The plains

31

were alive with buffalo, and herds could be seen every day coming to the Platte to drink. The meat of the young buffalo is excellent and so is that of the antelope, but the antelope are so fleet of foot it is difficult to get a shot at one. I witnessed many a buffalo hunt and more than once was in the chase close beside my father. A buffalo will not attack one unless wounded. When he sees the hunter he raises his shaggy head, gazes at him for a moment, then turns and runs; but when he is wounded he will face his pursuer. The only danger lay in a stampede, for nothing could withstand the onward rush of these massive creatures, whose tread seemed to shake the prairie.

Antelope and buffalo steaks were the main article on our bill-of-fare for weeks, and no tonic was needed to give zest for the food; our appetites were a marvel. Eliza soon discovered that cooking over a camp fire was far different from cooking on a stove or range, but all hands assisted her. I remember that she had the cream all ready for the churn as we drove into the South Fork of the Platte, and while we were fording the grand old stream she went on with her work, and made several pounds of butter. We found no trouble in crossing the Platte, the only danger being in quicksand. The stream being wide, we had to stop the wagon now and then to give the oxen a few moments' rest. At Fort Laramie, two hundred miles farther on, we celebrated the fourth of July in fine style. Camp was pitched earlier than usual and we prepared a grand dinner. Some of my father's friends in Springfield had given him a bottle of good old brandy, which he agreed to drink at a certain hour of this day looking to the east, while his friends in Illinois were to drink a toast to his success from a companion bottle with their faces turned west, the difference in time being carefully estimated; and at the hour agreed upon, the health of our friends in Springfield was drunk with great enthusiasm. At Fort Laramie was a party of Sioux, who were on the war path going to fight the Crows or Blackfeet. The Sioux are fine-looking Indians and I was not in the least afraid of them. They fell in love with my pony and set about bargaining to buy him. They brought buffalo robes and beautifully tanned buckskin, pretty beaded moccasins, and ropes made of grass, and placing these articles in a heap alongside several of their ponies, they made my father understand by signs that they would give them all for Billy and his rider. Papa smiled and shook his head; then the number of ponies was increased and, as a last tempting inducement, they brought an old coat, that had been worn by some poor soldier, thinking my father could not withstand the brass buttons!

On the sixth of July we were again on the march. The Sioux were several days in passing our caravan, not on account of the length of our train, but because there were so many Sioux. Owing to the fact that our wagons were strung so far apart, they could have massacred our whole party without much loss to themselves. Some of our company became alarmed, and the rifles were cleaned out and loaded, to let the warriors see that we were prepared to fight; but the Sioux never showed any inclination to disturb us. Their curiosity was annoying, however, and our wagon with its conspicuous stove-pipe and looking-glass attracted their attention. They were continually swarming about trying to get a look at themselves in the mirror, and their desire to possess my pony was so strong that at last I had to ride in the wagon and let one of the drivers take charge of Billy. This I did not like, and in order to see how far back the line of warriors extended, I picked up a large field-glass which hung on a rack, and as I pulled it out with a click, the warriors jumped back, wheeled their ponies and scattered. This pleased me greatly, and I told my mother I could fight the whole Sioux tribe with a spy-glass, and as revenge for forcing me to ride in the wagon, whenever they came near trying to get a peep at their war-paint and feathers, I would raise the glass and laugh to see them dart away in terror.

A new route had just been opened by Lansford W. Hastings, called the "Hastings Cutoff," which passed along the southern shore of the Great Salt Lake rejoining the old "Fort Hall Emigrant" road on the Humboldt. It was said to shorten the distance three hundred miles. Much time was lost in debating which course to pursue; Bridger and Vasquez, who were in charge of the fort, sounded the praises of the new road. My father was so eager to reach California that he was quick to take advantage of any means to shorten the distance, and we were assured by Hastings and his party that the only bad part was a forty-mile drive through the desert by the shore of the lake. None of our party knew then, as we learned afterwards, that these men had an interest in the road, being employed by Hastings. But for the advice of these parties we should have continued on the old Fort Hall road. Our company had increased in numbers all along the line, and was now composed of some of the very best people and some of the worst. The greater portion of our company went by the old road and reached California in safety. Eighty-seven persons took the "Hastings Cutoff," including the Donners, Breens, Reeds, Murphys (not the Murphys of Santa Clara County), C. T. Stanton, John Denton, Wm. McClutchen, Wm. Eddy, Louis Keseburg, and many others too numerous to mention in a short article like this. And these are the unfortunates who have since been known as the "Donner Party."

On the morning of July 31 we parted with our traveling companions, some of whom had become very dear friends, and, without a suspicion of impending disaster, set off in high spirits on the "Hastings Cut-off;" but a few days showed us that the road was not as it had been represented. We were seven days in reaching Weber Cañon, and Hastings, who was guiding a party in advance of our train, left a note by the wayside warning us that the road through Weber Cañon was impassable and advising us to select a road over the mountains, the outline of which he attempted to give on paper. These directions were so vague that C. T. Stanton, William Pike, and my father rode on in advance and overtook Hastings and tried to induce him to return and guide our party. He refused, but came back over a portion of the road, and from a high mountain endeavored to point out the general course. Over this road my father traveled alone, taking notes, and blazing trees, to assist him in retracing his course, and reaching camp after an absence of four days. Learning of the hardships of the advance train, the party decided to cross towards the lake. Only those who have passed through this country on horseback can appreciate the situation. There was absolutely no road, not even a trail. The cañon wound around among the hills. Heavy underbrush had to be cut away and used for making a road bed. While cutting our way step by step through the "Hastings Cut-off," we were overtaken and joined by the Graves family, consisting of W. F. Graves, his wife and eight children, his son-in-law Jay Fosdick, and a young man by the name of John Snyder. Finally we reached the end of the cañon where it looked as though our wagons would have to be abandoned. It seemed impossible for the oxen to pull them up the steep hill and the bluffs beyond, but we doubled teams and the work was, at last, accomplished, almost every yoke in the train being required to pull up each wagon. While in this cañon Stanton and Pike came into camp; they had suffered greatly on account of the exhaustion of their horses and had come near perishing. Worn with travel and greatly discouraged we reached the shore of the Great Salt Lake. It had taken an entire month, instead of a week, and our cattle were not fit to cross the desert.

We were now encamped in a valley called "Twenty Wells." The water in these wells was pure and cold, welcome enough after the alkaline pools from which we had been forced to drink. We prepared for the long drive across the desert and laid in, as we supposed, an ample supply of water and grass. This desert had been represented to us as only forty miles wide but we found it nearer eighty. It was a dreary, desolate alkali waste; not a living thing could be seen; it seemed as though the hand of death had been laid upon the country. We started in the evening, traveled all that night, and the following day and night - - two nights and one day of suffering from thirst and heat by day and piercing cold by night. When the third night fell and we saw the barren waste stretching away apparently as boundless as when we started, my father determined to go ahead in search of water. Before starting he instructed the drivers, if the cattle showed signs of giving out to take them from the wagons and follow him. He had not been gone long before the oxen began to fall to the ground from thirst and exhaustion. They were unhitched at once and driven ahead. My father coming back met the drivers with the cattle within ten miles of water and instructed them to return as soon as the animals had satisfied their thirst. He reached us about daylight. We waited all that day in the desert looking for the return of our drivers, the other wagons going on out of sight. Towards night the situation became desperate and we had only a few drops of water left; another night there meant death. We must set out on foot and try to reach some of the wagons. Can I ever forget that night in the desert, when we walked mile after mile in the darkness, every step seeming to be the very last we could take! Suddenly all fatigue was banished by fear; through the night came a swift rushing sound of one of the young steers crazed by thirst and apparently bent upon our destruction. My father, holding his youngest child in his arms and keeping us all close behind him, drew his pistol, but finally the maddened beast turned and dashed off into the darkness. Dragging ourselves along about ten miles, we reached the wagon of Jacob Donner. The family were all asleep, so we children lay down on the ground. A bitter wind swept over the desert, chilling us through and through. We crept closer together, and, when we complained of the cold, papa placed all five of our dogs around us, and only for the warmth of these faithful creatures we should doubtless have perished.

At daylight papa was off to learn the fate of his cattle, and was told that all were lost, except one cow and an ox. The stock, scenting the water, had rushed on ahead of the men, and had probably been stolen by the Indians, and driven into the mountains, where all traces of them were lost. A week was spent here on the edge of the desert in a fruitless search. Almost every man in the company turned out, hunting in all directions, but our eighteen head of cattle were never found. We had lost our best yoke of oxen before reaching Bridger's Fort from drinking poisoned water found standing in pools, and had bought at the fort two yoke of young steers, and now all were gone, and my father and his family were left in the desert, eight hundred miles from California, seemingly helpless. We realized that our wagons must be abandoned. The company kindly let us have two yoke of oxen, so with our ox and cow yoked together we could bring one wagon, but, alas! not the one which seemed so much like a home to us, and in which grandma had died. Some of the company went back with papa and assisted him in caching everything that could not be packed in one wagon. A cache was made by digging a hole in the ground, in which a box or the bed of a wagon was placed. Articles to be buried were packed into this box, covered with boards, and the earth thrown in upon them, and thus they were hidden from sight. Our provisions were divided among the company. Before leaving the desert camp, an inventory of provisions on hand was taken, and it was found that the supply was not sufficient to last us through to California, and as if to render the situation more terrible, a storm came on during the night and hill-tops became white with snow. Some one must go on to Sutter's Fort after provisions. A call was made for volunteers. C. T. Stanton and Wm. McCutchen bravely offered their services and started on bearing letters from the company to Captain Sutter asking for relief. We resumed our journey and soon reached Gravelly Ford on the Humboldt.

I now come to that part of my narrative which delicacy of feeling for both the dead and the living would induce me to pass over in silence, but which a correct and lucid chronicle of subsequent events of historical importance will not suffer to be omitted. On the 5th day of October, 1846, at Gravelly Ford, a tragedy was enacted which affected the subsequent lives and fortunes of more than one member of our company. At this point in our journey we were compelled to double our teams in order to ascend a steep, sandy hill. Milton Elliott, who was driving our wagon, and John Snyder, who was driving one of Mr. Graves's, became involved in a quarrel over the management of their oxen. Snyder was beating his cattle over the head with the butt end of his whip, when my father, returning on horse-back from a hunting trip, arrived and, appreciating the great importance of saving the remainder of the oxen, remonstrated with Snyder, telling him that they were our main dependence, and at the same time offering the assistance of our team. Snyder having taken offense at something Elliott had said declared that his team could pull up alone, and kept on using abusive language. Father tried to quiet the enraged man. Hard words followed. Then my father said: "We can settle this, John, when we get up the hill." "No," replied Snyder with an oath, "we will settle it now," and springing upon the tongue of a wagon, he struck my father a violent blow over the head with his heavy whip-stock. One blow followed another. Father was stunned for a moment and blinded by the blood streaming from the gashes in his head. Another blow was descending when my mother ran in between the men. Father saw the uplifted whip, but had only time to cry: "John, John," when down came the stroke upon mother. Quick as a thought my father's hunting knife was out and Snyder fell, fatally wounded. He was caught in the arms of W. C. Graves, carried up the hill-side, and laid on the ground. My father regretted the act, and dashing the blood from his eyes went quickly to the assistance of the dying man. I can see him now, as he knelt over Snyder, trying to stanch the wound, while the blood from the gashes in his own head, trickling down his face, mingled with that of the dying man. In a few moments Snyder expired. Camp was pitched immediately, our wagon being some distance from the others. My father, anxious to do what he could for the dead, offered the boards of our wagon, from which to make a coffin. Then, coming to me, he said: "Daughter, do you think you can dress these wounds in my head? Your mother is not able, and they must be attended to." I answered by saying: "Yes, if you will tell me what to do." I brought a basin of water and sponge, and we went into the wagon, so that we might not be disturbed. When my work was at last finished, I burst out crying. Papa clasped me in his arms, saying: "I should not have asked so much of you," and talked to me until I controlled my feelings, so that we could go to the tent where mama was lying.

We then learned that trouble was brewing in the camp where Snyder's body lay. At the funeral my father stood sorrowfully by until the last clod was placed upon the grave. He and John Snyder had been good friends, and no one could have regretted the taking of that young life more than my father.

The members of the Donner party then held a council to decide upon the fate of my father, while we anxiously awaited the verdict. They refused to accept the plea of self-defense and decided that my father should be banished from the company and sent into the wilderness alone. It was a cruel sentence. And all this animosity towards my father was caused by Louis Keseburg, a German who had joined our company away back on the plains. Keseburg was married to a young and pretty German girl, and used to abuse her, and was in the habit of beating her till she was black and blue. This aroused all the manhood in my father and he took Keseburg to task -- telling him it must be stopped or measures would be taken to that effect. Keseburg did not dare to strike his wife again, but he hated my father and nursed his wrath until papa was so unfortunate as to have to take the life of a fellow-creature in self-defense. Then Keseburg's hour for revenge had come. But how a man like Keseburg, brutal and overbearing by nature, although highly educated, could have such influence over the company is more than I can tell. I have thought the subject over for hours but failed to arrive at a conclusion. The feeling against my father at one time was so strong that lynching was proposed. He was no coward and he bared his neck, saying, "Come on, gentlemen," but no one moved. It was thought more humane, perhaps, to send him into the wilderness to die of slow starvation or be murdered by the Indians; but my father did not die. God took care of him and his family, and at Donner Lake we seemed especially favored by the Almighty as not one of our family perished, and we were the only family no one member of which was forced to eat of human flesh to keep body and soul together. When the sentence of banishment was communicated to my father, he refused to go, feeling that he was justified before God and man, as he had only acted in self-defense.

Then came a sacrifice on the part of my mother. Knowing only too well what her life would be without him, yet fearful that if he remained he would meet with violence at the hands of his enemies, she implored him to go, but all to no avail until she urged him to remember the destitution of the company, saying that if he remained and escaped violence at their hands, he might nevertheless see his children starving and be helpless to aid them, while if he went on he could return and meet them with food. It was a fearful struggle; at last he consented, but not before he had secured a promise from the company to care for his wife and little ones.

My father was sent out into an unknown country without provisions or arms -- even his horse was at first denied him. When we learned of this decision, I followed him through the darkness, taking Elliott with me, and carried him his rifle, pistols, ammunition and some food. I had determined to stay with him, and begged him to let me stay, but he would listen to no argument, saying it was impossible. Finally, unclasping my arms from around him, he placed me in charge of Elliott, who started back to camp with me -- and papa was left alone. I had cried until I had hardly strength to walk, but when we reached camp and I saw the distress of my mother, with the little ones clinging around her and no arm to lean upon, it seemed suddenly to make a woman of me. I realized that I must be strong and help mama bear her sorrows.

We traveled on, but all life seemed to have left the party, and the hours dragged slowly along. Every day we would search for some sign of papa, who would leave a letter by the way-side in the top of a bush or in a split stick, and when he succeeded in killing geese or birds would scatter the feathers about so that we might know that he was not suffering for food. When possible, our fire would always be kindled on the spot where his had been. But a time came when we found no letter, and no trace of him. Had he starved by the way-side, or been murdered by the Indians?

My mother's despair was pitiful. Patty and I thought we would be bereft of her also. But life and energy were again aroused by the danger that her children would starve. It was apparent that the whole company would soon be put on a short allowance of food, and the snow-capped mountains gave an ominous hint of the fate that really befell us in the Sierra. Our wagon was found to be too heavy, and was abandoned with everything we could spare, and the remaining things were packed in part of another wagon. We had two horses left from the wreck, which could hardly drag themselves along, but they managed to carry my too little brothers. The rest of us had to walk, one going beside the horse to hold on to my youngest brother who was only two and a half years of age. The Donners were not with us when my father was banished, but were several days in advance of our train. Walter Herron, one of our drivers, who was traveling with the Donners, left the wagons and joined my father.

On the 19th of October, while traveling along the Truckee, our hearts were gladdened by the return of Stanton, with seven mules loaded with provisions. Mr. McCutchen was ill and could not travel, but Captain Sutter had sent two of his Indian vaqueros, Luis and Salvador with Stanton. Hungry as we were, Stanton brought us something better than food -- news that my father was alive. Stanton had met him not far from Sutter's Fort; he had been three days without food, and his horse was not able to carry him. Stanton had given him a horse and some provisions and he had gone on. We now packed what little we had left on one mule and started with Stanton. My mother rode on a mule, carrying Tommy in her lap; Patty and Jim rode behind the two Indians, and I behind Mr. Stanton, and in this way we journeyed on through the rain, looking up with fear towards the mountains, where snow was already falling although it was only the last week in October. Winter had set in a month earlier than usual. All trails and roads were covered; and our only guide was the summit which it seemed we would never reach. Despair drove many nearly frantic. Each family tried to cross the mountains but found it impossible. When it was seen that the wagons could not be dragged through the snow, their goods and provisions were packed on oxen and another start was made, men and women walking in the snow up to their waists, carrying their children in their arms and trying to drive their cattle. The Indians said they could find no road, so a halt was called, and Stanton went ahead with the guides, and came back and reported that we could get across if we kept right on, but that it would be impossible if snow fell. He was in favor of a forced march until the other side of the summit should be reached, but some of our party were so tired and exhausted with the day's labor that they declared they could not take another step; so the few who knew the danger that the night might bring yielded to the many, and we camped within three miles of the summit.

That night came the dreaded snow. Around the camp-fires under the trees great feathery flakes came whirling down. The air was so full of them that one could see objects only a few feet away. The Indians knew we were doomed, and one of them wrapped his blanket about him and stood all night under a tree. We children slept soundly on our cold bed of snow with a soft white mantle falling over us so thickly that every few moments my mother would have to shake the shawl -- our only covering -- to keep us from being buried alive. In the morning the snow lay deep on mountain and valley. With heavy hearts we turned back to a cabin that had been built by the Murphy-Schallenberger party two years before. We built more cabins and prepared as best we could for the winter. That camp, which proved the camp of death to many in our company, was made on the shore of a lake, since known as "Donner Lake." The Donners were camped in Alder Creek Valley below the lake, and were, if possible, in a worse condition than ourselves. The snow came on so suddenly that they had no time to build cabins, but hastily put up brush sheds, covering them with pine boughs.

Three double cabins were built at Donner Lake, which were known as the "Breen Cabin," the "Murphy Cabin," and the "Reed-Graves Cabin." The cattle were all killed, and the meat was placed in snow for preservation. My mother had no cattle to kill, but she made arrangements for some, promising to give two for one in California. Stanton and the Indians made their home in my mother's cabin.

Many attempts were made to cross the mountains, but all who tried were driven back by the pitiless storms. Finally a party was organized, since known as the "Forlorn Hope." They made snow-shoes, and fifteen started, ten men and five women, but only seven lived to reach California; eight men perished. They were over a month on the way, and the horrors endured by that Forlorn Hope no pen can describe nor imagination conceive. The noble Stanton was one of the party, and perished the sixth day out, thus sacrificing his life for strangers. I can find no words in which to express a fitting tribute to the memory of Stanton.

The misery endured during those four months at Donner Lake in our little dark cabins under the snow would fill pages and make the coldest heart ache. Christmas was near, but to the starving its memory gave no comfort. It came and passed without observance, but my mother had determined weeks before that her children should have a treat on this one day. She had laid away a few dried apples, some beans, a bit of tripe, and a small piece of bacon. When this hoarded store was brought out, the delight of the little ones knew no bounds. The cooking was watched carefully, and when we sat down to our Christmas dinner mother said, "Children, eat slowly, for this one day you can have all you wish." So bitter was the misery relieved by that one bright day, that I have never since sat down to a Christmas dinner without my thoughts going back to Donner Lake.

The storms would often last ten days at a time, and we would have to cut chips from the logs inside which formed our cabins, in order to start a fire. We could scarcely walk, and the men had hardly strength to procure wood. We would drag ourselves through the snow from one cabin to another, and some mornings snow would have to be shoveled out of the fireplace before a fire could be made. Poor little children were crying with hunger, and mothers were crying because they had so little to give their children. We seldom thought of bread, we had been without it so long. Four months of such suffering would fill the bravest hearts with despair.

During the closing days of December, 1846, gold was found in my mother's cabin at Donner Lake by John Denton. I remember the night well. The storm fiends were shrieking in their wild mirth, we were sitting about the fire in our little dark home, busy with our thoughts. Denton with his cane kept knocking pieces off the large rocks used as fire-irons on which to place the wood. Something bright attracted his attention, and picking up pieces of the rock he examined them closely; then turning to my mother he said, "Mrs. Reed, this is gold." My mother replied that she wished it were bread. Denton knocked more chips from the rocks, and he hunted in the ashes for the shining particles until he had gathered about a teaspoonful. This he tied in a small piece of buckskin and placed in his pocket, saying, "If we every get away from here I am coming back for more." Denton started out with the first relief party but perished on the way, and no one thought of the gold in his pocket. Denton was about thirty years of age; he was born in Sheffield, England, and was a gunsmith and gold-beater by trade. Gold has never been found on the shore of the lake, but a few miles from there in the mountain cañons, from which this rock possibly came, rich mines have been discovered.

Time dragged slowly along till we were no longer on short allowance but were simply starving. My mother determined to make an effort to cross the mountains. She could not see her children die without trying to get them food. It was hard to leave them but she felt that it must be done. She told them she would bring them bread, so they were willing to stay, and with no guide but a compass we started -- my mother, Eliza, Milt Elliott and myself. Milt wore snow shoes and we followed in his tracks. We were five days in the mountains; Eliza gave out the first day and had to return, but we kept on and climbed one high mountain after another only to see others higher still ahead. Often I would have to crawl up the mountains, being too tired to walk. The nights were made hideous by the screams of wild beasts heard in the distance. Again, we would be lulled to sleep by the moan of the pine trees, which seemed to sympathize with our loneliness. One morning we awoke to find ourselves in a well of snow. During the night, while in the deep sleep of exhaustion, the heat of the fire had melted the snow and our little camp had gradually sunk many feet below the surface until we were literally buried in a well of snow. The danger was that any attempt to get out might bring an avalanche upon us, but finally steps were carefully made and we reached the surface. My foot was badly frozen, so we were compelled to return, and just in time, for that night a storm came on, the most fearful of the winter, and we should have perished had we not been in the cabins.

We now had nothing to eat but raw hides and they were on the roof of the cabin to keep out the snow; when prepared for cooking and boiled they were simply a pot of glue. When the hides were taken off our cabin and we were left without shelter Mr. Breen gave us a home with his family, and Mrs. Breen prolonged my life by slipping me little bits of meat now and then when she discovered that I could not eat the hide. Death had already claimed many in our party and it seemed as though relief never would reach us. Baylis Williams, who had been in delicate health before we left Springfield, was the first to die; he passed away before starvation had really set in.

I am a Catholic although my parents were not. I often went to the Catholic church before leaving home, but it was at Donner Lake that I made the vow to be a Catholic. The Breens were the only Catholic family in the Donner party and prayers were said aloud regularly in that cabin night and morning. Our only light was from little pine sticks split up like kindling wood and kept constantly on the hearth. I was very fond of kneeling by the side of Mr. Breen and holding these little torches so that he might see to read. One night we had all gone to bed -- I was with my mother and the little ones, all huddled together to keep from freezing -- but I could not sleep. It was a fearful night and I felt that the hour was not far distant when we would go to sleep -- never to wake again in this world. All at once I found myself on my knees with my hands clasped, looking up through the darkness, making a vow that if God would send us relief and let me see my father again I would be a Catholic. That prayer was answered.

On his arrival at Sutter's Fort, my father made known the situation of the emigrants, and Captain Sutter offered at once to do everything possible for their relief. He furnished horses and provisions and my father and Mr. McCutchen started for the mountains, coming as far as possible with horses and then with packs on their backs proceeding on foot; but they were finally compelled to return. Captain Sutter was not surprised at their defeat. He stated that there were no able-bodied men in that vicinity, all having gone down the country with Frémont to fight the Mexicans. He advised my father to go to Yerba Buena, now San Francisco, and make his case known to the naval officer in command. My father was in fact conducting parties there -- when the seven members of the Forlorn Hope arrived from across the mountains. Their famished faces told the story. Cattle were killed and men were up all night drying beef and making flour by hand mills, nearly 200 pounds being made in one night, and a party of seven, commanded by Captain Reasen P. Tucker, were sent to our relief by Captain Sutter and the alcalde, Mr. Sinclair. On the evening of February 19th, 1847, they reached our cabins, where all were starving. They shouted to attract attention. Mr. Breen, clambered up the icy steps from our cabin, and soon we heard the blessed words, "Relief, thank God, relief!" There was joy at Donner Lake that night, for we did not know the fate of the Forlorn Hope and we were told that relief parties would come and go until all were across the mountains. But with the joy sorrow was strangely blended. There were tears in other eyes than those of children; strong men sat down and wept. For the dead were lying about on the snow, some even unburied, since the living had not had strength to bury their dead. When Milt Elliott died -- our faithful friend, who seemed so like a brother -- my mother and I dragged him up out of the cabin and covered him with snow. Commencing at his feet, I patted the pure white snow down softly until I reached his face. Poor Milt! It was hard to cover that face from sight forever, for with his death our best friend was gone.

On the 22d of February the first relief started with a party of twenty-three men, women and children. My mother and her family were among the number. It was a bright sunny morning and we felt happy, but we had not gone far when Patty and Tommy gave out. They were not able to stand the fatigue and it was not thought safe to allow them to proceed, so Mr. Glover informed mama that they would have to be sent back to the cabins to await the next expedition. What language can express our feelings? My mother said that she would go back with her children -- that we would all go back together. This the relief party would not permit, and Mr. Glover promised mama that as soon as they reached Bear Valley he himself would return for her children. Finally my mother, turning to Mr. Glover said, "Are you a Mason?" He replied that he was. "Will you promise me on the word of a Mason that if we do not meet their father you will return and save my children?" He pledged himself that he would. My father was a member of the Mystic Tie and mama had great faith in the word of a Mason. It was a sad parting -- a fearful struggle. The men turned aside, not being able to hide their tears. Patty said, "I want to see papa, but I will take good care of Tommy and I do not want you to come back." Mr. Glover returned with the children and, providing them with food, left them in the care of Mr. Breen.

With sorrowful hearts we traveled on, walking through the snow in single file. The men wearing snow-shoes broke the way and we followed in their tracks. At night we lay down on the snow to sleep, to awake to find our clothing all frozen, even to our shoe-strings. At break of day we were again on the road, owing to the fact that we could make better time over the frozen snow. The sunshine, which it would seem would have been welcome, only added to our misery. The dazzling reflection of the snow was very trying to the eyes, while its heat melted our frozen clothing, making them cling to our bodies. My brother was too small to step in the track made by the men, and in order to travel he had to place his knee on the little hill of snow after each step and climb over. Mother coaxed him along, telling him that every step he took he was getting nearer to papa and nearer something to eat. He was the youngest child that walked over the Sierra Nevada. On our second day's journey John Denton gave out and declared it would be impossible for him to travel, but he begged his companions to continue their journey. A fire was built and he was left lying on a bed of freshly cut pine boughs, peacefully smoking. He looked so comfortable that my little brother wanted to stay with him; but when the second relief party reached him poor Denton was past waking. His last thoughts seemed to have gone back to his childhood's home, as a little poem was found by his side, the pencil apparently just dropped from his hand.

Captain Tucker's party on their way to the cabins had lightened their packs of a sufficient quantity of provisions to supply the sufferers on their way out. But when we reached the place where the cache had been made by hanging the food on a tree, we were horrified to find that wild animals had destroyed it, and again starvation stared us in the face. But my father was hurrying over the mountains, and met us in our hour of need with his hands full of bread. He had expected to meet us on this day, and had stayed up all night baking bread to give us. He brought with him fourteen men. Some of his party were ahead, and when they saw us coming they called out, "Is Mrs. Reed with you? If she is, tell her Mr. Reed is here." We heard the call; mother knelt on the snow, while I tried to run to meet papa.

When my father learned that two of his children were still at the cabins, he hurried on, so fearful was he that they might perish before he reached them. He seemed to fly over the snow, and made in two days the distance we had been five in traveling, and was overjoyed to find Patty and Tommy alive. He reached Donner Lake on the first of March, and what a sight met his gaze! The famished little children and the death-like look of all made his heart ache. He filled Patty's apron with biscuits, which she carried around, giving one to each person. He had soup made for the infirm, and rendered every assistance possible to the sufferers. Leaving them with about seven day's provisions, he started out with a party of seventeen, all that were able to travel. Three of his men were left at the cabins to procure wood and assist the helpless. My father's party (the second relief) had not traveled many miles when a storm broke upon them. With the snow came a perfect hurricane. The crying of half-frozen children, the lamenting of the mothers, and suffering of the whole party was heart-rending; and above all could be heard the shrieking of the storm King. One who has never witnessed a blizzard in the Sierra can form no idea of the situation. All night my father and his men worked unceasingly through the raging storm, trying to erect shelter for the dying women and children. At times the hurricane would burst forth with such violence that he felt alarmed on account of the tall timber surrounding the camp. The party was destitute of food, all supplies that could be spared having been left with those at the cabins. The relief party had cached provisions on their way over to the cabins, and my father had sent three of the men forward for food before the storm set in; but they could not return. Thus, again, death stared all in the face. At one time the fire was nearly gone; had it been lost, all would have perished. Three days and nights they were exposed to the fury of the elements. Finally my father became snow-blind and could do no more, and he would have died but for the exertions of William McCutchen and Hiram Miller, who worked over him all night. From this time forward, the toil and responsibility rested upon McCutchen and Miller.

The storm at last ceased, and these two determined to set out over the snow and send back relief to those not able to travel. Hiram Miller picked up Tommy and started. Patty thought she could walk, but gradually everything faded from her sight, and she too seemed to be dying. All other sufferings were now forgotten, and everything was done to revive the child. My father found some crumbs in the thumb of a woolen mitten; warming and moistening them between his own lips, he gave them to her and thus saved her life, and afterward she was carried along by different ones in the company. Patty was not alone in her travels. Hidden away in her bosom was a tiny doll, which she had carried day and night through all of our trials. Sitting before a nice, bright fire at Woodworth's Camp, she took dolly out to have a talk, and told her of all her new happiness.

There was untold suffering at that "Starved Camp," as the place has since been called. When my father reached Woodworth's Camp, a third relief started in at once and rescued the living. A fourth relief went on to Donner Lake, as many were still there -- and many remain there still, including George Donner and wife, Jacob Donner and wife and four of their children. George Donner had met with an accident which rendered him unable to travel; and his wife would not leave him to die alone. It would take pages to tell of the heroic acts and noble deeds of those who lie sleeping about Donner Lake.

Most of the survivors, when brought in from the mountains, were taken by the different relief parties to Sutter's Fort, and the generous hearted captain did everything possible for the sufferers. Out of the eighty-three persons who were snowed in at Donner Lake, forty-two perished, and of the thirty-one emigrants who left Springfield, Illinois, that spring morning, only eighteen lived to reach California. Alcalde Sinclair took my mother and her family to his own home, and we were surrounded with every comfort. Mrs. Sinclair was the dearest of women. Never can I forget their kindness. But our anxiety was not over, for we knew that my father's party had been caught in the storm. I can see my mother now, as she stood leaning against the door for hours at a time, looking towards the mountains. At last my father arrived at Mr. Sinclair's with the little ones, and our family were again united. That day's happiness repaid us for much that we had suffered; and it was spring in California.

Words cannot tell how beautiful the spring appeared to us coming out of the mountains from the long winter at Donner Lake in our little dark cabins under the snow. Before us now lay, in all its beauty, the broad valley of the Sacramento. I remember one day, when traveling down Napa Valley, we stopped at noon to have lunch under the shade of an oak; but I was not hungry; I was too full of the beautiful around me to think of eating. So I wandered off by myself to a lovely little knoll and stood there in a bed of wild flowers, looking up and down the green valley, all dotted with trees. The birds were singing with very joy in the branches over my head, and the blessed sun was smiling down upon all as though in benediction. I drank it in for a moment, and then began kissing my hand and wafting kisses to Heaven in thanksgiving to the Almighty for creating a world so beautiful. I felt so near God at that moment that it seemed to me I could feel His breath warm on my cheek. By and by I heard papa calling, "Daughter, where are you? Come, child, we are ready to start, and you have had no lunch." I ran and caught him by the hand, saying, "Buy this place, please, and let us make our home here." He stood looking around for a moment, and said, "It *is* a lovely spot," and then we passed on.

# FRÉMONT'S DISASTROUS COLORADO EXPEDITION
## (1848-49)

## Micajah McGehee

**Editors' Note:** John Charles Frémont, rightfully called "The Pathfinder," was one of the West's most energetic and charismatic explorers. He was also ambitious and headstrong. It may well be that these traits are mutually inclusive.

In 1838, at age twenty-five, Frémont was given a lieutenant's commission in the U.S. Army Corps of Topographical Engineers. Three years later, the dashing young lieutenant married Jessie Benton, the daughter of Senator Thomas Hart Benton of Missouri. Benton was one of the most powerful men in Washington and an enthusiastic believer in "Manifest Destiny," the doctrine which asserted that U.S. expansion from coast to coast was not only inevitable but morally just. With his father-in-law's support, Frémont led three expeditions between 1842 and 1846 to explore and map the Rocky Mountains, the Great Basin, and California and Oregon. He truly finished what Lewis and Clark had begun, and opened the way for the settlement of the American West. Frémont became a national hero.

Frémont had the good fortune to be in California when the Mexican war broke out in 1846, enabling him to figure prominently in its accession into the United States. Unfortunately, the following year he became embroiled in a bitter dispute with his superior, General Stephen W. Kearny. The result was that the general charged the fiery Frémont with insubordination and placed him under arrest. He was subsequently tried by court-martial in Washington and found guilty. Frémont was sentenced to dismissal from the Corps, but this punishment was set aside by Present James Polk. Distraught over the army's "injustice," he resigned his commission.

Even though he was now a private citizen, Frémont was not through exploring. In 1848, his mentor, Senator Benton, helped him organize a privately financed survey in search of a railroad passage through southern Colorado -- the scramble to locate transcontinental railway routes then being at its height. Frémont assembled a party of thirty-three men, several of whom had been West with him before. They reached Pueblo, Colorado, on November 21, 1848, a month after leaving St. Louis. Pueblo, the last outpost on the plains and the gateway to the Rockies was described by one of the party, Richard Kern, as "...a miserable looking place, the inside resembling a menagerie -- a compound of Spaniards, horses, mules, dogs, chickens and bad stench."

The late November nights were already cold and the fur trappers staying at Pueblo warned the explorers that the mountains that blocked their way were impassable in winter. But Frémont had negotiated the Sierra Nevada during the winter months, and he wanted to observe the southern Rocky Mountains at

49

their worst to better judge the suitability of any rail route he might discover. "Old Bill" Williams, one of the trappers then wintering at Pueblo, was hired to lead the party through the mountains. The next day, Frémont and his followers headed into the San Juan Mountains with sixty-one-year-old Bill Williams as their guide.

One of the members of the expedition was twenty-two-year-old Micajah McGehee who had joined Frémont at St. Louis purely for the adventure. In his graphic account of their attempts to cross the mountains, reprinted here, he described the miserable two months that followed. Frémont's fourth expedition was a disaster, resulting in the loss of ten lives to cold and starvation. Attempting to cross the San Juan Mountains in mid-winter would prove as foolish as attempting to explore the Sonoran desert in mid-summer, as the reader will note in comparing this event with the narrative by Jack Hoffman that appears later is this anthology.

McGehee's story was thought to have been written before the Civil War; however, it was not published until eleven years after his death. His brother, C. G. McGehee, sent the manuscript to *Century Magazine* where it was published in 1891.

Although the Pathfinder's railroad survey came to naught, Frémont went on to become a millionaire from gold found on land he acquired in California. He was elected to represent California in the U.S. Senate in 1850, and in 1856 he was nominated for president of the United States by the Republican Party, only to be defeated by James Buchanan. When the Civil War began, his court-martial was forgotten, and he was appointed a major general in the Union Army. His service during the war was undistinguished, however, and after the war bad business decisions resulted in the loss of his fortune. In 1878 he secured an appointment as the governor of Arizona, but his three years in that office are remembered more for his absences from the territory than his achievements in it. Frémont died in 1890, and although his later life was one of little accomplishment, the fame bought with his youthful explorations will not be forgotten. It has been truthfully said that great cities sprang from his campfires.

~ ~ ~ ~ ~

**Bill Williams was the most successful trapper in the mountains,** and the best acquainted with the ways and habits of the wild tribes among and near whom he spent his adventurous life. He first came to the West as a sort of missionary to the Osages. But "Old Bill" laid aside his Christianity and took up his rifle and came to the mountains. He was full of oddities in appearance, manner, conversation, and action. He generally went out alone into the mountains, and would remain there trapping by himself for several months together, his lonely camps being often pitched in the vicinity of hostile savages. But he was as well versed in stratagem as they, and though he bore the marks of balls and arrows, he was a terror to them in single fight. He had ingratiated himself into the favor of several tribes; he had two or three squaws among the Utahs, and spoke their language and also that of several other tribes.

He was a dead shot with a rifle, though he always shot with a "double wabble;" he never could hold his gun still, yet his ball went always to the spot on a single shot. Though a most indefatigable walker, he never could walk on a straight line, but went staggering along, first on one side and then the other. He was an expert horseman; scarce a horse or mule could unseat him. He rode leaning forward upon the pommel, with his rifle before him, his stirrups ridiculously short, and his breeches rubbed up to his knees, leaving his legs bare even in freezing cold weather. He wore a loose Monkey-jacket or a buckskin hunting-shirt, and for his head-covering a blanket-cap, the two top corners drawn up into two wolfish, satyr-like ears, giving him somewhat the appearance of the representations we generally meet with of his Satanic Majesty, at the same time rendering his tout ensemble exceedingly ludicrous. He was a perfect specimen of his kind, an embodiment of the reckless and extravagant propensity of the mountaineers, and he pursued his lucrative but perilous vocation from an innate love of its excitement and dangers. He had no other care for the gains of his labors than as a means of affording him a "big spree," and enabling him to procure more powder and lead. It is told of him that he once came into Taos and spent on one spree six thousand dollars, the result of a successful season of trapping, and then left the place in debt. One of his amusements on this occasion was to buy whole bolts of calico, then quite a costly article in Taos, and, going into the street, to take hold of one end and throw out the other as far as he could, unrolling it on the ground, and then call out the Mexican women to scramble for it. In this way, and with drinking and gambling, three or four weeks would suffice to run through his money. Taking his traps and rifle, and some provision on his mules, he would disappear among the mountains, and nothing would be heard of him for months, until he would come into the fort with a new supply of peltries. He would sometimes gamble until he lost all his money and animals; then borrowing as many as he wanted of the best horses belonging to his fellow trappers, who never opposed him, he would leave the fort, one or two thousand dollars in debt, and take to the mountains again, certain to return after a few months with another large supply. If he was much in need of a horse, or tired of his squaw, he would sell her, or "swap" her off for one or two horses. For twenty-one years he had lived in the mountains without returning to civilized life until he was taken back under guard, a year or two previous, by Captain Cook, for the offense of maneuvering and acting the Indian in his buckskin suit on the plains, thereby deceiving the captain into the belief that he was an Indian, and giving his men a fruitless chase of several miles over the prairies before they could overtake him on his pony, much to his diversion and the officer's chagrin.

Such was old Bill Williams -- he who was destined to be our guide at this time. But it was not without some hesitation that he consented to go, for most of the old trappers at the pueblo declared that it was impossible to cross the mountains at that time; that the cold upon the mountains was unprecedented, and the snow deeper than they had ever known it so early in the year. However, Old Bill concluded to go, for he thought we could manage to get through, though not without considerable suffering.

On the 26th of November [1848] we entered the Rocky Mountains, which had been for days looming up before us, presenting to view one continuous sheet of snow. The snow already covered the mountains and was rapidly deepening. I have frequently since called to mind the expression of one of the men as we rode along before entering Hard Scrabble. As we looked upon the stormy mountains so portentious of the future, he said, "Friends, I don't want my bones to bleach upon those mountains." Poor fellow, little did he dream of what the future would be!

In the evening, from our first camp, eight miles in the mountains, several of us climbed to a point to take a last look at the plains. The sight was beautiful; the snow-covered plain far beneath us stretching eastward as far as the eye could reach, while on the opposite side frowned the almost perpendicular wall of high mountains.

We entered the mountains on foot and the snow rapidly deepened and we continued on foot, packing our saddle mules with corn to sustain the animals. We traveled on, laboring through the deep snow upon the rugged mountain range, passing through successively what are called White Mountain Valley and Wet Mountain Valley, into San Luis Valley. The cold was intense and storms would frequently compel us to lie in camp, from the impossibility of forcing the mules against them, and the certainty of freezing if we attempted to proceed, for a number of the men were frozen in their limbs in such attempts before we could go a mile from camp. The animals became exhausted and poverty stricken from the inclemency of the weather, and the want of food, what little grass there had been being all buried in the snow.

Times grew worse and worse as we proceeded. The mules gave out, one by one and dropped down in the trail, and their packs were placed upon the saddle mules. The cold became more and more intense, even to such a degree that the thermometer would not indicate the temperature, it being many degrees below zero and the mercury sinking entirely into the bulb.

Crossing what we called the Sand Hills, and those bleak, bald ridges between the White Mountain and Wet Mountain Valleys, the very aspect of the men was chilling. The breath would freeze upon their faces and their lips be so stiff from the ice that it was almost impossible to speak, their eyelids in a similar condition from the freezing of the water which the cold wind would force from them, the ice standing on their lashes. Long icicles hung down from the nostrils, and the long beard and the hair stood out white and stiff with the frost, each hair standing to itself.

The aspect of the mules was suited to that of the men; their eyelashes and the long beards about their mouths stood like icicles and their breath passing back settled upon their breast and sides until they were perfectly white with frost, and the snow would clog upon their fetlocks and under their hoofs until it formed a ball six inches long, making them appear as though they were walking on stilts. With the deep snow around us, and the pendent frost upon the leafless trees, nature and ourselves presented a very compatible picture. Two trappers, Old Bill informed us, were frozen to death here the year previous.

We came through Robideau's Pass, the passage of which was exceedingly difficult, for it was completely filled with the fallen timber prostrated by some previous year's hurricane, amongst which the snow lay deep, and the mules were continually stumbling and falling over these and down the rocky slants. Emerging from this and camping near its extremity, the Colonel [Frémont], with several others, rode back to examine another pass, and soon returned, one or two with frozen feet.

We descended into San Luis Valley. The snow lay deep as elsewhere and there was no sign of vegetation. One broad, white, dreary looking plain lay before us, bounded by white mountains. High, precipitous, and frozen mountains were behind us, and this broad drear plain lay between us and the Rio Grande fifty miles ahead of us. So we entered with the determination of getting through it as quickly as possible. We travelled late and camped in the middle of it, without any shelter from the winds, and with no fuel but some wild sage, a small shrub which grew sparsely around. The cold was intense, the thermometer at night standing at 17 degrees below zero, and it was so cold during the day that Ducatel, a young fellow in the company, came very near freezing to death.

By collecting a quantity of the sage, we made sufficient fires to cook, or rather half cook, our suppers of deer meat, five of these animals having been killed this evening by two of the men, and, bolting down the half-cooked meat, we quickly turned into our blankets in order to keep somewhat warm and for protection against the driving snow for, since leaving the states, we had scarcely ever stretched tents. In the night, as ill luck would have it, our mules, poor creatures, which stood shivering in the cold with bowed backs and drooping heads, suffering from their exposed situation and half starved, being now reduced to a pint of corn twice a day, and having no other resource for food, broke loose from their weak fastenings of sage bushes and started off *en masse* on the back trail in order to obtain the shelter of the mountains we had left the day before or to find some shrubbery they could eat. As soon as it was ascertained that they were gone, in the middle of the night, we had to rise from our beds, lifting half a foot of snow with our top blankets, and strike out in pursuit of them through the severe cold. We overtook them several miles from camp and, taking them back, made them secure. But we rested little the balance of the night.

The next day we reached the Rio Grande del Norte, which we found frozen over, and camped in the river bottom, thickly timbered with cottonwood and willow. We had considerable difficulty in crossing the river, the mules slipping upon the ice and falling or breaking through in places, when we would have to raise them to their feet or draw them over the ice. We found some game, deer and elk, in the river bottom, of which we killed a few. The snow was deeper along here than we had seen it anywhere previously, and our camps, pitched upon it, presented a dreary prospect.

After traveling the whole day in a perfect storm of snow, towards night we would camp in the midst of it and, unpacking our mules, turn them loose to wander about and browse upon whatever shrubs or ends of twigs might chance to remain uncovered. Then digging out of the snow the fallen limbs of the dead fallen timber which lay buried beneath it, the ends here and there projecting out, we would build our fires in amongst the snow upon the top of which we slept at night, rolled in our blankets, first going through the process of thawing it from our feet where it would gather and become clogged while wading through the deep snow after our mules in order to feed and blanket them as night approached.

Here I first got my feet frozen as did several others, the result, in part, of wearing boots, for which I quickly substituted moccasins with blanket wrappers which are much warmer than socks. These are worn altogether by the mountain men whom experience has taught their advantages. They allow a freer exercise and consequently a more rapid circulation and greater warmth than is the case in wearing boots. Moccasins with blanket wrappers for the feet and with leggings of the same material afford the best protection for the lower extremities against severe cold.

Continuing up the river two or three days, we again entered the mountains, which soon assumed a very rugged character, and we continued ascending toward the main range. Nature here presents herself with all her features prominent and strongly marked, her figures bold and colossal. Peaks, crags, and gorges, of Alpine boldness, confronted us on all sides with their rocky barriers. Our progress became slow and laborious. Our track lay through deep mountain gorges, amid towering precipices and beetling crags, and along steep declivities where, at any other season, it would be next to impossible to travel, but where now the deep snows afforded a secure foothold.

In making the ascent of some of these precipitous mountain sides, now and then a mule would lose his footing and go tumbling and rolling many feet down with his pack until he lodged among the rocks below. My saddle mule took one of these tumbles. Losing her foothold, she got her rope hitched upon a large log which lay loosely balanced upon the rocks and knocking me down and jerking the log clear over my head they went tumbling down together. But fortunately no one was hurt.

A great obstacle to our progress were the rapid, rough-bottomed, but boggy streams that we had frequently to encounter in the narrow and deep ravines, where the mules would get balked, half a dozen at a time, with their packs on. Then we had to wade in up to our middle amongst the floating ice in the freezing water to help them out.

The farther we went the more obstacles we had to encounter, and difficulties beset us so thick and fast on every hand as we advanced that they seemed threatening to thwart our expedition; but it was determined to continue as long as one chance remained.

Our position assumed a threatening aspect. The snow became deeper daily and to advance was but adding dangers to difficulties. About one-third of the men were already frost-bitten more or less; some of the mules would freeze to death every night, and every day as many more would give out from exhaustion and be left on the trail, and it seemed like combatting fate to attempt to proceed, but we were bent on our course and we continued to advance.

At one time, men were sent ahead to report the prospect; they returned, stating that grass appeared in the distance before them and supposed the snow was abating, but, on coming up, what they saw proved to be the tops of bushes six feet high, projecting above the snow, nor did anything appear upon which the animals could subsist. The corn we had packed along for them was already consumed.

Sometimes we would attempt to move on and the severity of the weather would force us back into camp. In one of these attempts, before we could beat our way half a mile against the tempest, our guide, Old Bill Williams, had nearly frozen; he dropped down upon his mule in a stupor and was nearly senseless when we got into camp. A number of the men came in with their noses, ears, faces, fingers, and feet, partially frozen, and one or two of the mules dropped down and froze to death under their packs.

These times were tough. Poor mules! It was pitiable to see them; they would roam about all night generally on account of their extreme weakness, following back the path of the previous day, pawing in the snow three or four feet deep for some sign of vegetation to keep them alive. They would fall down every fifty yards under their packs and we would have to unpack them and lift them up, and that with fingers frozen and lacerated by the cold. Finally the mules began eating the ropes and rawhide lariats with which they were tied, until there were no more left in camp to tie them with, then they ate the blankets which we tied over them at night, then came in camp and ate the pads and rigging off the pack-saddles, and ate each others tails and manes entirely bare, even into the flesh, and would come to us while sleeping and begin to eat the blankets off us; would tumble into our fires over the cooking utensils, and even stick their noses into the kettles for something to eat. But, poor things, little relief could we afford them; for, though they suffered much, we were in no better condition. Our provisions were nearly exhausted, and we were more or less frozen.

Finally, on the 17th of December, after frequent ineffectual attempts, we found that we could force our way no further. By our utmost endeavors with mauls and spades, we could make but half a mile or a mile per day. The cold became more severe and storms constant so that nothing was visible at times through the thick driving snow. For days in succession, we would labor to beat a trail a few hundred yards in length, but the next day the storm would leave no trace of the previous day's work.

We were on the San Juan Mountains, a section of the main range of the Rocky Mountains proper, at an elevation of 11,000 feet. The cold was so intense and the atmosphere so rare at this great height that respiration became difficult and any exertion laborious and fatiguing; it would sometimes cause the blood to start from the lips and nose. The mercury in the thermometer stood 20 degrees below zero and the snow was here from four to twenty feet deep and probably, in places, as much as 100 feet, reaching within a few feet of the top of the tall pines.

When we built our campfires, deep pits were formed by the melting of the snow, completely concealing the different messes from each other. Down in these holes we slept, spreading our blankets upon the snow; every morning crawling out from under a deep covering of snow which had fallen upon us during the night. The strong pine smoke, for here there was no other timber but pine, together with the reflection from the snow, so affected our sight that at times we could scarcely see a particle, and the snow drifted over us continually, driven about by the violence of the chill blasts that swept over the mountains constantly.

Besides ourselves and our mules, no vestige of animal life appeared here in this lofty and dreary solitude; not even the ravens uttered their hoarse cry, nor the wolves their hollow and dismal howl, wonted visitants of unfrequented places. The mules stood huddled together on the mountain, after vainly searching for grass, their ears frozen and their limbs cracked and bleeding from cold; they would drop down and die, one by one, and, in a single night, nearly the entire band of over one hundred mules had frozen to death.

After remaining in this condition for five days without being able to move camp, with no prospect of better things, our provisions being almost entirely gone and the mules having nearly all perished, compelled to abandon our present course, the Colonel determined to endeavor as quickly as possible to return by a different direction to the Rio Grande. There we had left game upon which we could subsist until a party, to be previously despatched, should return with relief; and whence, having obtained a fresh supply of animals, we could, crossing the mountains by a different direction, still pursue a westerly course on the 38th degree.

So, on the 22nd of December, we commenced our move crossing over the bleak mountain thickly strewn with the frozen mules, and packing our baggage with us. We were more than a week moving our camp and equipage over the top of this mountain (a distance of two miles only from our first camp), owing to the intensity of the weather. The same day that we began to move, our provisions being all consumed except a small portion of macaroni and sugar, reserved against hard times, we commenced eating the carcasses of the frozen mules, for it was hoped that we might save the few that yet lived; but it was impossible, and we began to kill and eat the surviving ones. In butchering them, some of the men would return to camp with fingers perfectly hard frozen, such was the degree of cold. Capt. Cathcart said: "Who'd 'a thought it? A Captain in the 11th Prince Albert's Hussars eating mule meat and packing his baggage amongst the snows of the Rocky Mountains!"

On Christmas Day, the Colonel despatched a party of four men, King, Creutzfeldt, Breckenridge, and Bill Williams, to proceed down the Rio [Grande] del Norte with all possible speed to Abiquiu [New Mexico] where they were to procure provisions and mules to relieve us. He allowed them sixteen days to go and return. We made our Christmas and New Year's dinner on mule meat, not the fattest either as may be judged, and continued to feed upon it while it was within reach, for we had undertaken to pack all our baggage, saddles, pack saddles, etc., on our backs through the deep snow to the river, where we would be able to recover them. We made a sledge for this purpose, but it did not work well and we abandoned it.

Our way to the river was very rough, passing over rugged and precipitous mountain spurs, difficult of passage, and deep ravines with rapid streams frozen over in which the water was pitching and roaring beneath us as we crossed. We would move camp three or four miles at a time, then packing all the baggage down we would move again in the same way; on an average, at our best, scarcely making a mile per day, for wading through the deep snow was very laborious. It would bear us up for two or three steps with our load but, at the next step, we would break through and go in waist deep when we would have to scramble out the best way we could, and try it again.  We took advantage of every steep descent and, fixing our packs in the parfleches [rawhide bags] so that they would slide, we would give them a start and they would go sliding and bounding along down, fifty or a hundred yards at a stretch, when, acquiring a tremendous momentum, they would sometimes bolt out and, plunging ten or fifteen feet, come with great violence against a tree or rock which would stop their progress. Occasionally they would take a fellow before them about the heels and knocking his feet from under him away they would all go together.

But our labor became very exhausting, for we were now on short allowance, and our starvation also ill fitted us to endure the cold.  On our way the last provision was issued out, a little macaroni and sugar, and we began eating the rawhide tugropes and parfleches, cutting it in strips and boiling it to a sort of glue, or burning it on the coals until it was soft enough to bite.

Times were getting squally.  Between the last camps over a bleak and barren stretch of seven miles before reaching the river, the cold was unusually severe and perfectly unbearable, storms prevailing continually, which rendered it almost impossible for us to make the distance across in a single day, being compelled frequently to take a refuge under the shelter of the rocks, making a fire of what sticks or other material we could find to keep from freezing.

In crossing this stretch ere reaching the river, one of the party, Proue, had frozen to death beside the trail; we passed and repassed his lifeless body, not daring to stop long enough in this intense cold to perform the useless rites of burial.

One day I started across this stretch, determined to go on to the river that night or freeze.  Andrews started with me but, before we could get half way across, he became exhausted and lay down upon the snow, declaring that he could go no further, and that he would freeze to death if he attempted it.  I tried to urge him on, but he could not go and I could not leave him; so, proceeding a short distance, I got him into a cave of the rock, which afforded a shelter against the severity of the storm; then, climbing among the rocks, I ascended to the top of the mountain where the wind was blowing such a perfect hurricane that I would have to lie flat down, at times, to keep from being swept off. Taking advantage of the intervals between the gusts of winds, I rolled down some of the pinon logs which lay upon the mountainside, pitching them over the crags below and, descending to the cave, struck a fire.

By this time, two others, Capt. Cathcart and R. Kern, arrived to take shelter from the storm.  They had not a thing to eat, and we had our last portion; in the extremity of our starvation, we had the day before divided out the last morsel which remained of anything to eat, and the share that fell to each man was a cupful of boiled macaroni and a cup of sugar. This we had with us and we offered to share it with them, but, *miserabile vieu*, Andrews, in trying to warm it, by an unlucky move, upset it into the fire; thus went the last mouthful that we had to eat on earth, and we half starved.

The storm continued to rage with such violence that we could not leave, and here it kept us for two whole days. In looking around, I found a small roll of rawhide snowshoe strings which had been left by one of the men. These we cut into pieces and boiled them. I also found some dry bones in an old wolf den among the rocks; how many years they had been lying there, I will not undertake to say, but these we pounded to pieces between rocks and boiled them with the strings and, upon this mess, we four lived for two days. A number of others on their way had been forced, like us, to take shelter here and there among the rocks from the storm.

We reached the river. No game was there; the hope upon which we had depended was disappointed; the deer and elk had been driven off by the deep snow. For days we had been anxiously looking for the return of King's party with relief. The time allotted him had already expired and day after day passed by, but no prospect of relief came and we concluded that either the party had been attacked by Indians and had all been killed, or they had lost their way and perished.

The time allowed for King's return having passed (January 9), the Colonel, who had moved down to the river before us, waited two days longer, and then (January 11), taking just enough provision before it was all exhausted to do them down the river, himself started off with Mr. Preuss, Godey, Theodore (Godey's nephew) and Sanders, the Colonel's servant man, intending to find out what had become of the party and hasten them back; or, if our fears concerning them proved true, to push on himself to the nearest settlement and send relief.

He left an order that we scarce knew how to interpret, to the effect that we must finish packing the baggage to the river and hasten on down as speedily as possible to the mouth of Rabbit River where we would meet relief, and that if we wished to see him we must be in a hurry as he was going on to California. By this time, being forced to abandon his projected route, he had determined to proceed to California by a Southern route.

Two days after the Colonel left (about January 13), we had all collected on the river. The last of our provisions had been consumed and we had been living for several days upon parfleche. Our condition was perilous in the extreme. Starvation stared us in the face. To remain here longer was certain death. We held a consultation and determined to start down the river the next day, and try and make the best of our way to some settlement where we could get relief, in the meantime keeping as much together as possible, and hunting along as we went, as our only chance of safety.

The two Canadian Frenchmen, Tabeau, or "Sorrell" as we called him, and Moran, did not delay as long as we but, pinched by hunger, had started off the day before.

So, with a handful of sugar to each man, we divided some candles, pieces of rawhide, tugropes and parfleches and, strapping on a blanket apiece, and shouldering our rifles, we started on our gloomy march down the frozen river. Over its congealed surface a sombre shade was cast by the overhanging trees covered with the long white frost which hung like a thick fringe from their barren boughs. Tottering from weakness and some with frozen and bleeding feet, we made slow progress. We kept upon the ice down the middle of the river to get a level track, and to avoid as much as possible the deep snow. Now commenced a train of horrors which it is painful to force the mind to dwell upon, and which memory shrinks from. Before we had proceeded far, Manual, a California Indian of the Cosumne tribe, who had his feet badly frozen, stopped and begged Mr. Vincenthaler to shoot him and, failing to meet death in this way, turned back to the lodge at the camp we had left, there to await his fate. The same day Wise lay down upon the ice on the river and died; the Indian boys, Joaquin and Gregorio, who came along afterward, having stopped back to get some wood for Manuel, seeing his (Wise's) body, covered it over with brush and snow. That night, Carver, crazed by hunger, raved terribly all night, so that some in the camp with him became alarmed for their safety. He told them, if any would follow him back, he had a plan by which they might live. The next day he wandered off and we never saw him again. The next night "Sorrell," his system wrought upon by hunger, cold and exhaustion, took a violent fit, which lasted upon him for some time; it resulted in an entire prostration of all his faculties. At the same time, he was almost totally snowblind. Speaking to E. Kern of our situation, he said, "Oh, Kern, this is a *mise Dieu* (a visitation from God), and we can't avoid it." Poor fellow, the next day he traveled as long as his strength would allow, and then, telling us we would have to leave him, that he could go no farther, blind with snow, he lay down on the river bank to die. Moran soon joined him and they never came up again.

Late at night we all, arriving one by one, came into a camp together on the river bank. Gloom and despondency were depicted on every face. Our condition had become perfectly desperate. We knew not what to do; the candles and parfleche had kept us alive thus far, but these were gone. Our appearance was desolate as we sat in silence around the fires, in view of a fast approaching death by starvation, while hunger gnawed upon our vitals.

Then Vincenthaler, to whom the Colonel had left the charge of the camp, and whom, for that reason, we had allowed to have the chief direction, spoke up and told us then and there that he threw up all authority; that he could do nothing and knew not what to advise; that he looked upon our condition as hopeless, but he would suggest as the best advice he could give, that we break up into small parties and, hunting along, make the best of our way down separately, each party making use of all the advantages that might chance to fall in its way, to hasten on down without waiting for the others so that, if any chanced to get through to a settlement, they could forward relief to the others.

Accordingly, the next morning he joined himself with Scott, Martin, Hibbard, Bacon, Ducatel, Rohrer, and the two Indians, Joaquin and Gregorio, who had left the mess that they were in, for fear, as they said, that certain men in it would kill them to eat when it came to the worst.

Ferguson and Beedle went together; and the rest of us -- the three Kerns, Capt. Cathcart, Capt. Taplin, myself, Stepperfeldt, and Andrews -- went together, and we agreed not to leave each other while life lasted. Again we renewed our unsteady course down the river. We traveled hard all day and, late in the evening, weak and wornout, we staggered into a camp near the river side, some coming in far behind the rest. Dr. Kern came up so exhausted that he fell down, almost senseless, and remained in this torpid state a whole day. After a while Andrews came up; arriving within several hundred yards of camp, he raised a faint call and fell down, completely exhausted and senseless so that two or three of us had to go and pack him in. He never recovered from this exhaustion. Soon Rohrer came up. Vincenthaler's party, to which he belonged, was ahead of us; being too weak to proceed farther, he stopped with us.

Here we remained, determined, as we had promised, not to leave any while they lived. So we commenced hunting around, all that had strength and sight sufficient to do so, for most of us were so completely snowblind that we could not see to shoot. After long and frequent hunts, two prairie chickens or grouse were killed. These we divided with scrupulous exactness among the nine of us, dividing the entrails and all that appertained to them, even to the pin feathers. Taplin found part of a dead wolf upon the river and brought it in. All one side and the entrails had been eaten away, but we divided the skin and roasted it, hair and all, for one meal, drank the meagre broth for another, and then ate the meat and even devoured the bones. This was the last we got.

Day after day we stayed here but no game came near. Occasionally we could hear the distant, dismal howl of a wolf weary with waiting for its work, but none came near, and, at distant intervals, a raven would go screaming by, beyond our reach, but never stopping within sight. We found a handful or two of rosebuds along the river which we divided and ate, and Dr. Kern found a few small bugs upon the water where the ice was broken and ate them. We had already devoured our moccasin soles, and a small sack made of smoked lodge skin. We dug in the ground beneath the snow with our knives for roots, but it was a useless labor.

We became weaker daily, and to walk thirty steps once a day after some dry cottonwood sticks to keep up our fire fatigued us greatly. Our strength was rapidly failing. Andrews died in the course of the night as he lay by our side, after lingering out several days and, the next day, Rohrer was nearly gone, talking wildly, a fearful expression of despair resting upon his countenance. The mention of his family at home had served to rouse him and keep him going longer than his strength would otherwise have born him up; but now it was too late; his case was over. Taking from Andrews' pocket a small gilt-embossed Bible, carefully preserved, which we intended, in case any of us lived to get through, to hand over as a memento to his friends, we laid his body to one side and covered it with a blanket; then we sat down, waiting until Rohrer should die, intending (as soon as the breath had left his body), to commence another move down the river, continuing by slow degrees until our powers should entirely fail.

As we sat waiting, _____ came over to the fire where Taplin, I, and Stepperfeldt were sitting and, in a sad tone, said: "Men, I have come to make a proposition. I don't know how you will take it. It is a horrid one. We are starving. In two or three days more, except something is done, we will all be dead. Here lies a mass of useless flesh, from which the life has departed, which, as soon as we leave, will be the prey of wild beasts. There is enough to keep us all alive. It is nothing but our prejudices that causes us to look upon human flesh as anything more than any other flesh. Now, I propose that, instead of leaving it to become food for wolves, we make use of it to save human life. It is horrid, I know, but I will undertake to do the butchery, as you may call it, and you need have nothing to do with that part; you need not even see it done. Do you agree to my proposition?"

All sat in silence, then several of us objected, and I spoke up and said: "For my part, I have no conscientious scruples against such a procedure. I know that early prejudice and conventional opinion founded on prejudice are at the bottom of our objections to it, but these exist, and this is a horrid proposition to entertain. I fully appreciate our situation, but I think that by making up our minds to it and remaining quiet we can yet hold out three days longer, by which time, after finding that we cannot possibly bear up longer, there will then be time enough to think of adopting so horrible an alternative; then, if I do not approve, I will not censure it."

"And by that time," he said, "we will be too weak and too far gone ever to recover and we will all starve to death here in a mass. You see what they have come to and you see what you will come to."

"I can't help it," I said, "I am determined to risk it at the peril of my life," and, so saying, I walked over to the other fire. They talked about it a few minutes but were unwilling to do such a thing unless all did, and so we all waited together. We remained around the fire, stirring as little as possible and firing signal guns at frequent intervals during the day. Rohrer died. Two days passed and no relief came. Several times we imagined we heard an answer to our signal and would rise up to listen, but being as often disappointed we had ceased to notice.

The morning of the third day (January 25) arrived and was far advanced toward midday, and we sat in the deepest gloom. Suddenly we thought we heard a call.

"Hush!" said one, and we all listened intently.

Another call! "Relief, by God!" exclaimed one of the men, and we all started to our feet.

Relief it was, sure enough, for directly we spied Godey riding toward us, followed by a Mexican. We were all so snowblind that we took him to be the Colonel until he came up and some saluted him as the Colonel. We shook him by the hand heartily. Dismounting, he quickly distributed several loaves among us, with commendable forethought giving us but a small piece first, and making us wait until the Spaniard could boil some for us, or prepare some "tole" (boiled cornmeal), which he quickly made and this we more quickly devoured. It required considerable persuasion to prevent us from killing the old horse which the Spaniard had, in order to eat it; but Godey informed us there were two colts in the camp below, which, if we would wait, we might have. This was the 25th of January. There were men in the party who did not escape the horrible fate which came so near being ours.

Godey with the Colonel and the rest that were with them, after leaving the party, traveling on as rapidly as possible down the river, came upon two Indians with several old horses, and engaged them to pilot them in; going on they had overtaken King's party, who leaving the river, had undertaken to strike across the country to Abiquiu, but, becoming involved in the deep snow, their provisions being exhausted, they having eaten their knife scabbards and tried to eat their boots, and with no fuel, being compelled to lie out night after night, without fire, upon the barren plain, until they were more or less frozen from their hips down, had returned to the river, where King died; here the Colonel's party found them in a weak and emaciated condition, and nearly dead, with intellect shaken and scarcely any hearing, sight, or sense left, and half deranged and nearly sightless they took them along upon the Indian horses into the little outer settlement of the Rio Grande.

Here quickly obtaining what provisions he could, and hiring several Spaniards with mules, Godey set out as speedily as possible up the river. On his way he fell in with two other Mexicans, who, with mules loaded with bread and flour and cornmeal, were going out to trade with the Utah Indians. These he pressed into service with their cargoes, and, hastening on, traveling late and early, he met Vincenthaler's party about 20 miles below us, who had lived by killing a raven, hawk, or prairie chicken occasionally that they had the good luck to meet with; also they had eaten part of a dead horse they found. But two of their number were missing from among them. They had agreed among themselves that, when one became so exhausted that he could not travel, the rest should not wait for him. Hibbard had been first left, and soon after him Scott. Leaving most of the animals and provisions at Vincenthaler's camp, Godey proceeded rapidly up. He found Scott sitting in a listless manner by a fire he had just kindled, his head resting upon his hands, almost totally snowblind. Having strengthened him with food, Godey furnished him a horse and sent a Mexican with him to the camp below; then, proceeding on, he came to Hibbard, who had just died, his body yet warm. Failing in his attempt to restore him, he kept on.

Taking across a short bend in the river, he passed entirely by us without knowing it and found Ferguson a short distance above us. Beedle was dead, and his body was lying near by. Ferguson informed Godey that we were below him, and, coming down with him, he found us.

Leaving us and taking with him several Spaniards with pack-mules, he followed up along our track which was marked by the bodies of the dead as they had perished day by day, and now were lying the prey of wolves and ravens; the deep and gloomy silence of their solitude only broken by the snarls and yells of packs of wolves, quarreling over their remains. He found the bodies of "Sorrell" and Moran together. Friends in life they proved friends in death. "Sorrel" was lying prostrate on the snow and Moran apparently after having tried to strike a fire, had dropped his head upon the log against which he was sitting and expired by his side.

Godey found the Indian, Manuel, in the lodge, still alive, and brought him down. Manual afterward stated that Carver came up to the lodge with a piece of meat which he said was part of a deer he had killed, and that he undertook to go to the previous camp seven miles back for something and had frozen to death. Godey attempted to go back to this camp after some valuables of which we had made a *cache* in the snow before leaving, but two of the mules perished in the cold in the attempt, and he abandoned it and packed down only the lodge and its contents.

At the same time that Godey left us we had sent the Mexican to Vincenthaler's camp for animals to take us down, for we were wholly unable to walk. He returned with them the next day. Tying our blankets on for saddles and rigging rope stirrups, we were lifted (for we could not lift even our skeleton frames) upon as poor looking animals as were ever known to live on nothing, and after a two days journey, which, though the ride was almost killing, was the most welcome horseback excursion we had ever taken, reached the camp 20 miles below. We were pretty looking objects about then; lank, thin visaged, and eyes sunken, our hair and beard long, tangled and knotty, and our faces black with pine smoke which had not been washed off for two months, we resembled more the Spirits of Darkness, or, if anything mortal, a set of banditti, than anything else. Here we fell to eating enormously, and it required the exercise of all our self restraint to prevent plenty now from being as hurtful to us as want had been before. The abundance of food, when there had just been such a lack, made us all sick and kept us sick for some days, but that could not stop us. Our appetite was unbounded and we were eating constantly, at all hours of the day, and through the night. We had such cravings for meat of some kind that we killed two well grown colts and ate them. We were even more ravenous than the ravens themselves, which, now that we did not need them, came crowding around with hawks and wolves. We killed and devoured some of all these.

It was curious to hear different men tell of the workings of their minds when they were starving. Some were constantly dreaming or imagining that they saw before them a bountiful feast, and would make selections of different dishes. Others engaged their minds with other thoughts. For my part, I kept my mind amused by entering continually into all the minutiae of farming or some other systematic business which would keep up a train of thought, or by working a mental solution of mathematical problems, bringing in review the rudiments of some science, or by laying out plans for the future, all having a connection with home and after life. So, in this way, never allowing myself to think upon the hopelessness of our condition, yet always keeping my eyes open to every chance, I kept hope alive and never once suffered myself to despond, and to this course I greatly attribute my support for there were stronger men who, doubtless by worrying themselves, hastened their death.

Ten out of our party of thirty-three that entered the mountains had perished, and several days more would have finished the balance.

Vincenthaler's party, having been first relieved, soon recruited sufficiently to leave, and all except Ducatel and the two Indian boys, who remained with the rest of us, proceeded to the Rio Colorado [in Texas], distant three or four days' journey [to the east]. When Godey arrived we left together. On our way we were overtaken by a violent snowstorm. Having no compass to guide us, and not being able to see the sun or even the mountains through the thickly falling snow which rendered everything invisible a few rods distant, and without any subject to show us our course across the barren, snow-clad plain, we kept traveling all day in a circle, once coming in sight ouf our starting point. Once we were on the point of stopping in the midst of the stormy plain to take our chances, but before we could get to our intended camp we were almost frozen.

Late in the afternoon of February 9, cold, hungry, and weary, with no little joy we all at once hailed the sight of the little pueblo. We raised a yell as we came in sight which made the *Pueblaños* stand out and gaze. In a few minutes, with their assistance, we dismounted from our horses and sought the comfort which the place afforded. Here we met Mr. Preuss and Croitzfeldt -- one of the first relief party who had come very near perishing, and had not sufficiently recovered to proceed. Each had thought the other dead, and it was like the joy after a long parting with which we then grasped their hands. The rest of our companions, they told us, had gone on to Taos, where the Colonel had preceded them to make arrangements, for such as were able to proceed, to go on to California by the Gila route, or what is called the Lower California or Lower Spanish trail.

At Taos we first heard with certainty of the abundance of gold in California, the first account of which had reached the States immediately before our departure, but was scarcely believed.

On the 13th of February, having laid in a supply of provisions from the quartermaster's department, being facilitated by the generous kindness of the army officers, and having hired muleteers and a train of mules to take us down to Albuquerque, we set out for Santa Fe, leaving behind Captain Cathcart, who was not able to prosecute the journey farther, the three Kerns, Stepperfeldt, and Bill Williams, the guide, and taking Lindsay Carson and T. Bogg, son of the ex-governor of Missouri. From here, in the spring of the year, Bill Williams and Dr. Kern, with a company of Mexicans, went back into the mountains to recover some of the most valuable of the property left by us, and were attacked and killed, either by the Indians or by the Mexicans who went out with them, we never could ascertain which.

# THE CAPTIVITY OF THE OATMAN GIRLS
## (1851-56)

Lorenzo and Olive Oatman, as told to

Royal B. Stratton

**Editors' Note:** Like so many others, Royse Oatman caught "California fever" in 1849. It did not matter that he had carved a productive farm out of virgin Illinois prairie only four years earlier. The lure of new land was strong, and Royse was a pioneer. Troubled during the cold Illinois winters by an aching back due to an old injury, Royse was attracted by glowing promises of the salubrious climate of southern California. When a group of farmers proposed to colonize lands near the junction of the Gila and Colorado rivers, Royse joined up, unmindful of the fact that the colony's promoters had never been there. In the spring of 1850 he sold his farm for $1,500, packed up his wife and children, and, with several neighboring families, headed West.

When the emigrants arrived at the Mexican village of Tucson in January, 1851, they were bone-weary and much in need of rest. The party of fifty men, women, and children had been on the trail for five months, having left Independence, Missouri, the previous August. They had taken the southern emigrant trail to the Rio Grande in northern New Mexico, followed the river down into Mexican territory, and then headed west along the route blazed four years earlier by the Mormon Battalion. Their journey had thus far been relatively uneventful, but a struggle nonetheless. The draft animals pulling the wagons were nearly worn out and needed time to recuperate. Knowing that the dreaded desert lay ahead, the party elected to stay and rest for a month in Tucson.

After a month's halt, five of the families decided their oxen were still too weak to attempt the desert trek. Their plan was to plant crops near town and after the harvest continue on to California. Anxious to get to the Colorado River, the Oatman, Kelly, and Wilder families pushed on without them, crossing the ninety miles of waterless desert that lay between Tucson and the Pima ("Pimole") Indian villages on the Gila River.

In mid-February the would-be settlers reached the villages of the Pimas, peaceful farmers friendly to the Whites. By now the Kellys and the Wilders had had enough. Robert Kelly and Willard Wilder informed Royse Oatman that they intended to stay at the villages indefinitely. With food in short supply and the animals in poor condition, they thought it unwise to proceed further. Perhaps, they reasoned, in a few weeks they could resume the journey. Royse, however, was determined to continue.

Before leaving the villages, Royse had talked to Dr. John Le Conte, who, with a Mexican guide, had just come from Fort Yuma. An entomologist, Le

Conte had prospected and collected specimens along the way without encountering any serious difficulty. Fort Yuma, established at the confluence of the Gila and Colorado rivers the previous November, was only 160 miles distant -- not that far considering how far the family had come. Water would be no problem as the route lay along the Gila River; the main problem would be the lack of grass for the failing oxen. On March 11, Royse Oatman gathered up his large family and headed west. The Oatman family included Royse Sr., age 42; his wife Mary Ann, age 38; Lucy, age 17; Olive, age 15; Lorenzo, age 14; Mary Ann, age 7; Royse Jr., about 5; "C.A.," a girl age 3; and "Little Brother," age 1 year.

A week out from the villages, the Oatmans were overtaken by Le Conte on his way back to Fort Yuma. Le Conte could see that the family was in a bad way. The oxen were all but used up and their progress was painfully slow. Able to travel light, Le Conte agreed to hasten on and summon help at Yuma, now only 100 miles ahead. Before he could reach the fort, however, Le Conte's horses were stolen by Indians and he had to travel the last few miles on foot. As soon as he got to Yuma he reported the Oatmans' plight to the fort's commander, Captain Samuel Heintzelman. Heintzelman, however, was slow to respond. Not that it mattered. Two days after Le Conte's departure, the family was attacked by Western Yavapai Indians (erroneously called Apaches in the narrative).

The Yavapais fell upon the exhausted Oatmans with their war clubs. Two girls, Olive and Mary Ann, were taken captive. Lorenzo was bludgeoned and left for dead. All the others were killed. Lorenzo was later rescued by the Kellys and Wilders who had decided to proceed after all. He was then taken back to the Pima villages, then on to Fort Yuma, and eventually to California.

Olive and Mary Ann were kept by the Yavapais for one miserable year, then sold to Mohave Indians, a tribe living along the Colorado River upstream from Fort Yuma. A year later, Mary Ann died from the hardships of living with the Indians. Olive spent another four years with the Mohaves. Then, in 1856, news reached Fort Yuma that a White woman was living with Indians upriver. Henry Grinnell, a civilian employee of the fort, hired a Yuma Indian named Francisco to contact the Mohave Indians and arrange for the woman's release. The price finally agreed upon for her ransom was six pounds of white beads, four blankets, and a white horse. When Olive was brought to Fort Yuma, no one could believe she was White -- she was brown from exposure to the sun, dressed like a Mohave woman, and had tattoos on her chin.

Olive was reunited with her brother in California where they were befriended by the Reverend Royal B. Stratton. After hearing their stories, he incorporated their narratives in a book entitled *Captivity of the Oatman Girls*, published in 1857. The book proved extremely popular and quickly went through three editions. Stratton carefully identified the survivors' accounts with quotation marks, and augmented them with lengthy asides of his own -- pious lamentations regarding the Oatmans' plight that grate on the modern reader. For this anthology we have extracted the accounts of Lorenzo and

Olive Oatman from *Captivity of the Oatman Girls,* and omitted Stratton's tiresome commentary.

Despite her obvious suffering, Olive did not report having been tortured or sexually abused by the Indians, only forced to share the grim hand-to-mouth existence of her captors. Both Lorenzo and Olive eventually married and reportedly lived happy, productive lives. Olive's Mohave tatoos served as a constant reminder of her ordeal until her death at age 66 in Sherman, Texas.

~ ~ ~ ~ ~

### The Attack on the Oatman family -- Lorenzo Oatman's Account

**Wearied, heart-sick, and nearly destitute,** we arrived at the Pimo [Pima] Village, on or about the 16th of February, 1851. Here we found a settlement of Indians, who were in open hostility to the Apaches, and by whose skill and disciplined strength they were kept from pushing their depredations further in that direction. But so long had open and active hostilities been kept up, that they were short of provisions and in nearly a destitute situation. They had been wont to turn their attention and energies considerably to farming, but during the last two years, their habits in this respect had been greatly interfered with. We found the ninety miles that divides Tukjon [Tucson] from Pimole [the Pima settlements] to be the most dismal, desolate, and unfruitful of all the regions over which our way had led us as yet.

It was soon apparent to our family, that if we would proceed further we must venture the journey alone. Soon, and after a brief consultation, a full resolution was reached by the Wilders and Kellys to remain, and stake their existence upon traffic with the Pimoles, or upon a sufficient tarrying to produce for themselves; until from government or friends, they might be supplied with sufficient [food] to reach Fort Yuma. We were left to the severe alternative of starting with a meagre supply, which any considerable delay would exhaust ere we could reach a place of re-supply, or to stay among the apparently friendly Indians, who also were but poorly supplied at best to furnish us; and of whose *real* intentions it was impossible to form any reliable conclusion.

One of the many circumstances that conspired to spread a gloom over the way that was before us, was the jaded condition of our team, which by this time consisted of two yoke of cows and one yoke of oxen. My parents were in distress and perplexity for some time to determine the true course dictated by prudence, and their responsibility in the premises. One hundred and ninety miles of desert and mountain, each alike barren and verdureless, stretched out between us and the next settlement or habitation of man. We felt, deeply felt, the hazardous character of our undertaking; and for a time lingered in painful suspense over the proposed adventure. We felt and feared that a road

71

stretching to such a distance, through an uninhabited and wild region, might be infested with marauding bands of the Indians who were known to roam over the mountains that were piled up to the north of us; who, though they might be persuaded or intimidated to spare us the fate of falling by their savage hands, yet might plunder us of all we had as means for life's subsistence.

While in this dreadful suspense, one Dr. Lecount [Dr. John Le Conte], attended by a Mexican guide, came into the Pimole village. He was on his return from a tour that had been pushed westward, almost to the Pacific Ocean. As soon as we learned of his presence among us, father sought and obtained an interview with him. And it was upon information gained from him, that the decision to proceed was finally made. He had passed the whole distance to Fort Yuma, and returned, all within a few months, unharmed; and stated that he had not witnessed indications of even the neighborhood of Indians.

Accordingly on the 11th of March, finding provisions becoming scarce among the Pimoles, and our own rapidly wasting, unattended, in a country and upon a road where the residence, or even the trace of one of our own nation would be sought in vain, save that of the hurrying traveler who was upon some official mission, or, as in the case of Dr. Lecount, some scientific pursuit requiring dispatch, we resumed our travel. Our teams were reduced; we were disappointed in being abandoned by our fellow-travelers, and wearied, almost to exhaustion, by the long and fatiguing march that had conducted us to this point. For six days our course was due southwest, at a slow and patience-trying rate.

On the seventh day from Pimole, with our teams failing and sometimes in the most difficult and dangerous places utterly refusing to proceed, we were overtaken by Dr. Lecount, who with his Mexican guide was on his way back to Fort Yuma. The doctor saw our condition, and his large, generous heart poured upon us a flood of sympathy, which, with the words of good cheer he addressed us, was the only relief it was in his power to administer. Father sent by him, and at his own suggestion, to the fort for immediate assistance. This message the doctor promised should be conveyed to the fort, (we were about ninety miles distant from it at the time,) with all possible dispatch, also kindly assuring us that all within his power should be done to procure us help *at once.*

The roads had been made bad, at places almost impassable, by recent rains, and for the first time the strength and courage of my parents gave signs of exhaustion. The only method by which we could make the ascent of the frequent high hills that hindered our way, was by unloading the wagon and carrying the contents piece by piece to the top; and even then we were often compelled to aid a team of four cows and two oxen to lift the empty wagon.

Toward evening on the eighteenth day of March, we reached the Gila River, at a point over eighty miles from Pimole, and about the same distance from Fort Yuma. We descended to the ford from a high, bluff hill, and found it leading across at a point where the river armed, leaving a small island sand-bar in the middle of the stream. We attempted to cross the Gila about sunset; the stream was rapid and swollen to an unusual width and depth. After struggling with danger and every possible hinderance until long after dark, we reached the sand island in the middle of the stream. Here our teams mired, our wagon dragged heavily, and we found it impossible to proceed.

After reaching the center and driest portion of the island, with the wagon mired in the rear of us, we proceeded to detach the teams, and as best we could made preparations to spend the night. Well do I remember the forlorn countenance and dejected and jaded appearance of my father as he started to wade the lesser branch of the river ahead of us to gather material for a fire. At a late hour of that cold, clear, wind-swept night, a camp-fire was struck and our shivering group encircled it to await the preparation of our stinted allowance. At times the wind, which was blowing furiously most of the night, would lift the slight surges of the Gila quite to our camp-fire. We were compelled frequently to shift our position, as the fickle wind would change the point at which the light surges of the Gila would attack our camp-fire, in the center of that little island of about two hundred square feet, upon which we had of necessity halted for the night.

The longed-for twilight at length sent its earliest stray beams along the distant peaks, stole in upon our sand-bar camp, and gradually lifted the darkness from our dreary situation. Before us, and separating the shore from us, was a part of the river yet to be forded. At an early hour the teams were brought from the valley-neck of land, where they had found pasturage for the night, and attached to the wagon. We soon made the opposite bank. Before us was quite a steep declivity of some two hundred feet, by the way of the road. We had proceeded but a short distance when our galled and disarranged teams refused to go. We were again compelled to unload, and with our own hands and strength to bear the last parcel to the top of the hill. After this we found it next to impossible to compel the teams to drag the empty wagon to the summit.

After reaching the other bank we camped, and remained through the heat of the day intending to travel the next night by moonlight. About two hours and a half before sunset we started, and just before the sun sank behind the western hills we had made the ascent of the hill and about one mile advance. Here we halted to reload the remainder of our baggage. We found ourselves now upon the summit, which proved to be the east edge of a long table-land, stretching upon a level, a long distance westward, and lying between two deep gorges, one on the

73

right, the other on the left; the former coursed by the Gila River. We had hastily taken our refreshment, consisting of a few parcels of dry bread, and some bean-soup, preparatory to a night's travel. This purpose of night travel had been made out of mercy to our famished teams, so weak that it was with difficulty they could be driven during the extreme sultry heat of the day. Besides this, the moon was nearly in full, giving us light nearly the entire night; the nights were cool, and better for travel to man and beast, and the shortness of our provisions made it imperative that we should make the most of our time.

Though the sun had hid its glittering, dazzling face from us behind a tall peak in the distance, yet its rays lingered upon the summits that stretched away between us and the moon, and daylight was full upon us. Our hasty meal had been served. My father, sad, and seemingly spell-bound with his own struggling emotions, was a little on one side, as if oblivious of all immediately about him, and was about in the act of lifting some of the baggage to the wagon, that had as yet remained unloaded since the ascent of the hill, when, casting my eyes down the hill by the way we had come, I saw several Indians slowly and leisurely approaching us in the road. I was greatly alarmed, and for a moment dared not to speak. At the time, my father's back was turned. I spoke to him, at the same time pointing to the Indians. What I saw in my father's countenance excited in me a great fear, and took a deeper hold upon my feelings of the danger we were in, than the sight of the Indians. They were now approaching near us. The blood rushed to my father's face.

After the Indians approached, he became collected, and kindly motioned them to sit down; spoke to them in Spanish, to which they replied. They immediately sat down upon the stones about us, and still conversing with father in Spanish, made the most vehement professions of friendship. They asked for tobacco and a pipe, that they might smoke in token of their sincerity and of their friendly feelings toward us. This my father immediately prepared, took a whiff himself, then passed it around, even to the last.

After smoking, these Indians asked for something to eat. Father told them of our destitute condition and that he could not feed them without robbing his family; that unless we could soon reach a place of new supplies we must suffer. To all this they seemed to yield only a reluctant hearing. They became earnest and rather imperative, and every plea that we made to them of our distress, but increased their wild and furious clamors. Father reluctantly took some bread from the wagon and gave it to them, saying it was robbery, and perhaps starvation to his family. As soon as this was devoured they asked for more, meanwhile surveying us narrowly, and prying and looking into every part of the wagon. They were told that we could spare them no more. They immediately packed themselves into a secret council a little on one side, which they conducted in the Apache language, wholly unintelligible to us. We were totally in the dark as to their designs, save that their appearance and actions wore the threatening of some hellish deed. We were now about ready to start. Father had again returned to complete the reloading of the remainder of the articles; mother was in the wagon arranging them; Olive, with my older sister, was standing upon the opposite side of the wagon; Mary Ann, a little girl about seven years old, sat upon a stone holding to a rope attached to the horns of the foremost team; the rest of the children were on the opposite side of the wagon from the Indians. My eyes were turned away from the Indians.

Though each of the family was engaged in repairing the wagon, none were without manifestations of fear. For some time every movement of the Indians was closely watched by us. I well remember, however, that after a few moments my own fears were partially quieted, and from their appearance I judged it was so with the rest. In a subdued tone frequent expressions were made concerning the Indians, and their possible intentions; but we were guarded and cautious, lest they might understand our real dread and be emboldened to violence. Several minutes did they thus remain a few feet from us, occasionally turning an eye upon us, and constantly keeping up a low earnest babbling among themselves. At times they gazed eagerly in various directions, especially down the road by which we had come, as if struggling to discern the approach of some object or person either dreaded or expected by them.

Suddenly, as a clap of thunder from a clear sky, a defeaning yell broke upon us, the Indians jumping into the air, and uttering the most frightful shrieks, and at the same time springing toward us flourishing their war-clubs, which had hitherto been concealed under their wolf-skins. I was struck upon the top and back of my head, came to my knees, when with another blow, I was struck blind and senseless.

I soon must have recovered my consciousness after I had been struck down, for I heard distinctly the repeated yells of those fiendish Apaches. And these I heard mingling in the most terrible confusion with the shrieks and cries of my dear parents, brothers, and sisters, calling, in the most pitiful, heart-rending tones, for "Help, help! In the name of God, cannot any one help us?" Well do I remember coming to myself, with sensations as of waking from a long sleep but which soon gave place to the dreadful reality; at which time all would be silent for a moment, and then the silence broken by the low, subdued, but unintellitible gibberings of the Indians, intermingled with an occasional low, faint moan from some one of the family, as if in the last agonies of death. I could not move. I thought of trying to get up, but found I could not command a muscle or nerve.

While lying in this state, two of the wretches came up to me, rolling me over with their feet; they examined and rifled my pockets, took off my shoes and hat in a hurried manner; then laid hold of my feet and roughly dragged me a short distance, and then seemed to leave me for dead. After being left by the Indians, the thought I had, traces of which are still in my memory, were of opening my eyes, knowing perfectly my situation, and thinking still that each breath would be the last. The full moon was shining upon rock, and hill, and shrub about me; a more lovely evening indeed I never witnessed. I made an effort to turn my eye in search of the place where I supposed my kindred were cold in death, but could not stir. I felt the blood upon my mouth, and found it still flowing from my ears and nose. All was still as the grave.

The next period, the recollection of which conveys any distinct impression to my mind at this distance of time, was of again coming to myself, blind, but thinking my eyes were some way tied from without. As I rubbed them, and removed the clotted blood from my eyelids, I gathered strength to open them. The sun, seeming from mid-heaven, was looking me full in the face. My head was beating, and at times reeling under the grasp of a most torturing pain. I looked at my worn and tattered clothes, and they were besmeared with blood. I felt my head and found my scalp torn across the top. I found I had strength to turn my head, and it surprised me. I made an effort to get up, and succeeded in rising to my hands and knees; but then my strength gave way. I saw myself at the foot of a steep, rugged declivity of rocks, and all about me new. On looking up upon the rocks I discovered traces of blood marking the way by which I had reached my present situation from the brow above me. I soon determined in my mind that I had either fallen, or been hurled down upon my present position, from the place where I was first struck down. At first I concluded I had fallen myself, as I remembered to have made several efforts to get upon my hands and knees, but was baffled each time, and that during this I saw myself near a precipice of rocks, like that brow of the steep [bluff] near me now, and that I plainly recognized as the same place, and now sixty feet or more above me. My consciousness now fully returned, and with it a painful appreciation of the dreadful tragedies of which my reaching my present situation had formed a part. I dwelt upon what had overtaken my family-kin, and though I had no certain mode of determining, yet I concluded it must have been the day before.

I grew sick and faint, dizziness shook my brain, and my senses fled. I again awoke from the delirium, partly standing, and making a desperate effort. I felt the thrill of a strong resolution. "I will get up," said I, "and *will* walk or if not I will spend the last remnant of my shattered strength to crawl out of this place." I started, and slowly moved toward the rocks above me. I crept, snail-like, up the rock-stepped side of the table-land above me. As I drew near the top, having crawled almost fifty feet, I came in sight of the wagon wreck; then the scenes which had been wrought about it came back with horror, and nearly unloosed my hold upon the rocks. I could not look upon those faces and forms, yet they were within a few feet. The boxes, opened and broken, with numerous articles, were in sight. I could not trust my feelings to go further; I turned away, and began to crawl toward the east, round the brow of the hill. After carefully, and with much pain, struggling all the while against faintness, crawling some distance, I found myself at the slope leading down to the ford of the Gila, where I plainly saw the wagon track we had made, as I supposed, the day before. The hot sun affected me painfully; its burning rays kindled my fever, already oppressive, to the boiling point. I felt a giant determination urging me on. Frequently my weariness and faintness would bring me to the ground several times in a few moments. Then I would crawl aside, (as I did immediately after crossing the river), drag myself under some mountain shrub for escape from the sun, bathe my fevered head in its friendly shade, and lay me to rest.

I must have slept for three hours, for when I woke the sun was behind the western hills. I felt refreshed, though suffering still from thirst. The road crossed the bend in the river twice; to avoid this, I made my way over the bluff spur that turns the road and river to the north. I succeeded after much effort in sustaining myself upon my feet, with a cane. I walked slowly on and gained strength and courage that inspired within some hope of my escape. I traveled on, only taking rest two or three times during that evening and whole night. I made in all about fifteen miles by the next day-break.

About eleven o'clock of the next day I came to a pool of standing water; I was nearly exhausted when I reached it and lay me down by it, and drank freely, though the water was warm and muddy. I had no sooner slaked my thirst than I fell asleep and slept for some time. I awoke partially delirious, believing that my brain was trying to jump out of my head, while my hands were pressed to my head to keep it together, and prevent the exit of my excited brain. When I had proceeded about ten miles, which I had made by the middle of the afternoon, I suddenly became faint, my strength failed, and I fell to the ground. I was at that time upon a high table-land, sandy and barren. I marveled to know whether I might be dying; I was soon unconscious. When I came to myself I had hardly strength to move a muscle; it was a long time before I could get up. I concluded I must perish, and meditated seriously the eating of the flesh from my arm to satisfy my hunger and prevent starvation. I knew I had not sufficient of life to last to Pimole at this rate, and concluded it as well to lie there and die, as to put forth more of painful effort.

In the midst of these musings, too dreadful and full of horror to be described, I rose and started and was about turning a short corner, when two red-shirted Pimoles, mounted upon fine American horses, came in sight. They straightened in their stirrups, drew their bows, with arrows pointed at me. I raised my hand to my head and beckoned to them, and speaking in Spanish, begged them not to shoot. Quick as thought, when I spoke they dropped their bows, and rode up to me. I soon recognized one of them as an Indian with whom I had been acquainted at Pimole Village. They eyed me closely for a few minutes, when my acquaintance discovering through my disfigured features who it was, that I was one of the family that had gone on a little before, dismounted, laid hold of me, and embraced me with every expression of pity and condolence that could throb in an American heart. Taking me by the hand they asked me what could have happened. I told them as well as I could, and of the fate of the rest of the family. They took me one side under a tree, and laid me upon their blankets. They then took from their saddle a piece of their ash-baked bread, and a gourd of water. I ate the piece of bread, and have often thought of the mercy it was they had no more, for I might have easily killed myself by eating too much; my cravings were uncontrollable. They hung up the gourd of water in reach, and charged me to remain until they might return, promising to carry me to Pimole.

After sleeping a short time I awoke, and became fearful to trust myself with these Pimoles. They had gone on to the scene of the massacre; it was near night; I adjusted their blankets and laid them one side, and commenced the night's travel refreshed, and not a little cheered. But I soon found my body racked with more pain, and oppressed with more weariness than ever. I kept up all night, most of the time traveling. It was the loneliest, most horror-struck night of my life. I hastened my steps, staggering as I went; I found that I was compelled to rest oftener than usual, I plainly saw I could not hold much longer. My head was becoming inflamed within and without, and in places on my scalp was putrid. About mid-forenoon, after frequent attempts to proceed, I crawled under a shrub and was soon asleep. I slept two or three hours undistrubed.

"O my God!" were the words with which I woke, "could I get something to eat, and some one to dress my wounds, I might yet live." I had now a desire to sleep continually. I resisted this with all the power I had. While thus musing I cast my eyes down upon a long winding valley through which the road wandered, and plainly saw moving objects; I was sure they were Indians, and at the thought my heart sank within me. I meditated killing myself. For one hour I kept my aching eyes upon the strange appearance, when, all at once, as they rose upon a slight hill, I plainly recognized two white covered wagons. O what a moment was that. Hope, joy, confidence, now for the first time seemed to mount my soul, and hold glad empire over all my pains, doubts, and fears. In the excitement I lost my consciousness, and waked not until disturbed by some noise near me. I opened my eyes, and two covered wagons were halting close to me, and Robert [Kelly] was approaching me. I knew him, but my own appearance was so haggard and unnatural, it was some time before he detected who that "strange-looking boy, covered with blood, hatless and shoeless, could be, his visage scarred, and he pale as a ghost fresh from Pandemonium." After looking for some time, slowly and cautiously approaching, he broke out: "My God, Lorenzo! in the name of heaven, what, Lorenzo, has happened?" I felt my heart strangely swell in my bosom, and I could scarcely believe my sight. "Can it be?" I thought, "can it be that this is a familiar white face?" I could not speak; my heart could only pour out its emotions in the streaming tears that flowed most freely over my face. When I recovered myself sufficiently, I began to speak of the fate of the rest of the family. They could not speak, some of them; those tender-hearted women wept most bitterly, and sobbed aloud, begging me to desist, and hide the rest of the truth from them.

They immediately chose the course of prudence, and resolved not to venture with so small a company, where we had met such a doom. Mr. Wilder prepared me some bread and milk, which, without any necessity for a sharpening process, my appetite, for some reason, relished very well. They traveled a few miles on the back track that night, and camped. The next day we were safe at Pimole ere night came on. When the Indians learned what had happened, they, with much vehemence, charged it upon the Yumas; but for this we made allowance, as a deadly hostility burned between these tribes. Mr. Kelly and Mr. Wilder resolved upon proceeding immediately to the place of massacre, and burying the dead.

Accordingly, early the next day, with two Mexicans and several Pimoles, they started. They returned after an absence of three days, and reported that they could find but little more than the bones of six persons, and that they were able to find and distinguish the bodies of all but those of Olive and Mary Ann. If they had found the bodies of my sisters the news would have been less dreadful to me than the tidings that they had been carried off by the Indians. But my suspicions were now confirmed, and I could only see them as the victims of a barbarous captivity. During their absence, and for some time after, I was severely and dangerously ill, but with the kind attention and nursing rendered me I began after a week to revive. We were now only waiting the coming that way of some persons who might be westward bound, to accompany them to California.

When we had been there two weeks, six men came into Pimole, who, on learning of our situation, kindly consented to keep with us until we could reach Fort Yuma. The Kellys and Wilders had some time before abandoned their notion of a year's stay at Pimole. We were soon again upon that road, with every step of which I now had a painful familiarity.  On the sixth day we reached that place, of all others the most deeply memory-written.  I have no power to describe, nor can tongue or pen proclaim the feelings that heaved my sorrowing heart as I reached the fatal spot.  I could hear still the echo of those wild shrieks and hellish whoops, reverberating along the mountain cliffs! those groans, *those awful groans*.

With the exception of about eighteen miles of desert, we had a comfortable week of travel to Fort Yuma.  I still suffered much, at times was seriously worse, so that my life was despaired of; but more acute were my mental than my physical sufferings.  At the Fort every possible kindness, with the best of medical skill, ministered to my comfort and hastened my recovery.  To Dr. Hewitt I owe, and must forever owe, a debt of gratitude which I can never return.  The sense of obligations I still cherish finds but a poor expression in words.  He became a parent to me; and kindly extended his guardianship and unabating kindness, when the force was moved to San Diego, and then he took me to San Francisco, at a time when, but for his counsel and his affectionate oversight, I might have been turned out to wreck upon the cold world.  Here we found that Doctor Lecount had done all in his power to get up and hasten a party of men to our relief; but he was prevented by the commander, a Mr. Heintszelman [Captain Samuel Heintzelman], who was guilty of an unexplainable, if not an inexcusable delay -- a delay that was an afflicition to the doctor, and a calamity to us.

~ ~ ~ ~ ~

### The Oatman Girls Are Taken Captive -- Olive Oatman's Account

**They took me to one side,** and while one of the Indians were leading me off, I saw them strike Lorenzo, and almost at the same instant my father also.  I was so bewildered and taken by surprise by the suddenness of their movements, and their deafening yells, that it was some little time before I could realize the horrors of my situation. When I turned around, opened my eyes, and collected my thoughts, I saw my father, my own dear father! struggling, bleeding, and moaning in the most pitiful manner.  Lorenzo was lying with his face in the dust, the top of his head covered with blood, and his ears and mouth bleeding profusely.  I looked around and saw my poor mother, with her youngest child clasped in her arms, and both of them still, as if the work of death had already been completed; a little distance on the opposite side of the wagon, stood little Mary Ann, with her face covered with her hands, sobbing aloud, and a huge-looking Indian standing over her; the rest were motionless, save a younger brother and my father, all upon the ground dead or dying.  At this sight a thrill of icy coldness passed over me; I thought I had been struck; my thoughts began to reel and became irregular and confused; I fainted and sank to the earth, and for a while, I know not how long, I was insensible.

While I recovered my thought I could hardly realize where I was, though I remembered to have considered myself as having also been struck to the earth, and thought I was probably dying. I knew that all, or nearly all of the family had been murdered; thus bewildered, confused, half conscious and half insensible, I remained a short time, I know not how long, when suddenly I seemed awakened to the dreadful realities around me. My little sister was standing by my side, sobbing and crying, saying: "Mother, o mother! Olive, mother and father are killed, with all our poor brothers and sisters." I could no longer look upon the scene. Occasionally a low, piteous moan would come from some one of the family as in a dying state. I distinguished the groans of my poor mother, and sprang wildly toward her, but was held back by the merciless savage holding me in his cruel grasp, and lifting a club over my head, threatening me in the most taunting, barbarous manner.

After these cruel brutes had consummated their work of slaughter, which they did in a few moments, they then commenced to plunder our wagon, and the persons of the family whom they had killed. They broke open the boxes with stones and clubs, plundering them of such of their contents as they could make serviceable to themselves. They took off the wagon wheels, or a part of them, tore the wagon covering off from its frame, unyoked the teams and detached them from the wagons, and commenced to pack the little food, with many articles of their plunder, as if preparatory to start on a long journey. Coming to a feather bed, they seized it, tore it open, scattering its contents to the winds, manifesting meanwhile much wonder and surprise, as if in doubt what certain articles of furniture, and conveniences for the journey we had with us, could be intended for.

Such of these as they selected, with the little food we had with us that they could conveniently pack, they tied up in bundles, and started down the hill by the way they had come, driving us on before them. We descended the hill, not knowing their intentions concerning us, but under the expectation that they would probaby take our lives by slow torture. After we had descended the hill and crossed the river, and traveled about one half of a mile by a dim trail leading through a dark, rough, and narrow defile in the hills, we came to an open place where there had been an Indian camp before, and halted. The Indians took off their packs, struck a fire, and began in their own way to make preparations for a meal. They boiled some of the beans just from our wagon, mixed some flour with water, and baked it in the ashes. They offered us some food, but in the most insulting and taunting manner, continually making merry over every indication of grief in us, and with which our hearts were ready to break. We could not eat. After the meal, and about an hour's rest, they began to repack and make preparations to proceed.

The reader can perhaps imagine the nature of my thoughts while standing at that camp-fire, with my sister clinging to me in convulsive sobs and groans. From fear of the Indians, whose frowns and threats, mingled with hellish jests, were constantly glaring upon us, she struggled to repress and prevent any outburst of the grief that seemed to tear her little heart. And when her feelings became uncontrollable, she would hide her head in my arms, and most piteously sob aloud, but she was immediately hushed by the brandishing of a war-club over her head. While in this camp, awaiting the finished meal, and just after twilight, the full moon arose and looked in upon our rock-dirt gorge with a majesty and sereneness that seemed to mock our changeful doom.

We were started and kept upon a rapid pace for several hours. One of the Indians takes the lead, Mary Ann and myself follow, bareheaded and shoeless, the Indians having taken off our shoes and head covering. We were traveling at a rate, as we soon learned, much beyond our strength. Every slackening of our pace and utterance of grief, however, was the signal for new threats, and the suspended war-club, with the fiendish "*Yokoa*" in our ears, repressed all expression of sorrow, and pushed us on up steeper ascents and bolder hills with a quickened step. We must have traveled at the rate of four or five miles an hour. Our feet were soon lacerated, as in shadowed places we were unable to pick our way, and were frequently stumbling upon stone and rocks, which made them bleed freely. Little Mary Ann soon became unable to proceed at the rate we had been keeping, and sank down after a few miles, saying she could not go on. After threatening and beating her considerably, and finding this treatment as well as my entreaties useless, they threatened to dispatch and leave her, and showed by their movements and gestures that they had fully come to this determination. While thus halting, one of the stout Indians disloged his pack, and putting it upon the shoulders of another Indian, rudely threw Mary Ann across his back, and with vengeance in his eye bounded on.

Our way had been mostly over a succession of small bluff points of high mountain chains, these letting down to a rough winding valley, running principally northeast. These small rock hills that formed the bottom of the high cliffs on either side, were rough, with no perceptible trail. We halted for a few moments about the middle of the night; besides this we had no rest until about noon of the next day, when we came to an open place of a few acres of level, sandy soil, adorned with an occasional thrifty, beautiful tree, but high and seemingly impassable mountains hemming us in on every side. This appeared to be to our captors a familiar retreat. Almost exhausted, and suffering extremely, I dragged myself up to the place of halt, hoping that we had completed the travel of that day. We had tarried about two hours when the rest of the band, who had taken the stock in another direction, came up. They had with them the two oxen and the horse. The rest of the stock, we afterward learned, had been killed and hung up to dry, awaiting the roving of this plundering band when another expedition should lead them that way. Here they immediately proceeded to kill the other two. This being done they sliced them up, and closely packed the parcels in equalized packages for their backs. They then broiled some of the meat on the fire, and prepared another meal of this and burned dough and bean soup. They offered us of their fare and we ate with a good appetite. Never did the tender, well-prepared veal steak at home relish better than the tough, stringy piece of meat about the size of the hand, given us by our captors, and which with burned dough and a little bean soup constituted our meal. We were very sleepy, but such was my pain and suffering I could not sleep.

They endeavored now to compel Mary Ann again to go on foot; but this she could not do, and after beating her again, all of which she took without a murmur, one of them again took her upon his shoulder and we started. I had not gone far before I found it impossible to proceed on account of the soreness of my feet. They then gave me something very much of the substance of sole-leather which they tied upon the bottom of my feet. This was a relief, and though suffering much from thirst and the pain of over-exertion, I was enabled to keep up with the heavy-laden Indians. We halted in a snug, dark ravine about ten o'clock that night, and preparations were at once made for a night's stay. My present suffering had now made me almost callous as to the past, and never did rest seem so sweet as when I saw they were about to encamp. During the last six hours they had whipped Mary Ann in to walking. We were now shown a soft place in the sand, and directed to it as the place of our rest; and with two of our own blankets thrown over us, and three savages encircling us, we slept.

We were not roused until a full twilight had shone in upon our beautiful little retreat. The breakfast was served up, consisting of beef, burned dough, and beans, instead of beans, burned dough, and beef, as usual. The sun was now fairly upon us when, like cattle, we were driven forth to another day's travel. The roughest road (if road be a proper term) over which I ever passed, in all my captivity, was that day's route. Twice during the day, I gave up, and told Mary Ann I must consent to be murdered and left, for proceed I would not. But this they were not inclined to allow. When I could not be driven, I was pushed and hauled along. Stubs, rocks, and gravel-strewn mountain sides hedged up and embittered the travel of the whole day. *That day* is among the few days of my dreary stay among the savages, marked by the most pain and suffering every endured. I have since learned that they hurried for fear of the whites, emigrant trains of whom were not infrequently passing

83

that way. For protection they kept a close watch, having not less than three guards or sentinels stationed at a little distance from each camp we made during the entire night. We traveled until about midnight, when our captors called a halt, and gave us to understand we might sleep for the remainder of the night.

On the third day we came suddenly in sight of a cluster of low, thatched huts, each having an opening near the ground leading into them. We were soon ushered into camp, amid shouts and song, wild dancing, and the crudest, most irregular music. They lifted us on the top of a pile of brush and bark, then formed a circle about us of men, women, and children of all ages and sizes, some naked, some dressed in blankets, some in skins, some in bark. Music then commenced, which consisted of pounding upon stones with clubs and horn, and the drawing of a small string like a fiddle-bow across distended bark. They ran, and jumped, and danced in the wildest and most furious manner about us, but keeping a regular circle. Each, on coming to a certain point in the circle, marked by a removed piece of turf in the ground, would bend himself or herself nearly to the ground, uttering at the same time a most frightful yell, and making a violent gesticulation and stamping.

### Life Among the Apaches (Yavapais)

We found the tribe to consist of about three hundred living in all the extremes of filth. They subsisted principally upon deer, quail, and rabbit, with occasional mixtures of roots from the ground. And even this dealt out with the most sparing and parsimonious hand, and in quantity only up to a stern necessity. Their meat was boiled with water in a "Tusquin," (clay kettle,) and this meat-mush or soup was the staple of food among them, and of this they were frequently short, and obliged to quiet themselves with meted out allowance; to their captives it was always thus meted out.

These Apaches were without any settled habits of industry. They tilled not. It was a marvel to see how little was required to keep them alive; yet they were capable of the greatest endurance when occasion taxed their strength. They ate worms, grasshoppers, reptiles, *all flesh*. Their women were the laborers and principal burden-bearers, and during all our captivity it was our lot to serve under these enslaved women. We have often taken the time which was given to gather roots for our lazy captors, to gather and eat ourselves; and had it not been for supplies obtained by such means, we must have perished.

Seldom during our stay here were we cheered with any knowledge or circumstance that bid us hope for our escape. Hours were spent by us in talking of trying the experiment. Mary often would say: "I can find the way out and I can go the whole distance as quick as they."

84

Several times, after cruel treatment, or the passing of danger from starvation, have we made the resolution, and set the time for executing it, but were not bold enough to undertake it.

After we had been among these Apaches several months, their conduct toward us somewhat changed. They became more lenient and merciful, especially to my sister, so that, expecially on the part of those females connected in some way with the household of the chief, and who had the principal control of us, we could plainly see more forbearance, kindness, and interest exhibited toward their captives. This, slight as was the change, was a great relief to my mind, and comfort to Mary Ann. We had learned their language so as to hold converse with them quite understandingly, after a few months among them. They were much disposed at times to draw us into conversation; they asked our ages, inquired after our former place of living, and when we told them of the distance we had come to reach our home among them, they greatly marveled. They would gather about us frequently in large numbers, and ply their curious questions with eagerness and seeming interest.

They are much given to humor and fun, but it generally descends to low obscenity and meanness. They had great contempt for one that would complain under torture or suffering, even though of their own tribe, and said a person that could not uncomplainingly endure suffering was not fit to live.

### The Girls Are Sold to the Mohaves

During the autumn of 1851, late in the season, quite a large company of Mohaves came among us on a trading expedition. But the whole transactions of one of these expeditions did not comprise the amount of wealth or business of one hour's ordinary shopping of a country girl. This was the first acquaintance we had with these superior Indians. During their stay we had some faint hints that it was meditated to sell us to the Mohaves in exchange for vegetables, which they no doubt regarded as more useful for immediate consumption than their captives. But still it was only a hint that had been given us, and the curiosity and anxiety it created soon vanished, and we sank again into the daily drudging routine of our dark prison life. Months rolled by, finding us weary and late at our burden-bearing and torturing labors.

One day Mary Ann said: "Look! Who are those? They are Indians, they are those very Mohaves! See! They have a horse, and there is a squaw among them." The Mohave party descended a slope to the Apache village, and roaring, yelling, and dancing prevailed through the gathering crowd of Apaches. The party consisted of five men, and a young woman under twenty years. It was not long ere two of the chiefs came to us, and told us that these Mohaves had come after us, according to a contract made with them at a previous visit; that the party had been back to obtain the sanction of Espaniole, the Mohave chief, to the contract, and that now the chief had sent his own daughter to witness to his desire to purchase the white captives. The chief had, however, left it with his daughter to approve or annul the contract that had been made. This daughter of the chief was a beautiful, mild, and sympathizing woman.

Sunrise, which greeted us ere we had a moment's sleep, found the party prepared to leave, and we were cooly informed by our captors that we must go with them. Two horses, a few vegetables, a few pounds of beads, and three blankets we found to be our price in that market. We were informed at the outset that we had three hundred and fifty miles before us, and all to be made on foot. Our route we soon found to be in no way preferable to the one by which the Apache village had been reached. It was now about the first day of March, 1852. One year had been spent by us in a condition the most abject, the most desolate.

We had not proceeded far ere it was painfully impressed upon our feet, if not our aching hearts, that this trail to a second captivity was no improvement on the first, whatever might be the fate awaiting us at its termination. We had been under tutorage for one whole year in burden bearing, and labor even beyond our strength, but a long walk or run, as this proved, we had not been driven to during that time. Our feet soon became sore, and we were unable, on the second day after about noon, to keep up their rapid pace. A small piece of meat was put into our hands on starting, and this with the roots we were allowed to dig, and these but few, was our sole subsistence for ten days.

With much complaining, and some threatening from our recent captors, we were allowed to rest on the second day a short time. After this we were not compelled to go more than thirty-five miles any one day, and pieces of skins were furnished for our feet, but not until they had been needlessly bruised and mangled without them. The nights were cool, and, contrary to our expectations, the daughter of the chief showed us kindness throughout the journey by sharing her blankets with us at each camp. Of all rough, uncouth, irregular, and unattractive countries through which human beings trail, the one through which that ten days' march led us, must remain unsurpassed.

On the eleventh day, about two hours before sunset, we made a bold steep ascent (and of such we had been permitted to climb many) from which we had an extensive view on either side. Before us, commencing a little from the foot of our declivity, lay a narrow valley covered with a carpet of green, stretching a distance, seemingly, of twenty miles. On either side were the high, irregularly sloped mountains, with their foot hills robed in the same bright green as the valley, and with their bald humpbacks and sharp peaks, treeless, verdureless, and desolate, as if the tempests of ages had poured their rage upon their sides and summits.

Our guides soon halted. We immediately observed by their movements and manifestations that some object beyond the loveliness that nature had strewn upon that valley, was enrapturing their gaze. We had stood gazing a few moments only, when the smoke at the distance of a few miles, winding in gentle columns up the ridges, spoke to us of the abodes or tarrying of human beings. Very soon there came into the field of our steady view a large number of huts, clothing the valley in every direction. We could plainly see a large cluster of these huts huddled into a nook in the hills on our right and on the bank of a river, whose glassy waters threw the sunlight in our face; its winding, zigzag course pointed out to us by the row of beautiful cottonwood trees that thickly studded its vicinity.

We were soon ushered into the "Mohave Valley," and had not proceeded far before we began to pass the low, rude huts of the Mohave settlers. They greeted us with shouts, and dance, and song as we passed. Our guides kept up, however, a steady unheeding march for the village, occasionally joined by fierce, filthy-looking Mohaves, and their more filthy-looking children, who would come up, look rudely in our faces, fasten their deep-set, small, flashing eyes upon us, and trip along, with merry-making, hallooing, and dancing at our side.

We were conducted immediately to the home of the chief, and welcomed with the staring eyes of collecting groups, and an occasional smile from the members of the chief's family, who gave the warmest expressions of joy over the return of their daughter and sister so long absent. Seldom does our civilization furnish a more hearty exhibition of affection for kindred, than welcomed the coming in of this member of the chief's family, though she had been absent but a few days. The chief's house was on a beautiful but small elevation crowning the river bank, from which the eye could sweep a large section of the valley, and survey the entire village, a portion of which lined each bank of the stream.

As a model, and one that will give a correct idea of the form observed, especially in their village structures, we may speak of the chief's residence. When we reached the outskirts of the town we observed upon the bank of the river a row of beautiful cottonwood trees, just putting out their new leaves and foliage, their branches interlocking, standing in a row, about a perfect square of about one hundred feet, and arranged in taste. They were thrifty, and seemed fed from a rich soil, and other plots covered with the same growths, and abounding throughout the village, presented truly an oasis in the general desert of country upon which we had been trailing our painful walk for the last ten days, climbing and descending, with unshapen rocks, and sharp gravel, and burning sands for our pavement. Immediately behind the row of trees first spoken of, was a row of poles or logs, each about six inches in diameter and standing close to each other, one end firmly set in the ground and reaching up about twenty feet, forming an inclosure of about fifty feet square. We entered this inclosure through a door (never shut) and found a tidy yard, grass-plotted. Inside of this was still another inclosure of about twenty feet, walled by the same kind of fence, only about one third as high. Running from front to rear, and dividing this dwelling-place of the Mohave magnate into equal parts, stood a row of these logs stuck in the ground, and running up about three feet above the level top of the outside row, and forming a ridge for the resting of the roof. The roof was a thick mat of limbs and mud. A few blankets, a small smoking fire near the door, with naked walls over which the finishing hand of the upholsterer had never passed, a floor made when all *terra firma* was created, welcomed us to the interior.

The daughter of the chief had been kind to us, if kindness could be shown under their barbarous habits and those rates of travel while on our way. She was more intelligent and seemed capable of more true sympathy and affection, than any we had yet met in our one year's exile. She was of about seventeen years, sprightly, jovial, and good-natured, and at times manifested a deep sympathy for us, and a commiseration of our desolate condition. But though she was daughter of the chief, their habits of barbarousness could not bend to courtesy even toward those of rank. She had walked the whole distance to the Apaches, carrying a roll of blankets, while two horses were rode by two stalwart, healthy Mohaves by her side. On entering the house, Topeka, who had accompanied us, gave an immediate and practical evidence that her stinted stomach had not become utterly deaf to all the demands of hunger. Seeing a cake roasting in the ashes, she seized it, and dividing it into three parts, she gave me the Benjamin portion and bade us eat, which was done with greediness and pleasant surprise.

Night came on and with it the gathering of a large concourse of Indians, their brown, stout wives and daughters, and swarms of little ones. The Indians were mostly tall, stout, with large heads, broad faces, and of a much more intelligent appearance than the Apaches. Bark-clad, where clad at all, the scarcity of their covering indicating either a warm climate or a great destitution of the clothing material, or something else. They placed us out upon the green, and in the light of a large, brisk fire, and kept up their dancing, singing, jumping, and shouting, until near the break of day.

### Life Among the Mohaves

We found the location and scenery of our new home much pleasanter than the one last occupied. The valley extended about thirty or forty miles, northeast by southwest, and varying from two to five miles in width. Through its whole length flowed the beautiful Colorado, in places a rapid, leaping stream, in others making its way quietly, noiselessly over a deeper bed. It varied, like all streams whose sources are in immediate mountains, in depth, at different seasons of the year. During the melting of the snows that clothed the mountain-tops to the north, when we came among the Mohaves, it came roaring and thundering along its rock-bound banks, threatening the whole valley, and doing some damage.

We found the Mohaves accustomed to the tillage of the soil to a limited extent, and in a peculiar way. And it was a season of great rejoicing when the Colorado overflowed, as it was only after overflows that they could rely upon their soil for a crop. In the autumn they planted the wheat carefully in hills with their fingers, and in the spring they planted corn, melons, and a few garden vegetables. They had, however, but a few notions, and these were crude, about agriculture. When we first arrived among them the wheat sown the previous fall had come up, and looked green and thrifty, though it did not appear, nor was it, sufficient to maintain one-fifth of their population. It was to us however, an enlivening sight to see even these scattered parcels of grain growing, clothing sections of their valley. It was a remembrancer, and reminded us of home (now no more ours) and placed us in a nearness to the customs of a civilized mode of life that we had not realized before. The Colorado had overflown during the winter, and there had been considerable rain. The Mohaves were in high hopes for a bountiful crop during this season. What was to them a rich harvest would be considered in Yankee land, or in the Western states, a poor compensation for so much time and plodding labor. For two years before they had raised but little.

For a time after coming among them but little was said to us; none seemed desirous to enter into any intercourse, or inquire even, if it had been possible for us to understand them, as to our welfare, past or present. Topeka gave us to know that we were to remain in their house. Indeed we were merely regarded as strange intruders, with whom they had no sympathy, and their bearing for a while toward us seemed to say: "You may live here if you can eke out an existence, by bowing yourselves unmurmuringly to our barbarism and privations." In a few days they began to direct us to work in various ways, such as bringing wood and water, and to perform various errands of convenience to them.

At times, when some of their friends were visiting in the neighborhood of our valley, they would call for the captives that they might see them. One day, while one of the sub-chiefs and his family were visiting at Espaniola's house, Mary and I were out a little from the house singing, and were overheard. This aroused their curiosity, and we were called, and many questions were put to us as to what we were singing, where we learned to sing, and if the whites were good singers. Mary and I, at their request, sang them some of our Sabbath-school hymns, and some of the short children's songs we had learned. After this we were teased very much to sing to them. Several times a small string of beads was made up among them and presented to us for singing to them for two or three hours; also pieces of red flannel (an article that to them was the most valuable of any they could possess) of which after some time we had several pieces. These we managed to attach together with ravelings, and wore them upon our persons. The beads we wore about our necks, squaw fashion.

There was little game in the Mohave Valley, and of necessity little meat was used by this tribe. At some seasons of the year, winter and spring, they procure fish from a small lake in the vicinity. This was a beautiful little body of water at freshet seasons, but in the dry seasons became a loathsome mudhole. In the producing season, the Mohaves scarcely raised a four months' supply.

We spent most of this summer in hard work. We were, for a long time, roused at the break of day, baskets were swung upon our shoulders, and we were obliged to go from six to eight miles for the "Musquite," [mesquite] a seed or berry growing upon a bush about the size of our Manzanita. In the first part of the season, this tree bloomed a beautiful flower, and after a few weeks a large seed-bud could be gathered from it, and this furnished what is truly to be called their staple article of subsistence. We spent from twilight to twilight again, for a long time, in gathering this. And often we found it impossible, from its scarcity that year, to fill our basket in a day. This seed, when gathered, was hung up in their huts to be thoroughly dried, and to be used when their vegetables and grain should be exhausted.

One day, while we were sitting in the hut of the chief, having just returned from a root-digging excursion, there came two of their physicians attended by the chief and several others, to the door of the hut. The chief's wife then bade us go out upon the yard, and told us that the physicians were going to put marks on our faces. It was with much difficulty that we could understand, however, at first, what was their design. We soon, however, by the motions accompanying the commands of the wife of the chief, came to understand that they were going to tatoo our faces. We had seen them do this to some of their female children, and we had often conversed with each other about expressing the hope that we should be spared from receiving their marks upon us. I ventured to plead with them for a few moments that they would not put those ugly marks upon our faces. But it was in vain. To all our expostulations they only replied in substance that they knew why we objected to it; that we expected to return to the whites, and we would be ashamed of it then; but that it was their resolution we should never return, and that as we belonged to them we should wear their "Ki-e-chook." They said further, that if we should get away, and they should find us among other tribes, or if some other tribes should steal us, they would by this means know us.

They then pricked the skin in small regular rows on our chins with a very sharp stick, until they bled freely. They then dipped these same sticks in the juice of a certain weed that grew on the banks of the river, and then in the powder of a blue stone that was to be found in low water, in some places along the bed of the stream (the stone they first burned until it would pulverize easy, and in burning it turned nearly black) and pricked this fine powder into these lacerated parts of the face. The process was somewhat painful, though it pained us more for two or three days after than at the time of its being done. They told us this could never be taken from the face, and that they had given us a different mark from the one worn by their own females, as we saw, but the same with which they marked all their own captives, and that they could claim us in whatever tribe they might find us.

## Crop Failure and Famine

The autumn was by far the easiest portion of the year for us. To multiply words would not give any clearer idea to the reader of our condition. It was one continual routine of drudgery. Toward spring their grains were exhausted. There was but little rain, not enough to raise the Colorado near the top of its banks. The Mohaves became very uneasy about their wheat in the ground. It came much later than usual, and looked sickly and grew tardily after it was out of the ground. It gave a poor, wretched promise at the best for the next year. Ere it was fairly up there were not provisions or articles of any kind to eat in the village any one night to keep its population two days. We found that the people numbered really over fifteen hundred. We were now driven forth every morning by the first break of day, cold and sometimes damp, with rough, bleak winds, to glean the old, dry musquite seed that chanced to have escaped the fatiguing search of the summer and autumn months. From this on to the time of gathering the scanty harvest of that year, we were barely able to keep soul and body together. And the return for all our vigorous labor was a little dry seed in small quantities. And all this was put forth under the most sickening apprehensions of more privation awaiting us the next year. The harvest was next to nothing. No rain had fallen during the spring to do much good.

Above what was necessary for seeding again, there was not one month's supply when harvest was over. We had gathered less during the summer of "musquite," and nothing but starvation could be expected. We were now put upon a stinted allowance, and the restrictions upon us were next to the taking the life of Mary Ann. During the second autumn, and at the time spoken of above, the chief's wife gave us some seed-grain, corn and wheat, showed us about thirty feet square of ground marked off upon which we might plant it and raise something for ourselves. We planted our wheat, and carefully concealed the handful of corn and melon-seeds to plant in the spring. This we enjoyed very much.

The Indians said that about sixty miles away there was a "Taneta" (tree) [possbily squaw-berry] that bore a berry called "Oth-to-toa," upon which they had subsisted for some time several years before, but it could be reached only by a mountainous and wretched way of sixty miles. Soon a large party made preparations and set out in quest of this "life-preserver." Many of those accustomed to bear burdens were not able to go. Mary Ann started, but soon gave out and returned. A few Indians accompanied us, but it was a disgrace for them to bear burdens; this was befitting only to squaws and captives.

We reached the place on the third day, and found the taneta to be a bush, and very much resembling the musquite, only with a much larger leaf. It grew to a height of from five to thirty feet. The berry was much more pleasant to the taste than the musquite; the juice of it, when extracted and mixed with water, was very much like the orange. The tediousness and perils of this trip were very much enlivened with the hope of getting something with which to nourish and prolong the life of Mary Ann. She was very much depressed, and appeared quite ill when I left her.

After wandering about for two days with but little gathered, six of us started in quest of some place where the oth-to-toa might be more abundant. We traveled over twenty miles away from our temporary camp. We found tanetas in abundance, and loaded with the berry. We had reached a field of them we judged never found before. Our baskets being filled, we hastened to join the camp party before they should start for the village. We soon lost our way, the night being dark, and wandered without water the whole night, and were nearly all sick from eating our oth-to-toa berry. Toward day, nearly exhausted, and three of our number very sick, we were compelled to halt. We watched over and nursed the sick, sweating them with the medical leaf always kept with us and about the only medicine used by the Mohaves. But our efforts were in vain, for before noon the three had breathed their last. A fire was kindled and their bodies were burned; and for several hours I expected to be laid upon one of those funeral pyres in that deep, dark, and almost trackless wilderness. The next day we found the camp, and found we had been nearly around it. We were soon on our way, and by traveling all one night we were at the village.

I feared Mary Ann would not live and I found on reaching the village that she had materially failed, and had been furnished with scarcely food enough to keep her alive. I sought by every possible care to recruit her, and for a short time she revived. The berry we had gathered, while it would add to one's flesh, and give an appearance of healthiness (if the stomach could bear it) had but little strengthening properties in it. I cherished for a short time the hope that she might, by care and nursing, be kept up until spring, when we could get fish. Mary Ann failed fast. She and I were whole days at a time without anything to eat; when by some chance, or kindness of the chief's daughter, we would get a morsel to satisfy our cravings. Several children had died, and more were in a dying state. Each death that occurred was the occasion for a night or day of frantic howling and crocodile mourning. Mary Ann was weak and growing weaker, and I gave up in despair. I sat by her side for a few days, most of the time only begging of the passers-by to give something to keep Mary Ann alive. Sometimes I succeeded. Had it not been for the wife and daughter of the chief, we could have obtained nothing. They seemed really to *feel* for us, and I have no doubt would have done more if in their power. My sister would not complain, or beg for something to eat.

When I saw that she was dead, I could but give myself up to loneliness, to wailing and despair. There were two, however, who seemed not wholly insensible to my condition, these were the wife and daughter of the chief. They manifested a sympathy that had not gathered about me since the first closing in of the night of my capitivity upon me. The Indians, at the direction of the chief, began to make preparations to burn the body of my sister. This, it seemed, I could not endure. The wife of the chief came to me and gave me to understand that she had by much entreaty, obtained the permission of her lord to give me the privilege of disposing of the dead body as I should choose. This was a great consolation, and I thanked her most earnestly. It lifted a burden from my mind that caused me to weep tears of gratitude. The chief gave me two blankets, and in these they wrapped the corpse. Orders were then given to two Indians to follow my directions in disposing of the body. I selected a spot in that little garden ground, where I had planted and wept with my dear sister. In this they dug a grave about five feet deep, and into it they gently lowered the remains of my last, my only sister, and closed her last resting-place with the sand.

That same woman, the wife of the chief, came again to the solace and relief of my destitution and woe. I was now able to walk but little, and had resigned all care and anxiety. Just at this time the kind woman came to me with some corn gruel in a hollow stone. I marveled to know how she had obtained it. The handful of seed corn that my sister and I had hid in the ground, between two stones did not come to my mind. But this woman, this Indian woman, had uncovered a part of what she had deposited against spring planting, and ground it to a coarse meal, and of it prepared this gruel for me. I took it and soon she brought me more. I began to revive. I felt a new life and strength given me by this morsel, and was cheered by the unlooked-for exhibition of sympathy that attended it. She had the discretion to deny the unnatural cravings that had been kindled by the small quantity she brought first, and dealt a little at a time, until within three days I gained a vigor and cheerfulness I had not felt for weeks. She bestowed this kindness in a sly and unobserved manner, and enjoined secrecy upon me, for a reason which the reader can judge. She did it when deaths by starvation and sickness were occurring every day throughout the settlement. Had it not been for her, I must have perished. From this circumstance I learned to chide my hasty judgment against ALL the Indian race, and also, that kindness is not always a stranger to the untutored and untamed bosom.

By my own exertions I was able now to procure a little upon which to nourish my half-starved stomach. By using about half of my seed corn, and getting an occasional small dose of bitter, fermented oth-to-toa soup, I managed to drag my life along to March, 1854. During this month and April I procured a few small roots at a long distance from the village; also some fish from the lake. I took particular pains to guard the little wheat garden that we had planted the autumn before, and I also planted a few kernels of corn and some melon seeds. Day after day I watched this little "mutautea," lest the birds might bring upon me another winter like that now passed. In my absence Aespaneo would watch it for me. As the fruit of my care and vigilant watching, I gathered about one half bushel of corn, and about the same quanitity of wheat. My melons were destroyed. The same woman that had saved my life, and furnished me with ground and seed to raise corn and wheat, and watched it for me for many days now procured from the chief a place where I might store it, with the promise from him that every kernel should go for my own maintenance.

Good Crops and a Time of Plenty

I had to do my accustomed share of musquite gathering, also, in June and July. This we gathered in abundance. The Colorado overflowed this winter and spring, and the wheat and corn produced well, so that in autumn the tribe was better provided with food than it had been for several years.

The social habits of these Indians, and the traits of character on which they are founded, and to which they give expression, may be illustrated by a single instance as well as a thousand. The portion of the valley over which the populations extends, is about forty miles long. Their convivial seasons were occasions of large gatherings, tumultuous rejoicings, and (so far as their limited productions would allow) of excess in feasting. The year of 1854 was one of unusual bounty and thrift. They planted more than usual; and by labor and the overflow of the river, the seed deposited brought forth an unparalleled increase. During the autumn of that year, the residents of the north part of the valley set apart a day for feasting and merry-making. Notice was given about four weeks beforehand; great preparations were made, and a large number invited. Their supply for the appetite on that day consisted of wheat, corn, pumpkins, beans, etc. These were boiled, and portions of them mixed with ground seed, such as serececa (seed of a weed) or moeroco (of pumpkins). On the day of the feast the Indians masked themselves, some with bark, some with paint, some with skins.

On the day previous to the feast, the Indians of our part of the valley who had been favored with an invitation, were gathered at the house of the chief, preparatory to taking the trip in company to the place of the feast. Some daubed their faces and hair with mud, others with paint, so as to give to each an appearance totally different from his other natural state. I was told that I could go along with the rest. This to me was no privilege, as I knew too well what cruelty and violence they were capable of when excited, as on their days of public gathering they were liable to be. However, I was safer there than with those whom they left behind. The Indians went slowly, sometimes in regular, and sometimes in irregular march, yelling, howling, singing, and gesticulating, until toward night they were wrought up to a perfect phrenzy. They halted about one mile from the "north settlement," and after building a fire, commenced their war-dance, which they kept up until about midnight. On this occasion I witnessed some of the most shameful indecencies, on the part of both male and female, that came to my eye for the five years of my stay among Indians.

The next morning the Indians who had prepared the feast (some of whom had joined in the dance of the previous evening) came with their squaws, each bearing upon their heads a Coopoesech, containing a cake, or a stone dish filled with soup, or boiled vegetables. These cakes were made of wheat, ground, and mixed with boiled pumpkins. This dough was rolled out sometimes to two feet in diameter; then placed in hot sand, a leaf and a layer of sand laid over the loaf, and a fire built over the whole, until it was baked through. After depositing these dishes, filled with their prepared dainties, upon a slight mound near by, the whole tribe then joined in a war-dance, which lasted nearly twelve hours. After this the dishes and their contents were taken by our party and borne back to our homes, when and where feasting and dancing again commenced, and continued until their supplies were exhausted, and they from sheer weariness were glad to fly to the embrace of sleep.

The Mohaves had but a simple system or theory of medicine. They divide disease into spiritual and physical, or at least they used terms that conveyed such an impression as this to my mind. The latter they treated mainly to an application of their medical leaf, generally sweating the patient by wrapping him in blankets and placing him over the steam of the leaves warmed in water. For the treatment of their spiritual or more malignant diseases they have physicians. All diseases were ranked under the latter class that had baffled the virtue of the medical leaf, and that were considered dangerous.

In the summer of 1855 a sickness prevailed to a considerable extent, very much resembling in its workings the more malignant fevers. Several died. Members of the families of two of the sub-chiefs were sick, and their physicians were called. They performed their cures by manipulations, and all manner of contortions of their own bodies, which were performed with loud weeping and wailing of the most extravagant kind over the sick. They professed to be in league and intimacy with the spirits of the departed, and from whose superior knowledge and position they were guided in all their curative processes. Two of these were called to the sick bedside of the children of these chiefs. They wailed and wrung their hands, and twisted themselves into all manner of shapes over them for some time, but it was in vain, the patients died. They had lost several patients lately, and already their medical repute was low in the market. Threats had already followed them from house to house, as their failures were known. After the death of these children of rank, vengeance was sworn upon them, as they were accused of having bargained themselves to the evil spirits for purpose of injury to the tribe. They knew of their danger and hid themselves on the other side of the river. For several days search was made, but in vain. They had relatives and friends who kept constant guard over them. But such was the feeling created by the complainings of those who had lost children and friends by their alleged conspiracy with devils, that the tribe demanded their lives and the chief gave orders for their arrest. But their friends managed in a sly way to conceal them for some time, though they did not dare to let their managery be known to the rest of the tribe. They were found, arrested, and burned alive.

The Mohaves believe that when their friends die they depart to a certain high hill in the western section of their territory. That they there pursue their avocation free from the ills and pains of their present life, if they had been good and brave. But they held that all cowardly Indians (and bravery was *the* good with them) were tormented with hardships and failures, sickness and defeats. This hill or hades, they never dared visit. It was thronged with thousands who were ready to wreak vengeance upon the mortal who dared intrude upon this sacred ground.

## Americans at Fort Yuma Learn Olive is Alive

Each day I found myself, not without hope it is true, but settling down into such contentment as I could with my lot. For the next eighteen months during which I was witness to their conduct, these Mohaves took more care and exercised more forethought in the matter of their food. They did not suffer, and seemed to determine not to suffer the return of a season like 1853.

There were some with whom I had become intimately acquainted, and from whom I had received humane and friendly treatment, exhibiting real kindness. I thought it best now to conciliate the best wishes of all and by every possible means to avoid all occasions of awakening their displeasure, or enkindling their unrepentant, uncontrollable temper and passions. There were some few for whom I began to feel a degree of attachment. Every spot in that valley that had any attraction, or offered a retreat to the sorrowing soul, had become familiar, and upon much of its adjacent scenery I delighted to gaze. Everyday had its monotony of toil, and thus I plodded on. To escape secmed impossible, and to make an unsuccessful attempt would be worse than death. Friends or kindred to look after or care for me, I had none, as I then supposed. I thought it best to receive my daily allotment with submission, and not darken it with a borrowed trouble; to merit and covet the good-will of my captors, whether I received it or not.

Up to the middle of February, 1856, nothing occurred connected with my allotment that would be of interest to the reader. One day as I was grinding musquite near the door of our dwelling, a lad came running up to me in haste, and said that Francisco, a Yuma crier, was on his way to the Mohaves, and that he was coming to try to get me away to the whites. The report created a momentary strange sensation, but I thought it probably was a rumor. In a few moments, however, the report was circulating on good authority, and as a reality. One of the sub-chiefs came in and said that a Yuma Indian, named Francisco, was now on his way with possible orders for my immediate release and safe return to the fort. I knew that there were white persons at Fort Yuma, but did not know my distance from the place. I knew, too, that intercourse of some kind was constantly kept up with the Yumas and the tribes extending that way, and thought that they had perhaps gained traces of my situation by this means. But as yet I had nothing definite upon which to place confidence.

I saw in a few hours that full credit was given to the report by the Mohaves, for a sudden commotion was created, and it was enkindling excitement throughout the settlement. The report spread over the valley with astonishing speed, by means of their criers, and a crowd was gathering, and the chiefs and principal men were summoned to a council by their head "Aespaniola," with whom I stayed. Aespaniola was a tall, strongly built man, active and generally happy. He seemed to possess a mildness of disposition and to maintain a gravity and seriousness in deportment that was rare among them. He ruled a council (noisy as they sometimes were) with an ease and authority such as but few Indians can command, if the Mohaves be a fair example. This council presented the appearance of an aimless convening of wild maniacs, more than that of men, met to deliberate. I looked upon the scene as a silent but narrowly watched spectator but was not permitted to be in the crowd or to hear what was said. I knew the declared object of the gathering, and was the subject of most anxious thoughts as to its issue and results. I thought I saw upon the part of some of them, a designed working of themselves into a mad phrenzy, as if preparatory to some brutal deed. I queried whether yet the report was not false; and also as to the persons who had sent the reported message, and by whom it might be conveyed. I tried to detect the prevailing feeling among the most influential of the council, but could not. Sometimes I doubted whether all this excitement could have been gotten up on the mere question of my return to the whites. For some time past they had manifested but little watchfulness, care, or concern about me. But still, though I was debarred from the council, I had heard enough to know that it was only about me and the reported demand for my liberty.

In the midst of the uproar and confusion the approach of Francisco was announced. The debate suddenly ceased, and it was a matter of much interest to me to be able to mark, as I did, the various manifestations by which different ones received him. Some were sullen, and would hardly treat him with any cordiality; others were indifferent, and with a shake of the head would say, "Degee, degee, ontoa, ontoa" (I don't care for the captive); others were angry, and advised that he be kept out of the council and driven back at once; others were dignified and serious. I saw Francisco enter the council, and I was at once seized by two Indians and bade be off to another part of the village.

In the morning, Francisco and I were called before the chief and told, with much reluctance, that the decision had been to let me go. At this, and while yet in their presence, I found I could no longer control my feelings, and I burst into tears, no longer able to deny myself the pleasure of thus expressing the weight of feeling that struggled for relief and utterance within me. I found that it had been pleaded against my being given up, that Francisco was suspected of simply coming to get me away from the Mohaves that I might be retained by the Yumas.

The chief accused him of this, and said he believed it. This excited the anger of Francisco, and he boldly told them what he thought of them, and told them to go with their captive; that they would sorrow for it in the end. When it was determined that I might go, the chief said that his daughter should go and see that I was carried to the whites.

We ate our breakfast, supplied ourselves with mushed musquite, and started. Three Yuma Indians had come with Francisco, to accompany him to and from the Mohaves; his brother and two cousins. I now began to think of really leaving my Indian home. Involuntarily my eye strayed over that valley. I gazed on every familiar object. The mountains that stood about our valley home, like sentinels tall and bold, their every shape, color, and height, as familiar as the door-yard about the dwelling in which I had been reared. Again my emotions were distrusted, and I could hardly believe that what was passing was reality. "Is it true," I asked, "that they have concluded to let me escape? I fear they will change their mind. Can it be that I am to look upon the white face again?" I then felt like hastening as for my life, ere they could revoke their decision.

I went to the grave of Mary Ann, and took a last look of the little mound marking the resting place of my sister who had come with me to that lonely exile; and now I felt what it was to know she could not go with me from it.

# THE CRABB FILIBUSTERING EXPEDITION TO SONORA
## (1857)

## Charles Edward Evans

**Editors' Note:** Today "filibuster" means "to carry on an extended debate for the purpose of delaying or preventing action by a legislative body." In the mid-1800's, however, the word described a very different activity. At that time a "filibuster" was an unauthorized invasion of a foreign country by a private army with the intent of taking control of the government. The word filibuster comes from the Spanish *filibustero*, meaning a freebooter or pirate. Charles Edward Evans was a *filibustero* in the classic sense.

During the 1850's filibustering became an obsession in California. The discovery of gold in 1848 brought tens of thousands of '49ers flooding into the Sierra Nevada seeking a quick fortune. But, as in all gold rushes, the vast majority of gold hunters found little or no gold, only adventure. So when would-be soldiers-of-fortune concocted schemes to gain wealth and fame by "liberating" foreign lands, the gold fields provided a fertile source of volunteers.

Filibustering became popular partly because recent history had shown that the doctrine of "Manifest Destiny," which deemed it inevitable that the United State would extend from coast to coast, was more than just a patriotic idea. Settlers had successfully "liberated" Texas in 1836; the Northwest was annexed by the United States in 1846; and, in 1848, Mexico had been forced to cede half of its remaining territory, including California, to the Americans. It was only natural that frustrated '49ers coveted weakly-governed Latin American countries with the dream of being modern day *conquistadores*. Although patriotism undoubtedly explained some of their fervor, most filibusters were motivated by adventure and personal gain -- the same lures that had brought them to California in the first place.

In 1851 no fewer than five filibustering expeditons were organized in California. Campaigns were launched to conquer Equador, the Hawaiian Islands, Baja California, and Sonora (twice). All of these invasions were quickly repulsed. The two Sonoran adventures were mounted by French expatriots who had become disenchanted with their California prospects. French-led takeovers of Sonora were again attempted in 1852 and 1854 with similar results. The most famous filibustering Californian, however, was an American, William Walker, who after invading Baja California with forty-five mercenaries in 1854, had to flee for his life after a disasterous march to take Sonora. Not easily dissuaded, Walker successfully took control of Nicaragua for two years before being ousted in 1857.

The last American expedition to invade Mexican territory was organized by Henry A. Crabb in 1857. Crabb, a California state senator from Stockton, was married to Filomena Ainza, a member of a prominent Sonora family. Through her family, Crabb became acquainted with the chaotic political climate and the weakness of the Mexican federal government in this frontier province. Hoping to exploit the political situation and profit from Sonora's economic possibilities, Crabb decided to invade the state and set up his own government. While organizing his campaign, he was careful to claim that his was a mere colonizing venture (filibustering was against the law in the U. S.). However, when he arrived in Fort Yuma in February, 1857, it was with ninety well-armed men, not a contingent of farmers.

The little army marched up the Gila River for about fifty miles, then headed southeast toward the border town of Sonoyta. Crabb now sent two of his men to Tucson to enlist additional recruits from settlements along the Santa Cruz River. He also planned to bolster his forces with additional reinforcements from California once they had established a "beachhead" in northern Sonora. On approaching Sonoyta, Crabb divided his command, leaving twenty men and the wagons north of the border to come later, and moved forward with sixty-nine others.

Henry Crabb believed that many Sonorans would welcome him because of the domestic political turmoil and the Mexican government's inability to protect its northernmost citizens from Indians and bandits. In this assumption, he was terribly mistaken. Upon hearing of the filibusters' arrival, the Mexican population determined to repel the invading *Gringos*. When Crabb and his men arrived at the first important town, Caborca, the Mexicans were waiting for him. Although the Californians managed to fight their way into Caborca, the superior numbers of defenders forced them to seek refuge in a building across from the church. Here they held out for six days before surrendering. The Crabb expedition was to find out the same thing Texans learned during the war for Texas independence -- surrender to Mexican forces did not necessarily mean captivity and eventual repatriation. The next morning at Caborca, April 7, all of the Americans except for a fourteen-year-old boy were put to death by firing squads.

About three days later, a detachment of Mexican troops intercepted sixteen men of Crabb's rear guard proceeding toward Caborca. They too surrendered and met the same fate. The only survivors of the original expedition were now four men who had been left behind in Arizona as too sick to fight. On April 17, Mexican troops crossed over the line and shot all four of the invalids on American soil.

Although no reinforcements from California ever showed up to help Crabb, a column of twenty-four volunteers from the Tucson area set out for Caborca on April 1st. As they approached the town they were met by several hundred freshly victorious Mexicans. The Arizonans wisely fought their way back across the border, having four men killed and two others wounded. Thus ended Crabb's dreams of conquest in Mexico.

The boy spared by the Mexicans at Caborca, Charles Edward Evans, was detained in Sonora for a few months, and then released to American officials at the port of Mazatlán to tell his tale. The following account of the Crabb expedition and massacre by young Evans is taken from two sources. The first three paragraphs are from a statement given by Evans to the U. S. vice consul at Mazatlán which was subsequently published in the book *Reid's Tramp* in 1858. John C. Reid happened to be in Tucson when Crabb's recruiters came to town in search of volunteers. He joined the Arizonans who were repulsed outside of Caborca, and his book detailed his adventures as a filibuster. The remainder of Evan's account was published in the August 3, 1857, edition of the *Daily Alta California* on his arrival in San Francisco. Although Evans maintains the fiction that the Crabb expedition was a peaceful colonizing and prospecting venture, his story is otherwise thought to be accurate.

Each April, the citizens of Caborca, Altar, and other northwestern Sonora towns still celebrate the annihilation of Henry Crabb's little army and the end of invasions of Mexico by American filibusters.

~ ~ ~ ~ ~

**I was born in the city of New Orleans** on the 25th day of December, 1842, and removed to the state of California in the year 1849 in company with my mother and step-father, where I constantly resided until the year 1857.

On the 19th day of January, 1857, I was at the town of Sonora, Tuolumne County, State of California, and on that day joined an expedition at that time organizing in the town of Sonora and known as an expedition bound to Sonora, Mexico, for the purpose of mining. In company with about thirty men of said company, I left the town of Sonora on the following day en route for San Francisco, where we arrived on the 21st day of January. On the same day we embarked on board the steamer Sea Bird for San Pedro, accompanied by thirty or forty more members of the same expedition that had joined in San Francisco.

On the 24th day of January we arrived at San Pedro and, after disembarking from the steamer, took up our line of march for El Monte, Los Angeles County, where we arrived on the following day. After remaining there for one week for the purpose of purchasing horses, mules, wagons, and provisions, we took up our route for Fort Yuma on the Colorado River. Stopping for one week on the way at Warner's Ranch, we arrived at Fort Yuma on the 27th day of February. The company now consisted of ninety men and two wagons containing provisions. Part of the men were mounted and part on foot. Mr. Crabb acted in command of the expedition, assisted by Mr. McCoun, Mr. N. B. Wood, and Mr. David S. McDowell. The expedition remained at Fort Yuma one week, during which time Dr. Evans left the expedition and proceeded to Sonora alone. After recruiting more animals at Fort Yuma, we started for Sonora about the 4th of March.

Soon after arriving at Cabeza Prieta, the company held a meeting and selected volunteers to go forward to Sonoita, a distance of forty leagues. The object of this was to reduce the parties crossing the desert to such numbers as to allow them to carry the necessary amount of water. Twenty men then remained at Cabeza Prieta. Messrs. Crabb, McCoun, Wood and sundry others, including myself (sixty nine in all) were in the party that went forward. We arrived at Sonoita on the 25th of March. Here it was at first proposed to remain until the other party could come up and rejoin us; but provisions being scarce, and all anxious to press forward, Mr. Crabb ordered us to start for the interior of Sonora, which we did on the 27th, he leaving a letter with his brother-in-law, Jesus Ainsa, directing the others to follow immediately on their arrival. We kept the road several days, passing some haciendas, where we were treated with kindness by the people. We exchanged civilities with many of the inhabitants on the road. All of these appeared to look upon us as peaceable settlers, and evinced no alarm at our arms. We arrived in sight of Caborca about eight o'clock on the morning of April 1st. Up to his time we had received no intimation that we should be attacked, or be regarded as hostile invaders by the people. At Sonoita, Mr. Crabb and his brother-in-law, Mr. Cortelyou, held frequent private conversations, but upon what subject I could not learn. He showed, however, no anxiety as to the manner in which we were likely to be received and seemed confident that all would go well.

### The Attack at Caborca

We were traveling up a lane, between two wheat fields, in full security, as we supposed, and congratulating ourselves upon the success which had hitherto crowned the enterprise, when we were suddenly and unexpectedly fired upon by about one hundred and fifty Mexicans, hidden behind the adobe fences on both sides of the road. Though their firing made a terrible racket, and the air was filled with smoke, strange to say, none of us was wounded. Up to this time, not suspecting any hostilities, and confident in our own peaceable intentions, no military organization had been recommended or thought of. The object, this far, of Mr. Crabb and his advisers appears to have been to give the natives no cause for supposing us to be belligerents, and consequently no more military display was made than what travellers in a strange land would naturally adopt as precautionary measures.

The assault at first threw the party into confusion; but Mr. Crabb gave orders to return the fire, and our men shot from ten to fifteen of the enemy. Our first fire killed one of their principal officers. At the time of the attack we were no more than a quarter of a mile from the town -- a small collection of adobes, with a fine church. The enemy broke after our return of their fire, and ran for the church, and we continued our journey along the lane into town. We took shelter in a large house on the Plaza, directly opposite the church. The inhabitants seemed much frightened at our approach, and men, women and children had crowded into the convent, which formed part of the church. The Mexicans commenced and kept up a brisk and continuous fire with all kinds of small arms at us and our house; but they took care to keep out of sight so that we could not do much by returning their fire.

## Assault by Crabb on the Convent

We were soon convinced that we were considered as enemies and must regulate our conduct accordingly. Mr. Crabb called for volunteers to make an assault upon the church. Only fifteen out of the sixty-nine men came forward. These were headed by Mr. Crabb in person. (The only names I can remember at this moment, as forming part of this storming party, were David S. McDowell, and James Wood, of Sonora, Tuolumne County. The latter was shot dead, and the former received nine wounds in his right arm.) They took a keg of powder with them for the purpose of blowing open the door of the church. They crossed the Plaza in the midst of a murderous fire and Mr. Crabb gave the word to charge. They compelled the Mexicans to retreat out of the convent into the body of the church. Mr. Crabb then took possession of the convent with his men and placed a keg of powder under the door which connects with the church. By this time, Wm. Chaney, from Nevada, Clark Small, from Mariposa, and another person, whose name I had forgotten, had been killed. The slow match being damp, the powder did not explode. Crabb sat down and wrote a note on a leaf of his pocket-book, to his party on the opposite side of the Plaza, for a slow match. This he dispatched by a little Mexican child who had got separated from the other inhabitants. He had hardly finished the note when the Mexicans charged -- in number about one hundred and twenty. They entered the convent, and for several minutes a severe hand-to-hand fight continued. Mr. Crabb, having exhausted his shots, sat down deliberately by the door and commenced reloading his pistol. While in this act he was shot in the right arm above the elbow. He took his revolver in his left hand and fired all but one shot. Up to this time the efforts of the whole population were directed against those in the convent.

## The Siege

There were still forty-four Americans remaining in the adobe house opposite. We received no orders from any of our leaders to cross the plaza to the assistance of those in the convent, and many were not disposed to do so under any circumstances. After Mr. Crabb was wounded he retreated with his men to the adobe house, where the remainder of the party were. Here the wounded were attended to. We stood guard regularly while the Mexicans were shooting at us. I believe these were the longest days and nights I ever experienced. I am not capable, of course, of forming a reliable opinion on military matters, but I am convinced that if the whole party had taken the advice of a few bold spirits who wished to go out and meet the enemy, we could have retreated and escaped. But there was a strong conviction with many that, if we surrendered, we should be honorably treated. By rushing out we could have formed a formidable body, and kept at bay any reasonable force they could have sent against us and perhaps the whole might have succeeded in retreating safely out of the country, as the party of twenty-five did. There were long and animated discussions on this subject, but those for surrendering carried the day.

Two of our men were mortally wounded, who died soon after. These were William Allen, of Coyote Flat, Tuolumne county; and William Seaton, from Benicia, I believe. They both died before night. They were terribly wounded. In the convent, there were also killed James Woods and William Randolph, of Tuolumne county; also, another man of slim stature, from Los Angeles county. We remained in the adobe house all night the natives firing upon us incessantly. The next morning John George was shot through the body, and died in half an hour. He was from the northern mines, but from what part I do not recollect. The natives continued firing upon us during the second day (the 2nd of April). A larger number of people had collected in the town. We did not return their firing, except on the first day, as they were hidden behind the adobe walls. Often they raised caps and hats on their guns in order to deceive us. In nearly every instance these were perforated with a rifle ball, as soon as they appeared in sight.

On the nights of the 2nd, 3rd, 4th, and 5th of April, the natives continued their firing upon us, but did not see fit to attack us any nearer than by musket shots. We found in the house provisions, such as bread, beef, lard, etc.

### A Deserter and His Fate

On the 5th, one of our men deserted to the enemy. I do not recollect his name. The circumstances were these: We had retained, as a sort of hostage, the little boy by whom Mr. Crabb had sent the note for a slow match. The deserter, under the pretext of taking the boy with him into the yard to obtain some water, sprang over the fence and ran down the street, shouting to the natives, *"Viva, Mejico!"* The enemy pursued him, and carried him before the commander, who first extorted what news he could and then shot him.

## Arrival of Artillery

The enemy received on the 6th two pieces of artillery, with which they commended firing at point blank range upon our little fortress. Since the first day, we had fired but one shot, and that at a man in the belfry of the church, where he was hoisting the Mexican flag; he was killed. The cannon directed against us were loaded with chunks of lead instead of ball; but these did not have their desired effect in battering down the doors. The probability is that they had no cannon balls. They continued firing, however, all day during the 6th, until about sundown. About 9 o'clock the enemy began to set the house on fire. This was done by shooting lighted combustible materials affixed to arrows, into the straw thatch of the house. The roof took fire and commenced blazing. The house was soon filled with smoke, and Mr. Crabb gave orders to have two kegs of powder exploded for the purpose of blowing off the roof. The effect was to jar the house, and to burn one man slightly, but the flames were partially extinguished. The enemy were now surrounding the house, shouting "*Viva Mejico, y mueran los Yankees!*" They seemed firmly bent upon destroying us.

## The Surrender

Mr. Crabb now called a consultation, and advised a surrender. Many, however, were opposed to this, predicting and forseeing the death which awaited them, and urging that as the natives seemed determined to destroy us, they might as well sell their lives dearly. David S. McDowell had proposed to take command of the men, and take the Church; but Mr. Crabb opposed it. Col. Nathaniel Wood and Mr. McCoun agreed with Mr. Crabb in opinion, as did several others, whose names I cannot remember. There were a great many who wanted to sally out with McDowell, but they were overruled by the advice of Mr. Crabb, Col. Wood and others, who believed that if the whole party should surrender, the Mexicans would treat us as prisoners of war, and that it was better not to exasperate them by a useless resistance.

At half-past ten, Mr. ---- Hyne volunteered to be the bearer of a flag of truce to the natives. He accordingly attached a white handkerchief to a ramrod, and went out to the enemy. The Mexicans sent another flag to meet him halfway, and Mr. Hyne was taken into the convent; he was secured there and not allowed to return. The Mexicans made Hyne shout their conditions across the Plaza to us, which were that if we surrendered we should be taken to Altar, and tried the next day as prisoners of war; and that the wounded would be well attended to, as they (the Mexicans) had a good physician. Mr. Crabb not being satisfied, and not fully understanding these conditions, requested Cortelyou to ask a further explanation, which he did; and the terms being fully understood, the whole party surrendered. This was about eleven o'clock at night. It was very dark at the time, but the sky was clear.

We were required to go over one by one and leave the arms in the house as we departed. This was done. Mr. Crabb was the first who went over. He reported who he was. He was placed aside without being tied. The rest of us were searched, and tied with our hands in front. The party submitted without murmurs, as it was generally supposed that we should be soon set at liberty. We were then marched into their barracks and confined, Mr. Crabb being with us.

### The Party Condemned to Death

Mr. Crabb was soon taken out and interrogated by means of an interpreter. After about half an hour, he returned to us at the barracks, but the guard would not allow him to communicate to us the result of his conference with the Mexican leaders. This was about midnight. In about an hour more, an official appeared with a written paper, which we soon learned was our "sentence." Mr. Cortelyou, who read Spanish, translated it aloud to us. It was that we were all to be shot at sunrise. The effect upon us may be imagined. There appeared no means of averting our doom. We were in their power and felt that their barbarous resolution would certainly be executed. No attempts were made to intercede for us. In the course of an hour, a boy named Chapin, about 18 years of age, was released and taken out to be set at liberty, but soon after he was brought in again and tied, and I was released in his place. Chapin was shot with the rest. He had been slightly wounded in the late fight. I suppose I was substituted for him, as it was found that I was the youngest. I am in my sixteenth year.

After taking me out, they carried me to the adobe house, which our party had occupied and where I found nine of our party wounded. I remained there under guard, but not tied, until about daybreak, when I was taken by four men to Hilario Gabilondo, the second in command of the Mexicans, and he told me, through a Mexican, who spoke broken English, that I was the only one to be saved out of the party, and that the others were to be shot at sunrise. Gabilondo ordered the troops to mount. I was placed on a horse, and we started for Altar, where we arrived at half past 7 o'clock. The distance is said to be seven leagues. We rode the whole way in a canter. I remained in Altar two days. I was not allowed to go beyond the town limits. I was not questioned or molested in any way.

## Shocking Desecration of the Dead

On the 9th I returned, with Gabilondo, to Caborca. This was on the 3rd day after the execution of our party, which, of course, I did not witness, being absent. I went out to the cemetery and saw their bodies strewn about the ground, unburied. All were stripped of their clothing -- even of stockings. The stench arising from their bodies prevented my approaching nearer than to observe that they had been gnawed and mutilated by beasts. I saw a finger lying near me, which appeared to have been cut off -- perhaps to take a ring from it. From where I stood I was able to recognize several bodies -- among them those of Mr. McCoun and Col. Wood. I remained in Caborca fifteen days, and, up to the time of my departure, I saw no attempt made to bury them. It was a standing and exultant joke among the Mexicans that their hogs would get fat on the Yankee flesh -- ready for killing next fall. I recognized the clothing of our party, worn by the people around me.

## An Appalling Sight

On the day after my second arrival at Caborca, a Mexican came up and motioned me to go with him. I followed him into a small house, and he led me to a large earthen jar placed on the ground. He put his hand in and immediately drew out Mr. Crabb's head, holding it by the hair. It had been preserved in vinegar, and the liquid dripped down into the jar as he held the head up for me to look at. He laughed and asked me if I knew who it belonged to. I retreated with alarm and horror from the spectacle. He laughed, and put it back into the jar. I then left the house.

## Capture and Death of the Other Party

While I was in Altar, the news came that sixteen others of our party had been arrested on the same day that Crabb and his command were executed. These were the party of twenty, whom we had left, as above stated, at Cabeza Prieta. I understood that they had been captured within two leagues of Caborca. The other four of the twenty had been left on the American side. I was told that these sixteen had been surrounded about two leagues from Caborca, and that in taking them, the Americans had only fired one shot. The man who fired it gave his name to the Mexicans, just before the execution, as McKinney, from San Jose, Cal. The party were then taken into Caborca, and shot on the afternoon of the same day. These facts in relation to the sixteen, I give from the accounts of the Mexicans about me, not having been present. McKinney was in command of the party.

The commander-in-chief, Jiron, sent, on the 11th (of April) a company of lancers to Sonoita, with orders to kill every Yankee they should meet.


## The Dead and How They Were Treated

As I have said above, I was fifteen days at Caborca. During this time, the natives were constantly celebrating their victory over "*los Yankees,*" and the late execution was made the subject of constant conversations and merry makings. I repeat that, during this time, the bodies of our party lay unburied and putrifying in the sun. The hogs made it a daily place of resort, and at evening, when they came into the town, the stench, which, as they passed through the streets, was insupportable, showed too plainly how they had been occupied during the day. From these sickening sights, and the harrowing associations connected with them, I could not escape, and was only thankful that my life had been spared from this butchery.

I do not know what was the object in preserving Mr. Crabb's head. Many women and children passed into the house where it was kept, and it appeared to be a sort of trophy of their late victory.


## Treatment of Evans by the Mexicans

I can make no complaint of the treatment I received between Caborca and Hermosillo. On our route to Ures, and thence to Guaymas, there was nothing which they refused for my comfort. The soldiers themselves gave me everything I asked for, which they could obtain, and the women of the towns through which we passed always treated me kindly, and expressed great sympathy for my situation. But in Caborca, after my arrival there the second time, I was obliged to don a red jacket and a tri-colored ribbon (red, white and green) around my hat, on which was inscribed "*Libertad ó Muerto.*" I was also obliged to carry a lance, and to adopt, in full, the military uniform of the country.

### Celebration at the Capital

When I arrived at Ures, we were received with great demonstrations by the people. The whole city turned out to meet the conquerors of "los Yankees." The American flag above mentioned was fixed, union down, to a lance, and carried in advance of the cavalcade. The Governor and his staff met the troops at the entrance of the city, saluted them, and publicly congratulated them on their successful campaign. He then shouted with his hat off: "*Viva los gallantes oficiales de Caborca! Viva los valientes muchachos de la Caborca! Viva el Republica Mexicana!*" This was replied to by the troops, and the whole then paraded through the town. I followed with the servants and the pack animals.

I remained three days in Ures. Several public festivals were held in honor of the late event. The Governor, Don Ignacio Pesqueira, had me brought before him; he treated me very kindly.

While at Ures, I saw several brass field pieces -- 24 pounders. Two of these, accompanied by five hundred men, had started for Caborca for the purpose of taking part in the battle there. They had arrived at within a day's march of that place; when hearing of the surrender, they returned to Ures. Had the siege continued another day, the heavy ordinance would soon have battered down our adobe house.

# LEE'S CONFESSION -- THE MOUNTAIN MEADOWS MASSACRE
## (1857)

## John Doyle Lee

**Editors' Note:** So great is the horror of the Mountain Meadows massacre that to this day if one hears of it at all it is usually only in whispered bits and pieces. That this terrible episode actually occurred is not open to doubt. John D. Lee was a key participant and he told what happened and who was involved. The nagging question remains, why? To understand the motive for such a treacherous deed one needs to place the tragedy in historical perspective.

The relationship between the Church of Jesus Christ of Latter-Day Saints and the federal government had been strained ever since the Mormons arrived on the shores of Great Salt Lake, Utah, in 1847. Within ten years they were on the verge of open hostility. The Mormons looked to church president and Utah governor Brigham Young as their ultimate authority, and virtually ignored the territorial officials and federal judges appointed by the U. S. president. Outside of Utah, anti-polygamy and anti-Mormon sentiment had created an atmosphere of suspicion and hate.

A crises was reached in 1857 when President James Buchanan declared the territory to be in a state of rebellion. To restore federal authority in the territory,Colonel Albert S. Johnston was ordered to march into Utah with 2,500 troops. In retaliation, Brigham Young ordered the Nauvoo Legion, the Mormon militia, to prepare for war and sent Lot Smith and a band of guerrillas to harass Johnston's troops on their way west. The expectation was that the Mormons and the United States would soon be at war, and an aura of anxiety permeated the territory.

During this time of tension, a wagon train of California-bound, non-Mormon emigrants from Arkansas and Missouri arrived at Salt Lake City under the leadership of Charles Fancher. Too late in the year to cross the Sierra Nevada, the train headed south in August, 1857, taking the all-weather route to southern California. Considering the 140 men, women, and children aboard the wagons as enemies, the Saints refused to sell the emigrants supplies, and harsh words were exchanged. Some of the Mormons complained that members of the train allowed their livestock to invade their fields and damage crops. Towns along the route refused to allow the wagon train to pass through, forcing the Fancher caravan to make circuitous detours. Encouraged by their Mormon allies, Paiute Indians began to pester the emigrants and pilfer their goods.

No major confrontations occurred, however, until Fancher's party made camp in early September at Mountain Meadows, thirty-five miles west of the settlement of Cedar City. A well-watered, grassy valley at about 6,000 feet elevation, Mountain Meadows was a favorite spot for emigrants to rest their livestock before dropping down into the desert. Here about 200 Paiutes surrounded the camp and laid seige to the train. But the Missourians were well armed and skillfull at protecting themselves. A deadlock developed in which the Indians could not subdue the train, but neither could the Gentiles, as the Mormons called them, break out and continue their journey.

Meanwhile, at Cedar City, Mormon elders debated the fate of the emigrants. The people of southwestern Utah were known to be particularly zealous, even fanatical, in their beliefs. Emotional speeches were given detailing the persecution of the Mormons in Missouri, with special reference to the massacre at Haun's Mill in which eighteen Mormons, including a number of children, were murdered by an angry mob in 1838. Because many of the families in the Fancher party were from Missouri, it was reasoned that now might be a good time for vengeance. The Fancher emigrants also were well-off and had valuable livestock, wagons, and other goods, along with several thousands of dollars in gold. For whatever reason, a decision was made for the local militia to aid the Paiutes and annihilate the emigrants at the meadows. The Missourians' possessions would then be divided among the Indians and the participating "Saints." Because the Mormons' official liason with the Indians in southern Utah, Jacob Hamblin, was away, John D. Lee was summoned from the nearby village of Harmony to coordinate their plan with the Paiutes. On September 11, 1857, the plan was carried out.

Despite a blood oath that no participant would speak of what occurred on pain of death, rumors about the massacre began to circulate almost immediately. Wild animals uncovered many of the bodies and these were found by other travelers. But no one kept records of parties that headed west and there was no one waiting for the families to arrive in California. To this day the names of many of the victims are unknown. About all that the outside world was aware of was that apparently Indians had massacred a party of emigrants at Mountain Meadows.

In the meantime, relations between Utah and the federal govenment took a turn for the better. Slowed by Lot Smith's raiders, Colonel Johnston's troops had gone into winter quarters near Fort Bridger, Wyoming. Anxious to avoid an all-out fight, federal officials began negotiations with Brigham Young in an effort to defuse the situation without resorting to force of arms. Young agreed to step down as governor of Utah and cooperate with a replacement appointed by President Buchanan. In return, the president issued an order pardoning the Saints for destroying U. S. Army equipment and other offenses.

But rumors about a massacre of U. S. Citizens in Utah persisted. Jacob Forney, the new commissioner of Indian affairs for Utah, went to Cedar City in the spring of 1859 to learn more about the supposed killings. He traveled quietly throughout the region, discussing the matter with anyone who would talk with him. He discovered that some small children from the Fancher train were living with Mormon families. If only Indians were involved, how did these tots come to be among the Mormons? Little by little, he determined that the Mormons had somehow been involved in the massacre.

In April, 1859, a military detatchment was sent south from Salt Lake City to locate and arrest the guilty parties. Those Mormon men on the list to be arrested went into hiding. After a half-hearted search, the soldiers left without arresting anyone, and the fugitives returned home. Without some local cooperation, no case could be made against the perpetrators. The children, all of whom were too small to tell what happened, were gathered up and sent to live with strangers. By the time of the outbreak of the Civil War in 1861, the matter had been all but dropped.

Although they would not speak of it, most of the Mormons in southern Utah disapproved of the massacre. Several of the participants later reported regretting having been a part of the slaughter. And for reasons that are still unclear, blame for the massacre began to focus on a single individual. Perhaps, ineluctably, the situation called for a scapegoat; the guilt of the many would be pawned off on one man -- John D. Lee.

A convert while still in his twenties, the energetic Lee had helped organize the Mormons' exodus to Utah and had been instrumental in colonizing the southern portions of the territory. A polygamist, Lee eventually married nineteen wives and fathered scores of children. Yet, despite being a devout Mormon and having been one of Brigham Young's most trusted lieutenants, Lee began to be shunned by his neighbors and was the subject of all manner of rumors.

In 1870, John D. Lee and one Isaac Haight were excommunicated by the Mormon Church for participating in the Mountain Meadows massacre. Nonetheless, the following year Brigham Young sent Lee to establish a ferry across the Colorado River at the head of the Grand Canyon to facilitate the movement of Mormons into northern Arizona. Although technically outside the Church, and named in a federal warrant, Lee still looked to Young for guidance and obeyed the order. In 1872, Haight was readmitted to the church, leaving Lee, hiding at "Lonely Dell" (subsequently known as Lee's Ferry), to bear sole responsibility for the crimes at Mountain Meadows.

While on a clandestine visit to one of his many families in 1874, Lee was arrested by federal marshals in Panguitch, Utah, and charged with murder. The following year he was put on trial in Beaver City, Utah, but witnesses were few and testimony limited. The result was a hung jury -- non-Mormons voting for conviction, Mormon members voting for acquital. Lee was then taken to Salt Lake City, and pending a new trial, released on bail. By the time his case was reheard in September, 1876, the atmosphere had changed considerably. Witnesses were now numerous, and memories had greatly "improved." The all-Mormon jury quickly found Lee guilty of masterminding and conducting the massacre. He was sentenced to be executed by a firing squad.

While in prison awaitng execution, John Lee wrote his "confession," briefly telling his life story, but mainly detailing the planning, perpetration, and cover-up of the Mountain Meadows massacre. The confession was copied and prepared for publication by Lee's defense attorney, William W. Bishop, who swore in an affidavit that it had not been altered in any way. So inflamatory was the document at the time that it was shipped to Nevada by Wells Fargo & Co. under armed guard.

Some people believe that Lee's confession was either coerced by his jailors or that it was contrived in an attempt to save his own skin. Although his account has properly been criticized for being self-serving in that he deceptively minimized his role in the killings and falsely claimed to be opposed to the plot all along, most historians believe that it is otherwise accurate. Historian Juanita Brooks, herself a lifelong, practicing Mormon, was convinced that the document itself was genuine. In her definitive biography of Lee (*John Doyle Lee: Zealot, Pioneer Builder, Scapegoat*), Mrs. Brooks described how the confession was produced: "Lee did not make the public confession that would have spared him; however, he did start to write the story of his life [and] it became clear that he would not be able to finish it all before his execution. He laid down his pen and, encouraged by friendly officers, told the story of the massacre to stenographers who took it down in shorthand."

John Lee was taken to Mountain Meadows and shot while sitting on his coffin on March 23, 1877. His body was given to family members for burial in Panguitch, Utah.

~ ~ ~ ~ ~

**As a duty to myself, my family, and mankind at large,** I propose to give a full and true statement of all that I know and all that I did in that unfortunate affair, which has cursed my existence, and made me a wanderer from place to place for the last nineteen years, and which is known to the world as the *Mountain Meadows Massacre.*

I have no vindictive feeling against any one; no enemies to punish by this statement; and no *friends* to shield by keeping back, or longer keeping secret, any of the facts connected with the Massacre.

I believe that I must tell all that I do know, and tell everything just as the same transpired. I shall tell the truth and permit the public to judge who is most to blame for the crime that I am accused of committing. I did not act alone; I had many to assist me at the Mountain Meadows. I believe that most of those who were connected with the Massacre, and took part in the lamentable transaction that has blackened the character of all who were aiders or abettors in the same, were acting under the impression that they were performing a religious duty. I know all were acting under the orders and by the command of their Church leaders; and I firmly believe that the most of those who took part in the proceedings, considered it a religious duty to unquestioningly obey the orders which they had received. That they acted from a sense of duty to the Mormon Church, I never doubted. Believing that those with me acted from a sense of religious duty on that occasion, I have faithfully kept the secret of their guilt, and remained silent and true to the oath of secrecy which we took on the bloody field, for many long and bitter years. I have never betrayed those who acted with me and participated in the crime for which I am convicted, and for which I am to suffer death.

My attorneys, especially Wells Spicer and Wm. W. Bishop, have long tried, but tried in vain, to induce me to *tell all I knew* of the massacre and the causes which led to it. I have heretofore refused to tell the tale. Until the last few days I had intended to die, if die I must, without giving one word to the public concerning those who joined willingly, or unwillingly, in the work of destruction at Mountain Meadows.

To hesitate longer, or to die in silence, would be unjust and cowardly. I will not keep the secret any longer as my own, but will tell all I know.

At the earnest request of a *few* remaining friends, and by the advice of Mr. Bishop, my counsel, who had defended me thus far with all his ability, notwithstanding my want of money with which to pay even his expenses while attending to my case, I have concluded to write facts as I know them to exist.

I cannot go before the Judge of the quick and the dead without first revealing all that I know, as to what was done, who ordered me to do what I did do, and the motives that led to the commission of that unnatural and bloody deed.

The immediate orders for the killing of the emigrants came from those in authority at Cedar City. At the time of the massacre, I and those with me, acted by virtue of positive orders from Isaac C. Haight and his associates at Cedar City. Before I started on my mission to the Mountain Meadows, I was told by Isaac C. Haight that his orders to me were the result of full consultation with Colonel William H. Dame and all in authority. It is a new thing to me, if the massacre was not decided on by the head men of the Church, and it is a new thing for Mormons to condemn those who committed the deed.

Being forced to speak from memory alone, without the aid of my memorandum books, and not having time to correct the statements that I make, I will necessarily give many things out of their regular order. The superiority that I claim for my statement is this: ALL THAT I DO SAY IS TRUE AND NOTHING BUT THE TRUTH.

I will begin my statement by saying, I was born on the 6th day of September, A.D. 1812, in the town of Kaskaskia, Randolph County, State of Illinois. I am therefore in the sixty-fifth year of my age.

I joined the Mormon Church at Far West, Missouri, about thirty-nine years ago. To be with that Church and people I left my home on Luck Creek, Fayette County, Illinois, and went and joined the Mormons in Missouri, before the troubles at Gallatin, Far West and other points, between the Missourians and Mormons. I shared the fate of my brother Mormons, in being mistreated, arrested, robbed and driven from Missouri in a destitute condition, by a wild and fanatical mob. But of all this I shall speak in my life, which I shall write for publication if I have time to do so.

I took an active part with the leading men at Nauvoo, in building up that city. I induced many Saints to move to Nauvoo, for the sake of their souls. I traveled and preached the Mormon doctrine in many States. I was an honored man in the Church, and stood high with the Priesthood, until the last few years. I am now cut off from the Church for *obeying the orders* of my superiors, and doing so without asking questions -- for doing as my religion and my religious teachers had taught me to do. I am now used by the Mormon Church as a scape-goat to carry the sins of that people. My life is to be taken, so that my death may stop further enquiry into the acts of the members who are still in good standing in the Church. Will my death satisfy the nation for all the crimes committed by Mormons, at the command of the Priesthood, who have used and now have deserted me? Time will tell. I believe in a *just God,* and I know the day will come when others must answer for their acts, as I have had to do.

I first became acquainted with Brigham Young when I went to Far West, Missouri, to join the Church, in 1837. I got very intimately acquainted with all the great leaders of the Church. I was adopted by Brigham Young as one of his sons, and for many years I confess I looked upon him as an inspired and holy man. While in Nauvoo I took an active part in all that was done for the Church or the city. I had charge of building of the "Seventy Hall;" I was 7th Policeman. My duty as a policeman was to guard the residence and person of Joseph Smith, the Prophet. After the death of Joseph and Hyrum I was ordered to perform the same duty for Brigham Young. When Joseph Smith was a candidate for the Presidency of the United States I went to Kentucky as the chairman of the Board of Elders, or head of the delegation, to secure the vote of that State for him. When I returned to Nauvoo again I was General Clerk and Recorder for the Quorum of the Seventy. I was also head or Chief Clerk for the Church, and as such took an active part in organizing the Priesthood in the order of Seventy after the death of Joseph Smith.

After the destruction of Nauvoo, when the Mormons were driven from the State of Illinois, I again shared the fate of my brethren, and partook of the hardships and trials that befell them from that day up to the settlement of Salt Lake City, in the then-wilderness of the nation. I presented Brigham Young with seventeen ox teams, fully equipped, when he started with the people from Winter Quarters to cross the plains to the new resting place of the Saints. He accepted them and said, "God bless you, John." But I never received a cent for them -- I never wanted pay for them, for in giving property to Brigham Young I thought I was loaning it to the Lord.

118

After reaching Salt Lake City I stayed there but a short time, when I went to live at Cottonwood, where the mines were afterwards discovered by General Connor and his men during the late war.

I was just getting fixed to live there, when I was ordered to go out into the interior and aid in forming new settlements, and opening up the country. I then had no wish or desire, save that to know and be able to do the will of the Lord's anointed, Brigham Young, and until within the last few years I have never had a wish for anything else except to do his pleasure, since I became his adopted son. I believed it my duty to obey those in authority. I then believed that Brigham Young spoke by direction of the God of Heaven. I would have suffered death rather than have disobeyed any command of his. I had this feeling until he betrayed and deserted me. At the command of Brigham Young, I took one hundred and twenty-one men, went in a southern direction from Salt Lake City, and laid out and built up Parowan. George Smith was the leader and chief man in authority in that settlement. I acted under him as historian and clerk of the Iron County Mission, until January, 1851. I went with Brigham Young, and acted as a committee man, and located Provo, St. George, Fillmore, Parowan and other towns, and managed the location of many of the settlements in Southern Utah.

In 1852, I moved to Harmony, and built up that settlement. I remained there until the Indians declared war against the whites and drove the settlers into Cedar City and Parowan, for protection, in the year 1853.

I removed my then numerous family to Cedar City, where I was appointed a Captain of the militia, and commander of Cedar City Military Post.

I had commanded at Cedar City about one year, when I was ordered to return to Harmony, and build the Harmony Fort. This order, like all other orders, came from Brigham Young. When I returned to Harmony and commenced building the fort there, the orders were given by Brigham Young for the reorganization of the military at Cedar City. The old men were requested to resign their offices, and let younger men be appointed in their place. I resigned my office of Captain, but Isaac C. Haight and John M. Higbee refused to resign, and continued to hold on as Majors in the Iron Militia.

After returning to Harmony, I was President of the civil and local affairs, and Rufus Allen was President of that Stake of Zion, or head of the Church affairs.

I soon resigned my position as President of civil affairs, and became a private citizen, and was in no office for some time. In fact, I never held any position after that, except the office of Probate Judge of the County (which office I held before and after the massacre), and member of the Territorial Legislature, and Delegate to the Constitutional

119

convention which met and adopted a constitution for the State of Deseret, after the massacre.

I will here state that Brigham Young honored me in many ways after the affair at Mountain Meadows was fully reported to him by me, as I will more fully state hereafter in the course of what I have to relate concerning that unfortunate transaction.

Klingensmith, at my first trial, and White, at my last trial, swore falsely when they say that they met me near Cedar City, the Sunday before the massacre. They did not meet me as they have sworn, nor did they meet me at all on that occasion or on any similar occasion. I never had the conversations with them that they testify about. They are both perjurers, and bore false testimony against me.

There has never been a witness on the stand against me that has testified to the whole truth. Some have told part truths, while others lied clear through, but all of the witnesses who were at the massacre have tried to throw all the blame on me, and to protect the other men who took part in it.

About the 7th of September, 1857, I went to Cedar City from my home at Harmony, by order of President Haight. I did not know what he wanted of me, but he had ordered me to visit him and I obeyed. If I remember correctly, it was on Sunday evening that I went there. When I got to Cedar City, I met Isaac C. Haight on the public square of the town. Haight was then President of that Stake of Zion, and the highest man in the Mormon priesthood in that country, and next to Wm. H. Dame in all of Southern Utah, and as Lieutenant Colonel he was second to Dame in the command of the Iron Military District. The word and command of Isaac C. Haight were *the law* in Cedar City, at that time, and to disobey his orders was certain death; be they right or wrong, no Saint was permitted to question them, their duty was obedience or death.

When I met Haight, I asked him what he wanted with me. He said he wanted to have a long talk with me on private and particular business. We took some blankets and went over to the old Iron Works, and lay there that night, so that we could talk in private and in safety. After we got to the Iron Works, Haight told me all about the train of emigrants. He said (and I then believed every word that he spoke, for I believed it was an impossible thing for one so high in the Priesthood as he was, to be guilty of falsehood) that the emigrants were a rough and abusive set of men. They had, while traveling through Utah, been very abusive to all the Mormons they met. That they had insulted, outraged, and ravished many of the Mormon women. That the abuses heaped upon the people by the emigrants during their trip from Provo to Cedar City, had been constant and shameful; that they had burned fences and destroyed growing crops, that at many points on the road they had poisoned the water, so that all people and stock that drank of the water became sick, and many had died from the effects of the poison. That these vile Gentiles publicly proclaimed that they had the very pistol with which the Prophet, Joseph Smith, was murdered, and had threatened to kill Brigham Young and all of the Apostles. That when in Cedar City they said they would have friends in Utah who would hang Brigham Young by the neck until he was dead, before snow fell again in the Territory. They also said that Johnston was coming, with his army, from the East and they were going to return from California with soldiers, as soon as possible, and would then desolate the land, and kill every d--d Mormon man, woman and child that they could find in Utah. That they violated the ordinances of the town of Cedar, and had, by armed force, resisted the officers who tried to arrest them for violating the law. That after leaving Cedar City the emigrants camped by the company, or cooperative field, just below Cedar City, and burned a large portion of the fencing leaving the crops open to the large herds of stock in the surrounding country. Also that they had given poisoned meat to the Corn Creek tribe of Indians, which had killed several of them, and their Chief, Konosh, was on the trail of the emigrants, and would soon attack them. All of these things, and much more of a like kind, Haight told me as we lay in the dark at the old Iron Works. I believed all that he said, and, thinking that he had full right to do all that he wanted to do, I was easily induced to follow his instructions.

Haight said that unless something was done to prevent it, the emigrants would carry out their threats and rob every one of the outlying settlements in the South, and that the whole Mormon people were liable to be butchered by the troops that the emigrants would bring back with them from California. I was then told that the Council had held a meeting that day, to consider the matter, and that it was decided by the authorities to arm the Indians, give them provisions and ammunition, and send them after the emigrants, and have the Indians give them a *brush*, and if they killed part or all of them, so much the better.

I said, "Brother Haight, who is your authority for acting in the way?"

He replied, "It is the will of *all in authority*. The emigrants have no pass from any one to go through the country, and they are liable to be killed as common enemies, for the country is at war now. No man has a right to go through this country without a written pass."

We lay there and talked much of the night, and during that time Haight gave me very full instructions what to do, and how to proceed in the whole affair. He said he had consulted with Colonel Dame, and every one agreed to let the Indians use up the whole train if they could. Haight then said:

"I expect you to carry out your orders."

I knew I had to obey or die. I had no wish to disobey, for I then thought that my superiors in the Church were the mouthpieces of

Heaven, and that it was an act of godliness for me to obey any and all orders given by them to me, without my asking any questions.

My orders were to go home to Harmony, and Carl Shirts, my son-in-law, an Indian interpreter, and send him to the Indians in the South, to notify them that the Mormons and Indians were at war with the *"Mericats"* (as the Indians called all whites that were not Mormons) and bring all the Southern Indians up and have them join with those from the North, so that their force would be sufficient to make a successful attack on the emigrants.

It was agreed that Haight would send Nephi Johnson, another Indian interpreter, to *stir up* all the other Indians that he could find, in order to have a large enough force of Indians to give the emigrants a good *hush*. He said, "These are the orders that have been agreed upon by the Council, and it is in accordance with the feelings of the *entire people*." I asked him if it would not have been better to first send to Brigham Young for instructions, and find out what he thought about the matter.

"No," said Haight, "that is unnecessary, *we are acting by orders*. Some of the Indians are now on the war-path, and all of them must be sent out; all must go, so as to make the thing a success."

It was then intended that the Indians should kill the emigrants, and make it *an Indian massacre*, and not have any white interfere with them. No whites were to be known in the matter, it was to be all done by the Indians, so that it could be laid to them, if any questions were ever asked about it. I said to Haight:

"You know what the Indians are. They will kill all the party, women and children, as well as the men, and you know we are sworn not to shed innocent blood."

"Oh h--l," he said, "there will not be one drop of *innocent* blood shed, if every one of the d--d pack are killed, for they are the worse lot of outlaws and ruffians that I ever saw in my life."

We agreed upon the whole thing, how each one should act, and then left the iron works, and went to Haight's house and got breakfast.

After breakfast I got ready to start, and Haight said to me:

"Go, brother Lee, and see that the instructions of those in authority are obeyed, and as you are dutiful in this, so shall your reward be in the kingdom of God, for God will bless those who willingly obey counsel, and make all things fit for the people in these last days."

I left Cedar City for my home at Harmony, to carry out the instructions that I had received from my superior.

I then believed that he acted by the direct order and command of William H. Dame, and others even higher in authority than Colonel Dame. One reason for thinking so was from a talk I had only a few days before, with Apostle George A. Smith, and he had just then seen Haight, and talked with him, and I knew that George A. Smith never talked of things that Brigham Young had not talked over with him before-hand. Then the Mormons were at war with the United States, and the orders to the Mormons had been all the time to kill and waste away our enemies, but lose none of our people. These emigrants were from the section of country most hostile to our people, and I believed then as I do now, that it was the will of every true Mormon in Utah, at that time, that the enemies of the church should be killed as fast as possible, and that as this lot of people had men amongst them that were supposed to have helped kill the Prophets in the Carthage jail, the killing of all of them would be keeping our oaths and avenging the blood of the Prophets.

In justice to myself I will give the facts of my talk with George A. Smith.

In the latter part of the month of August, 1857, about ten days before the company of Captain Fancher, who met their doom at Mountain Meadows, arrived at that place, General George A. Smith called on me at one of my homes at Washington City, Washington County, Utah Territory, and wished me to take him round by Fort Clara, via Pinto Settlements, to Hamilton Fort, or Cedar City. He said:

"I have been sent down here by the old Boss, Brigham Young, to instruct the brethren of the different settlements not to sell any of their grain to our enemies. And to tell them not to feed it to their animals, for it will all be needed for ourselves. I am also to instruct the brethren to prepare for a *big fight*, for the enemy is coming in large force to attempt our destruction. But Johnston's army will not be allowed to approach our settlements from the east. God is on our side and will fight our battles for us, and deliver our enemies into our hands. Brigham Young has received revelations from God, giving him the right and the power to call down the curse of God on all our enemies who attempt to invade our Territory. Our greatest danger lies in the people of California -- a class of reckless miners who are strangers to God and his righteousness. They are likely to come upon us from the south and destroy the small settlements. But we will try and outwit them before we suffer much damage. The people of the United States who oppose our Church and people are a mob, from the President down, and as such it is impossible for their armies to prevail against the Saints who have gathered here in the mountains."

He continued this kind of talk for some hours to me and my friends who were with me.

General George A. Smith held high rank as a military leader. He was one of the twelve apostles of the Church of Jesus Christ of Latter Day Saints, and as such he was considered by me to be an inspired man. His orders were to me sacred commands, which I considered it my duty to obey, without question or hesitation.

I took my horses and carriage and drove with him to either Hamilton Fort or Cedar City, visiting the settlements with him, as he had requested. I did not go to hear him preach at any of our stopping places, nor did I pay attention to what he said to the leaders in the settlements.

The day we left Fort Clara, which was then the headquarters of the Indian missionaries under the presidency of Jacob Hamblin, we stopped to noon at the Clara River. While there the Indians gathered around us in large numbers, and were quite saucy and impudent. Their chiefs asked me where I was going and who I had with me. I told them that he was a big captain.

"Is he a Mericat Captain?"

"No," I said, "he is a Mormon."

The Indians then wanted to know more. They wanted to have a talk.

The General told me to tell the Indians that the Mormons were their friends, and that the Americans were their enemies, and the enemies of the Mormons, too; that he wanted the Indians to remain the fast friends of the Mormons, for the Mormons were all friends to the Indians; that the Americans had a large army just east of the mountains, and intended to come over the mountains into Utah and kill all of the Mormons and Indians in Utah Territory; that the Indians must get ready and keep ready for war against all of the Americans and keep friendly with the Mormons and obey what the Mormons told them to do -- that this was the will of the Great Spirit; that if the Indians were true to the Mormons and would help them against their enemies, then the Mormons would always keep them from want and sickness and give them guns and ammunition to hunt and kill game with, and would also help the Indians against their enemies when they went to war.

This talk pleased the Indians, and they agreed to all that I asked them to do.

I saw that my friend Smith was a little nervous and fearful of the Indians, notwithstanding their promises of friendship. To relieve him of his anxiety I hitched up and started on our way, as soon as I could do so without rousing the suspicions of the Indians.

We had ridden along about a mile or so when General Smith said:

"Those are savage looking fellows. I think they would make it lively for an emigrant train if one should come this way."

I said I thought they would attack any train that would come in their way. Then the General was in a deep study for some time, when he said:

"Suppose an emigrant train should come along through this southern country, making threats against our people and bragging of the part they took in helping kill our Prophets, what do you think the brethren would do with them? Would they be permitted to go their way, or would the brethren pitch into them and give them a good drubbing?"

I reflected a few moments, and then said,

"You know the brethren are now under the influence of late reformation, and are still red-hot for the gospel. The brethren believe the government wishes to destroy them. I really believe that any train of emigrants that may come through here will be attacked, and probably all destroyed. I am sure they would be wiped out if they had been making threats against our people. Unless emigrants have a pass from Brigham Young, or some one in authority, they will certainly never get safely through this country."

My reply pleased him very much, and he laughed heartily, and then said,

"Do you really believe the brethren would make it lively for such a train?"

I said, "Yes, sir, I know they will, unless they are protected by a pass, and I wish to inform you that unless *you want every train captured* that comes through here, you must inform Governor Young that if he wants emigrants to pass, without being molested, he must send orders to that effect to Colonel Wm. H. Dame or Major Isaac C. Haight, so that they can give passes to the emigrants, for *their passes will insure safety,* but nothing else will, except the positive orders of Governor Young, as the people are all bitter against the Gentiles, and full of religious zeal, and anxious to avenge the blood of the Prophets."

The only reply he made was to the effect that on his way down from Salt Lake City he had had a long talk with Major Haight on the same subject, and that Haight had assured him, and given him to understand, that emigrants who came along without a pass from Governor Young could not escape from the Territory.

We then rode along in silence for some distance, when he again turned to me and said,

"Brother Lee, I am satisfied that the brethren are under the full influence of the reformation, and I believe they will do just as you say they will with the wicked emigrants that come through the country making threats and abusing our people."

I repeated my views to him, but at much greater length, giving my reasons in full for thinking that Governor Young should give orders to protect all the emigrants that he did not wish destroyed. I went into a full statement of the wrongs of our people, and told him that the people were under the blaze of the reformation, full of wild fire and fanaticism, and that to shed the blood of those who would *dare to speak* against the Mormon Church or its leaders, they would consider doing the will of God, and that the people would do it as willingly and cheerfully as they would any other duty. That the apostle Paul, when he started forth to persecute the followers of Christ, was not any more sincere than every Mormon was then, who lived in Southern Utah.

My words served to cheer up the General very much; he was greatly delighted, and said,

"I am glad to hear so good an account of our people. God will bless them for all that they do to build up His Kingdon in the last days."

General Smith did not say one word to me or intimate to me, that he wished *any emigrants* to pass in safety through the Territory. But he led me to believe then, as I believe now, that he did want, and expected every emigrant to be killed that undertook to pass through the Territory while we were at war with the Government. I thought it was his *mission* to prepare the people for the bloody work.

I have always believed, since that day, that General George A. Smith was then visiting Southern Utah to prepare the people for the work of exterminating Captain Fancher's train of emigrants, and I now believe that he was sent for that purpose by the direct command of Brigham Young.

I have been told by Joseph Wood, Thomas T. Willis, and many others, that they heard George A. Smith preach at Cedar City during that trip, and that he told the people of Cedar City that the emigrants were coming, and he told them that they must not sell that company *any grain or provisions* of any kind, for they were a mob of villians and outlaws, and the enemies of God and the Mormon people.

Sidney Littlefield, of Panguitch, has told me that he was knowing to the fact of Colonel Wm. H. Dame sending orders from Parowan to Maj. Haight, at Cedar City, to exterminate the Fancher outfit, and to kill every emigrant without fail. Littlefield then lived at Parowan, and Dame was the Presiding Bishop. Dame still has all the wives he wants, and is a great friend of Brigham Young.

The knowledge of how George A. Smith felt toward the emigrants, and his telling me that he had a long talk with Haight on the subject, made me certain that it was the wish of the Church authorities that Fancher and his train should be wiped out, and knowing all this, I did not doubt then, and I do not doubt it now, either, that Haight was acting by full authority from the Church leaders, and that the orders he gave to me were just the orders that he had been directed to give, when he ordered me to raise the Indians and have them attack the emigrants.

On my way from Cedar City to my home at Harmony, I came up with a large band of Indians under Moquetas and Big Bill, two Cedar City Chiefs; they were in their war paint, and fully equipped for battle. They halted when I came up and said they had had a big talk with Haight, Higby and Klingensmith, and had got orders from them to follow up the emigrants and kill them all, and take their property as the spoil of their enemies.

These Indians wanted me to go with them and command their forces. I told them that I could not go with them that evening, that I had orders from Haight, the *Big Captain*, to send other Indians on the war-path to help them kill the emigrants, and that I must attend to that first; that I wanted them to go on near where the emigrants were and camp until the other Indians joined me; that I would meet them the next day and lead them.

This satisfied them, but they wanted me to send my little Indian boy, Clem, with them. After some time I consented to let Clem go with them, and I returned home.

When I got home I told Carl Shirts what the orders were that Haight had sent to him. Carl was naturally cowardly and was not willing to go, but I told him the orders must be obeyed. He then started off that night, or early next morning, to stir up the Indians of the South, and lead them against the emigrants. The emigrants were then camped at Mountain Meadows.

The Indians did not obey my instructions. They met, several hundred strong, at the Meadows, and attacked the emigrants Tuesday morning, just before daylight, and at the first fire, as I afterwards learned, they killed seven and wounded sixteen of the emigrants. The latter fought bravely, and repulsed the Indians, killing some of them and breaking the knees of two war chiefs, who afterwards died.

The news of the battle was carried all over the country by Indian runners, and the excitement was great in all the small settlements. I was notified of what had taken place, early Tuesday morning, by an Indian who came to my house and gave me a full account of all that had been done. The Indian said it was the wish of all the Indians that I should lead them, and that I must go back with him to the camp.

I started at once, and by taking the Indian trail over the mountain, I reached the camp in about twelve miles from Harmony. To go round by the wagon road it would have been between forty and fifty miles.

When I reached the camp I found the Indians in a frenzy of excitement. They threatened to kill me unless I agreed to lead them against the emigrants, and help them kill them. They also said they had been told that they could kill the emigrants without danger to themselves, but they had lost some of their braves, and others were wounded, and unless they could kill all the "Mericats," as they called them, they would declare war against the Mormons and kill every one in the settlements.

I did as well as I could under the circumstances. I was the only white man there, with a wild and excited band of several hundred Indians. I tried to persuade them that all would be well, that I was their friend and would see that they had their revenge, if I found out that they were entitled to revenge.

My talk only served to increase their excitement, and being afraid that they would kill me if I undertook to leave them, and I would not lead them against the emigrants, so I told them that I would go south and meet their friends, and hurry them up to help them. I intended to put a stop to the carnage if I had the power, for I believed that the emigrants had been sufficiently punished for what they had done, and I felt then, and always have felt that such wholesale murdering was wrong.

At first the Indians would not consent for me to leave them, but they finally said I might go and meet with their friends.

I then got on my horse and left the Meadows, and went south.

I had gone about sixteen miles, when I met Carl Shirts with about one hundred Indians, and a number of Mormons from the southern settlements. They were going to the scene of the conflict. How they learned of the emigrants being at the Meadows I never knew, but they did know it, and were there fully armed, and determined to obey *orders*.

Amongst those that I remember to have met there, were Samuel Knight, Oscar Hamblin, William Young, Carl Shirts, Harrison Pearce, James Pearce, John W. Clark, William Slade, Sr., James Matthews, Dudley Leavitt, William Hawley (now a resident of Fillmore, Utah Territory), William Slade Jr., and two others whose names I have forgotten. I think they were George W. Adair and John Hawley. I know they were at the Meadows at the time of the massacre, and I think I met them that night south of the Meadows, with Samuel Knight and the others.

The whites camped there that night with me, but most of the Indians rushed on to their friends at the camp on the Meadows.

I reported to the whites all that had taken place at the Meadows, but none of them were surprised in the least. They all seemed to know that the attack was to be made, and all about it. I spent one of the most miserable nights there that I ever passed in my life. I spent much of the night in tears and at prayer. I wrestled with God for wisdom to guide me. I asked for some sign, some evidence that would satisfy me that my mission was of Heaven, but I got no satisfaction from my God.

In the morning we all agreed to go on together to Mountain Meadows, and camp there, and then send a messenger to Haight, giving him full instructions of what had been done, and to ask him for further instructions. We knew that the original plan was for the Indians to do all the work, and the whites to do nothing, only to stay back and plan for them, and encourage them to do the work. Now we knew the Indians could not do the work alone, and we were in a sad fix.

I did not then know that a messenger had been sent to Brigham Young for instructions. Haight had not mentioned it to me. I now know that James Haslem was sent to Brigham Young, as a sharp play on the part of the authorities to protect themselves, if trouble ever grew out of the matter.

We went to the Meadows and camped at the springs, about half a mile from the emigrant camp. There was a larger number of Indians there then, fully three hundred, and I think as many as four hundred of them. The two Chiefs who were shot in the knee were in a bad fix. The Indians had killed a number of the emigrants horses, and about sixty or seventy head of cattle were lying dead on the Meadows, which the Indians had killed for spite and revenge.

Our company killed a small beef for dinner, and after eating a hearty meal of it we held a council and decided to send a messenger to Haight. I said to the messenger, who was either Edwards or Adair (I cannot now remember which it was), "Tell Haight, for my sake, for the people's sake, for God's sake, send me help to protect and save these emigrants, and pacify the Indians."

The messenger started for Cedar City, from our camp on the Meadows, about 2 o'clock P.M.

We all stayed on the field, and I tried to quiet and pacify the Indians, by telling them that I had sent to Haight the Big Captain, for orders, and when he sent his order I would know what to do. This appeared to satisfy the Indians, for they said,

"The Big Captain will send you word to kill all the Mericats."

Along toward evening the Indians again attacked the emigrants. This was Wednesday. I heard the report of their guns, and the screams of the women and children in the corral.

This was more than I could stand. So I ran with William Young and John Mangum, to where the Indians were, to stop the fight. While on the way to them they fired a volley, and three balls from their guns cut my clothing. One ball went through my hat and cut my hair on the side of my head. One ball went through my shirt and leaded my shoulder, the other cut my pants across my bowels. I thought this was rather warm work, but I kept on until I reached the place where the Indians were in force. When I got to them, I told them the Great Spirit would be mad at them if they killed the women and children. I talked to them some time, and cried with sorrow when I saw I could not pacify the savages.

When the Indians saw me in tears, they called me "Yaw Guts," which in the Indian language means "cry baby," and to this day they call me by that name, and consider me a coward.

Oscar Hamblin was a fine interpreter, and he came to my aid and helped me to induce the Indians to stop the attack. By his help we got the Indians to agree to be quiet until word was returned form Haight. (I do not know now but what the messenger started for Cedar City, after this night attack, but I was so worried and perplexed at that time, and so much has happened to distract my thoughts since then, that my mind is not clear on the subject).

On Thursday, about noon, several men came to us from Cedar City. I cannot remember the order in which all of the people came to the Meadows, but I do recollect that at this time and in this company Joel White, William C. Stewart, Benjamin Arthur, Alexander Wilden, Charles Hopkins and a man named Tate, came to us at the camp at the springs. These men said but little, but every man seemed to know just what he was there for. As our messenger had gone for further orders, we moved our camp about four hundred yards further up the valley on to a hill, where we made camp as long as we stayed there.

I soon learned that the whites were as wicked at heart as the Indians, for every little while during that day I saw white men taking aim and shooting at the emigrant's wagons. They said they were doing it to keep in practice and to *help pass off the time.*

I remember one man that was shooting, that rather amused me, for he was shooting at a mark over a quarter of a mile off, and his gun would not carry a ball two hundred yards. That man was Alexander Wilden. He took pains to fix up a seat under the shade of a tree, where he continued to load and shoot until he got tired. Many of the others acted just as wild and foolish as Wilden did.

The wagons were corraled after the Indians had made the first attack. On the second day after our arrival the emigrants drew their wagons near each other and chained the wheels one to the other. While they were doing this there was no shooting going on. Their camp was about one hundred yards above and north of the spring. They generally got their water from the spring at night.

Thursday morning I saw two men start from the corral with buckets, and run to the spring and fill their buckets with water, and go back again. The bullets flew around them thick and fast, but they got into their corral in safety.

The Indians had agreed to keep quiet until orders returned from Haight, but they did not keep their word. They made a determined attack on the train on Thursday morning about daylight. At this attack the Clara Indians had one brave killed and three wounded. This so enraged that band that they left for home that day and drove off quite a number of cattle with them. During the day I said to John Mangum,

"I will cross over the valley and go up on the other side, on the hills to the west of the corral, and take a look at the situation."

I did go. As I was crossing the valley I was seen by the emigrants, and as soon as they saw that I was a white man they ran up a *white* flag in the middle of their corral, or camp. They then sent two little boys from the camp to talk to me, but I could not talk to them at that time, for I did not know what orders Haight would send back to me, and until I did know his orders I did not know how to act. I hid, to keep away from the children. They came to the place where they had last seen me and hunted all around for me, but being unable to find me, they turned and went back to the camp in safety.

While the boys were looking for me several Indians came to me and asked for ammunition with which to kill them. I told them they must not hurt the children -- that if they did I would kill the first one that made the attempt to injure them. By this act I was able to save the boys.

It is all false that has been told about little girls being dressed in white and sent out to me. There never was anything of the kind done.

I stayed on the west side of the valley for about two hours, looking down into the emigrant camp, and feeling all the torture of mind that it is possible for a man to suffer who feels merciful, and yet knows, as I then knew, what was in store for that unfortunate company if the Indians were successful in their bloody designs.

While I was standing on the hill looking down into the corral, I saw two men leave the corral and go outside to cut some wood; the Indians and whites kept up a steady fire on them all the time, but they paid no attention to danger, and kept right along at their work until they had it done, and then they went back into camp. The men all acted so bravely that it was impossible to keep from respecting them.

After staying there and looking down into the camp until I was nearly dead from grief, I returned to the company at camp. I was worn out with trouble and grief; I was nearly wild waiting for word from the authorities at Cedar City. I prayed for word to come that would enable me to save that band of suffering people, but no such word came. It was never to come.

On Thursday evening John M. Higbee, Major of the Iron Militia, and Philip K. Smith, as he is called generally, but whose name is Klingensmith, Bishop of Cedar City, came to our camp with two or three wagons, and a number of men all well armed. I can remember the following as a portion of the men who came to take part in the work of death which was so soon to follow, viz: John M. Higbee, Major and commander of the Iron Militia, and also first counselor to Isaac C. Haight; Philip Klingensmith, Bishop of Cedar City; Ira Allen, of the High Council; Robert Wiley, of the High Council; Richard Harrison, of Pinto, also a member of the High Council; Samuel McMurdy, one of the Counselors of Klingensmith; Charles Hopkins, of the City Council of Cedar City; Samuel Pollock; Daniel McFarland, a son-in-law of Isaac C. Haight, and acting as Adjutant under Major Higbee; John Ure, of the City Council; George Hunter, of the City Council; and I honestly believe that John McFarland, now an attorney-at-law at St. George, Utah, was there -- I am not postive that he was, but my best impression is that he was there; Samuel Jukes; Nephi Johnson, with a number of Indians under his command; Irvin Jacobs; John Jacobs; E. Curtis, a Captain of

Ten; Thomas Cartwright of the City Council and High Council; William Bateman, who afterwards carried the flag of truce to the emigrant camp; Anthony Stratton; Al Loveridge; Joseph Clews; Jabez Durfey; Columbus Freeman; and some others whose names I cannot remember. I know that our total force was fifty-four whites and over three hundred Indians.

As soon as these persons gathered around the camp, I demanded of Major Higbee what orders he had brought. I then stated fully all that had happened at the Meadows, so that every person might understand the situation.

Major Higbee reported as follows: "It is the orders of the President, that all the emigrants must be *put out of the way.* President Haight has counseled with Colonel Dame, or has had orders from him to put all of the emigrants out of the way; none who are old enough to talk are to be spared."

He then went on and said substantially that the emigrants had come through the country as our enemies, and as the enemies of the Church of Jesus Christ of Latter Day Saints. That they had no pass from any one in authority to permit them to leave the Territory. That none but friends were permitted to leave the Territory, and that as these were our sworn enemies, they must be killed. That they were nothing but a portion of Johnston's army. That if they were allowed to go on to California, they would raise the war cloud in the West, and bring certain destruction upon all the settlements of Utah. That the only safety for the people was in the utter destruction of the whole rascally lot.

I told them that God would have to change my heart before I could consent to such a wicked thing as the wholesale killing of that people. I attempted to reason with Higbee and the brethren. I told them how strongly the emigrants were fortified, and how wicked it was to kill the women and children. I was ordered to be silent. Higbee said I was resisting authority.

He then said, "Brother Lee is afraid of shedding innocent blood. Why, brethren, there is not a drop of innocent blood in that entire camp of Gentile outlaws; they are a set of cut-throats, robbers and assassins; they are a part of the people who drove the Saints from Missouri, and who aided to shed the blood of our Prophets, Joseph and Hyrum, and it is our orders from all in authority, to get the emigrants from their stronghold, and help the Indians kill them."

I then said that Joseph Smith had told us never to betray any one. That we could not get the emigrants out of the corral unless we used treachery, and I was opposed to that.

I was interrupted by Higbee, Klingensmith and Hopkins, who said it was the orders of President Isaac C. Haight to us, and that Haight had his orders from Colonel Dame and the authorities at Parowan, and that

132

all in authority were of one mind, and that they had been sent by the Council at Cedar City to the Meadows to counsel and direct the way and manner that the company of emigrants should be disposed of.

The men then in council, I must here state, now knelt down in a prayer circle and prayed, invoking the Spirit of God to direct them how to act in the matter.

After prayer, Major Higbee said, "Here are the orders," and handed me a paper from Haight. It was in substance that it was the orders of Haight to *decoy* the emigrants from their position, and kill all of them that could talk. This order was in writing. Higbee handed it to me and I read it, and then dropped it on the ground, saying,

"I cannot do this."

The substance of the orders were that the emigrants should be *decoyed* from their strong-hold, and all exterminated, so that no one would be left to tell the tale, and then the authorities could say it was done by the Indians.

The words *decoy* and *exterminate* were used in that message or order, and these orders came to us as the orders from the Council at Cedar City, and as the orders of our military superior, that we were bound to obey. The order was signed by Haight, as commander of the troops at Cedar City.

Haight told me the next day after the massacre, while on the Meadows, that he got his orders from Colonel Dame.

I then left the Council, and went away to myself, and bowed myself in prayer before God, and asked Him to overrule the decision of that council. I shed many bitter tears, and my tortured soul was wrung nearly from the body by my great suffering. I will here say, calling upon Heaven, angels, and the spirits of just men to witness what I say, that if I could then have had a thousand worlds to command, I would have given them freely to save that company from death.

While in bitter anguish, lamenting the sad condition of myself and others, Charles Hopkins, a man that I had great confidence in, came to me from the Council, and tried to comfort me by saying that he believed it was all right, for the brethren in the Priesthood were all united in the thing, and it would not be well for me to oppose them.

I told him the Lord must change my heart before I could ever do such an act willingly. I will further state that there was a reign of terror in Utah, at that time, and many a man had been put out of the way, on short notice, for disobedience, and I had made some narrow escapes.

At the earnest solicitation of Brother Hopkins, I returned with him to the Council. When I got back, the Council again prayed for aid. The Council was called The City Counselors, the Church or High Counselors; and all in authority, together with the private citizens, then formed a circle, and kneeling down, so that elbows would touch each other, several of the brethren prayed for Divine instructions.

After prayer, Major Higbee said, "I have the evidence of God's approval of our mission. It is God's will that we carry out our instructions to the letter."

I said, "My God! this is more than I can do. I must and do refuse to take part in this matter."

Higbee then said to me, "Brother Lee, I am ordered by President Haight to inform you that you shall receive a crown of Celestial glory for your faithfulness, and your eternal joy shall be complete." I was much shaken by this offer, for I had full faith in the power of the Priesthood to bestow such rewards and blessings, but I was anxious to save the people. I then proposed that we give the Indians all of the stock of the emigrants, except sufficient to haul their wagons, and let them go. To this proposition all the leading men objected. No man there raised his voice or hand to favor the saving of life, except myself.

The meeting was then addressed by some one in authority, I do not remember who it was. He spoke in about this language: "Brethren, we have been sent here to perform a duty. It is a duty that we owe to God, and to our Church and people. The orders of those in authority are that all the emigrants *must* die. Our leaders speak with inspired tongues, and their orders come from the God of Heaven. We have no right to question what they have commanded us to do; it is our duty to obey. If we wished to act as some of our weak-kneed brethren desire us to do, it would be impossible; the thing has gone too far to allow us to stop now. The emigrants know that we have aided the Indians, and if we let them go they will bring certain destruction upon us. It is a fact that on Wednesday night, two of the emigrants got out of camp and started back to Cedar City for assistance to withstand the Indian attacks; they had reached Richards' Springs when they met William C. Stewart, Joel White and Benjamin Arthur, three of our brethren from Cedar City. The men stated their business to the brethren, and as their horses were drinking at the Spring, Brother Stewart, feeling *unusually* full of zeal for the glory of God and the upbuilding of the Kingdom of God on earth, shot and killed one of the emigrants, a young man by the name of Aden. When Aden fell from his horse, Joel White shot and wounded the other Gentile; but he unfortunately got away, and returned to his camp and reported that the Mormons were helping the Indians in all that they were doing against the emigrants. Now the emigrants will report these facts in California if we let them go. We must kill them all, and our orders are to get them out by treachery if no other thing can be done to get them into our power."

Many of the brethren spoke in the same way, all arguing that the orders must be carried out.

I was then told the plan of action had been agreed upon, and it was this: The emigrants were to be decoyed from their strong-hold under a promise of protection. Brother William Bateman was to carry a flag of truce and demand a parley, and then I was to go and arrange the terms of the surrender. I was to demand that all the children who were so young they could not talk should be put into a wagon, and the wounded were also to be put into a wagon. Then all the arms and ammunition of the emigrants should be put into a wagon, and I was to agree that the Mormons would protect the emigrants from the Indians and conduct them to Cedar City in safety, where they should be protected until an opportunity came for sending them to California.

It was agreed that when I had made the full agreement and treaty, as the brethren called it, the wagons should start for Hamblin's Ranch with the arms, the wounded and the children. The women were to march on foot and follow the wagons in single file; the men were to follow behind the women, they also to march in single file. Major John M. Higbee was to stand with his militia company about two hundred yards from the camp, and stand in double file, open order, with about twenty feet space between the files, so that the wagons could pass between them. The drivers were to keep right along, and not stop at the troops. The women were not to stop there, but to follow the wagons. The troops were to hold the men for a few minutes, until the women were some distance ahead, out into the cedars, where the Indians were hid in ambush. Then the march was to be resumed, the troops to form a single file, each soldier to walk by an emigrant, and on the right-hand side of his man, and the soldier was to carry his gun on his left arm, ready for instant use. The march was to continue until the wagons had massed beyond the ambush of the Indians, and until the women were right in the midst of the Indians. Higbee was then to give the orders and words, "Do Your Duty." At this the troops were to shoot down the men; the Indians were to kill all the women and larger children, and the drivers of the wagons and I were to kill the wounded and sick men that were in the wagons. Two men were to be placed on horses near by, to overtake and kill any of the emigrants that might escape from the first assault. The Indians were to kill the women and large children, so that it would be certain that no Mormon would be guilty of shedding innnocent blood -- if it should happen that there was any innocent blood in the company that were to die. Our leading men all said that there was no innocent blood in the whole company.

The Council broke up a little after daylight on Friday morning. All the horses, except two for the men to ride to overtake those who might escape, and one for Dan McFarland to ride as Adjutant, so that he could carry orders from one part of the field to another, were turned out on the range. Then breakfast was eaten, and the brethren prepared for the work in hand.

I was now satisfied that it was the wish of all of the Mormon priesthood to have the thing done. One reason for thinking so was that it was in keeping with the teachings of the leaders, and as Utah was then at war with the United States we believed all the Gentiles were to be killed as a war measure, and that the Mormons, as God's chosen people, were to hold and inhabit the earth and rule and govern the globe. Another, and one of my strongest reasons for believing that the leaders wished the thing done, was on account of the talk that I had with George A. Smith, which I have given in full in this statement. I was satisfied that Smith had passed the emigrants while on his way from Salt Lake City, and I then knew this was the train that he meant when he spoke of a train that would make threats and ill-treat our people, etc.

The people were in the full blaze of the reformation and anxious to do some act that would add to their reputation as zealous Churchmen.

I therefore, taking all things into consideration, and believing, as I then did, that my superiors were *inspired* men, who could not go wrong in any matter relating to the Church or the duty of its members, concluded to be obedient to the wishes of those in authority. I took up my cross and prepared to do my duty.

Soon after breakfast Major Higbee ordered the two Indians interpreters, Carl Shirts and Nephi Johnson, to inform the Indians of the plan of operations, and to place the Indians in ambush, so that they could not be seen by the emigrants until the work of death should commence.

This was done in order to make the emigrants believe that we had sent the Indians away, and that we were acting honestly and in good faith, when we agreed to protect them from the savages.

The orders were obeyed, and in five minutes not an Indian could be seen on the whole Meadows. They secreted themselves and lay still as logs of wood, until the order was given for them to rush out and kill the women.

Major Higbee then called all the people to order, and directed me to explain the whole plan to them. I did so, explaining just how every person was expected to act during the whole performance.

Major Higbee then gave the order for his men to advance. They marched to the spot agreed upon, and halted there. Wiliam Bateman was then selected to carry a flag of truce to the emigrants and demand their surrender, and I was ordered to go and make the treaty after some one had replied to our flag of truce. (The emigrants had kept a white flag flying in their camp ever since they saw me cross the valley).

Bateman took a white flag and started for the emigrant camp. When he got about half way to the corral, he was met by one of the emigrants, that I afterwards learned was named Hamilton. They talked some time, but I never knew what was said between them.

Brother Bateman returned to the command and said that the emigrants would accept our terms, and surrender as we required them to do.

I was then ordered by Major Higbee to go to the corral and negotiate the treaty, and superintend the whole matter. I was again ordered to be certain and get all the arms and ammunition into the wagons. Also to put the children and the sick and wounded in the wagons, as had been agreed upon in council. Then Major Higbee said to me:

"Brother Lee, we expect you to faithfully carry out all the instructions that have been given you by our council."

Samuel McMurdy and Samuel Knight were then ordered to drive their teams and follow me to the corral to haul off the children, arms, etc.

The troops formed in two lines, as had been agreed upon, and were standing in that way with arms at rest, when I left them.

I walked ahead of the wagons up to the corral. When I reached there I met Mr. Hamilton on the outside of the camp. He loosened the chains from some of their wagons, and moved one wagon out of the way, so that our teams could drive inside of the corral and into their camp. It was then noon, or a little after.

I found that the emigrants were strongly fortified; their wagons were chained to each other in a circle. In the centre was a rifle-pit, large enough to contain the entire company. This had served to shield them from the constant fire of their enemy, which had been poured into them from both sides of the valley, from a rocky range that served as a breastwork for their assailants. The valley at this point was not more than five hundred yards wide, and the emigrants had their camp near the center of the valley. On the east and west there was a low range of rugged, rocky mountains, affording a splendid place for the protection of the Indians and Mormons, and leaving them in comparative safety while they fired upon the emigrants. The valley at this place runs nearly due north and south.

When I entered the corral, I found the emigrants engaged in burying two men of note among them, who had died but a short time before from the effect of wounds received by them from the Indians at the time of the first attack on Tuesday morning. They wrapped the bodies up in buffalo robes, and buried them in a grave inside the corral. I was then told by some of the men that seven men were killed and seventeen others were wounded at the first attack made by the Indians, and that three of the wounded men had since died, making ten of their number killed during the siege.

As I entered the fortifications, men, women and children gathered around me in wild consternation. Some felt that the time of their happy deliverance had come, while others, though in deep distress, and all in tears, looked upon me with doubt, distrust and terror. My feelings at this time may be imagined (but I doubt the power of man being equal to even imagine how wretched I felt). No language can describe my feelings. My position was painful, trying and awful; my brain seemed to be on fire; my nerves were for a moment unstrung; humanity was overpowered, as I thought of the cruel, unmanly part that I was acting. Tears of bitter anguish fell in streams from my eyes; my tongue refused its office; my faculties were dormant, stupefied and deadened by grief. I wished that the earth would open and swallow me where I stood. God knows my suffering was great. I cannot describe my feelings. I knew that I was acting a cruel part and doing a damnable deed. Yet my faith in the godliness of my leaders was such that it forced me to think that I was not sufficiently spiritual to act the important part I was commanded to perform. My hesitation was only momentary. Then feeling that duty compelled *obedience to orders*, I laid aside my weakness and my humanity, and became an instrument in the hands of my superiors and my leaders. I delivered my message and told the people that they must put their arms in the wagon, so as not to arouse the animosity of the Indians. I ordered the children and wounded, some clothing and the arms, to be put into the wagons. Their guns were mostly Kentucky rifles of the muzzle-loading style. Their ammunition was about all gone -- I do not think there were twenty loads left in their whole camp. If the emigrants had had a good supply of ammunition they never would have surrendered, and I do not think we could have captured them without great loss, for they were brave men and very resolute and determined.

Just as the wagons were loaded, Dan McFarland came riding into the corral and said that Major Higbee had ordered great haste to be made, for he was afraid that the Indians would return and renew the attack before he could get the emigrants to a place of safety.

I hurried up the people and started the wagons off towards Cedar City. As we went out of the corral I ordered the wagons to turn to the left, so as to leave the troops to the right of us. Dan McFarland rode before the men and led them right up to the troops, where they still stood in open order as I left them. The women and larger children were walking ahead, as directed, and the men following them. The foremost man was about fifty yards behind the hindmost woman.

The women and children were hurried right on by the troops. When the men came up they cheered the soldiers as if they believed that they were acting honestly. Higbee then gave the orders for his men to form in single file and take their places as ordered before, that is, at the right of the emigrants.

I saw this much, but about this time our wagons passed out of sight of the troops, over the hill. I had disobeyed orders in part by turning off as I did, for I was anxious to be out of sight of the bloody deed that I knew was to follow. I knew that I had much to do yet that was of a cruel and unnatural character. It was my duty, with the two drivers, to kill the sick and wounded who were in the wagons, and to do so when we heard the guns of the troops fire. I was walking between the wagons: the horses were going in a fast walk, and we were fully half a mile from Major Higbee and his men, when we heard the firing. As we heard the guns, I ordered a halt and we proceeded to do our part.

I here pause in the recital of this horrid story of man's inhumanity, and ask myself the question, Is it honest in me, and can I clear my conscience before my God, if I screen myself while I accuse others? No, never! Heaven forbid that I should put a burden upon others' shoulders, that I am unwilling to bear my just portion of. I am not a traitor to my people, nor to my former friends and comrades who were with me on that dark day when the work of death was carried on in God's name, by a lot of deluded and religious fanatics. It is my duty to tell facts as they exist, and I will do so.

I have said that all of the small children were put into the wagons; that was wrong, for one little child, about six months old, was carried in its father's arms, and it was killed by the same bullet that entered its father's breast; it was shot through the head. I was told by Haight afterwards, that the child was killed by accident, but I cannot say whether that is a fact or not. I saw it lying dead when I returned to the place of slaughter.

When we had got out of sight, as I said before, and just as we were coming into the main road, I heard a volley of guns at the place where I knew the troops and emigrants were. Our teams were then going at a fast walk. I first heard one gun, then a volley at once followed.

McMurdy and Knight stopped their teams at once, for they were ordered by Higbee, the same as I was, to help kill all the sick and wounded who were in the wagons, and to do it as soon as they heard the guns of the troops. McMurdy was in front; his wagon was mostly loaded with the arms and small children. McMurdy and Knight got out of their wagons; each one had a rifle. McMurdy went up to Knight's wagon, where the sick and wounded were, and raising his rifle to his shoulder, said: "O Lord, my God, receive their spirits, it is for thy Kingdom that I do this." He then shot a man who was lying with his head on another man's breast; the ball killed both men.

I also went up to the wagon, intending to do my part of the killing. I drew my pistol and cocked it, but somehow it went off prematurely, and I shot McMurdy across the thigh, my pistol ball cutting his buck-skin pants. McMurdy turned to me and said:

"Brother Lee, keep cool, you are excited; you came very near killing me. Keep cool, there is no reason for being excited."

Knight then shot a man with his rifle; he shot the man in the head. Knight also brained a boy that was about fourteen years old. The boy came running up to our wagons, and Knight struck him on the head with the butt end of his gun, and crushed his skull. By this time many Indians reached our wagons, and all of the sick and wounded were killed almost instantly. I saw an Indian from Cedar City, called Joe, run up to the wagon and catch a man by the hair, and raise his head up and look into his face; the man shut his eyes, and Joe shot him in the head. The Indians then examined all of the wounded in the wagons, and all of the bodies, to see if any were alive, and all that showed signs of life were at once shot through the head. I did not kill any one there, but it was accident that kept me from it, for I fully intended to do my part of the killing, but by the time I got over the excitement of coming so near killing McMurdy, the whole of the killing of the wounded was done. There is no truth to the statement of Nephi Johnson, where he says I cut a man's throat.

Just after the wounded were all killed I saw a girl, some ten or eleven years old, running toward us, from the direction where the troops had attacked the main body of emigrants; she was covered with blood. An Indian shot her before she got within sixty yards of us. That was the last person that I saw killed on that occasion.

About this time an Indian rushed to the front wagon, and grabbed a little boy, and was going to kill him. The lad got away from the Indian and ran to me, and caught me by the knees; and begged me to save him, and not let the Indian kill him. The Indian had hurt the little fellow's chin on the wagon-bed, when he first caught hold of him. I told the Indian to let the boy alone. I took the child up in my arms, and put him back in the wagon, and saved his life. This little boy said his name was Charley Fancher, and that his father was Captain of the train. He was a bright boy. I afterwards adopted him, and gave him to Caroline. She kept him until Dr. Forney took all the children East. I believe that William Sloan, alias Idaho Bill, is the same boy.

After all the parties were dead, I ordered Knight to drive out on one side, and throw out the dead bodies. He did so, and threw them out of his wagon at a place about one hundred yards from the road, and then came back to where I was standing. I then ordered Knight and McMurdy to take the children that were saved alive, (sixteen was the number, some say seventeen, I say sixteen,) and drive on to Hamblin's ranch. They did as I ordered them to do. Before the wagons started, Nephi Johnson came up in company with the Indians that were under his command, and Carl Shirts I think came up too, but I know that I then considered that Carl Shirts was a coward, and I afterwards made him suffer for being a coward. Several white men came up too, but I cannot tell their names, as I have forgotten who they were.

Knight lied when he said I went to the ranch and ordered him to go to the field with his team. I never knew anything of his team, or heard of it, until he came with a load of armed men in his wagon, on the evening of Thursday. If any one ordered him to go to the Meadows, it was Higbee. Every witness that claims that he went to the Meadows without knowing what he was going to do, has lied, for they all knew, as well as Haight or any one else did, and they all voted, every man of them, in the Council, on Friday morning, a little before daylight, to kill all the emigrants.

After the wagons, with the children, had started for Hamblin's ranch, I turned and walked back to where the brethren were. Nephi Johnson lies when he says he was on horse-back, and met me, or that I gave him orders to go to guard the wagons. He is a perjured wretch, and has sworn to every thing he could to injure me. God knows what I did do was bad enough, but he has lied to suit the leaders of the Church, who want me out of the way.

While going back to the brethren, I passed the bodies of several women. In one place I saw six or seven bodies near each other; they were stripped perfectly naked, and all of their clothing was torn from their bodies by the Indians.

I walked along the line where the emigrants had been killed, and saw many bodies lying dead and naked on the field, near by where the women lay. I saw ten children; they had been killed close to each other; they were from ten to sixteen years of age. The bodies of the women and children were scattered along the ground for quite a distance before I came to where the men were killed.

I do not know how many were killed, but I thought then that there were some fifteen women, about ten children, and about forty men killed, but the statement of others that I have since talked with about the massacre, makes me think there were fully one hundred and ten killed that day on the Mountain Meadows, and the ten who had died in the corral, and young Aden killed by Stewart at Richards' Springs, would make the total number one hundred and twenty-one.

When I reached the place where the dead men lay, I was told how the orders had been obeyed. Major Higbee said, "The boys have acted admirably, they took good aim, and all of the d--d Gentiles but two or three fell at the *first fire.*"

He said that three or four got away some distance, but the men on horses soon overtook them and cut their throats. Higbee said the Indians did their part of the work well, that it did not take over a minute to finish up when they got fairly started. I found that the first orders had been carried out to the letter.

Three of the emigrants did get away, but the Indians were put on their trail and they overtook and killed them before they reached the settlements in California. But it would take more time than I have to spare to give the details of their chase and capture. I may do so in my writings hereafter, but not now.

141

I found Major Higbee, Klingensmith, and most of the brethren standing near by where the largest number of the dead men lay. When I went up to the brethren, Major Higbee said,

"We must now examine the bodies for valuables."

I said I did not wish to do any such work.

Higbee then said, "Well, you hold my hat and I will examine the bodies, and put what valuables I get into the hat."

The bodies were all searched by Higbee, Klingensmith and Wm. C. Stewart. I did hold the hat a while, but I soon got so sick that I had to give it to some other person, as I was unable to stand for a few minutes. The search resulted in getting a little money and a few watches, but there was not much money. Higbee and Klingensmith kept the property, I suppose, for I never knew what became of it, unless they did keep it. I think they kept it all.

After the dead were searched, as I have just said, the brethren were called up, and Higbee and Klingensmith, as well as myself, made speeches, and *ordered* the people to keep the matter a secret from the *entire* world. Not to tell their wives, or their most intimate friends, and we pledged ourselves to keep everything relating to the affair a secret during life. We also took the most binding oaths to stand by each other, and to always insist that the massacre was committed by Indians alone. This was the advice of Brigham Young too, as I will show hereafter.

The men were mostly ordered to camp there on the field for that night, but Higbee and Klingensmith went with me to Hamblin's ranch, where we got something to eat, and stayed there all night. I was nearly dead for rest and sleep; in fact I had rested but little since the Saturday night before. I took my saddle-blanket and spread it on the ground soon after I had eaten my supper, and lay down on the saddle-blanket, using my saddle for a pillow, and slept soundly until next morning.

I was awakened in the morning by loud talking between Isaac C. Haight and William H. Dame. They were very much excited, and quarreling with each other. I got up at once, but was unable to hear what they were quarreling about, for they cooled down as soon as they saw that others were paying attention to them.

I soon learned that Col. Dame, Judge Lewis of Parowan, and Isaac C. Haight, with several others, had arrived at the Hamblin ranch in the night, but I do not know what time they got there.

After breakfast we all went back in a body to the Meadows, to bury the dead and take care of the property that was left there.

When we reached the Meadows we all rode up to that part of the field where the women were lying dead. The bodies of men, women and children had been stripped entirely naked, making the scene one of the most loathsome and ghastly that can be imagined.

Knowing that Dame and Haight had quarreled at Hamblin's that morning, I wanted to know how they would act in sight of the dead, who lay there as a result of their orders. I was greatly interested to know what Dame had to say, so I kept close to them, without appearing to be watching them.

Colonel Dame was silent for some time. He looked all over the field, and was quite pale, and looked uneasy and frightened. I thought then that he was just finding out the difference between giving and executing orders for wholesale killing. He spoke to Haight, and said:

"I must report this matter to the authorities."

"How will you report it?" said Haight.

Dame said, "I will report it just as it is."

"Yes, I suppose so, and implicate yourself with the rest?" said Haight.

"No," said Dame. "I will not implicate myself, for I had nothing to do with it."

Haight then said, "That will not do, for you know a d--d sight better. You ordered it done. Nothing has been done except by your orders, and it is too late in the day for you to order things done and then go back on it, and go back on the men who have carried out your orders. You cannot *sow pig* on me, and I will be d--d if I will stand it. You are as much to blame as any one, and you know that we have done nothing except what you ordered done. I know that I have obeyed orders, and by G-d I will not be lied on."

Colonel Dame was much excited. He choked up, and would have gone away, but he knew Haight was a man of determination, and would not stand any foolishness.

As soon as Colonel Dame could collect himself, he said:

*"I did not think there were so many of them, or I would not have had anything to do with it."*

I thought it was now time for me to chip in, so I said:

"Brethren, what is the trouble between you? It will not do for our chief men to disagree."

Haight stepped up to my side, a little in front of me, and facing Colonel Dame. He was very mad, and said:

"The trouble is just this: Colonel Dame *counseled* and *ordered* me to do this thing, and now he wants to back out, and go back on me, and by G-d he shall not do it. He shall not lay it *all* on me. He cannot do it. He must not try to do it. I will *blow him to h--l* before he shall lay it all on me. He has got to stand up to what he did, like a little man. He knows he ordered it done, and I dare him to deny it."

Colonel Dame was perfectly cowed. He did not offer to deny it again, but said:

"Isaac, I did not know there were so many of them."

"That makes no difference," said Haight, "you ordered me to do it, and you have got to stand up for your *orders*."

I thought it was now time to stop the fuss, for many of the young brethren were coming around. So I said:

"Brethren, this is no place to talk over such a matter. You will agree when you get where you can be quiet, and talk it over."

Haight said, "There is no more to say, for he knows he ordered it done, and he has got to stand by it."

That ended the trouble between them, and I never heard of Colonel Dame denying the giving of the orders any more, until after the Church authorities concluded to offer me up for the sins of the Church.

We then went along the field, and passed by where the brethren were at work covering up the bodies. They piled the dead bodies up in heaps, in little gullies, and threw dirt over them. The bodies were only lightly covered, for the ground was hard, and the brethren did not have sufficient tools to dig with. I suppose it is true that the first rain washed the bodies all out again, but I never went back to examine whether it did or not.

We then went along the field to where the corral and camp had been, to where the wagons were standing. We found that the Indians had carried off all the wagon covers, and the clothing, and the provisions, and had emptied the feathers out of the feather-beds, and carried off all the ticks.

After the dead were covered up or buried (but it was not much of a burial), the brethren were called together, and a council was held at the emigrant camp. All the leading men made speeches; Colonel Dame, President Haight, Klingensmith, John M. Higbee, Hopkins and myself. The speeches were first -- Thanks to God for delivering our enemies into our hands; next, thanking the brethren for their zeal in God's cause; and then the necessity of always saying the Indians did it alone, and that the Mormons had nothing to do with it. The most of the speeches, however, were in the shape of exhortations and commands to keep the whole matter secret from every one but Brigham Young. It was voted unanimously that any man who should divulge the secret, or tell who was present, or do anything that would lead to discovery of the truth, should suffer death.

The brethren then all took a most solemn oath, binding themselves under the most dreadful and awful penalties, to keep the whole matter secret from every human being, as long as they should live. No man was to know the facts. The brethren were sworn not to talk of it among themselves, and each one swore to help kill all who proved to be traitors to the Church or people in this matter.

It was then agreed that Brigham Young should be informed of the whole matter, by some one to be selected by the Church Council, after the brethren had returned home.

It was also voted to turn all the property over to Klingensmith, as Bishop of the Church at Cedar City, and he was to take care of the property for the benefit of the Church, until Brigham Young was notified, and should give further orders what to do with it.

Colonel Dame then blest the brethren and we prepared to go to our homes. I took my little Indian boy, Clem, on the horse behind me, and started home. I crossed the mountains and returned the same way I had come.

When I got in about two miles of Harmony, I overtook a body of about forty Indians, on their way home from the massacre. They had a large amount of bloody clothing, and were driving several head of cattle that they had taken from the emigrants.

The Indians were very glad to see me, and said I was their Captain, and that they were going to Harmony with me as my men. It was the orders from the Church authorities to do everything we could to pacify the Indians, and make them the fast friends of the Mormons, so I concluded to humor them.

I started on and they marched after me until we reached the fort at Harmony. We went into the fort and marched round inside, after which they halted and gave their whoop of victory, which means much the same with them as the *cheers* do with the whites. I then ordered the Indians to be fed; my family gave them some bread and melons, which they ate, and then they left me and went to their tribe.

I will here state again that on the field, before and after the massacre, and again at the council at the emigrant camp, the day after the massacre, orders were given to keep everything *secret*, and if any man told the secret to any human being, he was to be killed, and I assert as a fact that if any man had told it then, or for *many years afterwards, he would have died*, for some "Destroying Angel" would have followed his trail and sent him over the "*rim of the basin.*"

From that day to this it has been the understanding with all concerned in that massacre, that the man who divulged the secret should die; he was to be killed, wherever he was found, for treason to the men who killed the emigrants, and for his *treason to the Church.* No man was at liberty to tell his wife, or any one else, nor were the brethren permitted to talk of it *even among themselves.* Such were the *orders* and *instructions*, from *Brigham Young* down to the lowest in authority. The orders to lay it all to the Indians, were just as positive as they were to keep it all secret. This was the counsel from all in authority, and for years it was faithfully observed.

The children that were saved were taken to Cedar City, and other settlements, and put out among different families, where they were kept until they were given up to Dr. Forney, the Agent of the United States, who came for them.

I did not have anything to do with the property taken from the emigrants, or the cattle, or anything else, for some three months after the massacre, and then I only took charge of the cattle because I was ordered to do so by Brigham Young.

There were eighteen wagons in all at the emigrant camp. They were all wooden axles but one, and that was a light iron axle; it had been hauled by four mules. There were something over five hundred head of cattle, but I never got the half of them. The Indians killed a large number at the time of the massacre, and drove others to their tribes when they went home from Mountain Meadows. Klingensmith put the Church brand on fifty head or more, of the best of the cattle, and then he and Haight and Higbee drove the cattle to Salt Lake City and sold them for goods that they brought back to Cedar City to trade on.

The Indians got about twenty head of horses and mules. Samuel Knight, one of the witnesses on my trial, got a large sorrel mare; Haight got a span of average American mules; Joel White got a fine mare; Higbee got a good large mule; Klingensmith got a span of mules. Haight, Higbee and Allen each took a wagon. The people all took what they wanted, and they had divided and used up much over half of it before I was put in charge.

# PASSAGE THROUGH THE GREAT CAÑON OF THE COLORADO
## (1867)

James White, as told to

## Dr. Charles C. Parry and Alfred R. Calhoun

**Editors' Note:** On September 7, 1867, the residents of Callville, a tiny Mormon outpost in southern Nevada, seventy miles downstream from the Grand Canyon, saw a strange object floating down the Colorado River. It was a crude raft of cottonwoods logs, and sprawled on it was a man. Pulling the raft ashore, they helped the weak and nearly incoherent stranger into one of their houses. He was in horrible shape -- his clothes were in tatters, his skin was sunburned and badly lacerated, and he was suffering from starvation. Obviously he had undergone a terible ordeal.

In a few days the man's strength began to return and he could tell his story. His name was James White and he was thirty years old. He had been a member of a prospecting party, and had taken to the river to escape from hostile Indians. Only semi-literate, not especially articulate, and not knowledgeable about Southwest geography, he nonetheless described an incredible journey. If his tale was to be believed, he must have floated through the Grand Canyon -- thc first and only man to have done so. His story created a sensation.

In January, 1868, Dr. Charles C. Parry, a botanist, met James White and carefully interviewed him concerning his adventure. Like others who had heard White's story, Parry was impressed with the fellow's sincerity and lack of guile. In short, Parry concluded that White was telling the truth. Later, Major Alfred Calhoun, who, along with Parry and others, was surveying a railroad route through Arizona, prepared a narrative of White's trip from Parry's notes. The story was printed in 1870 in William Bell's book, *New Tracks In North America,* which presented the results of the railroad survey. It is this version of White's adventure that is reprinted here.

White's story generated a controversy that continues to this day. Many Colorado River experts reject the notion that White floated through the Grand Canyon on a raft two years before John Wesley Powell and his men accomplished their epic feat in 1869. Major Powell didn't believe White's account, nor did Robert Stanton who led the second (third?) successful journey through the canyon in 1889. White's account has been discounted in that it is considered physically impossible to push an unwieldy bundle of cottonwood logs some five hundred miles through canyons and rapids in the fourteen days alloted. A log when tossed into the wild Colorado didn't simply float along unimpeded to the sea. Rocks jut out into the river and catch logs with a grip so firm that no one man can free them. Below the numerous rapids are eddies and

149

backwaters that can trap debris for months and even years. It could take several years and a number of spring floods for a log (or raft) to work its way through the Grand Canyon. Even today, boats that float away from their moorings in the canyon are usually found hung up in the rocks after traveling only a few miles. And White was alone and without oars or other means to control his crude craft. For White to maneuver a raft through the rapids, keep it in the current, and get it to shore and back out in the river again would have required a superhuman effort.

But there remain nagging questions about James White's journey and his claim cannot be dismissed out of hand. Where did he come from if not through the Grand Canyon? Some have suggested that he entered the river below the canyon. But White did not fake his miserable physical condition which could not have resulted from a two or three day's float trip on calm water. Moreover, it appears certain that he was indeed in southwestern Colorado, the supposed starting point of his odyssey, in the summer of 1867. White lived to be ninety years old and was interviewed many times about his experience. All of the interviewers agreed that he truly believed that he had come through the Grand Canyon. We will let the reader decide whom to believe.

~ ~ ~ ~ ~

**Twenty years ago the trapper and hunter** were the romantic characters of the Far West. They still figure in fiction, and there is a fascination about their daring deeds which, in America, makes Boone a household name, and throws an air of chivalry, seldom to be felt now-a-day, around the exploits of such men as Carson, Crockett, and Williams. Nor is our admiration for these hardy men undeserved; they have trapped on every Western stream, and hunted on every mountain-side, despite the opposition of the Indian and the barrier of winter snows. They have been the skirmish line of that great army of occupation which is daily pushing westward, and they have taught the savage to respect the white man's courage and to fear the white man's power.

While the field for the trapper and hunter has been gradually growing less, another class of adventurers has come into existense -- the "prospectors" in search of precious metals. Within the last nineteen years these men have traversed every mountain slope, from the rugged peaks of British Columbia to the rich plateaux of old Mexico; and have searched the sands of every stream from the Mississippi to the shores of the Pacific, stimulated by the same hope of reward that led the early Spaniards to explore places, still unsettled, in their search for an "El Dorado." Could the varied and adventurous experiences of these searchers for gold be written we should have a record of daring and peril that no fiction could approach, and the very sight of gold would suggest to our minds some scene of startling tragedy, some story of hair-breadth escape. Could we but gather and set down in proper form

150

the geographical knowledge possessed by these men, we should know as much of the western wilds as we now do of the long-settled portions of the American continent.

It has fallen to the lot of one of these prospectors to be the hero of an adventure more thrilling than any heretofore recorded, while, at the same time, he has solved a geographical problem which has long attracted the attention of the learned at home and abroad, who could but theorise before his voyage as to the stupendous chasms or cañons through which the Colorado cleaves its course.

James White, our hero, now lives at Callville, Arizona Territory, the present head of navigation on the Colorado River. His home is in Kenosha, Wisconsin. He is thirty-two years of age, and in person is a good type of the Saxon; being of medium height and heavy build, with light hair and blue eyes. He is a man of average intelligence, simple and unassuming in his manner and address, and without any of the swagger or bravado peculiar to the majority of frontier men. Like thousands of our own young men, well enough off at home, he grew weary of the slow but certain method of earning his bread by regular employment at a stated salary. He had heard of men leaping into wealth at a single bound in the Western gold-fields, and for years he yearned to go to the land where fortune was so lavish of her favours. He readily consented then to be one of a party from his neighborhood who, in the spring of 1867, started for the plains and the gold-fields beyond. When they left Fort Dodge, on the Arkansas River, April 13th, 1867, the party consisted of four men, of whom Captain Baker, an old miner and ex-officer in the Confederate army, was the acknowledged leader. The destination of this little party was the San Juan valley west of the Rocky Mountains, about the gold-fields of which prospectors spoke in the most extravagant terms, stating that they were only deterred from working the rich placers of the San Juan by fear of the Indians. Baker and his companions reached Colorado "city," at the foot of Pike's Peak, lat. 38 degrees, in safety. This place was, and is still, the depot for supplying the miners who work the diggings scattered through South Park, and is the more important for being situated at the entrance of Ute Pass, through which there is a wagon-road crossing the Rocky Mountains, and descending to the plateau beyond. The people of Colorado "city" tried to dissuade Baker from what they considered a rash project, but he was determined to carry out the original plan. These representations, however, affected one of the men so much that he left the party, and the others, Captain Baker, James White, and Henry Strole, completed their outfit for their prospecting tour.

The journey was undertaken on foot, with two pack mules to carry the provisions, mining tools, and the blankets they considered necessary for the expedition. On the 25th of May they left Colorado "city" and crossing the Rocky Mountains, through the Ute Pass, they entered

South Park, being still on the Atlantic slope of the continent. Ninety miles brought them across the Park to the Upper Arkansas, near the Twin Lakes. They then crossed the Snowy Range, or Sierra Madre, and descended towards the Pacific. Turning southwest, they passed around the head-waters of the Rio Grande del Norte, and after a journey of 400 miles, they reached in safety the Animas, the most northern branch of the San Juan River, which flows into the Great Colorado from the east.

They were now in the land of where their hopes centered, and to reach which they had crossed plains and mountains, and forded rapid streams, leaving the nearest abodes of the white man hundreds of miles to the east. Their prospecting for gold began in the bed of the Animas, and though they were partially successful, the result did not by any means reach their expectations; so they followed down the stream into the main valley of the San Juan. There was gold there, but not in the quantity they expected; so they gradually moved west, along the beautiful valley, for 200 miles, when they found that the San Juan entered a deep and gloomy cañon. To avoid this they forded the river to the right bank, and struck across a rough timbered country, directing their course toward the great Colorado.

Having travelled through this rough country for a distance estimated at fifty miles, they reached Grand River [now the upper Colorado River], being still above the junction of Green River, the united waters of which two streams form the Colorado proper. At the point where they struck the river it was hemmed in by cliffs of perpendicular rock, down which they could gaze at the coveted water, dashing and foaming two thousand feet below. Men and animals were suffering for water, so they pushed up the stream along the rocky uneven cañon wall, hoping to find a place where they could descend to the river. After a day spent in clambering over and around the huge rocks that blocked their way, they came upon a side cañon, which they succeeded in descending with their animals, and where they obtained the water of which all stood so much in need.

On the night of the 23rd of August they encamped at the bottom of the cañon, where they found plenty of fuel, and grass in abundance for their animals. As they sat around the camp fire they lamented their failure in the San Juan country, and Strole began to regret that they had undertaken the expedition. But Baker, who was a brave, sanguine fellow, spoke of the *placeres* up the river about which he had heard, and promised his companions that all their hopes should be realized, and that they should return to their homes to enjoy the gains and laugh at the trials of their trip. So glowingly did he picture the future, that his companions even speculated as to how they should spend their princely fortunes when they returned to the States. Baker sang songs of home and hope, and the others lent their voices to the chorus till, far into the night, they sank to sleep unguarded, to dream of coming opulence, and to rise refreshed for the morrow's journey.

Early next morning they breakfasted, and began the ascent of the side cañon up the opposite bank to that by which they had entered it. Baker was in the advance with his rifle slung at his back, gaily springing up the rocks towards the tableland above. Behind him came White; Strole, with the mules, brought up the rear. Nothing disturbed the stillness of the beautiful summer morning but the tramping of the mules and the short heavy breathing of the climbers. They had ascended but half the distance to the top, when stopping for a moment to rest, suddenly the war-whoop of a band of savages rang out, sounding as if every rock had a demon's voice. Simultaneously with the first whoop a shower of arrows and bullets was poured into the little party. With the first fire Baker fell against a rock, but, rallying for a moment, he unslung his carbine and fired at the Indians, who now began to show themselves in large numbers, and then, with the blood flowing from his mouth, he fell to the ground. White, firing at the Indians as he advanced and followed by Strole, hurried to the aid of his wounded leader. Baker, with an effort, turned to his comrades and said with his last breath, "Back boys, back! save yourselves; I am dying." To the credit of White and Strole be it said, they faced the savages and fought till the last tremor of the powerful frame told them that Baker was dead.

Then slowly they began to retreat, followed by the exultant Indians, who, stopping to strip and mutilate the dead body in their path, gave the white men a chance to secure their animals, and retrace their steps into the side cañon, beyond the immediate reach of the Indians' arrows. Here they held a hurried consultation. To the east, for 300 miles, stretched an uninhabited country, over which, if they attempted to escape in that direction, the Indians, like bloodhounds, would follow their track. North, south, and west, was the Colorado with its tributaries, all flowing through deep chasms across which it would be impossible for men or animals to travel. Their deliberations were necessarily short, and resulted in a decision to abandon the animals -- first securing their arms, a small stock of provisions, and the ropes or lariats of the mules. Through the descending side cañon they travelled due west for four hours, and emerged at last on a low strip of bottomland on Grand River, above which, for 2,000 feet on either bank, the cold grey walls rose to block their path, leaving to them but one avenue for escape -- the dashing current of the river.

They found considerable quantities of drift-wood along the banks, from which they collected enough to enable them to construct a raft capable of floating themselves, with their arms and provisions. This raft consisted of three sticks of cotton-wood, about ten feet in length and eight inches in diameter, lashed firmly together with their lariats.

Procuring two stout poles with which to guide the raft, and fastening the bag of provisions to the logs, they waited for midnight to come with the waning moon, so as to drift off unnoticed by the Indians. They did not consider that even the sun looked down into that chasm for but one short hour in the twenty-four, and then left it to the angry waters and blackening shadows; and that the faint moonlight reaching the bottom of the cañon would hardly serve to reveal the horror of their situation. Midnight came, as they thought, by the measurement of the dark, dreary hours; when, seizing the poles, they untied the rope that held the raft, and, tossed about by the current, they rushed through the yawning cañon on their adventurous voyage to an unknown landing. Through the long night they clung to the raft as it dashed against half-concealed rocks, or whirled about like a plaything in some eddy, whose white foam was perceptible even in the blackness. They prayed for the daylight, which came at last, and with it a smoother current and less rugged banks, though the cañon walls appeared to have increased in height. Early in the morning (August 25th) they found a spot where they could make a landing, and went ashore. After eating a little of their water-soaked provisions, they returned and strengthened their raft by the addition of some light pieces of cedar, which had been lodged in clefts of the rocks by recent floods. White estimates the width of the river where they landed at 200 yards, and the current at three miles per hour. After a short stay at this place they again embarked, and during the rest of the day they had no difficulty in avoiding the rocks and whirlpools that met them at every bend of the river.

In the afternoon, and after having floated over a distance estimated at thirty miles from the point of starting, they reached the mouth of Green River, or rather where the Green and the Grand unite to form the Colorado proper. Here the cañons of both streams form one of but little greater width, but far surpassing either in the height and grandeur of its walls. At the junction, the walls were estimated at 4,000 feet in height. Detached pinnacles appeared to rise, one above the other, for 1,000 feet higher, from amidst huge masses of rock, confusedly piled, like grand monuments to commemorate this "meeting of the waters." The fugitives felt the sublimity of the scene, and in contemplating its stupendous and unearthly grandeur, they forgot for the time their own sorrows.

The night of the day upon which they entered the Great Cañon, and indeed on nearly all the subsequent nights of the voyage, the raft was fastened to a loose rock, or hauled up on some strip of bottom-land, where they rested till daylight next morning.

As they floated down the cañon the grey sandstone walls increased in height; the lower portion was smooth from the action of floods, but the perpendicular wall-rock above became more and more rugged, until the far-off sky appeared to rest upon a fringe of pinnacles on either side. Here and there a stunted cedar clung to the cliff-side 2,000 feet overhead, or a prickly cactus tried to suck sustenance from the bare rock. No living thing in sight beyond the raft, for even the wing of bird which could pass the chasms in the upper world never fanned the dark air in those subterranean depths. Nought to gaze on but their own pale faces and the cold grey walls that hemmed them in, and mocked at their escape. Here and there the raft shot past side cañons, black and forbidding, like cells set in the walls of a mighty prison.

Baker had informed his comrades as to the geography of the country, and while floating down they remembered that Callville was at the mouth of the cañon, which could not be far off; "such wonderful walls could not last." Then hope came with the promise of escape. A few days would take them to Callville; their provisions could be made to last for five. So these two men, thus shut *in* from the world, buried, as it were, in the very bowels of the earth, in the midst of a great unknown desert, began to console themselves, and even to jest at their situation.

Forty miles below their entrance into the cañon of the Colorado, they reached the mouth of the San Juan River. They attempted to enter it, but its swift current cast them back. The perpendicular walls, high as those of the Colorado, with the water flowing from bank to bank, forbade their abandoning their raft to attempt escape in that direction. So they floated away. At every bend of the river it seemed as if they were descending deeper into the earth, and that the walls were coming closer together above them, shutting out the narrow belt of sky, thickening the black shadows, and redoubling the echoes that went up from the foaming waters.

Four days had elapsed since they embarked on the frail raft; it was now August 28th. So far they had been constantly wet, but the water was comparatively warm, and the current more regular than they could have expected. Strole had taken upon himself to steer the raft, and, against the advice of White, he often set one end of the pole against the bank or some opposing rock, and then leaned with the other end against his shoulder, to push the raft away. As yet they had seen no natural bridge spanning the chasm above them, nor had fall or cataract prevented their safe advance. About three o'clock on the afternoon of the 28th, they heard the deep roar as of a waterfall in front of them. They felt the raft agitated, then whirled along with frightful rapidity towards a wall that seemed to bar all farther progress. As they approached the cliff, the river made a sharp bend, around which the raft swept, disclosing to them, in a long vista, the water lashed into foam, as it poured through a narrow precipitous gorge, caused by huge masses of rock detached from the main wall. There was no time to think. The logs strained as if they would break their fastenings. The waves dashed around the men, and the raft was buried in the seething waters. White clung to the logs with the grip of death. His comrade stood up for an instant with the pole in his hands, as if to guide the raft from the rocks against which it was plunging; but he had scarcely straightened, before the raft seemed to leap down a chasm, and, amid the deafening roar of waters, White heard a shriek that thrilled him to the heart, and looking round he saw, through the mist and spray, the form of his comrade tossed for an instant on the water, then sinking out of sight in the whirlpool.

White still clung to the logs, and it was only when the raft seemed to be floating smoothly, and the sound of the rapids was left behind, that he dared to look up; then it was to find himself alone, the provisions lost, and the lengthening shadows warning him of the approaching night. A feeling of despair seized him, and clasping his hands he prayed for the death he was fleeing from. He was made cognizant of more immediate danger by the shaking of his raft, the logs were separating; then he worked, and succeeded in effecting a landing near some flat rocks, where he made his raft fast for the night. After this he sat down, to spend the long gloomy hours in contemplating the horror of his situation, and the small chance for completing the adventurous voyage he had undertaken. He blamed himself for not having fought the Indians till he had fallen with Baker. He might have escaped through the San Juan valley and the mountains beyond to the settlements. Had he done so, he would have returned to his home, and rested satisfied with his experience as a prospector. And when he thought of "home," it called up the strongest inducements for life, and he resolved, to use his own words, "to die hard, and like a man."

Gradually the dawn, long perceptible in the upper world, began to creep down the black cañon, and gave him light to strengthen his raft, and launch it again into the treacherous river. As he floated down he remembered the sad fate of Strole, and took the precaution to lash himself firmly to the raft, so as to preclude the possibility of his being separated from it. This forethought subsequently saved his life. His course through the cañon was now over a succession of rapids, blocked up by masses of rock, over which his frail raft thumped and whirled, at times wholly submerged in the foaming water. At one of these rapids, in the distance of about a hundred yards, he thinks the river must have fallen between thirty and forty feet. In going over this place the logs composing the raft became separated at the upper end, and, spreading out like a fan, White was thrown into the water. He struggled to the side by means of his rope, and with a desperate strength held the logs together till they floated into calmer water, when he succeeded in refastening them.

White's trials were not yet at an end, and in relating the following incident he showed the only sign of emotion exhibited during his long series of answers.

About four miles below where the raft separated he reached the mouth of a large stream, which he afterwards learned was the Colorado Chiquito [Little Colorado]. The cañon through which it enters the main river is very much like that of the San Juan, and though it does not discharge so large a body of water, the current is much more rapid, and sweeps across the Great Colorado, causing, in a black chasm on the opposite bank, a large and dangerous whirlpool. White saw this and tried to avoid it, but he was too weak for the task. His raft, borne by the current of the Colorado proper, rushed down with such force, that aided by his paddle he hoped to pass the waters that appeared to sweep at right angles across his course from the Chiquito. When he reached the mouth of the latter stream the raft suddenly stopped, and swinging round for an instant as if balanced on a point, it yielded to the current of the Chiquito and was swept into the whirlpool.

White felt now that all further exertion was useless, and dropping his paddle, he clasped his hands and fell upon the raft. He heard the gurgling waters around him, and every moment he felt that he must be plunged into the boiling vortex. He waited with his eyes closed for some minutes, when, feeling a strange swinging sensation, he opened them and found that he was circling round the whirlpool, sometimes close to the vortex, and at others thrown back by some invisible cause to the outer edge only to whirl again towards the centre. Thus borne by the circling waters he looked up, up, up, through the mighty chasm that seemed bending over him as if about to fall and crush him. He saw in the blue belt of sky which hung above him like an ethereal river the red tinged clouds floating, and knew that the sun was setting in the upper world. Still around the whirlpool the raft swung, like a circular pendulum measuring the long moments before expected death. He felt a dizzy sensation, and thinks he must have fainted; he knows he was unconscious for a time, for when he looked up between the walls, whose rugged summits towered 5,000 feet above him, the red clouds had changed to black, and the heavy shadows of night had crept down the cañon.

Then, for the first time, he remembered that there was a strength greater than that of man, a power that holds the ocean in the hollow of His hand. "I fell on my knees," he said, "and as the raft swept around in the current, I asked God to aid me. I spoke as if from my very soul, and said, 'Oh, God! if there is a way out of this fearful place show it to me; take me to it.'" Here White's voice became husky, and his somewhat heavy features quivered as he continued -- "I was still looking up with my hands clasped when I felt a different movement in the raft, and turning to look at the whirlpool, it was some distance behind, and I was floating down the smoothest current I had yet seen in the cañon."

This statement is the only information White volunteered; all the rest was obtained by close questioning. One of his friends who was present during the examination smiled when White repeated his prayer. He noticed it, and said with some feeling: "It is true, Bob, and I'm sure God took me out."

Below the mouth of the Colorado Chiquito the current was very slow, and White felt what he subsequently found to be the case -- viz., that the rapids were past, though he was not equally fortunate in guessing his proximity to Callville. The course of the river below this he describes as exceedingly "crooked, with short, sharp turns," the view on every side being shut in by flat precipitous walls of "white sand-rock." These walls presented white perpendicular surfaces to the high water-level, which had a distinct mark of about forty feet above the August stage. The highest part of the cañon, White thinks, is between the San Juan and the Colorado Chiquito, where the wall appeared to him more than one mile (5,280 feet) in perpendicular height, and at a few points even higher. Dr. Newberry states, from barometrical observations, that for a long distance the altitude is nearly 7,000 feet. But we must not begin to draw conclusions too soon, much of interest remains to be told of this unparalleled adventure.

The current bore White from the Colorado Chiquito slowly down the main river. His clothing was torn to shreds, and the few rags which clung to his frame were constantly saturated with water. Each noon the sun looked into the cañon only to pour his almost vertical rays on the famishing man, and to burn and blister those parts of his body that the scanty rags did not cover. One, two, three, four days dragged slowly past since he tasted food, and still the current bore him through the towering walls of the cañon. The hunger maddened him. He felt it burning into his vitals. His thoughts were of food! food! food! and his sleeping moments were filled with Tantalus-like dreams. Once he raised his arm to open some vein and draw nutriment from his own blood, but its shrivelled, blistered length frighted him. For hours as he floated down he would sit looking into the water, yet lacking courage to make the plunge that would rid him of all earthly pain. On the morning of the fifth day since he had tasted food, he saw a flat bank with some mezquit bushes upon it, and by using all his strength he succeeded in reaching it with his raft. He devoured the few green pods and the leaves of the bushes, but they only increased his desire for more. The journey was resumed, and he remembers that during the last two days of unbroken cañon wall, the rocks became very black, with shining surfaces -- probably where the igneous took the place of the cretaceous rocks.

Six days without food, save the few green leaves, and eleven days since starting, and still the uneven current bore on the raft with its wretched occupant. He saw occasional breaks in the wall, and here and there a bush. Too weak to move his raft, he floated past and felt no pain, for the over-wrought nerves refused to convey sensation.

On the afternoon of this, the sixth day, he was roused by hearing the sound of human voices, and, raising himself on one arm, he looked towards the shore, and saw men beckoning to him. A momentary strength came to his arms, and, grasping the paddle, he urged the raft to the bank. On reaching it he found himself surrounded by a band of Yampais Indians, who for many years have lived on a low strip of alluvial land along the bottom of the cañon, the trail to which, from the upper world, is only known to themselves. One of the Indians made fast the raft, while another seized White roughly and dragged him up the bank. He could not remonstrate; his tongue refused to give a sound, so he pointed to his mouth and made signs for food. The fiend that pulled him up the bank, tore from his blistered shoulders the shreds that had once been a shirt, and was proceeding to take off the torn trousers, when, to the credit of the savage be it said, one of the Indians interfered, and pushed back his companions. He gave White some meat, and roasted mezquit beans to eat, which the famished man devoured, and after a little rest he made signs that he wanted to go to the nearest dwellings of white men. The Indians told him he could reach them in "two suns" by his raft, so he stayed with them all night, and with a revolver that remained fastened to the logs, he purchased some mezquit beans, and the half of a dog.

Early the next morning he tottered to the bank, and again pushed into the current. The first day out he gave way to the yearnings for food, and, despite his resolution to the contrary, he ate up his entire stock of provisions, which did not, by any means, satisfy his craving. Three long days of hope and dread passed slowly by, and still no signs of friends. Reason tottered, and White stretched himself on the raft; all his energies exhausted, life and death were to him alike indifferent.

Late in the evening of the third day after leaving the Indians, and fourteen days from the time of starting on this perilous voyage, White again heard voices, accompanied by the rapid dash of oars. He understood the words, but could make no reply. He felt a strong arm thrown around him, and he was lifted into a boat, to see manly bearded faces looking on him with pity. The great objective point, Callville, was reached at last; the battle for a life was won, but with the price of unparalleled suffering. The people of this Mormon settlement had warm, generous hearts, and, like good Samaritans, lavishly bestowed every care on the unfortunate man, so miraculously thrown into their midst from the bowels of the unknown cañon. His constitution, naturally strong, soon recovered its terrible shock, and he told his new-found friends his wonderful story, the first recital of which led them to doubt his sanity.

Charles McAllister, at present an assistant in the store of Mr. Todd at Fort Mojave, was one of the three men who went in the boat to White's assistance. He said that he never saw so wretched a looking man as White when he first met him; his feet, legs, and body were literally flayed, from exposure to drenching from water and the scorching rays of the sun. His reason was almost gone, his form stooped, and his eyes were so hollow and dreary, that he looked like an old and imbecile man. Mr. W.H. Hardy, of Hardyville, near Fort Mojave, brought White thither, that we might see and talk with him. Mr. Hardy corroborates the statements of McAllister, and from his knowledge of the country above Callville, says that it would be impossible for White to have come for any distance by the river, without travelling through the whole length of the Great Cañon of the Colorado. Mr. Ballard, a mail contractor, in whose employment White is now earning money to take him home, says he believes him to be a sober, truthful man; but, apart from White's statement, Ballard is confident he must have traversed, and in the manner stated, that hitherto unexplored chasm which completes the missing link between the upper and lower course of the Great Colorado.

# THE CAMP GRANT MASSACRE
## (1871)

## William S. Oury

**Editors' Note:** Camp Grant, a small army post established in 1865 at the mouth of Aravaipa Creek in southeast Arizona, was only in existence for eight years. In 1873 the post was moved fifty miles to the east to Sulphur Springs Valley at the foot of the Pinaleño Mountains. Today, nothing remains of the adobe buildings of "Old Camp Grant." But its name lives on, owing to one of the most controversial events in the history of the West -- the Camp Grant Massacre of 1871.

The purpose of Camp Grant, indeed the mission of all military posts in southeast Arizona, was to pacify the Apache Indians. The Apaches were a nomadic people, and several bands had perfected the raiding and plundering of their neighbors to a fine art. Sedentary farmers such as the Pima and Papago Indians had long suffered Apache depredations, as had the struggling Mexican villages of the region. With the arrival of large numbers of Anglo-American settlers after the Civil War, confict with the Apaches was inevitable.

The pacification policy of the U.S. government involved encouraging Apache bands to come in from the mountains, lay down their arms, and take up sedentary agricultural pursuits under the watchful eye of a military fort or camp. There they would be fed and protected from their enemies, and eventually settled on a suitable reservation. Although the pacification policy was bitterly criticized by White settlers, the program had its successes, and early in 1871 a large number of Apaches began gathering near Camp Grant. The post commander, Lieutenant Royal E. Whitman, allowed the Indians to establish a semi-permanent village or *rancheria* on Arivaipa Creek, about five miles upstream from the post. Here the Indians built their wickiups, traditional conical shelters made of brush, while the women cut wild hay for use at the post. In return, the Indians were issued food and clothing. Soon their numbers swelled to five hundred, and Whitman felt that good progress was being made in their domestication.

But taming Apaches was a gradual process. Apache raids continued, and, as always, the band committing the attack was often difficult to ascertain. The people of Tucson looked on the growing population of Apaches fifty miles to the north at Camp Grant with alarm and suspicion, convinced that many of Whitman's Indians were responsible for a recent spate of thefts and murders. As the victims of Apache raids, these citizens were not interested in the government's program of gradual pacification -- they wanted to be rid of the Apache menace. Nor was this attitude confined to Anglo-Americans. Hatred for the Apaches in southern Arizona cut across ethnic lines. The Papagos and

Mexican-Americans also considered the Apaches as unredeemable vermin, deserving of extermination.

Army officers charged with carrying out the government's resettlement policy came to be despised by the local civilian population almost as much as the Apaches themselves. The settlers believed that any program that fed and protected Apaches was so cockeyed that the officers must be grafters making illegal profits from military post appropriations. General George Stoneman, commander of the Department of Arizona, and Lieutenant Whitman were especially reviled and viciously excoriated in the Tucson newspapers. The army posts were considered as mere havens for the raiders where the Apaches could rest and regroup between their deadly forays afield.

Attitudes toward the Camp Grant Indians reached a flash point in the spring of 1871. In a May 17 letter to a superior, Lieutenant Whitman described how he learned of the carnage that had been wrought at the Apaches' camp.

"On the morning of April 30, I was at breakfast at 7:30 o'clock, when a dispatch was brought to me by a sergeant of Company P, Twenty-first Infantry, from Captain Penn, commanding Camp Lowell, informing me that a large party had left Tucson on the 28th, with the avowed purpose of killing all the Indians at this post. I immediately sent two interpreters, mounted, to the Indian camp, with orders to tell the chiefs the exact state of things, and for them to bring their entire party inside the post... My messengers returned in about an hour, with intelligence that they could find no living Indians.

The camp was burning and the ground strewn with their dead and mutilated women and children. I immediately mounted a party of about twenty soldiers and citizens, and sent them with the post surgeon, with a wagon to bring in the wounded, if any could be found. The party returned late in the p.m., having found no wounded. Early the next morning I took a similar party, with spades and shovels, and went out and buried all the dead in and immediately about the camp...

Their camp was surrounded and attacked at day-break. So sudden and unexpected was it, that no one was awake to give the alarm, and I found quite a number of women shot while asleep beside their bundles of hay which they had collected to bring in on that morning. The wounded, who were unable to get away, had their brains beaten out with clubs or stones, while some were shot full of arrows after having been mortally wounded by gunshot. The bodies were all stripped... Of the whole number killed and missing, about one hundred and twenty-five, eight only were men..."

The assailants, Anglos, Mexican-Americans, and Papago Indians from the Tucson area, had been thorough in their work. The only survivors of the slaughter were about twenty-five infants who were taken by the Papagos and sold into slavery in Sonora. Only about a half-dozen of these children were ever repatriated. Exactly how many Apaches were killed was never determined, but about one hundred is a good estimate. Many of the five hundred Indians previously counted were obviously absent during the attack, and almost all of the men were somewhere else. The whereabouts of the missing Indians never was made clear. The Tucsonans were positive that they were on a sinister mission; Lieutenant Whitman was sure they were not. In any event, the absent Apaches were soon resettled at San Carlos, a remote reservation on the Gila River. The citizens of Tucson were pleased with what they had achieved.

News of the massacre was received in the East with horror and dismay. President Ulysses S. Grant was said to have been outraged, calling the killing of Apache women and children "purely murder." He demanded an immediate, full investigation of the incident. It was the residents of Tucson who now received rough treatment in the newspapers.

In December, 1871, one hundred men were put on trial in Tucson, each charged with murder for having taken part in the killings at Camp Grant. Their defense rested on the assertion that a state of war existed between the Apaches and the other people of the region, and that the attack was an act of war. The defense also stated that the Apaches at Camp Grant were not well supervised, but left their *rancheria* at will to prey upon nearby settlers. That most of the men were absent on the morning of the massacre was cited as proof that the military had no knowledge, much less any control, of Apache comings and goings. After five days of testimony, the jury deliberated nineteen minutes before finding the men not guilty.

The following account of the Camp Grant Massacre was read before the Society of Arizona Pioneers (now the Arizona Historical Society) at Tucson on April 6, 1885. The author, William S. Oury, one of the leaders of the attack, served as sheriff of Pima County from 1873 to 1876 and was the Society's first president. A park in Tucson is named in his honor.

~ ~ ~ ~ ~

**Having been chosen by our president** to give a paper upon some event connected with the early history of Arizona, the writer has selected as his theme the so-called Camp Grant Massacre, believing it to be one of the events most important in its results to the peace and progress of our Apache-cursed land. To give a mere recital of the act of killing a few, more or less, of bloodthirsty savages, without the details of the causes and provocations which drove a long-suffering and patient people to the adoption of remedial measures so apparently cruel in their results, would be a great wrong and injustice to those of our friends and neighbors who in various ways gave sanction and aid to the undertaking, and would fall far short of the object and aim of the writer to give fair and impartial history.

In the year 1870, in accordance with the peace policy which had been decided upon by the U.S. Government, the Pinal and Aravaipa bands of the Apache Indians were collected together and placed upon a reservation around old Camp Grant at the junction of the San Pedro and Aravaipa creeks, about fifty-five miles from Tucson, under the supervision of the military stationed at that post. One or two agents for them had been taken from civilian life, but in a short time their management proving unsatisfactory, one Royal E. Whitman, a lieutenant of the Third Cavalry, U.S. Army, was assigned to duty as their agent. Being what is termed a sharp man and of thrifty disposition, he soon saw there was money in the Apache and lost no time in practical application of that knowledge, to do which successfully required outside partners, who were soon found in Tucson. A sutler's store was first started, followed by a blacksmith, butcher, and a number of others chosen in various capacities, ostensibly for the benefit of poor "Lo," but really "affidavy," easy-conscience witness-men for the boss. As a trite saying goes, "Hell was fully inaugurated."

The Indians soon commenced plundering and murdering the citizens of Tucson, San Xavier, Tubac, Sonoita, San Pedro, and every other settlement within a radius of one hundred miles of old Camp Grant, in the confidence that if they escaped to their reservation they reached a secure haven. During the winter of 1870-71, these murders and depredations were so numerous as to threaten the abandonment of nearly all the settlements outside of Tucson, especially that of San Pedro. In the meantime, the citizens of Tucson were aroused and meetings were held upon the occurrence of each new murder or outrage. Representations were made to the Right Royal Whitman that his Indians were plundering and murdering our people, which he denied, and stood ready to prove, by every striker [flunky] on the reservation, that his Indians never left the place. Meanwhile, the work of death and destruction kept up with ever-increasing force until the slaughter of Wooster and his wife on the Santa Cruz above Tubac so inflamed the people that an indignation meeting was held at Tucson.

A great amount of resoluting and speechifying was indulged in, and it was determined to raise a military company at once, for which a paper was drawn up and signers called for, to which eighty-two Americans signed their names. The writer was selected captain, and all hands pledged to eat up blood-raw every Apache in the land upon the recurrence of a new outrage. A committee was appointed to visit the department commander, General Stoneman, at the time on the Gila near Florence, consisting of S.R. DeLong, J.W. Hopkins, and the writer, the remaining names are not now remembered, which committee started at once for its destination.

The result of the conference with that august personage, General Stoneman, was that he had but few troops and could give no aid, that Tucson had the largest population in the territory, and he gave us to understand that we must protect ourselves. With this cold comfort, after a trip of one hundred and fifty miles and the loss of a valuable mule, we returned to our constituents. Although no public demonstration was made, at a quiet assemblage of some of our ablest and most substantial citizens, it was resolved that the recommendation of General Stoneman should be adopted, and that to the best of our ability we would endeavor to protect ourselves.

A few days afterwards, at the beginning of April, 1871, the arrival of a courier from San Xavier brought the sad intelligence that the Indians had just made a descent on that place and had driven off a large number of cattle and horses. The alarm drum (the usual way of collecting our people) was beaten. A flaring cartoon carried by a man who accompanied the drummer was displayed with the following inscription: "Injuns--Injuns--Injuns. Big meeting at the court house. Come everybody. Time for action has arrived." This device had been so frequently resorted to, and the result obtained so unsatisfactory, that it failed to draw. Meanwhile, a party of citizens had saddled their horses, and learning from the two San Xavier couriers the direction the marauding Indians had taken, rode off, hoping to intercept them before they reached Cebadilla Pass. In this they were disappointed, for the Indians had gone into the pass before they arrived, but they met the pursuing party from San Xavier and the whole party followed through the pass and overtook the rear Indian, driving the stock on a tired horse, and killed him and recovered some of the cattle. The other Indians escaped with the horses and the freshest cattle.

Upon the return of the party to Tucson, I hunted up Jesús Elias and had a long conference with him, in which he said to me, "Don Guillermo, I have always been satisfied, and have repeatedly told you, that the Camp Grant Indians were the ones that were destroying us. I now have proof positive. The Indian we have just killed I will swear, and others will also swear, is a Camp Grant Indian. I have frequently seen him there and know him well by having his front tooth out. As a further proof, when we overtook the Indians they were making a direct course for Camp Grant. Now it devolves upon you, as one of the oldest American residents of this country, to devise some means of saving us from the total ruin which the present state of affairs must inevitably lead to, if not remedied. See your countrymen, they are the only ones who have money to furnish the supplies necessary to make a formal and effective campaign against our implacable enemies. I know my countrymen will vouch that if arms and ammunition and provisions, however scant, are furnished them, they will be ready at the first call."

I replied, "Don Jesús, for myself I will answer that I will at all times be ready to do my part, and will at once issue a call for the assemblage of my people at the court house, where you can publicly state what you have just told me, and some concerted plan can be adopted which may give the desired relief."

With a sad shake of his head, he answered, "Don Guillermo, for months we have repeatedly held public meetings at which many patriotic speeches have been made and many glowing resolutions passed, meanwhile our means of subsistence have been rapidly diminishing and nothing accomplished. We cannot resolute the remorseless Apache out of existence. If that could have been done, every one of them would have been dead long since. Besides, giving publicity to the course we might pursue would surely defeat any plan we might adopt. You are aware that there are wealthy and influential men in this community whose interest is to have the Indians of Camp Grant left undisturbed, and who would, at the first intimation of an intent to inquire seriously into their operations, appeal to the military, whose ear they have, and frustrate all our plans and hopes."

I saw at once the force of his arguments and replied, "Lay out the plan of action and I will aid you with all the zeal and energy I possess."

He then developed the following plan: "You and I will go first to San Xavier and see Francisco, the head Papago there, and have him send runners to the various Papago villages, notifying them that on the 28th day of April we want them to be at San Xavier early in the morning, with all the force they can muster, for a campaign against our common enemy, the Apaches. Francisco is to be prepared to give them a good breakfast on their arrival, and to send messengers to me at once. If this matter is satisfactory, upon returning to Tucson I will see all the Mexicans who may desire to participate in the campaign, and have them all ready to move on the day fixed. You make arrangements with the Americans you can trust, either to take active part in the campaign or render such assistance in supplies, arms, ammunition, and horses as will be required to carry out the expedition. And on the day fixed, April 28th, news of the arrival of the Papagoes at San Xavier having first been received, all who are to be active participants in the campaign will leave town quietly and singly, to avoid giving alarm, and rendezvous on the Rillito opposite San Xavier, where the Papagoes will be advised to meet us, and where, as per arrangements, the arms, ammunition, and provisions will be delivered and distributed. All hands having arrived at the rendezvous, the command will be fully organized by the election of a commander who all shall be pledged to obey implicitly. When thus organized, the company will march up the Rillito until the trail of the Indians who had committed the recent depredations at San Xavier is struck, which will be followed to where it ought to lead, and all Indians found on it killed, if possible."

Here you have the whole plan of the Camp Grant campaign as proposed by Mr. Elias and concurred in by the writer. For its successful fulfillment, we both went to work with all our hearts, he with his countrymen, the Mexicans, I with mine, the Americans, and both together with our auxiliaries, the Papagoes. And early on the morning of April 28th, 1871, we received the welcome news of the arrival of the Papagoes at San Xavier, and that after a short rest and a feed they would march to the general rendezvous on the Rillito.

Soon after, Elias informed me that the Mexicans' contingent was quietly and singly leaving town for the same destination, and soon after, the writer, having given proper directions to the extremely small contingent of his own countrymen, silently and alone took up the line of march to the common rendezvous. By three p.m., all the command had arrived, also that which was still more essential to the successful issue of the campaign, to wit: the wagon with the arms, ammunition, and grub, thanks to our old companion the adjutant general of the territory, whose name it might not be discreet to give in this connection, but who is well known to almost every member of the Society of Arizona Pioneers.

As soon as the writer was convinced that no further increase was to be expected, he proceeded to take account of the stock, with the following result: Papagoes, ninety-two; Mexicans, forty-eight; Americans, six. In all, one hundred and forty-six men, good and true. During our short stay at the general rendezvous, a number of pleasantries were indulged in by the different members of the party upon the motley appearance of the troop. Your historian got a blow squarely in the right eye from an old neighbor who quietly said to him, "Don Guillermo, your countrymen are grand on resoluting and speechifying, but when it comes to actions, they show up exceedingly thin." Which in view of the fact that eighty-two Americans had solemnly pledged themselves to be ready at any moment for the campaign, and only six finally showed up, was to say the least rather humiliating. However, everything was taken pleasantly.

Jesús Elias was elected commander of the expedition, and at four p.m. the company was in the saddle, ready for the march. Just here it seemed to me that we had neglected a very important precautionary measure and I penciled the following note to H.S. Stevens, Esq., Tucson: "Send a party to the Cañada del Oro, on the main road from Tucson to Camp Grant, with orders to stop any and all persons going towards Camp Grant until seven a.m. of April 30th, 1871." This note I gave to the teamster, who had not yet left our camp, who delivered it promptly, and it was as promptly attended to by Mr. Stevens. But for this precaution, our campaign would have resulted in complete failure, from the fact that the absence of so many men from so small a population as Tucson then contained was noted by a person of large influence in the community, and at whose urgent command the military commander sent an express of two soldiers with dispatches to Camp Grant. They were quietly detained at Cañada del Oro and did not reach that post until it was too late to harm us.

After writing and dispatching the note, the order "forward" was given and the command moved gaily and confidently on its mission. About six p.m., the trail was struck which we proposed to follow, and the march continued through the Cebadilla Pass and down the slopes of the San Pedro to the point where the San Xavier party had killed the Indian. The order to camp was given, as it was about midnight, the moon going down, and the trail could not well be followed in the dark.

Just at break of day of the morning of April 29th, we marched down into the San Pedro bottom, where our commander determined to remain until nightfall lest our command should be discovered by roving Indians and alarm given at their *rancheria*. We had followed all this time the trail of the Indians who had raided San Xavier, and every man in the command was now fully satisfied that it would lead up to the reservation, and arrangements were made accordingly.

Commander Elias gave the order to march as soon as it was dark. He detailed three men as scouts, whose duty it was, when the command arrived conveniently near the *rancheria*, to go ahead and ascertain its exact locality and report to him the result of their reconnaissance, in order to have no guess-work about their actual position, and our attack, consequently, be a haphazard affair. We believed that we were much nearer the *rancheria* than we really were, and that we would reach its neighborhood by midnight. Everything being now ready for the final march, we moved out of the San Pedro bottom just at dark.

It soon became evident that our captain and all those who thought they knew the distance had made a grave mistake, and that instead of being about sixteen miles as estimated, it was nearer thirty miles. After a continuous march through the whole night, it was near daybreak before we reached the Aravaipa Canyon, and when we did reach it there was no time left to make the proposed reconnaissance so as to ascertain the exact location of the Indian camp. This involved the necessity of a change of our plan of attack. We knew that the *rancheria* was in the Aravaipa Canyon, somewhere above the post, but the exact location nobody knew. We were in a critical position. We were in sight of the post, day was approaching, and it was plain that in a very short time we would be discovered, either by the Indians or the people at the post. In either case our expedition would be an absolute failure. But our gallant captain was equal to the emergency. Promptly he gave orders to divide the command into two wings, the one to comprise the Papagoes, the other the Mexicans and Americans, and to skirmish up the creek until we struck the *rancheria*.

When the order "forward" was given, a new difficulty arose which, if it had not been speedily overcome, would have been fatal. The command was now in plain view of the military post. The Papagoes had all the time been afraid of military interference with us. I had assured them that no such thing would occur and vouched for it. It happened that just as the command was halting, I had dropped the canteen from the horn of my saddle, and dismounting to look for it in the dust and semi-darkness got behind the troops. The Papagoes, not seeing me at the front when the order "forward for the skirmish" was given, refused to move, inquiring where Don Guillermo was. Word was immediately passed down the line to me and I galloped to the front, and with a motion of my hand, without a word spoken, the Papagoes bounded forward like deer, and the skirmish began -- a better executed one I never witnessed, even from veteran soldiers.

There was not a break in either line from beginning to end of the affair, which covered a distance of nearly four miles before the Indians were struck. They were completely surprised and sleeping in absolute security in their wickiups, with only a buck and a squaw as lookouts on a bluff above the *rancheria*. They were playing cards by a small fire and were both clubbed to death before they could give the alarm. The Papagoes attacked them in their wickiups with clubs and guns, and all who escaped them took to the bluffs and were received and dispatched by the other wing, which occupied a position above them. The attack was so swift and fierce that within a half hour the whole work was ended and not an adult Indians left to tell the tale. Some twenty-eight or thirty small papooses were spared and brought to Tucson as captives. Not a single man of our command was hurt to mar the full measure of our triumph. At eight o'clock on the bright morning of April 30th, 1871, our tired troops were resting on the San Pedro, a few miles above the post, in the full satisfaction of a work well done.

Here, also, might your historian lay down his pen and rest, but believing that in order to fully vindicate those who were aid-and-abettors, he craves your indulgence whilst he gives a brief summary of the causes which drove our people to such extreme measures, and the happy effects resulting therefrom.

Through the greater part of the year 1870, and the first part of 1871, these Indians had held a carnival of murder and plunder in all our settlements, until our people were appalled and almost paralyzed. On the San Pedro, the bravest and best of its pioneers had fallen by the wayside, instance Henry Long, Alex McKenzie, Sam Brown, Simms, and many others well known to all of you. On the Santa Cruz, noble Wooster, his wife, Sanders, and an innumerable host sleep the sleep that knows no waking. On the Sonoita, the gallant Pennington, Jackson, Carroll, Rotherwell, and others were slain without a chance of defense, and our secretary, William J. Osborn, severely wounded. In the vicinity of Tucson, mail drivers and riders, and almost all others whom temerity or necessity caused to leave the protection of our adobe walls were pitilessly slaughtered. The array is truly appalling. Add to this the fact that the remaining settlers on the San Pedro, not knowing who the next victim would be, had at last resolved to abandon their crops in the fields and fly with their wives and little ones to Tucson for safety, and the picture is complete up to that glorious and memorable day of April 30th, 1871. Then swift punishment was dealt out to those red-handed butchers, and they were wiped from the face of the earth.

Behold now the happy result immediately following that episode. The farmers of the San Pedro returned with their wives and babies to gather their abandoned crops. On the Sonoita, Santa Cruz, and all other settlements of southern Arizona, new life springs up, confidence is restored, and industry bounds forward with an impetus that has known no check in the whole fourteen years that have elapsed since that occurrence. In view of these facts, I call on all Arizonians to answer, on their consciences, can you call the killing of the Apaches at Camp Grant on the morning of April 30th, 1871, a massacre?

# CUSTER'S LAST BATTLE
## (1876)

## Captain Edward S. Godfrey

**Editors' Note:** Probably no event in the history of the West has been the subject of more analysis than the annihilation of General George Armstrong Custer and his entire command by Sioux Indians in the Battle of the Little Bighorn on June 25, 1876. When news of the Custer disaster reached the East, the nation was stunned. Custer was a Civil War hero and a notable Indian fighter. It had been believed that a contingent the size of Custer's was a match for anything the Indians could throw against it. While the Seventh Cavalry's total loss of 265 lives in the engagement was hardly comparable with the Civil War casualties of little more than a decade earlier, in which thousands of men were killed in a single battle, the U. S. Army had nonetheless been humiliated by men with names like Crazy Horse, Gall, Crow King and Sitting Bull, and white Americans were dismayed.

Then, as now, such a disaster required someone to blame. Custer himself received much criticism and has been characterized by some historians as rash and foolhardy. Others have pointed an accusing finger at Major Marcus Reno, charging that he was too timid and overcautious. Still others were of the opinion that bad intelligence was at fault -- the Sioux were more numerous and better armed than anyone had expected and may have outnumbered the soldiers in fighting men by as much as four to one. A court of inquiry convened in Chicago in 1879 to look into causes for the defeat. It exonerated Major Reno of any overt wrongdoing, but was otherwise inconclusive in its findings. Hence, the controversy has continued to this day.

When Captain Edward Godfrey published his "Custer's Last Battle" in 1892 in *Century Magazine,* it was hailed as *the* authoritative account. For Godfrey was at the time of the battle a Lieutenant in charge of troop "K" attached to Captain Benteen's battalion on Custer's flank and fought the same encampment of Sioux that Custer did. Godfrey was fighting for his life just over the ridge from where Custer and his men were losing theirs; no one survived from Custer's battalion to tell the story of the Last Stand and Godfrey's narrative is as near as we come to an eye-witness account by a soldier. Thus Godfrey's evenhanded and much praised recollection was, and is, regarded as must reading for anyone interested in Custer and the Battle of the Little Bighorn.

Godfrey tells us more than his version of the battle itself. Events leading up to the U. S. Government's campaign against the Sioux are described along with the role of some key personalities, Indian as well as White. The intricacies of cavalry life are detailed. Godfrey not only carefully reconstructs the events leading up to Custer's demise, he vividly tells us what it was like to be a horse soldier that hot June afternoon on the Little Bighorn River in Montana.

~ ~ ~ ~ ~

**There were a number of Sioux Indians** who never went to an agency except to visit friends and relatives. They camped in and roamed about the Buffalo Country. Their camp was the rendezvous for the agency Indians when they went out for their annual hunts for meat and robes. They were known as the "Hostiles" and comprised representatives from all the different tribes of the Sioux nation. Many of them were renegade outlaws from the agencies. In their visits to the agencies they were usually arrogant and fomenters of discord. Depredations had been made upon the commerce to the Black Hills, and a number of lives taken by them or by others, for which they were blamed. The authorities at Washington had determined to compel these Indians to reside at the agencies -- hence the Sioux War. Sitting Bull, an Uncpapa Sioux Indian, was the chief of the hostile camp; he had about sixty lodges of followers on whom he could at all times depend. He was the host of the Hostiles, and as such received and entertained their visitors. These vistors gave him many presents, and he was thus enabled to make many presents in return. All visitors paid tribute to him, so he gave liberally to the most influential, the chiefs; i.e., he "put it where it would do the most good." In this way he became known as the chief of the hostile Indian camp, and the camp was generally known as "Sitting Bull's camp." Sitting Bull was a heavy-set, muscular man, about five feet eight inches in stature, and at the time of the battle of the Little Big Horn was forty-two years of age. He was the autocrat of the camp -- chiefly because he was the host. In council his views had great weight, because he was known as a great medicine man. He was a chief, but not a warrior chief. In the war councils he had a voice and vote the same as any other chief. A short time previous to the battle he had "made medicine," had predicted that the soldiers would attack them and that the soldiers would all be killed. He took no active part in the battle, but as was his custom in time of danger, remained in the village "making medicine." Personally he was regarded as a great coward and a very great liar, "a man with a big head and a little heart."

Major James McLaughlin, United States Indian Agent, stationed at the Devil's Lake Agency, Dakota, from 1870 to 1881, and at Standing Rock Agency, Dakota, from 1881 to the present time, has made it a point to get estimates of the number of Indians at the hostile camp at the time of the battle. In his opinion, and all who know him will accept it with confidence, about one-third of the whole Sioux nation, including the northern Cheyennes and Arapahoes, were present at the battle; he estimated the number present as between twelve and fifteen thousand;

that one out of four is a low estimate in determining the number of warriors present; every male over fourteen years of age may be considered a warrior in a general fight such as was the battle of the Little Big Horn; also, considering the extra hazards of the hunt and expected battle, fewer squaws would accompany the recruits from the agencies. The minimum strength of their fighting men may then be put down as between twenty-five hundred and three thousand. Information was despatched from General Sheridan that from one agency alone about eighteen hundred lodges had set out to join the hostile camp; but that information did not reach General Terry until several days after the battle. The principal warrior chiefs of the hostile Indians were: "Gall," "Crow King," and "Black Moon," Uncpapa Sioux; "Low Dog," "Crazy Horse," and "Big Road," Ogallala Sioux; "Spotted Eagle," Sans-Arc Sioux; "Hump" of the Minneconjous; and "White Bull" and "Little Horse," of the Cheyennes. To these belong the chief honors of conducting the battle, of whom, however, "Gall," "Crow King," and "Crazy Horse" were the ruling spirits.

On the 16th of April, 1876, at McComb City, Missouri, I received orders to report my troop ("K," 7th Cavalry) to the Commanding General of the Department of Dakota, at St. Paul, Minnesota. At the latter place about twenty-five recruits fresh from civil life joined the troop, and we were ordered to proceed to Fort Abraham Lincoln, Dakota, where the Yellowstone Expedition was being organized. This expedition consisted of the 7th United States Cavalry, commanded by General George A. Custer, 28 officers and about 700 men; two companies of the 17th United States Infantry, and one company of the 6th United States Infantry, 8 officers and 135 men; one platoon of Gatling guns, 2 officers and 32 men (of the 20th United States Infantry); and 40 "Ree" Scouts. The expeditionary forces were commanded by Brigadier-General Alfred H. Terry, the Department Commander, who with his staff arrived several days prior to our departure.

On the 17th day of May, at 5 A.M., the "general" [signal to take down tents and break camp] was sounded, the wagons were packed and sent to the Quartermaster, and by six o'clock the wagon-train was on the road escorted by the infantry. By seven o'clock the 7th Cavalry was marching in column of platoon around the parade-ground of Fort Lincoln, headed by the band playing "Garry Owen," the Seventh's battle tune, first used when the regiment charged at the battle of Washita. The column was halted and dismounted just outside the garrison. The officers and married men were permitted to leave the ranks to say "good-bye" to their families. General Terry, knowing the anxiety of the ladies, had assented to, or ordered, this demonstration, in order to allay their fears and satisfy them, by the formidable appearance we made, that we were able to cope with any enemy that we might expect to meet. Not many came out to witness the pageant, but many tear-filled eyes looked from the windows.

During this halt the wagon-train was assembled on the plateau west of the post and formed in column of fours. When it started off the "assembly" was sounded, and the regiment marched away, the band playing "The Girl I Left Behind Me."

The 7th Cavalry was divided into two columns, designated right and left wings, commanded by Major Marcus A. Reno and Captain F. W. Benteen. Each wing was subdivided into two battalions of three troops each.

Nothing of special interest occurred until the 27th of May, when we came to the Bad Lands of the Little Missouri River. On the 30th General Custer was sent with four troops to make a scout up the Little Missouri, for about twenty miles. He returned the same day, without having discovered any recent "Indian signs." On the 31st we crossed the Little Missouri without difficulty. On the 1st and 2nd of June we were obliged to remain in camp on account of a snow-storm.

We remained in camp on the Powder River for three days. General Terry went to the Yellowstone to communicate with the supply steamer *Far West*, which was at the mouth of the Powder River. He also went up the Yellowstone to communicate with General Gibbon's command, known as the "Montana Column," composed of four troops of the 2nd Cavalry and several companies of the 7th Infantry. Before General Terry left it was given out that the 7th Cavalry would be sent to scout up the Powder River, while the wagon-train, escorted by the infantry, would be sent to establish a supply camp at the mouth of the Powder.

General Terry having returned, orders were issued on the 10th for the right wing, six troops, under Major Reno, to make a scout up the Powder, provided with twelve days' rations.

The left wing was ordered to turn over all forage and rations; also the pack-mules, except four to each troop. Major Reno left at 3 p.m., and the next day the rest of the command marched to the mouth of the Powder. My troop was rear-guard, and at times we were over three miles in rear of the wagon-train waiting on the packers, for we had taken this opportunity to give them practical instruction.

Up to this time we had not seen an Indian, nor any recent signs of them, except one small trail of perhaps a dozen tepees, evidently of a party of agency Indians on their way to join the hostile camps. The buffalo had all gone west; other game was scarce and wild. The indications were that the Indians were west of the Powder, and information from General Gibbon placed them south of the Yellowstone. Some of the officers of the right wing before they left expressed their belief that we would not find any Indians, and were sanguine that we would all get home by the middle of August.

Major Reno was ordered to scout to the forks of the Powder, then across the Mizpah Creek, follow it down to near its confluence with the Powder; then cross over to Pumpkin Creek, follow it down to the Tongue River, scout up that stream, and then rejoin the regiment at the mouth of the Tongue by the time his supplies were exhausted; unless, in the mean time, he should make some discovery that made it necessary to return sooner to make preparations for pursuit. A supply depot was established at the mouth of the Powder, guarded by the infantry, at which the wagon train was left.

General Terry, with his staff and some supplies, took passage on the supply steamer *Far West*, and went up to the mouth of the Tongue. General Custer, with the left wing, marched to the mouth of the Tongue, where we remained until the 19th waiting tidings from Reno's scout. The grounds where we camped had been occupied by the Indians the previous winter. (Miles City, Montana, was first built on the site of this camp.) The rude shelters for their ponies, built of driftwood, were still standing and furnished fuel for our camp-fires. A number of their dead, placed upon scaffolds, or tied to the branches of trees, were disturbed and robbed of their trinkets. Several persons rode about exhibiting trinkets with as much gusto as if they were trophies of their valor, and showed no more concern for their desecration than if they had won them at a raffle. Ten days later I saw the bodies of these same persons dead, naked, and mutilated.

On the 19th of June tidings came from Reno that he had found a large trail that led up the Rosebud River. The particulars were not generally known. The camp was full of rumors; credulity was raised to the highest pitch, and we were filled with anxiety and curiosity until we reached Reno's command, and learned the details of their discoveries. They had found a large trail on the Tongue River, and had followed it up the Rosebud about forty miles. The number of lodges in the deserted villages was estimated by the number of camp-fires remaining to be about three hundred and fifty. The indications were that the trail was about three weeks old. No Indians had been seen, nor any recent signs. It is not probable that Reno's movements were known to the Indians, for on the very day Reno reached his farthest point up the Rosebud, the battle of the Rosebud, between General Crook's forces and the Indians, was fought. The two commands were then not more than forty miles apart, but neither knew or even suspected the proximity of the other.

We reached the mouth of the Rosebud about noon on the 21st, and began preparations for the march.

Generals Terry, Gibbon, and Custer had a conference on board the steamer *Far West*. It was decided that the 7th Cavalry, under General Custer, should follow the trail discovered by Reno.

At twelve o'clock, noon, on the 22nd of June, the "Forward" was sounded, and the regiment marched out of camp in column of fours, each troop followed by its pack-mules. Generals Terry, Gibbon, and Custer stationed themselves near our line of march and reviewed the regiment. General Terry had a pleasant word for each officer as he returned the salute. Our pack-trains proved troublesome at the start, as the cargoes began falling off before we got out of camp, and during all that day the mules straggled badly. After that day, however, they were placed under the charge of an officer, who was directed to report at the end of each day's march the order of merit of the efficiency of the troop packers. Doubtless General Custer had some ulterior design in this. It is quite probable that if he had had occasion to detach troops requiring rapid marching, he would have selected those troops whose packers had the best records. At all events the efficiency was much increased, and after we struck the Indian trail the pack-trains kept well closed.

We went into camp about 4 p.m., having marched twelve miles. About sunset "officers' call" was sounded, and we assembled at General Custer's bivouac and squatted in groups about the General's bed. It was not a cheerful assemblage; everybody seemed to be in a serious mood, and the little conversation carried on, before all had arrived, was in undertones. When all had assembled the General said that until further orders trumpet-calls would not be sounded except in an emergency; the marches would begin at 5 a.m. sharp; the troop commanders were all experienced officers, and knew well enough what to do, and when to do what was necessary for their troops; there were two things that would be regulated from his headquarters, *i.e.*, when to move out of and when to go into camp. All other details, such as reveille, stables, watering, halting, grazing, etc., on the march would be left to the judgment and discretion of the troop commanders; they were to keep within supporting distance of each other, not to get ahead of scouts, or very far to the rear of the column. He took particular pains to impress upon the officers his reliance upon their judgment, discretion, and loyalty. He thought, judging from the number of lodge-fires reported by Reno, that we might meet at least a thousand warriors; there might be enough young men from the agencies, visiting their hostile friends, to make a total of fifteen hundred. He had consulted the reports of the Commissioner of Indian Affairs as to the probable number of "Hostiles" (those who had persistently refused to live or enroll themselves at the Indian agencies), and he was confident, if any reliance was to be placed upon those reports, that there would not be an opposing force of more than fifteen hundred. General Terry had offered him the additional force of the battalion of the 2nd Cavalry, but he had declined it because he felt sure that the 7th Cavalry could whip any force that would be able to combine against him; that if the regiment could not, no other regiment in the service could; if they could whip the regiment, they would be able to defeat a much larger force, or, in other words, the reinforcement of this battalion could not save us from defeat. With the regiment acting alone there would be harmony, but another organization would be sure to cause jealousy. He had declined the offer of the Gatling guns for the reason that they might hamper our movements or march at a critical moment, because of the difficult nature of the country through which we would march. The marches would be from twenty-five to thirty miles a day. Troop officers were cautioned to husband their rations and the strength of their mules and horses, as we might be out for a great deal longer time than that for which we were rationed, as he intended to follow the trail until we could get the Indians, even if it took us to the Indian agencies on the Missouri River or in Nebraska. All officers were requested to make to him, then or at any time, any suggestions they thought fit.

This "talk" of his, as we called it, was considered at the time as something extraordinary for General Custer, for it was not his habit to unbosom himself to his officers. In it he showed a lack of self-confidence, a reliance on somebody else; there was an indefinable something that was not Custer. His manner and tone, usually brusque and aggressive, or somewhat rasping, was on this occasion conciliating and subdued. There was something akin to an appeal, as if depressed, that made a deep impression on all present. We compared watches to get the official time, and separated to attend to our various duties. Lieutenants McIntosh, Wallace, and myself walked to our bivouac, for some distance in silence, when Wallace remarked: "Godfrey, I believe General Custer is going to be killed." "Why, Wallace," I replied, "what makes you think so?" "Because," said he, "I have never heard Custer talk in that way before."

I went to my troop and gave orders what time the "silent" reveille should be and as to other details for the morning preparations; also the following directions in case of a night attack: the stable guard, packers, and cooks were to go out at once to the horses and mules to quiet and guard them; the other men were to go at once to a designated rendezvous and await orders; no man should fire a shot until he received orders from an officer to do so. When they retired for the night they should put their arms and equipments where they could get them without leaving their beds. I then went through the herd to satisfy myself as to the security of the animals. During the performance of this duty I came to the bivouac of the Indian scouts. "Mitch" Bouyer, the half-breed interpreter, "Bloody Knife," the chief of the Ree scouts, "Half-Yellow-Face," the chief of the Crow scouts, and others were having a "talk." I observed them for a few minutes, when Bouyer turned toward me, apparently at the suggestion of "Half-Yellow-Face," and said, "Have you ever fought against these Sioux?" "Yes," I replied. Then he asked, "Well, how many do you expect fo find?" I answered, "It is said we may find between one thousand and fifteen hundred." "Well, do you think we can whip that many?" "Oh, yes, I guess so." After he interpreted our conversation, he said to me with a good deal of emphasis, "Well, I can tell you we are going to have a ---- big fight."

At five o'clock, sharp, on the morning of the 23rd, General Custer mounted and started up the Rosebud, followed by two sergeants, one carrying the regimental standard and the other his personal or headquarters flag, the same kind of flag as used while commanding his cavalry division during the Rebellion. This was the signal for the command to mount and take up the march. Eight miles out we came to the first of the Indian camping-places. It certainly indicated a large village and numerous population. There were a great many "wicki-ups" (bushes stuck in the ground with the tops drawn together over which they placed canvas or blankets). These we supposed at the time were for the dogs, but subsequent events developed the fact that they were the temporary shelters of the transients from the agencies. During the day we passed through three of these camping-places and made halts at each one. Everybody was busy studying the age of pony droppings and tracks and lodge trails, and endeavoring to determine the number of lodges. These points were the all-absorbing topics of conversation. We went into camp about five o'clock, having marched about thirty-three miles.

June 24th we passed a great many camping-places, all appearing to be of nearly the same strength. One would naturally suppose these were the successive camping-places of the same village, when in fact they were the continuous camps of the several bands. The fact that they appeared to be of nearly the same age, that is, having been made at the same time, did not impress us then. We passed through one much larger than any of the others. The grass for a considerable distance around it had been cropped close, indicating that large herds had been grazed there. The frame of a large "sun-dance" lodge was standing, and in it we found the scalp of a white man, probably one of General Gibbon's command who had been killed some weeks previously. It was whilst here that the Indians from the agencies had joined the Hostiles' camp. The command halted here and "officers' call" was sounded. Upon assembling we were informed that our Crow scouts, who had been very active and efficient, had discovered fresh signs, the tracks of three or four ponies and of one Indian on foot. At this time a stiff southerly breeze was blowing; as we were about to separate, the General's headquarters flag was blown down, falling toward our rear. Being near the flag, I picked it up and stuck the staff in the ground, but it fell again to the rear. I then bored the staff into the ground where it would have the support of a sage-bush. This circumstance made no impression on me at the time, but after the battle an officer asked me if I remembered the incident; he had observed it, and regarded the fact of its falling to the rear as a bad omen, and felt sure we would suffer a defeat.

The march during the day was tedious. We made many long halts so as not to get ahead of the scouts, who seemed to be doing their work thoroughly, giving special attention to the right, toward Tulloch's Creek, the valley of which was in general view from the divide. Once or twice signal smokes were reported in that direction. The weather was dry and had been for some time, consequently the trail was very dusty. The troops were required to march on separate trails so that the dust clouds would not rise so high. The valley was heavily marked with lodge-pole trails and pony tracks, showing that immense herds of ponies had been driven over it. About sundown we went into camp under the cover of a bluff, so as to hide the command as much as possible. We had marched about twenty-eight miles. The fires were ordered to be put out as soon as supper was over, and we were to be in readiness to march again at 11:30 p.m. Lieutenant Hare and myself lay down about 9:30 to take a nap; when comfortably fixed we heard some one say, "He's over there by that tree." As that described our locality pretty well, I called out to know what was wanted, and the reply came: "The General's compliments and wants to see all the officers at headquarters immediately." So we gave up our much-needed rest and groped our way through horse herds, over sleeping men, and through thickets of bushes trying to find headquarters. No one could tell us, and as all fires and lights were out we could not keep our bearings. We finally espied a solitary candle-light, toward which we traveled, and found most of the officers assembled at the General's bivouac. The General said that the trail led over the divide to the Little Big Horn; the march would be taken up at once, as he was anxious to get as near the divide as possible before daylight, where the command would be concealed during the day, and give ample time for the country to be studied, to locate the village and to make plans for the attack on the 26th. We then returned to our troops, except Lieutenant Hare, who was put on duty with the scouts. Because of the dust it was impossible to see any distance, and the rattle of equipments and clattering of the horses' feet made it difficult to hear distinctly beyond our immediate surroundings. We could not see the trail, and we could only follow it by keeping in the dust cloud. The night was very calm, but occasionally a slight breeze would waft the cloud and disconcert our bearings; then we were obliged to halt to catch a sound from those in advance, sometimes whistling or hallooing, and getting a response we would start forward again. Finally troopers were put ahead, away from the noise of our column, and where they could hear the noise of those in front. A little after 2 a.m., June 25, the command was halted to await further tidings from the scouts; we had marched about ten miles. Part of the command unsaddled to rest the horses. After daylight some coffee was made, but it was almost impossible to drink it; the water was so alkaline that the horses refused to drink it. Some time before eight o'clock, General

Custer rode bareback to the several troops and gave orders to be ready to march at eight o'clock, and gave information that scouts had discovered the locality of the Indian villages or camps in the valley of the Little Big Horn, about twelve or fifteen miles beyond the divide. Just before setting out on the march I went to where General Custer's bivouac was. The General, "Bloody Knife," and several Ree scouts and a half-breed interpreter were squatted in a circle having a "talk," after the Indian fashion. The General wore a serious expression and was apparently abstracted. The scouts were doing the talking, and seemed nervous and disturbed. Finally "Bloody Knife" made a remark that recalled the General from his reverie, and he asked in his usual quick, brusque manner, "What's that he says?" The interpreter replied, "He said we'll find enough Sioux to keep us fighting two or three days." The General smiled and remarked, "I guess we'll get through with them in one day."

We started promptly at eight o'clock and marched uninterruptedly until 10:30 a.m., when we halted in a ravine and were ordered to preserve quiet, keep concealed, and not do anything that would be likely to reveal our presence to the enemy; we had marched about ten miles.

It is a rare occurrence in Indian warfare that gives a commander the opportunity to reconnoiter the enemy's position in daylight. This is particularly true if the Indians have a knowledge of the presence of troops in the country. When following an Indian trail the "signs" indicate the length of time elapsed since the presence of Indians. When the "signs" indicate a "hot trail," i.e., near approach, the commander judges his distance and by a forced march, usually in the night-time, tries to reach the Indian village at night and make his disposition for a surprise attack at daylight. At all events his attack must be made with celerity, and generally without other knowledge of the numbers of the opposing force than that discovered or conjectured while following the trail. The dispositions for the attack may be said to be "made in the dark," and successful surprise to depend upon luck. If the advance to the attack be made in daylight it is next to impossible that a near approach can be made without discovery. In all our previous experiences, when the immediate presence of the troops was once known to them, the warriors swarmed to the attack, and resorted to all kinds of ruses to mislead the troops, to delay the advance toward their camp or village, while the squaws and children secured what personal effects they could, drove off the pony herd, and by flight put themselves beyond danger, and then scattering made successful pursuit next to impossible. In civilized warfare the hostile forces may confront each other for hours, days, or weeks, and the battle may be conducted with a tolerable knowledge of the numbers, position, etc., of each other. A full knowledge of the immediate presence of the enemy does not imply immediate attack. In Indian warfare the rule is "touch and go." These remarks are made because the firebrand nature of Indian warfare is not generally understood. In meditating upon the preliminaries of an Indian battle, old soldiers who have participated only in the battles of the Rebellion are apt to draw upon their own experiences for comparison, when there is no comparison.

The Little Big Horn River, or the "Greasy Grass" as it is known to the Indians, is a rapid mountain stream, from twenty to forty yards wide, with pebbled bottom, but abrupt, soft banks. The water at the ordinary stage is from two to five feet in depth, depending upon the width of the channel. The general direction of its course is northeasterly down to the Little Big Horn battle-field, where it trends northwesterly to its confluence with the Big Horn River. The other topographical features of the country which concerns us in this narrative may be briefly described as follows: Between the Little Big Horn and Big Horn Rivers is a plateau of undulating prairie; between the Little Big Horn and the Rosebud are the Little Chetish or Wolf Mountains. By this it must not be misunderstood as a rocky upheaval chain or spur of mountains, but it is a rough, broken country of considerable elevation, of high precipitous hills and deep narrow gulches. The command had followed the trail up a branch of the Rosebud to within, say, a mile of the summit of these mountains, which form the "divide." Not many miles to our right was the divide between the Little Big Horn and Tulloch's Fork. The creek that drained the watershed to our right and front is now called "Sundance," or Benteen's, Creek. The trail, very tortuous, and sometimes dangerous, followed down the bed and valley of this creek, which at that time was dry for the greater part of its length. It was from the divide between the Little Big Horn and the Rosebud that the scouts had discovered the smoke rising above the village, and the pony herds grazing in the valley of the Little Big Horn, somewhere about twelve or fifteen miles away. It was to their point of view that General Custer had gone while the column was halted in the ravine. It was impossible for him to discover more of the enemy than had already been reported by the scouts. In consequence of the high bluffs which screened the village, it was not possible in following the trail to discover more. Nor was there a point of observation near the trail from which further discoveries could be made until the battle was at hand.

It was well known to the Indians that the troops were in the field, and a battle was fully expected by them; but the close proximity of our column was not known to them until the morning of the day of the battle. Several young men had left the hostile camp on that morning to go to one of the agencies in Nebraska. They saw the dust made by the column of troops; some of their number returned to the village and gave warning that the troops were coming, so the attack was not a surprise. For two or three days their camp had been pitched on the site where they were attacked. The place was not selected with the view of making that the battle-field of the campaign, but whoever was in the van on their march thought it a good place to camp, put up his tepee, and the others as they arrived followed his example. It is customary among the Indians to camp by bands. The bands usually camp some distance apart, and Indians of the number then together would occupy a territory of several miles along the river valley, and not necessarily within supporting distance of each other. But in view of the possible fulfilment of Sitting Bull's prophecy the village had massed.

Our officers had generally collected in groups and discussed the situation. Some sought solitude and sleep, or meditation. The Ree scouts, who had not been very active for the past day or two, were together and their "medicine man" was anointing them and invoking the Great Spirit to protect them from the Sioux. They seemed to have become satisfied that we were going to find more Sioux that we could well take care of. Captain Yates's troop had lost one of its packs of hard bread during the night march from our last halting-place on the 24th. He had sent a detail back on the trail to recover it. Captain Keogh came to where a group of officers were, and said this detail had returned and reported that when near the pack they discovered an Indian opening one of the boxes of hard bread with his tomahawk, and that as soon as the Indian saw the soldiers he galloped away to the hills out of range and then moved along leisurely. This information was taken to the General at once by his brother, Colonel Tom Custer. The General came back and had "officers' call" sounded. He recounted Captain Keogh's report, and also said that the scouts had seen several Indians moving along the ridge overlooking the valley through which we had marched, as if observing our movements; he thought the Indians must have seen the dust made by the command. At all events our presence had been discovered and further concealment was unnecessary; that we would march at once to attack the village; that he had not intended to make the attack until the next morning, the 26th, but our discovery made it imperative to act at once, as delay would allow the village to scatter and escape. Troop commanders were ordered to make a detail of one non-commissioned officer and six men to accompany the pack; to inspect their troops and report as soon as they were ready to march; that the troops would take their places in the column of march in the order in which reports of readiness were received, and that the last one to report would escort the pack-train.

The inspections were quickly made and the column was soon en route. We crossed the dividing ridge between the Rosebud and Little Big Horn valleys a little before noon. Shortly afterward the regiment was divided into battalions. The advance battalion, under Major Reno, consisted of troop "M," Captain French; troop "A," Captain Moylan and Lieutenant De Rudio; troop "G," Lieutenants McIntosh and Wallace;

the Indian scouts under Lieutenant Varnum and Hare and the interpreter Girard; Lieutenant Hodgson was Acting Adjutant and Doctors De Wolf and Porter were the medical officers. The battalion under General Custer was composed of troop "I," Captain Keogh and Lieutenant Porter; troop "F," Captain Yates and Lieutenant Reily; troop "C," Captain Custer and Lieutenant Harrington; troop "E," Lieutenants Smith and Sturgis; troop "L," Lieutenants Calhoun and Crittenden; Lieutenant Cook was the Adjutant, and Dr. G. E. Lord was medical officer. The battalion under Captain Benteen consisted of troop "H," Captain Benteen and Lieutenant Gibson; troop "D," Captain Weir and Lieutenant Edgerly, and troop "K," Lieutenant Godfrey. The pack-train, Lieutenant Mathey in charge, was under the escort of troop "B," Captain McDougall.

Major Reno's battalion marched down a valley that developed into the small tributary to the Little Big Horn, now called "Sun-dance," or Benteen's, Creek. The Indian trail followed the meanderings of this valley. Custer's column followed Reno's closely, and the pack-train followed their trail. Benteen's battalion was ordered to the left and front, to a line of high bluffs about three or four miles distant. Benteen was ordered if he saw anything to send word to Custer, but to pitch into anything he came across; if, when he arrived at the high bluffs, he could not see any enemy, he should continue his march to the next line of bluffs and so on, until he could see the Little Big Horn Valley. He marched over a succession of rough, steep hills and deep valleys. The view from the point where the regiment was organized into battalions did not discover the difficult nature of the country, but as we advanced farther it became more and more difficult and more forbidding. Lieutenant Gibson was sent some distance in advance but saw no enemy, and so signaled the result of his reconnaissance to Benteen. The obstacles threw the battalion by degrees to the right until we came in sight of and not more than a mile from the trail. Many of our horses were greatly jaded by the climbing and descending, some getting far to the rear of the column. Benteen very wisely determined to follow the trail of the rest of the command, and we got into it just in advance of the pack-train. During this march on the left we could see occasionally the battalion under Custer, distinguished by the troop mounted on gray horses, marching at a rapid gait. Two or three times we heard loud cheering and also some few shots, but the occasion of these demonstrations is not known.

Some time after getting on the trail we came to a water-hole, or morass, at which a stream of running water had its source. Benteen halted the battalion. While watering we heard some firing in advance, and Weir became a little impatient at the delay of watering and started off with his troop, taking the advance, whereas his place in column was second. The rest of the battalion moved out very soon afterward and soon caught up with him. Just as we were leaving the water-hole the pack-train was arriving, and the poor thirsty mules plunged into the morass in spite of the efforts of the packers to prevent them, for they had not had water since the previous evening. We passed a burning tepee, fired presumably by our scouts, in which was the body of a warrior who had been killed in the battle with Crook's troops on the Rosebud on the 17th of June.

## The Fighting Begins

The battalions under Reno and Custer did not meet any Indians until Reno arrived at the burning tepee; here a few were seen. These Indians did not act as if surprised by the appearance of troops; they made no effort to delay the column, but simply kept far enough in advance to invite pursuit. Reno's command and the scouts followed them closely, until he received orders "to move forward at as rapid a gait as he thought prudent, and charge the village afterward, and the whole outfit would support him." The order was received when Reno was not very far from the Little Big Horn River. His battalion moved at a trot to the river, where Reno delayed about ten or fifteen minutes watering the horses and reforming the column on the left bank of the stream. Reno now sent word to Custer that he had everything in front of him and that the enemy was strong. Custer had moved off to the right, being separated from Reno by a line of high bluffs and the river. Reno moved forward in column of fours about half a mile, then formed the battalion in line of battle across the valley with the scouts on the left; after advancing about a mile further he deployed the battalion as skirmishers. In the mean time the Hostiles, continually reinforced, fell back, firing occasionally, but made no decided effort to check Reno's advance. The horses of two men became unmanageable and carried them into the Indian camp. The Indians now developed great force, opened a brisk fire, mounted, and made a dash toward the foot-hills on the left flank where the Ree scouts were. The scouts ignominiously fled, most of them abandoning the field altogether.

Reno, not seeing the "whole outfit" within supporting distance, did not obey his orders to charge the village, but dismounted his command to fight on foot. The movements of the Indians around the left flank and the flight of the scouts caused the left to fall back until the command was on the defensive in the timber and covered by the bank of the old river-bed. Reno's loss thus far was one wounded. The position was a strong one, well protected in front by the bank and fringe of timber, somewhat open in the rear, but sheltered by timber in the bottom. Those present differ in their estimates of the length of time the command remained in the bottom after they were attacked in force.

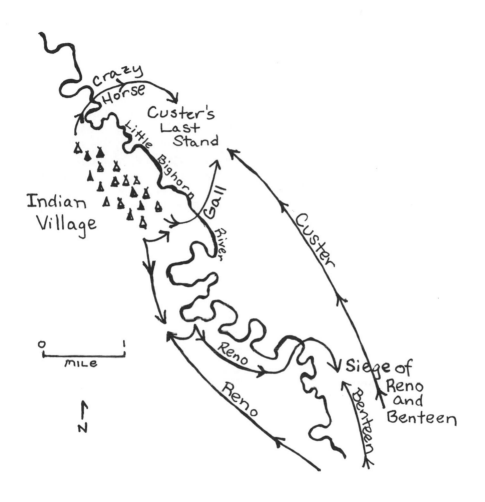

Little Bighorn Battlefield, July, 1876

Some say "a few minutes"; others, "about an hour." While Reno remained there his casualties were few. The Hostiles had him nearly surrounded, and there was some firing from the rear of the position by Indians on the opposite bank of the river. One man was killed close to where Reno was, and directly afterward Reno gave orders to those near him to "mount and get to the bluffs." This order was not generally heard or communicated; while those who did hear it were preparing to execute it, he countermanded the order, but soon afterward he repeated the same order, "to mount and get to the bluffs," and again it was not generally understood. Individuals, observing the preparations of those on the left, near Reno, informed their troop commanders, who then gave orders to mount. Owing to the noise of the firing and to the absorbed attention they were giving to the enemy, many did not know of the order until too late to accompany the command. Some remained concealed until the Indians left and then came out. Four others remained until night and then escaped. Reno's command left the bottom by troop organizations in column. Reno was with the foremost in this retreat or "charge," as he termed it in his report, and after he had exhausted the shots of his revolvers he threw them away. The hostile strength pushed Reno's retreat to the left, so he could not get to the ford where he had entered the valley, but they were fortunate in striking the river at a fordable place; a pony-trail led up a funnel-shaped ravine into the bluffs. Here the command got jammed and lost all semblance of organization. The Indians fired into them, but not very effectively. There does not appear to have been any resistance, certainly no organized resistance, during this retreat. On the right and left of the ravine into which the pony-path led were rough precipitous clay bluffs. It was surprising to see what steep inclines men and horses clambered up under the excitement of danger.

Lieutenant Donald McIntosh was killed soon after leaving the timber. Dr. DeWolf was killed while climbing one of the bluffs a short distance from the command. Lieutenant B. H. Hodgson's horse leaped from the bank into the river and fell dead; the lieutenant was wounded in the leg, probably by the same bullet that killed the horse. Hodgson called out, "For God's sake, don't abandon me"; he was assured that he would not be left behind. Hodgson then took hold of a comrade's stirrup-strap and was taken across the stream, but soon after was shot and killed. Hodgson, some days before the battle, had said that if he was dismounted in battle or wounded, he intended to take hold of somebody's stirrup to assist himself from the field. During the retreat Private Dalvern, troop "F," had a hand-to-hand conflict with an Indian; his horse was killed; he then shot the Indian, caught the Indian's pony, and rode to the command.

Reno's casualties thus far were three officers, including Dr. J. M. DeWolf, and twenty-nine enlisted men and scouts killed; seven enlisted men wounded; and one officer, one interpreter, and fourteen soldiers and scouts missing. Nearly all the casualties occurred during the retreat and after leaving the timber. The Ree scouts continued their flight until they reached the supply camp at the mouth of the Powder, on the 27th. The Crow scouts remained with the command.

We will now go back to Benteen's battalion. Not long after leaving the water-hole a sergeant met him with an order from Custer to the commanding officer of the pack-train to hurry it up. The sergeant was sent back to the train with the message; as he passed the column he said to the men, "We've got 'em, boys." From this and other remarks we inferred that Custer had attacked and captured the village.

Shortly afterward we were met by a trumpeter bearing this message signed by Colonel Cook, Adjutant: "Benteen, come on. Big village. Be quick. Bring packs," with the postscript, "Bring packs." The column had been marching at a trot and walk, according as the ground was smooth or broken. We now heard firing, first straggling shots, and as we advanced the engagement became more and more pronounced and appeared to be coming toward us. The column took the gallop with pistols drawn, expecting to meet the enemy which we thought Custer was driving before him in his effort to communicate with the pack-train, never suspecting that our force had been defeated. We were forming in line to meet our supposed enemy, when we came in full view of the valley of the Little Big Horn. The valley was full of horsemen riding to and fro in clouds of dust and smoke, for the grass had been fired by the Indians to drive the troops out and cover their own movements. On the bluffs to our right we saw a body of troops and that they were engaged. But an engagement appeared to be going on in the valley too. Owing to the distance, smoke, and dust, it was impossible to distinguish if those in the valley were friends or foes. There was a short time of uncertainty as to the direction in which we should go, but some Crow scouts came by, driving a small herd of ponies, one of whom said "Soldiers," and motioned for the command to go to the right. Following his directions, we soon joined Reno's battalion, which was still firing. Reno had lost his hat and had a handkerchief tied about his head, and appeared to be very much excited.

Benteen's battalion was ordered to dismount and deploy as skirmishers on the edge of the bluffs overlooking the valley. Very soon after this the Indians withdrew from the attack. Lieutenant Hare came to where I was standing and, grasping my hand heartily, said with a good deal of emphasis: "We've had a big fight in the bottom, got whipped, and I am ---- glad to see you." I was satisfied that he meant what he said, for I had already suspected that something was wrong, but was not quite prepared for such startling information. Benteen's battalion was ordered to divide its ammunition with Reno's men, who had aparently expended nearly all in their personal possession. It has often been a matter of doubt whether this was fact, or the effect of imagination. It seems most improbable, in view of their active movements and the short time the command was firing, that the "most of the men" should have expended one hundred and fifty rounds of ammunition per man.

While waiting for the ammunition pack-mules, Major Reno concluded to make an effort to recover and bury the body of Lieutenant Hodgson. At the same time we loaded up a few men with canteens to get water for the command; they were to accompany the rescuing party. The effort was futile; the party was ordered back after being fired upon by some Indians who doubtless were scalping the dead near the foot of the bluffs.

A number of officers collected on the edge of the bluff overlooking the valley and were discussing the situation; among our number was Captain Moylan, a veteran soldier, and a good one too, watching intently the scene below. Moylan remarked, quite emphatically: "Gentlemen, in my opinion General Custer has made the biggest mistake of his life, by not taking the whole regiment in at once in the first attack." At this time there were a large number of horsemen, Indians, in the valley. Suddenly they all started down the valley, and in a few minutes scarcely a horseman was to be seen. Heavy firing was heard down the river. During this time the questions were being asked: "What's the matter with Custer, that he don't send word what we shall do?" "Wonder what we are staying here for?" etc., thus showing some uneasiness; but still no one seemed to show great anxiety, nor do I know that any one felt any serious apprehension but that Custer could and would take care of himself. Some of Reno's men had seen a party of Custer's command, including Custer himself, on the bluffs about the time the Indians began to develop in Reno's front. This party was heard to cheer, and seen to wave their hats as if to give encouragement, and then they disappeared behind the hills or escaped further attention from those below. It was about the time of this incident that Trumpeter Martini left Cook with Custer's last orders to Benteen, viz.: "Benteen, come on. Big village. Be quick. Bring packs. Cook, Adjutant. P.S. Bring packs." The repetition in the order would seem to indicate that Cook was excited, flurried, or that he wanted to emphasize the necessity for escorting the packs. It is possible, yes probable, that from the high point Custer could then see nearly the whole camp and force of the Indians and realized that the chances were desperate; but it was too late to reunite his forces for the attack. Reno was already in the fight and his (Custer's) own battalion was separated from the attack by a distance of two and a half to three miles. He had no reason to think that Reno would not push his attack vigorously. The commander seldom goes into battle counting upon the failure of his lieutenant; if he did, he certainly would provide that such failure should not turn into disaster.

During a long time after the junction of Reno and Benteen we heard firing down the river in the direction of Custer's command. We were satisfied that Custer was fighting the Indians somewhere, and the conviction was expressed that "our command ought to be doing something or Custer would be after Reno with a sharp stick." We heard two distinct volleys which excited some surprise, and, if I mistake not, brought out the remark from some one that "Custer was giving it to them for all he was worth." I have but little doubt now that these volleys were fired by Custer's orders as signals of distress and to indicate where he was.

Captain Weir and Lieuteant Edgerly, after driving the Indians away from Reno's command, on their side, heard the firing, became impatient at the delay, and thought they would move down that way, if they should be permitted. Weir started to get this permission, but changed his mind and concluded to take a survey from the high bluffs first. Edgerly, seeing Weir going in the direction of the firing, supposed it was all right and started down the ravine with the troop. Weir, from the high point, saw the Indians in large numbers start for Edgerly, and signaled for him to change his direction, and Edgerly went over to the high point, where they remained, not seriously molested, until the remainder of the troops marched down there; the Indians were seen by them to ride about what after proved to be Custer's battle-field, shooting into the bodies of the dead men.

McDougall came up with the pack-train and reported the firing when he reported his arrival to Reno. I remember distinctly looking at my watch at twenty minutes past four, and made a note of it in my memorandum-book, and although I have never satisfactorily been able to recall what particular incident happened at that time, it was some important event before we started down the river. It is my impression, however, that it was the arrival of the pack-train. It was about this time that thirteen men and a scout named Herendeen rejoined the command; they had been missing since Reno's flight from the bottom; several of them were wounded. These men had lost their horses in the stampede from the bottom and had remained in the timber; when leaving the timber to rejoin, they were fired upon by five Indians, but they drove them away and were not again molested.

My recollection is that it was about half-past two when we joined Reno. About five o'clock the command moved down toward Custer's supposed whereabouts, intending to join him. The advance went as far as the high bluffs where the command was halted. Persons who have been on the plains and have seen stationary objects dancing before them, now in view and now obscured, or a weed on the top of a hill, projected against the sky, magnified to appear as a tree, will readily understand why our views would be unsatisfactory. We could see stationary groups of horsemen, and individual horsemen moving about; from their grouping and the manner in which they sat their horses we knew they were Indians. On the left of the valley a strange sight attracted our attention. Some one remarked that there had been a fire that scorched the leaves of the bushes, which caused the reddish-brown appearance, but this appearance was changeable; watching this intently for a short time with field-glasses, it was discovered that this strange sight was the immense pony-herds of the Indians.

Looking toward Custer's field, on a hill two miles away we saw a large assemblage. At first our command did not appear to attract their attention, although there was some commotion observable among those nearer to our position. We heard occasional shots, most of which seemed to be a great distance off, beyond the large groups on the hill. While watching this group the conclusion was arrived at that Custer had been repulsed, and the firing was the parting shots of the rear-guard. The firing ceased, the groups dispersed, clouds of dust arose from all parts of the field, and the horsemen converged toward our position. The command was now dismounted to fight on foot. Weir's and French's troops were posted on the high bluffs and to the front of them; my own troop along the crest of the bluffs next to the river; the rest of the command moved to the rear, as I supposed to occupy other points in the vicinity, to make this our defensive position. Busying myself with posting my men, giving direction about the use of ammunition, etc., I was a little startled by the remark that the command was out of sight. At this time Weir's and French's troops were being attacked. Orders were soon brought to me by Lieutenant Hare, Acting-Adjutant, to join the main command. I had gone some distance in the execution of this order when, looking back, I saw French's troop come tearing over the bluffs, and soon after Weir's troop followed in hot haste. Edgerly was near the top of the bluff trying to mount his frantic horse, and it did seem that he would not succeed, but he vaulted into his saddle and then joined the troop. The Indians almost immediately followed to the top of the bluff, and commenced firing into the retreating troops, killing one man, wounding others and several horses. They then started down the hillside in pursuit. I at once made up my mind that such a retreat and close pursuit would throw the whole command into confusion, and perhaps, prove disastrous. I dismounted my men to fight on foot, deploying as rapidly as possible without waiting for the formation laid down in tactics. Lieutenant Hare expressed his intention of staying with me, "Adjutant or no Adjutant." The led horses were sent to the main command. Our fire in a short time compelled the Indians to halt and take cover, but before this was accomplished, a second order came for me to fall back as quickly as possible to the main command. Having checked the pursuit we began our retreat, slowly at first, but kept up our firing. After proceeding some distance the men began to group together, and to move a little faster and faster, and our fire slackened. This was pretty good evidence that they were getting demoralized. The Indians were being heavily reinforced, and began to come from their cover, but kept up a heavy fire. I halted the line, made the men take their intervals, and again drove the Indians to cover; then once more began to retreat. The firing of the Indians was very heavy; the bullets struck the ground all about us; but the "ping-ping" of the bullets overhead seemed to have a more terrifying influence than the "swish-thud" of the bullets that struck the ground immediately about us. When we got to the ridge in front of Reno's position I observed some Indians making all haste to get possession of a hill to the right. I could not see the rest of the command, and I knew that that hill would command Reno's position. Supposing that my troop was to occupy the line we were then on, I ordered Hare to take ten men and hold the hill, but, just as he was moving off, an order came from Reno to get back as quickly as possible; so I recalled Hare and ordered the men to run to the lines. This movement was executed, strange to say, without a single casualty.

The Indians now took possession of all the surrounding high points, and opened a heavy fire. They had in the mean time sent a large force up the valley, and soon our position was entirely surrounded. It was now about seven o'clock.

Our position next the river was protected by the rough, rugged steep bluffs which were cut up by irregular deep ravines. From the crest of these bluffs the ground gently declined away from the river. On the north there was a short ridge, the ground sloping gently to the front and rear. This ridge, during the first day, was occupied by five troops. Directly in rear of the ridge was a small hill; in the ravine on the south of this hill our hospital was established, and the horses and pack-mules were secured. Across this ravine one troop, Moylan's, was posted, the packs and dead animals being utilized for breastworks. The high hill on the south was occupied by Benteen's troop. Everybody now lay down and spread himself out as thin as possible. After lying there a few minutes I was horrified to find myself wondering if a small sagebush, about as thick as my finger, would turn a bullet, so I got up and walked along the line, cautioned the men not to waste their ammunition; ordered certain men who were good shots to do the firing, and others to keep them supplied with loaded guns.

The firing continued till nearly dark (between nine and ten o'clock), although after dusk but little attention was paid to the firing, as everybody moved about freely.

Of course everybody was wondering about Custer -- why he did not communicate by courier or signal. But the general opinion seemed to prevail that he had been defeated and driven down the river, where he would probably join General Terry, and with whom he would return to our relief. Quite frequently, too, the question, "What's the matter with Custer?" would evoke an impatient reply.

Indians are proverbial economists of fuel, but they did not stint themselves that night. The long twilight was prolonged by numerous bonfires, located throughout their village. The long shadows of the hills and the refracted light gave a supernatural aspect to the surrounding country, which may account for the illusions of those who imagined they could see columns of troops, etc. Although our dusky foes did not molest us with obtrusive attentions during the night, yet it must not be inferred that we were allowed to pass the night in perfect rest; or that they were endeavoring to soothe us into forgetfulness of their proximity, or trying to conceal their situation. They were a good deal happier than we were; nor did they strive to conceal their joy. Their camp was a veritable pandemonium. All night long they continued their frantic revels; beating tom-toms, dancing, whooping, yelling with demoniacal screams and discharging firearms. We knew they were having a scalp-dance. In this connection the question has often been asked "if they did not have prisoners at the torture?" The Indians deny that they took any prisoners. We did not discover any evidence of torture in their camps. It is true that we did find human heads severed from their bodies, but these probably had been paraded in their orgies during that terrible night.

Our casualties had been comparatively few since taking position on the hill. The question of moving was discussed, but the conditions coupled to the proposition caused it to be indignantly rejected. Some of the scouts were sent out soon after dark to look for signs of Custer's command, but they returned after a short absence saying that the country was full of Sioux. Lieutenant Varnum volunteered to go out, but was either discouraged from the venture or forbidden to go out.

After dark the troops were arranged a little differently. The horses were unsaddled, and the mules were relieved of their packs; all animals were secured to lariats stretched and picketed to the ground.

Soon after all firing had ceased the wildest confusion prevailed. Men imagined they could see a column of troops over on the hills or ridges, that they could hear the tramp of the horses, the command of officers, or even the trumpet-calls. Stable-call was sounded by one of our trumpeters; shots were fired by some of our men, and familiar trumpet-calls were sounded by our trumpeter immediately after, to let the supposed marching column know that we were friends. Every favorable expression or opinion was received with credulity, and then ratified with a cheer. Somebody suggested that General Crook might be coming, so some one, a civilian packer, I think, mounted a horse, and galloping along the line yelled: "Don't be discouraged, boys, Crook is coming." But they gradually realized that the much-wished-for reinforcements were but the phantasma of their imaginations, and settled down to their work of digging rifle-pits. They worked in pairs, in threes and fours. The ground was hard and dry. There were only three or four spades and shovels in the whole command; axes, hatchets, knives, table-forks, tin cups, and halves of canteens were brought into use. However, everybody worked hard, and some were still digging when the enemy opened fire at early dawn, between half-past two and three o'clock, so that all had some sort of shelter, except Benteen's men. The enemy's first salutations were rather feeble, and our side made scarcely any response; but as dawn advanced to daylight their lines were heavily reinforced, and both sides kept up a continuous fusillade. Of course it was their policy to draw our fire as much as possible to exhaust our ammunition. As they exposed their persons very little we forbade our men, except well-known good shots, to fire without orders. The Indians amused themselves by standing erect, in full view for an instant, and then dropping down again before a bullet could reach them, but of that they soon seemed to grow tired or found it too dangerous; then they resorted to the old ruse of raising a hat or blouse or a blanket, on a stick to draw our fire; we soon understood their tactics. Occasionally they fired volleys at command. Their fire, however, was not very effective. Benteen's troop suffered greater losses than any other, because their rear was exposed to the long-range firing from the hills on the north. The horses and mules suffered greatly, as they were fully exposed to long-range fire from the east.

Benteen came over to where Reno was lying, and asked for reinforcements to be sent to his line. Before he left his line, however, he ordered Gibson not to fall back under any circumstances, as this was the key of the position. Gibson's men had expended nearly all their ammunition, some men being reduced to as few as four or five cartridges. He was embarrassed, too, with quite a number of wounded men. Indeed, the situation here was most critical, for if the Indians had made a rush, a retreat was inevitable. Private McDermott volunteered to carry a message from Gibson to Benteen urging him to hasten the reinforcements. After considerable urging by Benteen, Reno finally ordered French to take "M" troop over to the south side. On his way over Benteen picked up some men then with the horses. Just previous to his arrival an Indian had shot one of Gibson's men, then rushed up and touched the body with his "coup-stick," and started back to cover, but he was killed. He was in such close proximity to the lines and so exposed to the fire that the other Indians could not carry his body away. This, I believe, was the only dead Indian left in our possession. This boldness determined Benteen to make a charge, and the Indians were driven nearly to the river. On their retreat they dragged several dead and wounded warriors away with them.

The firing almost ceased for a while, and then it recommenced with greater fury. From this fact, and their more active movements, it became evident that they contemplated something more serious than a mere fusillade. Benteen came back to where Reno was, and said if something was not done pretty soon the Indians would run into our lines. Waiting a short time, and no action being taken on his suggestion, he said rather impatiently: "You've got to do something here pretty quick; this won't do, you must drive them back." Reno then directed us to get ready for a charge, and told Benteen to give the word. Benteen called out "All ready now, men. Now's your time. Give them hell. Hip, hip, here we go!" and away we went with a hurrah, every man, but one who lay in his pit crying like a child. The Indians fired more rapidly than before from their whole line. Our men left the pits with their carbines loaded, and they began firing without orders soon after we started. A large body of Indians had assembled at the foot of one of the hills, intending probably to make a charge, as Benteen had divined, but they broke as soon as our line started. When we had advanced 75 or 100 yards, Reno called out "Get back, men, get back," and back the whole line came. A most singular fact of this sortie was that not a man who advanced with the lines was hit; but directly after every one had gotten into the pits again, the one man who did not go out was shot in the head and killed instantly. The poor fellow had a premonition that he would be killed, and had so told one of his comrades.

Up to this time the command had been without water. The excitement and heat made our thirst almost maddening. The men were forbidden to use tobacco. They put pebbles in their mouths to excite the glands; some ate grass roots, but did not find relief; some tried to eat hard bread, but after chewing it awhile would blow it out of their mouths like so much flour. A few potatoes were given out and afforded some relief. About 11 a.m. the firing was slack, and parties of volunteers were formed to get water under the protection of Benteen's lines. The parties worked their way down the ravines to within a few yards of the river. The men would get ready, make a rush to the river, fill the camp-kettles, and return to fill the canteens. Some Indians stationed in a copse of woods, a short distance away, opened fire whenever a man exposed himself, which made this a particularly hazardous service. Several men were wounded, and the additional danger was incurred of rescuing their wounded comrades. I think all these men were rewarded with medals of honor. By about one o'clock the Indians had nearly all left us, but they still guarded the river; by that time, however, we had about all the water we needed for immediate use. About two o'clock the Indians came back, opened fire, and drove us to the trenches again, but by three o'clock the firing had ceased altogether.

Late in the afternoon we saw a few horsemen in the bottom apparently to observe us, and then fire was set to the grass in the valley. About 7 p.m. we saw emerge from behind this screen of smoke an immense moving mass crossing the plateau, going toward the Big Horn Mountians. A fervent "Thank God" that they had at last given up the contest was soon followed by grave doubts as to their motive for moving. Perhaps Custer had met Terry, and was coming to our relief. Perhaps they were short of ammunition, and were moving their village to a safe distance before making a final desperate effort to overwhelm us. Perhaps it was only a ruse to get us on the move, and then clean us out.

The stench from the dead men and horses was now exceedingly offensive, and it was decided to take up a new position nearer the river. The companies were assigned positions, and the men were put to work digging pits with the expectation of a renewal of the attack. Our loss on the hill had been eighteen killed and fifty-two wounded.

During the night Lieutenant DeRudio, Private O'Neal, Mr. Girard, the interpreter, and Jackson, a half-breed scout, came to our line. They had been left in the bottom when Reno made his retreat.

Tuesday morning, June 27, we had reveille without the "morning guns," enjoyed the pleasure of a square meal, and had our stock properly cared for. Our commanding officer seemed to think the Indians had some "trap" set for us, and required our men to hold themselves in readiness to occupy the pits at a moment's notice. Nothing seemed determined except to stay where we were. Not an Indian was in sight, but a few ponies were seen grazing down in the valley.

About 9:30 a.m. a cloud of dust was observed several miles down the river. The assembly was sounded, the horses placed in a protected situation, and camp-kettles and canteens filled with water. An hour of suspense followed; but from the slow advance we concluded that they were our own troops. "But whose command is it?" We looked in vain for a gray-horse troop. It could not be Custer; it must then be Crook, for if it was Terry, Custer would be with him. Cheer after cheer was given Crook. A white man, Harris, I think, soon came up with a note from General Terry, addressed to General Custer, dated June 26, stating that two of our Crow scouts had given information that our column had been whipped and nearly all had been killed; that he did not believe their story, but was coming with medical assistance. The scout said that he could not get to our lines the night before, as the Indians were on the alert. Very soon after this Lieutenant Bradley, 7th Infantry, came into our lines, and asked where I was. Greeting most cordially my old friend, I immediately asked, "Where is Custer?" He replied, "I don't know, but I suppose he was killed, as we counted 197 dead bodies. I don't suppose any escaped." We were simply dumfounded. This was the first intimation we had of his fate. It was hard to realize; it did seem impossible.

General Terry and staff, and officers of General Gibbon's column soon after approached, and their coming was greeted with prolonged, hearty cheers. The grave countenance of the General awed the men to silence. The officers assembled to meet their guests. There was scarcely a dry eye; hardly a word was spoken, but quivering lips and hearty grasping of hands gave token of thankfulness for the relief and grief for the misfortune.

During the rest of that day we were busy collecting our effects and destroying surplus property. The wounded were cared for and taken to the camp of our new friends of the Montana column. Among the wounded was saddler "Mike" Madden of my troop, whom I promoted to be sergeant, on the field, for gallantry. Madden was very fond of his grog. His long abstinence had given him a famous thirst. It was necessary to amputate his leg, which was done without administering any anesthetic; but after the amputation the surgeon gave him a good, stiff drink of brandy. Madden eagerly gulped it down, and his eyes fairly danced as he smacked his lips and said, "M-eh, doctor, cut off my other leg."

On the morning of the 28th we left our intrenchments to bury the dead of Custer's command. The morning was bright, and from the high bluffs we had a clear view of Custer's battle-field. We saw a large number of objects that looked like white boulders scattered over the field. Glasses were brought into requisition, and it was announced that these objects were the dead bodies. Captain Weir exclaimed, "Oh, how white they look!"

All the bodies, except a few, were stripped of their clothing. According to my recollection nearly all were scalped or mutilated, but there was one notable exception, that of General Custer, whose face and expression were natural; he had been shot in the temple and in the left side. Many faces had a pained, almost terrified expression. It is said that "Rain-in-the-face," a Sioux warrier, has gloried that he had cut out and had eaten the heart and liver of one of the officers. Other bodies were mutilated in a disgusting manner. The bodies of Dr. Lord and Lieutenants Porter, Harrington, and Sturgis were not found, at least not recognized. The clothing of Porter and Sturgis was found in the village, and showed that they had been killed. We buried, according to my memoranda, 212 bodies. The killed of the entire command was 265, and of wounded we had 52.

### Reconstructing the Massacre of General Custer's Command

In 1886, on the tenth anniversary, an effort was made to have a reunion of the survivors at the battle-field. Colonel Benteen, Captains McDougall and Edgerly, Dr. Porter, Sergeant Hall, Trumpeter Penwell, and myself met there on the 25th of June. Through the kind efforts of the officers and of the ladies at Fort Custer our visit was made as pleasant as possible. Through the personal influence of Major McLaughlin, Indian agent at Standing Rock Agency, Chief Gall was prevailed upon to accompany the party and describe Custer's part in the battle.

In this narrative of the movements immediately preceding, and resulting in, the annihilation of the men with Custer, I have related facts substantially as observed by myself or as given to me by Chief Gall of the Sioux. His statements have been corroborated by other Indians, notably the wife of "Spotted Horn Bull," an intelligent Sioux squaw, one of the first who had the courage to talk freely to any who participated in the battle.

It has been previously noted that General Custer separated from Reno before the latter crossed the Little Big Horn under orders to charge the village. Custer's column bore to the right of the river (a sudden change of plan, probably); a ridge of high bluffs and the river separated the two commands, and they could not see each other. On this ridge, however, Custer and staff were seen to wave their hats, and heard to cheer just as Reno was beginning the attack; but Custer's troops were at that time a mile or more to his right. It was about this time that the trumpeter was sent back with Custer's last order to Benteen. From this place Custer could survey the valley for several miles above and for a short distance below Reno; yet he could only see a part of the village; he must, then, have felt confident that all the Indians were below him; hence, I presume, his message to Benteen. The view of the main body of the village was cut off by the highest points of the ridge, a short distance from him. Had he gone to this high point he would have understood the magnitude of his undertaking, and it is probable that his plan battle would have been changed. We have no evidence that he did not go there. He could see, however, that the village was not breaking away toward the Big Horn Mountains. He must, then, have expected to find the squaws and children fleeing to the bluffs on the north, for in no other way do I account for his wide detour to the right. He must have counted upon Reno's success and fully expected the "scatteration" of the non-combatants with the pony herds. The probable attack upon the families and the capture of the herds were in that event counted upon to strike consternation in the hearts of the warriors, and were elements for success upon which General Custer fully counted in the event of a daylight attack.

When Reno's advance was checked, and his left began to fall back, Chief Gall started with some of his warriors to cut off Reno's retreat to the bluffs. On his way he was excitedly hailed by "Iron Cedar," one of his warriors who was on the high point, to hurry to him, that more soldiers were coming. This was the first intimation the Indians had of Custer's column; up to the time of this incident they had supposed that all the troops were in at Reno's attack. Custer had then crossed the valley of the dry creek, and was marching along and well up the slope of the bluff forming the second ridge back from the river, and nearly parallel to it. The command was marching rapidly in column of fours, and there was some confusion in the ranks, due probably to the unmanageableness of some excited horses.

The accepted theory for many years after the battle, and still persisted in by some writers, was that Custer's column had turned the high bluffs near the river, moved down the dry (Reno's) creek, and attempted to ford the river near the lowest point of these bluffs; that he was there met by an overpowering force and driven back; that he then divided his battalion, moved down the river with the view of attacking the village, but met with such resistance from the enemy posted along the river bank and ravines that he was compelled to fall back, fighting, to the position on the ridge. The numerous bodies found scattered between the river and ridge were supposed to be the first victims of the fight. I am now satisfied that these were men who either survived those on the ridge or attempted to escape the massacre.

Custer's column was never nearer the river or village than his final position on the ridge. The wife of Spotted Horn Bull, when giving me her account of the battle, persisted in saying that Custer's column did not attempt to cross at the ford, and appealed to her husband, who supported her statement. On the battle-field, in 1886, Chief Gall indicated Custer's route to me, and it then flashed upon me that I myself had seen Custer's trail. On June 28, while we were burying the dead, I asked Major Reno's permission to go on the high ridge east or back of the field to look for tracks of shod horses to ascertain if some of the command might not have escaped. When I reached the ridge I saw this trail, and wondered who could have made it, but dismissed the thought that it had been made by Custer's column, because it did not accord with the theory with which we were then filled, that Custer had attempted to cross at the ford, and this trail was too far back, and showed no indication of leading toward the ford. Trumpeter Pewell was my orderly and accompanied me. It was a singular coincidence that in 1886 Penwell was stationed at Fort Custer, and was my orderly when visiting the battle-field. Penwell corroborated my recollection of the trail.

The ford theory arose from the fact that we found there numerous tracks of shod horses, but they evidently had been made after the Indians had possessed themselves of the cavalry horses, for they rode them after capturing them. No bodies of men or horses were found anywhere near the ford, and these facts are conclusive to my mind that Custer did not go to the ford with any body of men.

As soon as Gall had personally confirmed Iron Cedar's report he sent word to the warriors battling against Reno, and to the people in the village. The greatest consternation prevailed among the families, and orders were given for them to leave at once. Before they could do so the great body of warriors had left Reno, and hastened to attack Custer. This explains why Reno was not pushed when so much confusion at the river crossing gave the Indians every opportunity of annihilating his command. Not long after the Indians began to show a strong force in Custer's front, Custer turned his column to the left, and advanced in the direction of the village to near a place now marked as a spring, halted at the junction of the ravines just below it, and dismounted two troops, Keogh's and Calhoun's, to fight on foot. These two troops advanced at double-time to a knoll, now marked by Crittenden's monument. The other three troops, mounted, followed them a short distance in their rear. The led horses remained where the troops dismounted. When Keogh and Calhoun got to the knoll the other troops marched rapidly to the right; Smith's troop deployed as skirmishers, mounted, and took position on a ridge, which, on Smith's left, ended in Keogh's position (now marked by Crittenden's monument), and, on Smith's right, ended at the hill on which Custer took position with Yates and Tom Custer's troops, now known as Custer's Hill, and marked by the monument erected to the command. Smith's skirmishers, holding their gray horses, remained in groups of fours.

The line occupied by Custer's battalion was the first considerable ridge back from the river, the nearest point being about half a mile from it. His front was extended about three fourths of a mile. The whole village was in full view. A few hundred yards from his line was another but lower ridge, the further slope of which was not commanded by his line. It was here that the Indians under Crazy Horse from the lower part of the village, among whom were the Cheyennes, formed for the charge on Custer's Hill. All Indians had now left Reno. Gall collected his warriors, and moved up a ravine south of Keogh and Calhoun. As they were turning this flank they discovered the led horses without any other guard than the horse-holders. They opened fire upon the horse-holders, and used the usual devices to stampede the horses -- that is, yelling, waving blankets, etc.; in this they succeeded very soon, and the horses were caught up by the squaws. In this disaster Keogh and Calhoun probably lost their reserve ammunition, which was carried in the saddle-bags. Gall's warriors now moved to the foot of the knoll held by Calhoun. A large force dismounted and advanced up the slope far enough to be able to see the soldiers when standing erect, but were protected when squatting or lying down. By jumping up and firing quickly, they exposed themselves only for an instant, but drew the fire of the soldiers, causing a waste of ammunition. In the mean time Gall was massing his mounted warriors under the protection of the slope. When everything was in readiness, at a signal from Gall the dismounted warriors rose, fired, and every Indian gave voice to the war-whoop; the mounted Indians put whip to their ponies, and the whole mass rushed upon and crushed Calhoun. The maddened mass of Indians was carried forward by its own momentum over Calhoun and Crittenden down into the depression where Keogh was, with over thirty men, and all was over on that part of the field.

In the mean time the same tactics were being pursued and executed around Custer's Hill. The warriors, under the leadership of Crow-King, Crazy Horse, White Bull, "Hump," and others, moved up the ravine west of Custer's Hill, and concentrated under the shelter of the ridges on his right flank and back of his position. Gall's bloody work was finished before the annihilation of Custer was accomplished, and his victorious warriors hurried forward to the hot encounter then going on, and the frightful massacre was completed.

Smith's men had disappeared from the ridge, but not without leaving enough dead bodies to mark their line. About twenty-eight bodies of men belonging to this troop and other organizations were found in one ravine nearer the river. Many corpses were found scattered over the field between Custer's line of defense, the river, and in the direction of Reno's Hill. These, doubtless, were of men who had attempted to escape; some of them may have been sent as couriers by Custer. One of the first bodies I recognized and one of the nearest to the ford was that of Sergeant Butler of Tom Custer's troop. Sergeant Butler was a soldier of many years' experience and of known courage. The indications were that he had sold his life dearly, for near and under him were found many empty cartridge-shells.

All the Indian accounts that I know of agree that there was no organized close-quarters fighting, except on the two flanks; that with the annihilation at Custer's Hill the battle was virtually over. It does not appear that the Indians made any advance to the attack from the direction of the river; they did have a defensive force along the river and in the ravines which destroyed those who left Custer's line.

There was a great deal of firing going on over the field after the battle by the young men and boys riding about and shooting into the dead bodies.

The question has been often asked, "What were the causes of Custer's defeat?" I should say :

*First.* The overpowering numbers of the enemy and their unexpected cohesion.

*Second.* Reno's panic rout from the valley.

*Third.* The defective extraction of the empty cartridge-shells from the carbines.

Of the first, I will say that we had nothing conclusive on which to base calculations of the numbers -- and to this day it seems almost incredible that such great numbers of Indians should have left the agencies, to combine against the troops, without information relating thereto having been communicated to the commanders of troops in the field, further than that heretofore mentioned. The second has been mentioned incidentally. The Indians say if Reno's position in the valley had been held, they would have been compelled to divide their strength for the different attacks, which would have caused confusion and apprehension, and prevented the concentration of every able-bodied warrior upon the battalion under Custer; that, at the time of the discovery of Custer's advance to attack, the chiefs gave orders for the village to move, to break up; that, at the time of Reno's retreat, this order was being carried out, but as soon as Reno's retreat was assured the order was countermanded, and the squaws were compelled to return with the pony herds; that the order would not have been countermanded had Reno's forces remained fighting in the bottom. Custer's attack did not begin until after Reno had reached the bluffs.

Of the third we can only judge by our own experience. When cartridges were dirty and corroded the ejectors did not always extract the empty shells from the chambers, and the men were compelled to use knives to get them out. When the shells were clean no great difficulty was experienced. To what extent this was a factor in causing the disaster we have no means of knowing.

A battle was unavoidable. Every man in Terry's and Custer's commands expected a battle; it was for that purpose, to punish the Indians, that the command was sent out, and with that determination Custer made his preparations. Had Custer continued his march southward -- that is, left the Indian trail -- the Indians would have known of our movement on the 25th, and a battle would have been fought very near the same field on which Crook had been attacked and forced back only a week before; the Indians never would have remained in camp and allowed a concentration of several columns to attack them. If they had escaped without punishment or battle Custer undoubtedly would have been blamed.

# HOW I ROUTED A GANG OF ARIZONA OUTLAWS
## (1879-81)

## Wyatt S. Earp

**Editors' Note:** By coincidence, the West's two most durable gunfighter legends are based on incidents that occurred in the same year: On July 14, 1881, Pat Garrett shot Billy the Kid in Lincoln Country, New Mexico; on October 26, 1881, Wyatt Earp, his brothers Virgil and Morgan, and "Doc" Holliday shot it out with the Clanton-McLowery gang at the O.K. Corral in Tombstone, Arizona. While both shoot-outs were widely reported in the press, neither was considered especially important at the time. Decades and dozens of retellings were needed for the legends to grow to their present proportions. News takes more than a day or a year to become myth.

Billy the Kid got a head start toward immortality with the publication of Pat Garrett's *Authentic Life of Billy the Kid* in 1882. But Garrett's book was not a big seller in the 1880's, and did not become well known until it was reprinted in 1927. The legends of both Billy and Earp got a big boost in the 1920's after novelist Walter Nobel Burns wrote the popular books *The Saga of Billy the Kid* (1926) and *Tombstone, An Illiad of the Southwest* (1927). The first nonfiction book about Tombstone in the turbulent 1880's, *Heldorado* by William Breakenridge, came out in 1928. Breakenridge was a deputy Cochise County sheriff at the time of the famous gunfight at the O.K. Corral and no friend of the Earps. Neither Wyatt nor his brothers fare well in *Heldorado*. It was not until 1931, with the publication of Stewart Lake's biography, *Wyatt Earp, Frontier Marshal*, that Earp was portrayed as an unblemished hero. Lake's book, which has been reprinted many times, laid the foundation for the legend of Wyatt Earp as an upright, fearless lawman without peer.

Still, it was not until the mid-1950's that Wyatt Earp's fame caught up with Billy's. In September, 1955, the television program "The Life and Legend of Wyatt Earp" began its six-year run. Each Tuesday night, Hugh O'Brian portrayed the frontier marshal in heroic western fashion -- "Wyatt Earp, Wyatt Earp...brave, courgeous, and bold," trumpeted the show's theme song. Millions of viewers and a whole generation of Americans would come to know Earp as a model of courage and integrity.

The real Wyatt Earp was, of course, something less, or at least different. His true character remains an enigma, as is the case of Billy the Kid, and this accounts for much of Earp's appeal. The question was, and continues: Were the Earps heroic lawmen who were "in the right," or thieves and cutthroats hiding behind badges as their detractors claimed?

Wyatt and his brothers Virgil and Morgan arrived in Tombstone in December, 1879. The previous year Ed Schieffelin had discovered silver on the site and a classic "boom" was in progress. By the time the Earps arrived on the

207

scene, Tombstone was on its way to becoming the largest town in the territory. As all boomtowns do, Tombstone eventually went bust -- by 1885 the mines were playing out and by 1890 it was practically a ghost town. But it was a great show while it lasted, and the Earps were the sort of frontiersmen who sought to be part of the action.

Before coming to Arizona, Wyatt Earp had held law enforcement postions in Kansas, first as a policeman in Wichita, and then as town marshal for the notorious Dodge City. By the time he arrived in Tombstone, he already had a reputation as a pretty tough hombre. And there was an unsavory side to his persona. He was a known gambler and sometime saloon keeper with friends like Big-Nosed Kate and the gambling gunman Doc Holliday. At the time of the famous shoot-out, the 33-year-old Wyatt was a deputy U. S. marshal, his older brother Virgil (38) was town marshal, and Morgan (30) was Virgil's deputy. These were all political offices and there were strong political overtones to the Tombstone saga. The Earps were Republicans, as was their supporter, Mayor John Clum, editor of the Tombstone *Epitaph*. Allied against them were the Democrats, including Cochise County Sheriff Johnny Behan and the editors of the other town newspaper, the *Nugget*. As reported in the *Epitaph*, the Earps could do no wrong; the *Nugget's* readers were routinely told that the Earps were bad characters; and modern day historians continue to take sides.

After the fight at the O.K. Corral, Sheriff Behan arrested Wyatt and Doc Holliday, charging them with murder. Although exonerated at a hearing before a local judge, the matter did not end there. Numerous reprisal shootings and killings took place on both sides over the next several months.

With another warrant out for his arrest, an embattled Wyatt Earp left Arizona in March, 1882, to seek refuge in Colorado. During the next several years he wandered all over the West. In 1890 he moved to San Francisco, and on December 2, 1896, he was referee for the Sharkey-Fitzsimmons prizefight. The next year Earp followed the gold rush to Alaska, but after a few years drifted down to Nevada, and then back to California. In 1906 he settled down in Los Angeles where he lived until his death in 1929.

The following version of the O.K. Corral fight, first published in the San Francisco *Examiner* in 1896, is unique in two respects. It is the earliest summary of Wyatt Earp's Tombstone exploits that we know about, and it is the only account of the famous gunfight under the by-line of a participant. It does, of course, tell the story from Earp's perspective. And while Earp probably had help from one of the *Examiner's* reporters in writing the article, it is truly his account and agrees with the version he told to Stewart Lake many years later.

~ ~ ~ ~ ~

**It may be that the trail of blood** will seem to lie too thickly over the pages that I write. If I had it in me to invent a tale I would fain lighten the crimson stain so that it would glow no deeper than demure pink. But half a lifetime on the frontier attunes a man's hand to the six-shooter rather than the pen, and it is lucky that I am asked only for facts, for more than facts I could not give. Half a lifetime of such turbulent days and nights as will never again be seen in this, or, I believe, in any land, might be expected to tangle a man's brain with memories none too easy to sift apart. But for the corner-stone of this episodic narrative, I cannot make better choice than the bloody feud in Tombstone, Arizona, which cost me a brave brother and cost more than one worthless life among the murderous dogs who pursued me and mine only slightly less bitterly than I pursued them.

And so I marshal my characters. My stalwart brothers, Virgil and Morgan, shall stand on the right of the stage with my dear old comrade, Doc Holliday; on the left shall be arrayed Ike Clanton, Sheriff Behan, Curly Bill and the rest. Fill in the stage with miners, gamblers, rustlers, stage robbers, murderers and cowboys, and the melodrama is ready to begin. Nor shall a heroine be wanting, for Big-Nose Kate was shaped for the part both by nature and circumstances. Poor Kate! Frontier whiskey must have laid her low long since. And that gives me an opportunity to introduce the reader to both Doc Holliday and Kate by telling of an episode in their checkered lives two years before the action of my melodrama begins.

It happened in '77, when I was city marshal of Dodge City, Kansas. I had followed the trail of some cattle thieves across the border into Texas, and during a short stay in Fort Griffen I first met Doc Holliday and the woman who was known variously as Big-Nose Kate, Kate Fisher, and, on occasions of ceremony, Mrs. Doc Holliday. Holliday asked me a good many questions about Dodge City and seemed inclined to go there, but before he had made up his mind about it my business called me over to Fort Clark. It was while I was on my way back to Fort Griffen that my new friend and his Kate found it necessary to pull their stakes hurriedly. Whereof the plain, unvarnished facts were these:

Doc Holliday was spending the evening in a poker game, which was his custom whenever faro bank did not present superior claims on his attention. On his right sat Ed Bailey, who needs no description because he is soon to drop out of this narrative. The trouble began, as it was related to me afterward, by Ed Bailey monkeying with the "deadwood," or what people who live in cities call discards. Doc Holliday admonished him once or twice to "play poker" -- which is your seasoned gambler's method of cautioning a friend to stop cheating -- but the misguided Bailey persisted in his furtive attentions to the deadwood. Finally, having detected him again, Holliday pulled down a pot without showing his hand, which he had a perfect right to do. Thereupon Bailey started to throw his gun on Holliday, as might have been expected. But before he could pull the trigger Doc Holliday had jerked a knife out of his breast pocket and with one sideways sweep had caught Bailey just below the brisket.

Well, that broke up the game, and pretty soon Doc Holliday was sitting cheerfully in the front room of the hotel, guarded by the city marshal and a couple of policemen, while a hundred miners and gamblers clamored for his blood. You see, he had not lived in Fort Griffen very long, while Ed Bailey was well liked. It wasn't long before Big-Nose Kate, who had a room downtown, heard about the trouble and went up to take a look at her Doc through the window. What she saw and heard led her to think that his life wasn't worth ten minutes purchase, and I don't believe it was. There was a shed at the back of the lot, and a horse stabled in it. She was a kind-hearted girl, was Kate, for she went to the trouble of leading the horse into the alley and tethering it there before she set fire to the shed. She also got a six-shooter from a friend down the street, which, with the one she always carried, made two.

It all happened just as she had planned it. The shed blazed up and she hammered at the door yelling, "Fire!" Everybody rushed out, except the marshal and the constables and their prisoner. Kate walked in as bold as a lion, threw one of her six-shooters on the marshal and handed the other to Doc Holliday. "Come on, Doc," she said with a laugh. He didn't need any second invitation and the two of them backed out of the hotel, keeping the officers covered. All that night they hid among the willows down by the creek, and early next morning a friend of Kate's brought them two horses and some of Doc Holliday's clothes from his room. Kate dressed up in a pair of pants, a pair of boots, a shirt and a hat, and the pair of them got away safely and rode the 400 miles to Dodge City, where they were installed in great style when I got back home. Which reminds me that during my absence the man whom I had left behind as a deputy had been killed by some cowboys who were engaged in the fascinating recreation known as "shootin' up the town." This incident is merely mentioned as a further sign of the time, and a further excuse for the blood which cannot but trickle through the web of my remembrance.

Such then was the beginning of my acquaintance with Doc Holliday, the mad, merry scamp with heart of gold and nerves of steel, who, in the dark years that followed, stood at my elbow in many a battle to the death. He was a dentist, but preferred to be a gambler. He was a Virginian, but he preferred to be a frontiersman and a vagabond. He was a philosopher, but he preferred to be a wag. He was long, lean, and ash-blond, and the quickest man with a six-shooter I ever knew. It wasn't long after I returned to Dodge City that his quickness saved my life. He saw a man draw on me behind my back. "Look out Wyatt!" he shouted, but while the words were coming out of his mouth he had jerked his pistol out of his pocket and shot the other fellow before the latter could fire. On such incidents as that are built the friendships of the frontier.

In 1879 Dodge City was beginning to lose much of the snap which had given it a charm to men of restless blood, and I decided to move to Tombstone, which was just building up a reputation. Doc Holliday thought he would move with me. Big-Nose Kate had left him long before -- they were always a quarrelsome couple -- and settled in Las Vegas, New Mexico. He looked her up en route, and, the old tenderness reasserted itself; she resolved to throw in her lot with his in Arizona.

As for me, I was tired of the trials of a peace officer's life and wanted no more of it. But as luck would have it I stopped at Prescott, Arizona, to see my brother Virgil and while there I met C. P. Dake, the United States marshal of the territory. Dake had heard of me before, and he begged me so hard to take the deputy-ship in Tombstone that I finally consented. It was then that the the real troubles of a lifetime began.

The boom had not struck Tombstone then, but it did a few months later, when the mills for treating the ore were completed, and tales about the fabulous richness of the silver mines were bruited abroad. Before long the town had a population of 10,000 to 12,000, of whom about 300 were cattle thieves, stage robbers, murderers and outlaws.

For the first eight months I worked as a shotgun messenger for Wells, Fargo & Co., and beyond the occasional excitement of an abortive hold-up, a few excursions after cattle thieves, and homicides in my official capacity, everything was quiet as the grave. Then the proprietors of "The Oriental," the biggest gambling house in town, offered to take me into partnership. One of them -- his name was Rickabaugh and he was a San Francisco man -- was unpopular, and a coterie of the tough gamblers were trying to run the firm out of town. The proprietors had an idea that their troubles would cease if they had the deputy United States marshal for a partner, and so it proved, for a time at least. So I turned over my position with Wells, Fargo & Co. to my brother Morgan, who held it for six months, after which I gave him a job in "The Oriental." My brother Virgil had also joined me, and when the town was incorporated, he was appointed chief of police.

About this time was laid the foundation of the vendetta which became the talk of the frontier and resulted in no end of bloodshed. A band of rustlers held up the stage coach and killed the driver and one of the passengers. Virgil and I, with another man, followed them into the mountains for seventeen days, but our horses gave out and they got away from us. When we got back to town I went to Ike Clanton, who was a sort of leader among the rustlers, and offered to give him all the $6,000 reward offered by Wells, Fargo & Co. if he would lead me to where I could arrest the murderers. After thinking about it deeply, he agreed to send a partner of his named Joe Hill to lead them from where they were hiding to some place within twenty-five miles of Tombstone, where I could get them. But in case I killed them he wanted to be sure that the reward would be paid alive or dead. In order to assure him I got Wells-Fargo Agent Marshall Williams to telegraph to San Francisco about it, and a reply came in the affirmative.

So Clanton sent Hill off to decoy the men I wanted. That was to take several days, and in the meantime Marshall Williams got drunk, and, suspecting that I was using Ike Clanton for some purpose, tried to pump him about it. Clanton was terrified at the thought of any third person knowing of our bargain and accused me of having told Williams. I denied it, and then he accused me of having told Doc Holliday, who had known nothing about it. Doc Holliday, who was the soul of honor, berated him vigorously for his treachery, and the conversation was heard by several people. That was enough for Clanton. He knew that his only alternative was to kill us or be killed by his own people.

Early next morning Virgil and I were told that Clanton was out with a Winchester and a six-shooter looking for us. So we went out looking for him, taking different routes. Virgil was going down Fourth Street when Clanton came out of a hallway, looking in the opposite direction. "I want you, Ike," said Virgil, walking up behind him. Clanton threw his gun around and tried to take a shot, but Virgil knocked it away, pulled his own and arrested his man. Ike was fined $25 for disturbing the peace.

Ike Clanton's next move was to telegraph to Charleston, ten miles away, for Billy Clanton, Tom McLowery, Frank McLowery and Billy Clayton [Billy Claiborne] -- hard men, every one. They came galloping into town, loaded up with ammunition and swearing to kill us off in short order. Thirty or forty citizens offered us their help, but we said we could manage the job alone.

"What had we better do?" asked Virgil.

"Go and arrest 'em," said I.

The four newcomers and Ike Clanton stationed themselves on a fifteen-foot lot between two buildings and sent us word that if we did not come down there and fight they would waylay and kill us. So we started down after them -- Doc Holliday, Virgil, Morgan and I. As we came to the lot they moved back and backed against one of the buildings.

"I'm going to arrest you boys," said Virgil.

For answer, their six-shooters began to spit. Frank McLowery fired at me, and Billy Clanton at Morgan. Both missed. I had a gun in my overcoat pocket and I jerked it out and shot at Frank McLowery, hitting him in the stomach. At the same time Morgan shot Billy Clanton in the breast. So far we had got the best of it, but just then Tom McLowery, who had got behind his horse, fired under the animal's neck and bored a hole right through Morgan sideways. The bullet entered one shoulder and came out the other.

"I've got it, Wyatt!" said Morgan.

"Then get behind me and keep quiet," I said -- but he didn't.

By this time bullets were flying so fast that I could not keep track of them. Frank McLowery had given a yell when I shot him and made for the street with his hand over his stomach. Ike Clanton and Billy Clayton [sic] were shooting fast, and so was Virgil, and the former two made a break for the street. I fired a shot which hit Tom McLowery's horse and made it break away, and Doc Holliday took the opportunity to pump a charge of buckshot out of a Wells-Fargo shotgun into Tom McLowery, who promptly fell dead. In the excitement of the moment, Doc Holliday didn't know what he had done and flung away the shotgun in disgust, pulling his six-shooter instead.

Then I witnessed a strange spectacle. Frank McLowery and Billy Clanton were sitting in the middle of the street, both badly wounded but emptying their six-shooters like lightning. One of them shot Virgil through the leg, and he shot Billy Clanton. Then Frank McLowery started to his feet and staggered across the street, though he was full of bullets. On the way he came face to face with Doc Holliday.

"I've got ye now, Doc." he said.

"Well, you're a good one if you have," said Holliday with a laugh.

With that they both aimed. But before you can understand what happened next, I must carry the narrative back half a minute. After the first exchange in the lot, Ike Clanton had got into one of the buildings from the rear and when I reached the street he was shooting out of one of the front windows. Seeing him aim at Morgan, I shouted, "Look out, Morg, you're getting it in the back!" Morgan wheeled round and in doing so fell on his side. While in that position he caught sight of Doc Holliday and Frank McLowery aiming at each other. With a quick drop he shot McLowery in the head. At the same instant, McLowery's pistol flashed and Doc Holliday was shot in the hip. That ended the fight. Ike Clanton and Billy Clayton [sic] ran off and made haste to give themselves up to the sheriff, for the citizens were out a hundred strong to back us up.

I have described this battle with as much particularity as possible, partly because there are not many city dwellers who have more than a vague idea of what such a fight really means, and partly because I was rather curious to see how it would look in cold type. It may or may not surprise some readers to learn that from the first to the last shot fired not more than a minute elapsed.

Of the exciting events which followed, I can give no more than a brief account. The principal factor in all that happened was Sheriff Johnny Behan, my political rival and personal enemy. Doc Holliday and I were arrested on a charge of murder. My two brothers were exempt from this proceeding because they were both disabled. We were acquitted at the preliminary hearing and rearrested on another warrant charging the same offense. This time the hearing was held at Contention, nine miles from Tombstone, and we would have been assassinated on the road had not a posse of the best citizens insisted on accompanying the sheriff as a guard. The hearing was never completed because Holliday and I were released on a writ of habeas corpus. In the meantime, the grand jury persistently refused to indict us.

But the determination to assassinate us never relaxed. Three months later, Virgil was returning home to the hotel, and when he was half way across the street five double-barreled shotguns were discharged at him from an ambuscade. One shot shattered his left arm and another passed through his body. I arrested several of the assassins, but twenty or thirty rustlers swore to an alibi and they were released.

Three months later, before Virgil had recovered from his wounds, Morgan was shot dead through the glass door of a saloon while he was playing a game of pool. I sent his body home to Colton, Cal. [his parents' home], and shipped off Virgil -- a physical wreck -- on the same train from Tucson. But even at the depot I was forced to fight Ike Clanton and four or five of his friends who had followed us to do murder. One of them, Frank Stilwell, who was believed to be Morgan's murderer, was killed by my gun going off when he grasped it.

When I returned to Tombstone, Sheriff Behan came to arrest me, but I refused to surrender and he weakened. For a long time thereafter I occupied the anomalous position of being a fugitive from the county authorities and performing the duties of deputy United States marshal with the sanction and moral support of my chief. With Doc Holliday and one or two faithful comrades, I went into camp among the hills and withstood more than one attack from outlaws who had been implicated in the death of one brother and the disablement of another -- attacks which resulted fatally to some of my enemies and left me without a scratch.

One such encounter I will describe because it illustrates as well as anything what could come of the exigencies of a frontier vendetta. We had ridden twenty-five miles over the mountains with the intention of camping at a certain spring. When we got near the place I had a presentiment that something was wrong, and unlimbered my shotgun. Sure enough, nine cowboys sprang up from the bank where the spring was and began firing at us. I jumped off my horse to return fire, thinking my men would do the same, but they retreated. One of the cowboys, who was trying to pump some lead into me with a Winchester, was a fellow named Curly Bill [William Brocius], a stage robber whom I had been after for eight months, and for whom I had a warrant in my pocket. I fired both barrels of my gun into him, blowing him all to pieces.

With that the others jumped into a clump of willows and kept on firing, so I retreated, keeping behind my horse. He was a high-strung beast, and the firing frightened him so that whenever I tried to get my Winchester from the saddle he would rear up and keep it out of my reach. When I had backed out about a hundred yards, I started to mount. Now, it was a hot day and I had loosened my cartridge belt two or three holes. When I tried to get astride, I found that it had fallen down over my thighs, keeping my legs together. While I was perched up thus, trying to pull my belt higher with one hand, the horn of the saddle was shot off. However, I got away all right, and just then my men rallied. But I did not care to go back at the rustlers, so we sought out another water hole for camp. The skirt of my overcoat was shot to pieces on both sides, but not a bullet touched me.

Sheriff Behan trailed us with a big posse composed of rustlers, but it was only a bluff, for when I left word for him where he could find us and waited for him to come, he failed to appear. My best friends advised me to leave the territory, so I crossed into Colorado. While I was there, they tried to get a requisition for me, but the governor refused to sign it.

It's an old story now. I have been in Arizona of recent years -- as near Tombstone as Tucson in fact -- but no one sought to molest me. The outlaws who were my worst enemies are mostly killed off or in the penitentiary. Poor Doc Holliday died of consumption three years ago in Colorado. My brother Virgil is running a stock ranch in Texas. A large section of his upper arm is entirely without bone, and yet he can use his fingers.

On reading it over it seems to me that there is not only too much blood, but too much of myself in my story. However, a man gets in the habit of thinking about himself when he spends half a lifetime on the frontier.

# THE LAST DAYS OF BILLY THE KID
## (1881)

## Pat F. Garrett

**Editors' Note:** No Wild West desperado has attained more notoriety than Henry McCarty, later known as Henry Antrim, then William Bonney, then "The Kid," and finally, Billy the Kid. He has been the star character in hundreds of stories, dozens of books, more than forty movies, and at least one ballet! Said to have killed twenty-one men (one for each year of his life) before his youthful demise, Billy the Kid is considered by many to epitomize the West in which a man made his own rules by which to live and die. To others he remains the quintessential folk hero, a symbol of a rebellious young America, a frontier Robin Hood to whom romance was more important than convention, and who only killed for honor or in self defense. Still others regard the Kid as little more than a pathological killer.

Although it has been more than 100 years since his death, Billy the Kid continues to evoke a curiosity and admiration that can only be described as remarkable. A large and growing clan of Billy the Kid aficionados eagerly absorbs every scrap of information they can glean about his life and times. So skewed have become the few facts known about Billy that his persona is almost as individual as the investigator. One source says he was born in New York City, another says he was not; some claim that he killed close to 40 men, others -- probably more accurately -- say the number was more like four; a few even believe that he did not die at Fort Sumner, New Mexico, that he somehow survived to live a long and secret life. What is known beyond a reasonable doubt is that Billy was a participant in New Mexico's infamous Lincoln County War, that he was a rustler and a killer, and that he was shot dead by an ex-buffalo hunter named Pat Garrett on July 14, 1881.

No sooner had Pat Garrett been elected sheriff of Lincoln County, New Mexico Territory, in November, 1880, than he set off after Billy the Kid and his his gang of outlaws. At that time, Lincoln County was much larger than it is now, encompassing almost the entire southeast quarter of New Mexico. It was thinly populated, far from the territorial government in Santa Fe, and harbored some of the worst criminals in the West. For years, effective law inforcement had been Lincoln County's most scarce commodity.

During the 1870's, southeast New Mexico had been the scene of a violent feud known as the Lincoln County War. This was not a dispute between embittered families, but a complex struggle between two groups vying for political and economic power. In simple terms, the rival antagonists were the Murphy faction, named after an Irishman, Laurence Murphy, which attempted to set up a mercantile and grazing monopoly throughout Lincoln County; and the Tunstall group, named after an Englishman, John Tunstall, which attempted to break that monopoly with its own enterprises beginning in 1876. Billy the Kid was a cowboy for the Tunstall outfit and an admirer of John Tunstall, who would become one of the first victims of the Lincoln County War. At stake were the grazing lands of the Pecos Valley and the lucrative government contracts for supplying beef to western army posts and Indian reservations. This rivalry developed into a vicious conflict with numerous shootings and killings before reaching a climax in July, 1878, with a "Five Days Fight" in the town of Lincoln. This protracted shoot-out involved more than one hundred gunmen and resulted in at least five deaths. With the help of the U. S. Cavalry, the Murphy outfit prevailed in the Five Days Fight, forcing Billy the Kid and several of his compadres into a life of banditry.

The "generals" in the "war" were wealthy ranch owners, powerful politicians, and businessmen. The "soldiers" were young toughs like Billy the Kid. And a kid he was -- although he was a prominent figure in the Five Days Fight, he was only eighteen years old at that time. The Kid's specialty, however, was rustling cattle and stealing horses. Should the lawful owner resist, a shootout would result. By 1880 the Kid was wanted by the law in connection with several murders, including the shootings of Lincoln County Sheriff William Brady, and Jimmy Carlyle, a blacksmith from the mining town of White Oaks. As long as the Lincoln County War continued, outlaws such as Billy the Kid flourished. By stealing from one faction, they received support and protection from the other. But the climate was changing, and the Kid's time was running out.

In September, 1878, President Rutherford B. Hayes appointed General Lew Wallace (author of the novel *Ben Hur*) governor of New Mexico Territory with the mission of halting the outrageous lawlessness. Governor Wallace took strong measures to restore law and order, and by mid-December, 1880, the "war" was all but over. Billy and his comrades were now vulnerable to determined lawmen like Pat Garrett who soon had traced the gang's whereabouts to a ranch twelve miles east of the hamlet of Fort Sumner. At this time the Kid's gang consisted of his old compadres Tom Foliard (or O'Folliard) and Charles Bowdre, and new members Billy Wilson, Dave Rudabaugh and Tom Pickett. The ranch was owned by two men named Wilcox and Brazil, who, while on friendly terms with the outlaws, were secretly keeping the sheriff informed about the gang's comings and goings.

Garrett assembled a formidable thirteen-man posse. Six were local men, one of whom was Barney Mason, a young man of dubious background who had once been a good friend of Billy's. Also on hand were seven West Texas vigilantes who were looking for cattle stolen by the Kid's band. The Texans were led by a man named Frank Stewart, and the others were identified by Garrett as Lon Chambers, Lee Hall, Jim East, Poker Tom, The Animal, and Tenderfoot Bob. With characters like these after him, Billy the Kid was in serious trouble. Garrett's description of what followed, written with the assistance of a newspaper man named Ash Upson, opens as he and his posse quietly enter Fort Sumner and prepare to ambush the outlaws when they come to town.

~ ~ ~ ~ ~

## Fort Sumner, New Mexico -- December 18, 1880

**I was confident that the gang would be in Fort Sumner** that night, and made arrangements to receive them. There was an old hospital building on the eastern boundary of the plaza -- the direction from which they would come -- the wife of Bowdre occupied a room of the building, and I felt sure they would pay their first visit to her. I took my posse there, placed a guard about the house, and awaited the game.

They came fully two hours before we expected them. We were passing away the time playing cards. There were several Mexicans in the plaza, some of whom, I feared, would convey information to the gang, so I had them with me, in custody. Snow was lying on the ground, increasing the light outside. About eight o'clock a guard cautiously called from the door -- "Pat, someone is coming!" "Get your guns, boys," said I; "None but the men we want are riding this time of night."

The Kid, with all his reckless bravery, had a strong infusion of caution in his composition when not excited. He afterwards told me that, as they approached the building that night he was riding in front with Foliard. As they bore down close upon us, he said a strong suspicion arose in his mind that they might be running into unseen danger. "Well," said I, "what did you do?" He replied: "I wanted a chew of tobacco, bad. Wilson had some that was good, and he was in the rear. I went back after tobacco, don't you see?" -- and his eye twinkled mischievously.

One of the Mexicans followed me out, and we two joined the guard, Lon Chambers, on one side, and Mason, with the rest of the party, went round the building to intercept them should they aim to pass on into the plaza. The gang were in full sight approaching. In front rode Foliard and Pickett. I was under the porch, and close against the wall, partly hidden by some harness hanging there, Chambers close behind me and the Mexican behind him. I whispered: "That's them." They rode up until Foliard's horse's head was under the porch, when I called, "Halt!" Foliard reached for his pistol -- Chambers and I both fired; his horse wheeled and ran at least one hundred and fifty yards. Quick as possible I fired at Pickett. The flash of Chambers' gun disconcerted my aim and I missed him; but one would have thought, by the way he ran and yelled, that he had a dozen balls in him. When Foliard's horse ran with him, he was uttering cries of mortal agony, and we were convicted that he had received his death. He, however, wheeled his horse, and, as he rode

219

slowly back, he said: "Don't shoot, Garrett. I'm killed." Mason called: "Take your medicine old boy, take your medicine," and was going to Foliard. I called to Mason and told him that Foliard was killed, and might want revenge. He could pull a trigger yet, and to be careful how he approached him. I called to Tom, to throw up his hands, that I would give him no chance to kill me. He said he was dying and could not throw up his hands, and begged that we would take him off his horse and let him die as easy as possible. Holding our guns down on him we went up, took his gun out of the scabbard, lifted him off his horse, carried him into the house and laid him down; took off his pistol, which was full-cocked, and found that he was shot through the left side, just below the heart, and his coat was cut across the front by a bullet.

During this encounter with Foliard and Pickett, the party on the other side had seen The Kid and the rest of the gang, had fired on them and killed Rudabaugh's horse, which, however, ran twelve miles with him, to Wilcox's ranch, before he died. Soon as Mason and his party fired, these four ran like a bunch of wild Nueces steers. They were completely surprised and demoralized. As soon as The Kid and companions disappeared, Mason came round the building just as Foliard was returning, reeling in his saddle. After we had laid him down inside, he begged me to kill him, said if I was a friend of his I would put him out of his misery. I told him I was no friend to men of his kind, who sought to murder me because I tried to do my duty, and that I did not shoot up my friends as he was shot. Just then Mason entered the room again. Foliard changed his tone at once, and cried: "Don't shoot anymore for God's sake, I'm already killed." Perhaps he guessed that if he called on Mason to put him out of his misery he would comply with his request. Mason told him again to "take his medicine." He replied: "It's the best medicine I ever took." He also asked Mason to tell McKinney to write to his grandmother in Texas, and inform her of his death. Once he exclaimed: "O! my God, is it possible I must die?" I said to him, just before he died: "Tom, your time is short." He answered: "The sooner the better; I will be out of pain." He died about three quarters of an hour after he was shot.

Pickett was unhurt, but was nearly scared to death. He went howling over the prairie, yelling bloody murder, and was lost until the next night. He ran his horse down and then took it on foot, reached Wilcox's ranch about dark the next night, and hid in a hay-stack. He had run his horse full twenty-five miles in a northeast direction, before he gave out, and had then walked twelve or fifteen miles to the ranch. Here he remained, crouching in fear and trembling in the hay-stack, until he saw his companions ride in from the hills.

The Kid, Rudabaugh, Bowdre, and Wilson fled to Wilcox's ranch, where Rudabaugh got another horse. They then lost no time in getting to the hills, from which they watched the ranch and surrounding country throughout all the next day, with their field glasses. At dark they rode back to the house, when Pickett showed himself. It must have been amusing to witness this fellow's sudden change from abject cowardice to excessive bravado so soon as he realized that he was actually alive and unharmed, and that he had friends within reach to whom he could look for protection. He swaggered about and blowed his bugle something in this strain. "Boys, I got that d----d long-legged fellow [Pat Garrett was a lean 6'4"] that hollered, 'Halt.' I had my gun lying on my saddle, in front of me, and, just as he hailed, I poured it into him. O, I got him sure."

The gang, now reduced to five, remained at Wilcox's ranch that night. They were depressed and disheartened. After a long consultation, they concluded to send some one to Fort Sumner the following morning to spy out the lay of the land. They relieved guard through the night to prevent surprise, and sent Wilcox's partner, Mr. Brazil, to the plaza the next day. They had suspected Wilcox and Brazil of treachery, when they were so effectually surprised at the hospital building, but had been entirely reassured by them, since their return.

Brazil came to me at Fort Sumner on the morning of December 20th. He described the condition of the crestfallen band, and told me they had sent him in to take items and report to them. I told him to return and tell them that I was at Sumner with only Mason and three Mexicans; that I was considerably scared up and wanted to go back to Roswell, but feared to leave the plaza. Brazil did not return until the following day. When he was ready to start, I told him if he found the gang at the ranch, when he arrived there, to remain. If they had left, or did leave after his arrival, to come and report to me; that if he did not come to me sooner, I would start for the ranch at 2 o'clock in the morning; and that, if I did not meet him on the road, I would feel sure they were at the ranch.

This faithful friend went home and returned, reaching Sumner about 12 o'clock in the night. There was snow on the ground, it was desperately cold, and Brazil's beard was full of icicles. He reported that The Kid and his four companions had taken supper at Wilcox's ranch, then mounted and left. We all started for the ranch. I sent Brazil ahead to see whether the gang had returned, whilst, with my posse, I took a circuitous route by Lake Ranch, a mile or two off the road, thinking they might be there. We rounded up the house, found it vacant, and rode on towards Wilcox's. About three miles from there we met Brazil. He said the outlaws had not returned, and showed me their trail on the snow. After following this trail a short distance, I was convinced that they had made for Stinking Spring, where there was an old deserted house, built by Alejandro Perea. When within a half-mile of the house, we halted and held a consultation. I told my companions I was confident we had them trapped, and cautioned them to preserve silence. When within about four hundred yards, we divided our party and left Juan Roybal in charge of the horses. With one-half the force I circled the house. Finding a dry arroyo we took its bed and were able to approach pretty close. Stewart, with the rest of the posse, found concealment within about two hundred yards of the building on the other side. There were three horses tied to projecting rafters of the house, and, knowing that there were five of the gang, and that they were all mounted when they left Wilcox's, we concluded they had led two horses inside. There was no door; only an opening, where a door had once been. I sent a messenger, who crept around to Stewart, proposing that, as they were surely there, we would stealthily enter the house, cover them with our guns, and hold them until daylight. Stewart demurred. Lee Hall was in favor of the plan. Shivering with cold, we awaited daylight for a movement from the inmates of the house.

I had a perfect description of The Kid's dress, especially his hat. I had told all the posse that, should The Kid make his appearance, it was my intention to kill him and the rest would surrender. The Kid had sworn that he would never yield himself a prisoner, but would die fighting, with a revolver at each hand, and I knew he would keep his word. I was in a position to command a view of the door-way, and told my men that when I brought up my gun, to all raise and fire.

Before it was fairly daylight, a man appeared at the entrance with a nose-bag in his hand, whom I firmly believed to be The Kid. His size and dress, especially the hat, corresponded with his descripton exactly. I gave the signal by bringing my gun to my shoulder, my men raised, and seven bullets sped on their errand of death. Our victim was Charlie Bowdre. Turning, he reeled back into the house. In a moment Wilson's voice was heard. He called to me and said the Bowdre was killed and wanted to come out. I told him to have Bowdre come out with his hands up. As Bowdre started out, The Kid caught hold of his belt, drew his revolver around in front of him and said: "They have murdered you, Charlie, but you can get revenge. Kill some of the sons-of-b-----s before you die." Bowdre came out, his pistol still hanging in front of him, but with his hands up. He walked towards our ranks until he recognized me, then came straight to me, motioned with his hand towards the house, and strangling with blood, said: "I wish -- I wish -- I wish -- I wish -- " then, in a whisper: "I'm dying!" I took hold of him, laid him gently on my blankets, and he died almost immediately.

Watching every movement about the house, in the increasing light, I shortly saw a motion of one of the ropes by which the horses were tied, and dropped on the fact that they were attempting to lead one of them inside. My first impulse was to shoot the rope in two, but it was shaking so, I feared to miss. I did better -- just as the horse was fairly in the opening, I shot him and he fell dead, partially barricading the outlet.

They had two horses in the house, one of them The Kid's favorite mare, celebrated for speed, bottom and beauty.

I now opened a conversation with the besieged, of whom The Kid was spokesman. I asked him how he was fixed in there.

"Pretty well," answered The Kid, "but we have no wood to get breakfast."

"Come out," said I, "and get some. Be a little sociable."

"Can't do it, Pat," replied he. "Business is too confining. No time to run around."

"Didn't you fellows forget a part of your programme yesterday?" said I. "You know you were to come in on us at Fort Sumner, from some other direction, give us a square fight, set us afoot, and drive us down the Pecos."

Our party were becoming very hungry, and, getting together, we arranged to go to Wilcox's ranch for breakfast. I went first, with one half the men. The distance was only about three miles. When we reached there, Brazil asked me what news I brought. I told him the news was bad; that we had killed the very man we did not want to kill. When he learned that it was Bowdre, he said: "I don't see why you should be sorry for having killed him. After you had the interview with him the other day, and was doing your best to get him out of his troubles, he said to me, as we were riding home, 'I wish you would get that d----d long-legged son-of-a----- out to meet me once more; I would just kill him and end all this trouble!' Now, how sorry are you?"

I made arrangements with Wilcox to haul out to our camp some provisions, wood and forage for our horses. I did not know how long the outlaws might hold out, and concluded I would make it as comfortable as possible for myself and the boys. Charley Rudolph had frozen his feet slightly, the night previous. On my return, Stewart and the balance of the boys went to breakfast.

About 3 o'clock, the gang turned loose the two horses from the inside. We picked them up, as we had the other two. About 4 o'clock the wagon arrived from Wilcox's with provisions and wood. We built a rousing fire and went to cooking. The odor of roasting meat was too much for the famished lads, who were without provisions. Craving stomachs overcame brave hearts. Rudabaugh stuck out from the window a handkerchief that had once been white, at the end of a stick, and called to us that they wanted to surrender. I told them that they could all come out, with their hands up, if they wanted to. Rudabaugh then came out to our camp and said they would all surrender if I would guarantee them protection from violence. This, of course, I did. Rudabaugh returned to the house, where they held a short consultation. In a few moments they all, The Kid, Wilson, Pickett and Rudabaugh, came out, were disarmed, got their supper, and we took them to Wilcox's. I sent Brazil, Mason and Rudolph back to the ranch, with a wagon, after the body of Bowdre. On their arrival with the corpse at Wilcox's ranch, the cortege started for Fort Sumner, getting there before night. We turned Bowdre's body over to his wife, ironed the prisoners, and by sundown Stewart, Mason, Jim East, "Poker Tom" and myself, with the prisoners in charge, started for Las Vegas.

The Kid and Rudabaugh were cheerful and gay, during the trip. Wilson seemed dejected, and Pickett frightened. The Kid said that, had they succeeded in leading the three horses, or two of them, or one of them, into the house, they would have made a break to get away. He said, also, that he, alone, would have made a target of himself until his mare could have carried him out of range of our guns, or we had killed him, if it had not been for the dead horse barring his way. He said he knew she would not try to pass that [dead horse], and, if she did, she would have knocked the top of his head off against the lentel of the doorway. Whilst at Fort Sumner, The Kid had made Stewart a present of the mare, remarking that he expected his business would be so confining for the next few months, that he would hardly find time for horse-back exercise.

We reached Gayheart's ranch, with our prisoners, about midnight, rested until 8 in the morning, and reached Puerto de Luna at 2 o'clock p.m., on Christmas day. My friend Grzelachowski gave us all a splendid dinner.

With a fresh team, we got away from Puerta de Luna about 4 o'clock. Broke our wagon; borrowed one of Capt. Clarency, and reached Hay's ranch for breakfast. At 2 o'clock p.m., December 26, we reached Las Vegas, and, through a crowd of citizens, made our way to the jail. Our objective point was the Santa Fe jail, as there were United States warrants against all our prisoners except Pickett. Him we intended to leave at Las Vegas. The other three we proposed to go on to Santa Fe with in the morning, although we expected, and so did Rudabaugh, that the authorities of Las Vegas would insist on holding him for the killing of the jailor. We had promised Rudabaugh to take him to Santa Fe, and were determined to do it. So Stewart went and made oath that we were holding this prisoner on a United States warrant; armed with which instrument and our warrant, we intended to hold this prisoner and take him to Santa Fe.

On the morning of December 27th, I had fresh irons placed on The Kid, Rudabaugh and Wilson. Michael Cosgrove, Esq., mail contractor, being well acquainted in Santa Fe, I induced him to accompany me there with the prisoners. I therefore released two of my guards, and started with Cosgrove, Stewart and Mason.

After breakfast, we went to the jail for our prisoners. They turned out The Kid and Wilson to us, who were handcuffed together. We demanded Rudabaugh. They refused to yield him up, saying he had escaped from that jail, and they wanted him for murder. I told them that our right to the prisoner ranked theirs, as I was a Deputy United States Marshal, and had arrested Rudabaugh for an offense against laws of the United States; that I knew nothing of any other offense or arrest; that he was my prisoner, I was responsible for him, and intended to have him. Stewart drew his affidavit on them, and they, at last, turned Rudabaugh out to us.

We had been on the train with our three prisoners but a few minutes when we noticed that a good many Mexicans, scattered through the crowd, were armed with rifles and revolvers, and seemed consideraby excited. Stewart and I concluded their object was to take Rudabaugh off the train. I asked Stewart if we should make a fight for it; he said we would, of course. I said "Let's make it a good one." We felt sure they intended to mob him, or we might have given him up. Besides, he acknowledged that he was afraid of them, and we were pledged to protect him and take him to Santa Fe.

Stewart guarded one door of the car, and I the other. These armed ruffians crowded about the car, but none of them made a formal demand for Rudabaugh, or stated their business. Deputy Sheriff Romero, brother to the Sheriff who had so distinguished himself when I brought Webb to him at Hay's ranch, headed a mob of five, who approached the platform where I was standing, flourishing their revolvers. One of the mob said: "Let's go right in and take him out of there, and they pushed this Deputy up on the platform, crowding after him. I merely requested them, in my mildest tones, to get down, and they slid to the ground like a covey of hardback turtles off the banks of the Pecos. They did not seem at all frightened, but modest and bashful-like.

Rudabaugh was excited. The Kid and Wilson seemed unconcerned. I told them not to be uneasy; that we were going to make a fight if they tried to enter the car, and if the fight came off, I would arm them all, and let them take a hand. The Kid's eyes glistened, as he said: "All right, Pat. All I want is a six shooter. There is no danger, though. Those fellows won't fight." The mob were weakening, and all they wanted was for some one to coax them to desist, so it not look so much like a square back-down. Some influential Mexicans reasoned a little with them and they subsided. We were detained by them about three-quarters of an hour. I understood, afterwards, that they had presented their guns to the engineer and threatened him if he moved the train. One of the railroad officials threatened them with the law for detaining the United States mail. At last Deputy United States Marshal Mollay mounted the cab and pulled the train out.

I had telegraphed to Deputy United States Marshal Charles Conklin, and found him at the Santa Fe depot, waiting for us. I turned the prisoners over to him, on the 27th day of December, 1880, and he placed them in the Santa Fe jail. Whilst there they made an attempt to escape by digging a hole through the adobe walls, hiding the dirt under their bedding. This attempt was frustrated through the vigilance of officials.

Rudabaugh was tried and convicted for robbing the United States mail, but no sentence was passed. On demand of territorial authorities he was taken to San Miguel County, tried for the murder of the jailer, convicted, and sentenced to be hung. He took an appeal and languished in the Las Vegas jail awaiting a new trial. He has since escaped.

Billy Wilson has been twice arraigned for passing counterfeit money, first at Mesilla and then at Santa Fe; but has not, as yet, had a trial. Should he clear himself on this charge, he is in jeopardy for complicity in the murder of Carlyle.

Deputy United States Marshal Tony Neis took The Kid and Wilson from Santa Fe to Mesilla, where The Kid was first tried, at the March, 1881, term for the District Court, for the murder of Roberts, at the Mescalero Apache Indian Agency, in March, 1878. Judge Bristol assigned Judge Ira E. Leonard, of Lincoln, to defend him. He was acquitted. He was again tried, at the same term, for the murder of Sheriff William Brady, at Lincoln, on the 1st day of April, 1878, was convicted, and sentenced to be hung on the 13th day of May, 1881, at Lincoln, the county seat of Lincoln County. He was brought from Mesilla by Deputy Marshal Robert Olinger and Deputy Sheriff David Woods, of Doña Ana County, and turned over to me by them at Fort Stanton, nine miles west of Lincoln, April 21, 1881.

Lincoln County has never had a jail, until within the last few weeks, that would hold a cripple. The county had just purchased the large two-story building, formerly the mercantile house of Murphy & Dolan, for the use of the county as a public building, but no jail had been constructed; hence I was obliged to place a guard over The Kid. I selected Deputy Sheriff J. W. Bell, and Deputy Marshal Robert Olinger, for this duty, and assigned them a guard room in the second story of the county building, separate and apart from other prisoners. This room was at the north-east corner of the building, and one had to pass from a hall, through another large room, to gain the only door to it. There were two windows -- one on the north, opening to the street, and the other on the east, opening into a large yard, which ran east a hundred yards, or more, and projected into the street twelve or fourteen feet past the north, or front, walls of the building. At the projecting corner of the yard, next to the house on the north-west, was a gate; a path running from this gate along the east end of the building to the rear, or south wall, where was a smaller gate opening into a corral, in the rear of the house. Passing through this corral to the south-west corner of the building, we come to a door leading to a small hall and a broad staircase, which was the only, then, means of access to the second story of the building. Facing the north, we ascend five or six steps, reach a square landing, turn to the right, facing the east, and ascend twelve or fourteen steps, reaching the hall which extends through the building from north to south. Turning to the right, we find two doors, one on each side of the hall. The one to the right leads into a room in the south-west corner of the building, where we kept surplus arms. Turning to the left, from the head of the staircase we find two other doors, one on each side of the hall, and still another at the north end, which opens on a porch, facing the street on the north. The door on the left, or west side of the hall, led to a room appropriated to the confinement of prisoners, over whom I kept a guard. The door on the right, or east side of the hall, opened into a large room, occupied by me as an office, passing through which, another door opens into the north-east apartment, which I assigned to the guard, in which to confine The Kid. The necessity of this description will soon be understood by the reader, whether the description is lucid or not.

During the few days The Kid remained in confinement, I had several conversations with him. He appeared to have a plausible excuse for each and every crime charged against him, except, perhaps, the killing of Carlyle. I said to him one day: "Billy, I pass no opinion as to whether your sentence is just for the killing of Brady, but, had you been acquitted on that charge, you would, most surely, have been hung for the murder of Jimmy Carlyle, and I would have pronounced that sentence just. That was the most detestable crime ever charged against you." He seemed abashed and dejected, and only remarked: "There's more about that than people know of." In our conversations, he would sometimes seem on the point of opening his heart, either in confession or justification, but it always ended in an unspoken intimation that it would all be of no avail, as no one would give him credence, and he scorned to beg for sympathy. He expressed no enmity towards me for having been the instrument through which he was brought to justice, but evinced respect and confidence in me, acknowledging that I had only done my duty, without malice, and had treated him with marked leniency and kindness.

As to his guards, he placed confidence in Deputy Sheriff Bell, and appeared to have taken a liking to him. Bell was in no manner connected with the Lincoln County War, and had no animosity or old grudge against The Kid. The natural abhorence of an honest man towards a well known violator of the law was intensified in Bell's case, by the murder of Carlyle, who was a friend of his; but never, by word or action, did he betray his prejudice, if it existed. As to Deputy Marshal Olinger, the case was altogether different. They had met, opposed in arms, frequently during the past years of anarchy. Ben Beckwith was a bosom friend of Olinger's -- The Kid had killed him. The Kid charged that Olinger had killed friends of his. There existed a reciprocal hatred between these two, and neither attempted to disguise or conceal his antipathy from the other.

On the evening of April 28, 1881, Olinger took all the other prisoners across the street to supper, leaving Bell in charge of The Kid, in the guard room. We have but The Kid's tale, and the sparse information elicited from Mr. Geiss, a German employed about the building, to determine facts in regard to events immediately following Olinger's departure. From circumstances, indications, information from Geiss, and The Kid's admissions, the popular conclusion is that:

At the Kid's request, Bell accompanied him down stairs and into the back corral. As they returned, Bell allowed The Kid to get considerably in advance. As the Kid turned on the landing of the stairs, he was hidden from Bell. He was light and active, and, with a few noiseless bounds, reached the head of the stairs, turned to the right, put his shoulder to the door of the room used as an armory, (though locked, this door was well-known to open by a firm push), entered, seized a six-shooter, returned to the head of the stairs just as Bell faced him on the landing of the stair-case, some twelve steps beneath, and fired. Bell turned, ran out into the corral and towards the little gate. He fell dead before reaching it. The Kid ran to the window of the south end of the hall, saw Bell fall, then slipped his handcuffs over his hands, threw them at the body, and said: "Here, d--n you, take these, too." He then ran to my office and got a double-barreled shot-gun. This gun was a very fine one, a breech-loader, and belonged to Olinger. He had loaded it that morning, in presence of The Kid, putting eighteen buckshot in each barrel, and remarked: "The man that gets one of those loads will feel it." The Kid then entered the guard-room and stationed himself at the east window, opening on the yard.

Olinger heard the shot and started back across the street, accompanied by L. M. Clements. Olinger entered the gate leading into the yard, as Geiss appeared at the little corral gate and said, "Bob, The Kid has killed Bell." At the same instant The Kid's voice was heard above: "Hello, old boy," said he. "Yes, and he's killed me, too," exclaimed Olinger, and fell dead, with eighteen buckshot in his right shoulder, breast and side. The Kid went back through the guard-room, through my office, into the hall and out on the balcony. From here he could see the body of Olinger, as it lay in the projecting corner of the yard, near the gate. He took deliberate aim and fired the other barrel, the charge taking effect in nearly the same place at the first; then breaking the gun across the railing of the balcony, he threw the pieces at Olinger, saying: "Take it, d---n you, you won't follow me any more with that gun." He then returned to the back room, armed himself with a Winchester and two revolvers. He was still encumbered with his shackles, but hailing old man Geiss, he commanded him to bring a file. Geiss did so, and threw it up to him in the window. The Kid then ordered the old man to go and saddle a horse that was in the stable, the property of Billy Burt, Deputy Clerk of Probate, then went to the front window, commanding a view of the street, seated himself and filed the shackles from one leg. Bob Brookshire came out on the street from the hotel opposite, and started down towards the plaza. The Kid brought his Winchester down on him and said: "Go back, young fellow, go back. I don't want to hurt you, but I am fighting for my life. I don't want to see any body leave that house."

In the meantime, Geiss was having trouble with the horse, which broke loose and ran around the corral and yard a while, but was at last brought to the front of the house. The Kid was all over the building, on the porch, and watching from the windows. He danced about the balcony, laughed and shouted as though he had not a care on earth. He remained at the house for nearly an hour after the killing, before he made a motion to leave. As he approached to mount, the horse again broke loose and ran down towards the Rio Bonito. The Kid called to Andrew Nimley, a prisoner, who was standing by, to go and catch him. Nimley hesitated, but a quick, imperative motion by The Kid started him. He brought the horse back and The Kid remarked: "Old fellow, if you hadn't gone for this horse I would have killed you." And now he mounted and said to those in hearing: "Tell Billy Burt I will send his horse back to him," then galloped away, the shackles still hanging to one leg. He was armed with a Winchester and two revolvers. He took the road west, leading to Fort Stanton, but turned north about four miles from town, and rode in the direction of Las Tablas.

It is in order to again visit the scene of the tragedy. It was found that Bell was hit under the right arm, the ball passing through the body and coming out under the left arm. On examination it was evident that The Kid had made a very poor shot, for him, and his hitting Bell at all was a scratch. The ball had hit the wall on Bell's right, caromed, passed through his body and buried itself in an adobe on his left. There was other proof besides the marks in the wall  The ball had surely been indented and creased before it entered the body, as these scars were filled with flesh. The Kid afterwards told Peter Maxwell that Bell shot at him twice, and just missed him. There is no doubt but this statement was false. One other shot was heard before Olinger appeared on the scene, but it is believed to have been an accidental one by The Kid whilst prospecting with the arms. Olinger was shot in the right shoulder, breast and side. He was literally riddled by thirty-six buckshot.

The inhabitants of the whole town of Lincoln appeared to be terror-stricken. The Kid, it is my firm belief, could have ridden up and down the plaza until dark, without a shot having been fired at him, nor an attempt made to arrest him. A little sympathy might have actuated some of them, but most of the people were, doubtless, paralyzed with fear when it was whispered that the dreaded desperado, The Kid, was at liberty and had slain his guards.

This, to me, was a most distressing calamity, for which I do not hold myself guiltless. The Kid's escape, and the murder of his two guards, was the result of mismanagement and carelessness, to a great extent. I knew the desperate character of the man who the authorities would look for at my hands on the 13th day of May -- that he was daring and unscrupulous, and that he would sacrifice the lives of a hundred men who stood between him and liberty, when the gallows stared him in the face, with as little compunction as he would kill a coyote. And now I realize how all inadequate my precautions were. Yet, in self-defense, and hazarding the charge of shirking the responsibility and laying it upon dead men's shoulders, I must say that my instructions as to caution and the routine of duty, were not heeded and followed.

On the bloody 28th of April, I was at White Oaks. I left Lincoln on the day previous, to meet engagements to receive taxes. Was at Las Tablas on the 27th, and went from there to White Oaks. On the 29th, I received a letter from John C. Delaney, Esq., of Fort Stanton, merely stating the fact of The Kid's escape and the killing of the guard. The same day Billy Nickey arrived from Lincoln and gave me the particulars. I returned to Lincoln on the 30th, and went out with some volunteer scouts to try and find The Kid's trail, but was unsuccessful. A few days later, Billy Burt's horse came in dragging a rope. The Kid had either turned him loose, or sent him in by some friend, who had brought him into the vicinity of the town, and headed him for home.

The next I heard of The Kid, after his escapade at Lincoln, was that he had been at Las Tablas and had there stolen a horse from Andy Richardson. He rode this horse to a point a few miles from Fort Sumner, where he got away from him, and The Kid walked into the town. If he made his presence known to any one there, I have not heard of it. At Sumner he stole a horse from Montgomery Bell, who lives some fifty miles above, but was there on business. He rode this horse out of town bareback, going in a southerly direction. Bell supposed the horse had been stolen by some Mexican, and got Barney Mason and Mr. Curington to go with him and hunt him up. Bell left his companions and went down the Rio Pecos. Mason and Curington took another direction. Mason had a rifle and a six-shooter, whilst Curington was unarmed. They came to a Mexican sheep-camp, rode up close to it, and The Kid stepped out and hailed them. The Kid had designated Mason as an object of his direct vengeance. On the sudden and unexpected appearance of The Kid, Mason's business "laid rolling." He had *no sight on his gun*, but wore *a new pair of spurs*. In short, Mason left. Curington stopped and talked to The Kid, who told him that he had Bell's horse, and to tell Bell he was afoot, and must have something to ride out of the country; that, if he could make any other arrangements, he would send the horse to him; if not, he would pay for him.

It is known that, subsequent to The Kid's interview with Curington, he stayed for some time with one of Pete Maxwell's sheep-herders, about thirty-five miles east of Sumner. He spent his time at cow and sheep-camps, was often at Cañaditas, Arenoso and Fort Sumner. He was almost constantly on the move. And thus, for about two and a-half months, The Kid led a fugitive life, hovering, in spite of danger, around the scenes of his past two years of lawless adventure. He had many friends who were true to him, harbored him, kept him supplied with territorial newspapers, and with valuable information concerning his safety. The end was not yet, but fast approaching.

During the weeks following The Kid's escape, I was censured by some for my seeming unconcern and inactivity in the matter of his re-arrest. I was egotistical enough to think I knew my own business best, and preferred to accomplish this duty, if possible at all, in my own way. I was constantly, but quietly, at work, seeking sure information and maturing my plans of action. I did not lay about The Kid's old haunts, nor disclose my intentions and operations to any one. I stayed at home, most of the time, and busied myself about the ranch. If my seeming unconcern deceived the people and gave The Kid confidence in his security, my end was accomplished. It was my belief that The Kid was still in the country and haunted the vicinity of Fort Sumner; yet there was some doubt mingled with my belief. He was never taken for a fool, but was credited with the possession of extraordinary forethought and cool judgment, for one of his age. It seems incredible that, in his situation, with the extreme penalty of the law, the reward of detection, and the way of successful flight and safety open to him -- with no known tie to bind him to that dangerous locality -- it seemed incredible that he should linger in the Territory. My first task was to solve my doubts.

Early in July I received a reply from a letter I had written to Mr. Brazil. I was at Lincoln when this letter came to me. Mr. Brazil was dodging and hiding from The Kid. He feared his vengeance on account of the part which he, Brazil, had taken in his capture. There were many others who "trembled in their boots" at the knowledge of his escape; but most of them talked him out of his resentment, or conciliated him in some manner.

Brazil's letter gave me no positive information. He said he had not seen The Kid since his escape, but, from many indications, believed he was still in the country. He offered me any assistance in his power to re-capture him. I again wrote to Brazil, requesting him to meet me at the mouth of Tayban Arroyo, an hour after dark, on the night of the 13th day of July.

A gentleman named John W. Poe, who had superceded Frank Stewart, in the employ of the stockmen of the Canadian, was at Lincoln on business, as was one of my deputies, Thomas K. McKinney. I first went to McKinney, and told him I wanted him to accompany me on a business trip to Arizona; that we would go down home and start from there. He consented. I then went to Poe, and, to him, I disclosed my business and all its particulars, showing him my correspondence. He, also, complied with my request that he should accompany me.

We three went to Roswell, and started up the Rio Pecos from there on the night of July 10th. We rode mostly in the night, followed no roads, but taking unfrequented routes, and arrived at the mouth of Tayban Arroyo, five miles south of Fort Sumner, one hour after dark, on the night of the 13th. Brazil was not there. We waited nearly two hours, but he did not come. We rode off a mile or two, staked our horses and slept until daylight. Early in the morning we rode up into the hills and prospected awhile with our field-glasses.

Poe was a stranger in the county and there was little danger that he would meet any one who knew him at Sumner. So, after an hour or two spent in the hills, he went into Sumner to take observations. I advised him, also, to go on to Sunnyside, seven miles above Sumner, and interview M. Rudolph, Esq., in whose judgment and discretion I had great confidence. I arranged with Poe to meet us that night at moonrise, at La Punta de la Glorietta, four miles north of Fort Sumner. Poe went on to the Plaza, and McKinney and myself rode down into the Pecos Valley, where we remained during the day. At night we started out circling around the town, and met Poe exactly on time at the trysting place.

Poe's appearance at Sumner had excited no particular observation, and he had gleaned no news there. Rudolph thought, from all indications, that The Kid was about; and yet, at times, he doubted. His cause for doubt seemed to be based on no evidence except the fact that The Kid was no fool, and no man in his senses, under the circumstances, would brave such danger.

I then concluded to go and have a talk with Peter Maxwell, Esq., in whom I felt sure I could rely. We had ridden to within a short distance of Maxwell's grounds, when we found a man in camp, and stopped. To Poe's great surprise, he recognized in the camper an old friend and former partner, in Texas, named Jacobs. We unsaddled here, got some coffee, and, on foot, entered an orchard which runs from this point down to a row of old buildings, some of them occupied by Mexicans, not more than sixty yards from Maxwell's house. We approached these houses cautiously, and when within ear-shot, heard the sound of voices conversing in Spanish. We concealed ourselves quickly and listened; but the distance was too great to hear words, or even distinguish voices. Soon a man arose from the ground, in full view; but too far away to recognize. He wore a broad-brimmed hat, a dark vest and pants, and was in his shirtsleeves. With a few words, which fell like a murmur on our ears, he went to the fence, jumped it, and walked down towards Maxwell's house.

Little as we then suspected it, this man was The Kid. We learned, subsequently, that, when he left his companions that night, he went to the house of a Mexican friend, pulled off his hat and boots, threw himself on a bed and commenced reading a newspaper. He soon, however, hailed his friend, who was sleeping in the room, told him to get up and make some coffee, adding: "Give me a butcher knife and I will go over to Pete's and get some beef; I'm hungry." The Mexican arose, handed him the knife, and The Kid, hatless and in his stocking-feet, started to Maxwell's room, which was but a few steps distant.

When The Kid, unrecognized by me, left the orchard, I motioned to my companions, and we cautiously retreated a short distance, and, to avoid the persons whom we had heard at the houses, took another route, approaching Maxwell's house from the opposite direction. When we reached the porch in front of the building, I left Poe and McKinney at the end of the porch, about twenty feet from the door of Pete's room, and went in. It was near midnight and Pete was in bed. I walked to the head of the bed and sat down on it, beside him, near the pillow. I asked him as to the whereabouts of The Kid. He said that The Kid had certainly been about, but did not know whether he had left or not. At that moment a man sprang quickly into the door, looking back, and called twice in Spanish, "Who comes there?" No one replied and he came on in. He was bareheaded. From his step I could perceive he was either barefooted or in his stocking-feet, and had a revolver in his right hand and a butcher knife in his left.

He came directly towards me. Before he reached the bed, I whispered: "Who is it, Pete?" but received no reply for a moment. It struck me that it might be Pete's brother-in-law, Manuel Abreu, who had seen Poe and McKinney, and wanted to know their business. The intruder came close to me, leaned both hands on the bed, his right hand almost touching my knee, and asked, in a low tone: "Who are they Pete?" at the same instant Maxwell whispered to me. "That's him!" Simultaneously The Kid must have seen, or felt, the presence of a third person at the head of the bed. He raised quickly his pistol, a self-cocker, within a foot of my breast. Retreating rapidly across the room he cried: *"Quien es? Quien es?"* (Who's that? Who's that?) All this occurred in a moment. Quickly as possible I drew my revolver and fired, threw my body aside and fired again. The second shot was useless; The Kid fell dead. He never spoke. A struggle or two, a little strangling sound as he gasped for breath, and The Kid was with his many victims.

Maxwell had plunged over the foot of the bed on the floor, dragging the bed-clothes with him. I went to the door and met Poe and McKinney there. Maxwell rushed past me, out on the porch; they drew their guns down on him, when he cried: "Don't shoot, don't shoot." I told my companions I had got The Kid. They asked me if I had not shot the wrong man. I told them I had made no blunder; that I knew The Kid's voice too well to be mistaken. The Kid was entirely unknown to either of them. They had seen him pass in, and, as he stepped on the porch, McKinney, who was sitting, rose to his feet; one of his spurs caught under the boards, and nearly threw him. The Kid laughed, but, probably, saw their guns, as he drew his revolver and sprang into the door-way, as he hailed: "Who comes there?" Seeing a bareheaded, barefooted man, in his shirt-sleeves, with a butcher knife in his hand, and hearing his hail in excellent Spanish, they naturally supposed him to be a Mexican and an attaché of the establishment, hence their suspicion that I had shot the wrong man.

We now entered the room and examined the body. The ball struck him just above the heart, and must have cut through the ventricles. Poe asked me how many shots I fired; I told him two, but that I had no idea where the second one went. Both Poe and McKinney said The Kid must have fired then, as there were surely three shots fired. I told them that he had fired one shot, between my two. Maxwell said that The Kid fired; yet, when we came to look for bullet marks, none from his pistol could be found. We searched long and faithfully -- found both my bullet marks and none other; so, against the impression and senses of four men, we had to conclude that The Kid did not fire at all. We examined his pistol -- a self-cocker, calibre .41. It had five cartridges and one shell in the chambers, the hammer resting on the shell, but this proves nothing, as many carry their revolvers in this way for safety; besides, this shell looked as though it had been shot some time before.

It will never be known whether The Kid recognized me or not. If he did, it was the first time, during all his life of peril, that he ever lost his presence of mind, or failed to shoot first, and hesitate afterwards. He knew that a meeting with me meant surrender or fight. He told several persons about Sumner that he bore no animosity against me, and had no desire to do me injury. He also said that he knew, should we meet, he would have to surrender, kill me, or get killed himself. So, he declared his intention, should we meet, to commence shooting on sight.

On the following morning, the Alcalde, Alejandro Segura, held an inquest on the body. Hon. M. Randolph, of Sunnyside, was foreman of the Coroner's Jury. They found a verdict that William H. Bonney came to his death from a gun-shot wound, the weapon in the hands of Pat F. Garrett; that the fatal wound was inflicted by the said Garrett in the discharge of his official duty as Sheriff, and that the homicide was justifiable.

The body was neatly and property dressed and buried in the Military Cemetery at Fort Sumner, July 15, 1881. His exact age, on the day of his death, was 21 years, 7 months and 21 days.

I said that the body was buried in the cemetery at Fort Sumner; I wish to add that it is there to-day intact. Skull, fingers, toes, bones and every hair of the head that was buried with the body on that 15th day of July, doctors, newspaper editors and paragraphers to the contrary notwithstanding. Some presuming swindlers have claimed to have The Kid's skull on exhibition, or one of his fingers, or some other portion of his body, and one medical gentleman has persuaded credulous idiots that he has all the bones strung upon wires. It is possible that there is a skeleton on exhibition somewhere in the States, or even this Territory, which was procured somewhere down the Rio Pecos. We have them, lots of them, in this section. The banks of the Pecos are dotted from Fort Sumner to the Rio Grande with unmarked graves, and the skeletons are of all sizes, ages and complexions. Any showman of ghastly curiosities can resurrect one or all of them, and place them on exhibition as the remains of Dick Turpin, Jack Shepherd, Cartouche, or The Kid, with no one to say him nay, so long as they don't ask the people of the Rio Pecos to believe it.

Again I say that The Kid's body lies undisturbed in the grave -- and I speak of what I know.

# CHASING GERONIMO THROUGH THE SIERRA MADRE
## (1885-86)

## Captain Marion P. Maus

**Editors' Note:** No Indians were more feared by both American and Mexican settlers than the Apaches of the Southwest. Semi-nomadic hunters and raiders, the Apaches were expert guerrilla fighters and almost impossible to pursue and hunt down in their rugged mountain sanctuaries. After preying upon sedentary Southwest Indian tribes for generations, it was only natural that they took to stealing livestock from Mexican and American ranches, and raiding homesteads and settlements that increasingly threatened traditional Apache territory. And woe be it to any poor souls who found themselves caught out alone or outnumbered when the Apaches were on the warpath.

Despite numerous skirmishes and some serious defeats at the hands of their American and Mexican foes, the Apaches continued to take their toll of lives and property until the early 1870's. Then the U. S. War Department put Lieutenant Colonel George Crook in command of the Apache campaign in Arizona Territory. Crook's tactic was to use Apaches to fight Apaches. Some of the Apaches, having already been pacified, were encouraged to enlist as army "scouts." The term "scout" did not imply that these men were only trackers and guides -- which they were -- for they were also armed and paid wages to fight like regular troops. Formed into companies under the command of the legendary Al Sieber, these Apache scouts tracked down and killed or captured renegade Apaches and Yavapais. So succesful were Crook's troops that when he was promoted to General and sent to serve against the Sioux in 1875, virtually all of the Apaches had been rounded up and placed on reservations.

But this was not to last. Many Apache warriors found the confines of reservation life demeaning and longed for their lost freedom. Soon Apaches were once again terrorizing the countryside. Knowing that they could not elude Sieber's scouts in U.S. Territory, they concentrated their raiding along the international border, operating from hideouts deep in the Sierra Madre of Mexico where the army could not follow them.

In September, 1882, General Crook was again placed in charge of the U. S. Army's Department of Arizona. Now his assignment was to hunt down and capture Chiricahua Apache renegades who had fled the San Carlos Reservation in Arizona and the Warm Springs Reservation in New Mexico. Once again the Indians were hiding out in the Sierra Madre and depredating villages on both sides of the border. The principal leader of the renegades was Geronimo.

Earlier in the year, a treaty had been signed with Mexican officials allowing U. S. Troops to enter Mexico in pursuit of Apaches. The Sierra Madre was no longer a sanctuary beyond the reach of American forces. After a campaign of eight difficult months, Crook induced Geronimo to surrender, and in June, 1883, the chief and about three hundred of his followers were taken back to San Carlos.

For nearly two years all went fairly smoothly, but in May, 1885, Geronimo and his Chiricahuas again jumped the reservation. In groups of ten to twenty, they slipped away at night and headed for the border, leaving a trail of despoiled ranches and dead settlers in their wake. Eventually, some two hundred Chiricahuas, including women and children, had fled their reservations. The citizens of Arizona and New Mexico demanded immediate action. The cat-and-mouse game of chasing Apaches in Mexico began anew.

In November, 1885, another expedition was sent south into Mexico in search of Geronimo and his band. This time the commander was Captain Emmet Crawford; other officers were Lieutenant W. E. Shipp, Lieutenant S. L. Faison, army surgeon T. B. Davis, and Marion P. Maus, at the time a Lieutenant in the U.S. Cavalry and second in command to Captain Crawford. The fighting force was a company of one hundred Apache scouts. As chief of scouts, Sieber sent Tom Horn, a flamboyant frontiersman of longstanding and his right-hand man. The highest ranking Apache under Crawford's command was a man named Chato (Spanish for pug-nosed). Ironically, before becoming a scout, Chato had been a renegade leader in his own right. In 1883 he led a small band of Apache raiders that murdered Judge Charles McComas and his wife along the Silver City to Lordsburg wagon road in southwest New Mexico, and carried the McComas child, Charlie, into Apache captivity in Mexico.

Pursuing Apaches through rough terrain was always a tough assignment, as the Chiricahuas lived off the land and were constantly on the move. Had it not been for the fact that the renegades were encumbered with women and children, it is doubtful if even the scouts could have caught up with them. There were also problems with operating in Mexico. Despite the 1882 treaty, Mexican troops regarded all Apaches as the enemy, whether renegades or U. S. Army scouts. Mexican troops were also less than enamored with the idea of American regulars operating in Mexico, as the expedition was to find out.

Despite the hardships endured and a supreme effort by the scouts and their officers, Crawford and his men were unsuccessful in bringing in the wily Geronimo. The following account of this frustrating, yet deadly, five-month foray into Mexico, written by then-Lieutenant Marion P. Maus, was first published in 1896 in General Nelson A. Miles' book *Personal Recollections*. General Miles relieved Crook as commander of the Department of Arizona in April, 1886, politicians and army brass having become impatient with Crook's failure to bring Geronimo to bay. They need not have worried. The old chief and his band had grown weary of the constant harassment by soldiers and scouts. Geronimo and most of his band surrendered to Miles' men at Skeleton Canyon, just north of Mexico, on the Arizona-New Mexico border, in August, 1886. Unlike Crook, who had always returned the renegades to reservations in the Southwest, Miles had Geronimo and the other Chiricahuas loaded into railroad cars and sent into exile at Fort Marion, Florida. Thus ended the military campaign against the Apaches and the Indian Wars in the American West.

~ ~ ~ ~ ~

**The command, fully equipped for field service, left Fort Apache,** Arizona, on November 11, 1885, for Fort Bowie. Here it was inspected by Lieutenant-General Sheridan and Brigadier-General Crook, and with words of encouragement from these officers, the command started south by way of the Dragoon Mountains, endeavoring to find the trail of a band of Indians who were returning to Mexico after a raid into the United States. Thoroughly scouting these mountains without finding the trail, we went on to the border and crossed into Mexico twenty miles north of the town of Fronteras, with the object of pursuing the renegades to their haunts in southern Sonora. We believed that if we could trace this band we could find the entire hostile camp under Geronimo and Natchez. Under instructions from Captain Crawford, I preceded the command to the town of Fronteras to notify the Presidente of the town of our approach, of our object in coming, and to gain information. It was a small place, composed of the usual adobe buildings, and its people lived in a constant state of alarm about the movements of the hostiles. The command arriving, we proceeded to Nocozari, a small mining town in the Madre Mountains. On account of the roughness of these mountains we found great difficulty in crossing them with the pack-train. We found one horse which had evidently been abandoned by the hostiles, but no distinct trail.

In marching the command it was interesting to notice the methods adopted by our Indians in scouting the country to gain information and prevent surprise. It illustrated to us very clearly what we must expect from the hostiles, who would employ the same methods. It was impossible to march these scouts as soldiers, or to control them as such, nor was it deemed advisable to attempt it. Among them were many who had bloody records; one named Dutchy had killed, in cold blood, a white man near Fort Thomas, and for this murder the civil authorities were at this time seeking to arrest him. Their system of advance guards and flankers was perfect, and as soon as the command went into camp, outposts were at once put out, guarding every approach. All this was done noiselessly and in secret, and without giving a single order. As scouts for a command in time of war they would be ideal. Small of stature, and apparently no match physically for the white man, yet when it came to climbing mountains or making long marches, they were swift and tireless. The little clothing they wore consisted of a soldier's blouse, discarded in time of action, light undergarments and a waist cloth, and on the march the blouse was often turned inside out to show only the gray lining. Nothing escaped their watchful eyes as they marched silently in their moccasined feet. By day small fires were built of dry wood to avoid smoke, and at night they were made in hidden places so as to be invisible. If a high point was in view, you could be sure that a scout had crawled to the summit and, himself unseen, with a glass or his keen eyes had searched the country around. At night only was the watch relaxed, for these savages dread the night with a superstitious fear. It was necessary to allow them their way, and we followed, preserving order as best we could by exercising tact and by a careful study of their habits. Under the influence of mescal, which is a liquor made in parts of Mexico and easily procured, they often became violent and troublesome and we could not help realizing how perfectly we were in their power. However, no distrust of them was shown. One of my Indians, a sergeant named Rubie, followed me one day while I was hunting. I thought his actions were curious, but they were explained when he suddenly came from the front and told me to go back. He had seen the footprints of hostiles near by. In the action which followed later he came to me and warned me to cover. There was, however, very little evidence of affection or gratitude in them as a class.

Continuing the march, we reached the town of Huasavas in the valley of the Bavispe. Orange and lemon trees were filled with golden fruit, although it was now the 22nd of December. This valley, surrounded by high mountains, was fertile though but little cultivated. The only vehicles in use were carts, the wheels of which were sections sawed from logs. The plows were pieces of pointed wood. The people were devoid of all the comforts of life. Corn flour was obtained by pounding the grains on stones. They were a most desolate people, and completely terrorized by the Apaches, who were a constant menace to them, as they were to inhabitants of all these towns. Here occurred the first serious trouble with the Indian scouts. One of them, who was drunk but unarmed, was shot by a Mexican policeman. At the time I was on my way to the town and met the Indian, who was running down the road toward me, followed by two policemen or guards firing rapidly. One ball passed through his face, coming out through the jaw. The other Indian scouts were much incensed, and at once began to prepare for an attack on the town, giving us much trouble before we were able to stop them. The officers were unable to sleep that night, as many of the Indians had been drinking and continued to be so angry that they fired off their rifles in the camp. The next day I released one of them from prison, and subsequently had to pay a fine of five dollars for him. It was claimed by the Mexicans that the Indians had committed some breach of the peace.

Here we got the first reliable news of the hostiles who were murdering people and killing cattle to the south. Crossing the mountains we passed the towns of Granadas and Bacadehuachi, the latter being the site of one of the fine old missions built by the daring priests who had sought to plant their religion among the natives many years before.

Proceeding on our way over a mountainous country, we finally came to the town of Nacori. This place was in a continual state of alarm, a wall having been built around it as a protection against the Apaches, the very name of whom was a terror. From our camp, sixteen miles south of this town, two of our pack-trains were sent back to Lang's Ranch, New Mexico, for supplies. To our surprise a deputy United States marshal from Tombstone came here to arrest Dutchy. Captain Crawford declined to permit the arrest, and in a letter to the marshal (now on file in the State Department) asked him to "delay the arrest till I may be near the border where protection for myself, officers and white men, with my pack-trains, may be afforded by United States troops other than Indians," offering to return if desired. The scouts were intensely excited, and under the circumstances the marshal did not wish to attempt to arrest Dutchy, and returned without delay.

We had now penetrated over two hundred miles into the mountains of Mexico, and we were sure the hostiles were near. It was decided to move immediately in on them. In this wild and unknown land even our Indians looked more stolid and serious. One by one they gathered together for a medicine dance. The Medicine Man, Noh-wah-zhe-tah, unrolled the sacred buckskin he had worn since he left Fort Apache. There was something very solemn in all this. The dance, the marching, the kneeling before the sacred buckskin as each pressed his lips to it and the old man blessed him, impressed us too, as we looked on in silence. Afterward, the Indians held a council. They said they meant to do their duty, and would prove that they would fight to those who said they would not, and they seemed very much in earnest. I am satisfied that they desired to get the hostiles to surrender, but do not believe they intended or desired to kill them -- their own people. In view of their relations it was little wonder that they felt in this way.

It was decided that all must go on foot, and that officer and scout alike must carry his own blanket, all else being left behind. Leaving a few scouts (the weakest and the sick) to guard the camp, a force of seventy-nine was equipped with twelve days' rations, carried on three or four of the toughest mules best suited for the purpose, and we started forward. We marched to the Aros River, which we forded, and then ascending the high hills beyond, we discovered first a small trail, and then a large, well-beaten one, evidently that of the entire band of hostiles. The trail was about six days old, and as we passed over it, here and there, the bodies of dead cattle, only partially used, were found. The hostiles had but a short time previously moved their camp from the junction of the Aros and Yaqui Rivers a few miles to the west, and were going to the east to the fastnesses of some extremely rugged

241

mountains: the *Espinosa del Diablo*, or the Devil's Backbone -- a most appropriate name, as the country was broken and rough beyond description. The march was now conducted mostly by night. We suffered much from the cold, and the one blanket to each man used when we slept was scanty covering. Often it was impossible to sleep at all. At times we made our coffee and cooked our food in the daytime, choosing points where the light could not be seen, and using dry wood to avoid smoke. Our moccasins were thin and the rocks were hard on the feet. Shoes had been abandoned, as the noise made by them could be heard a long distance. The advance scouts kept far ahead. Several abandoned camps of the hostiles were found, the selection of which showed their constant care. They were placed on high points, to which the hostiles ascended in such a way that it was impossible for them to be seen; while in descending, any pursuing party would have to appear in full view of the lookout they always kept in the rear. The labor of the Indian women in bringing the water and wood to these points was no apparent objection.

Crossing the Aros River the trail led direct to the Devil's Backbone, situated between the Aros and Satachi Rivers. The difficulties of marching over a country like this by night, where it was necessary to climb over rocks and descend into deep and dark cañons, can hardly be imagined. When we halted, which was sometimes not until midnight, we were sore and tired. We could never move until late in the day, as it was necessary to examine the country a long distance ahead before we started. No human being seemed ever to have been here. Deer were plentiful, but we could not shoot them. Once I saw a leopard [jaguar] that bounded away with a shriek. It was spotted and seemed as large as a tiger. At last, after a weary march, at sunset on the 9th of January, 1886, Noche, our Indian sergeant-major and guide, sent word that the hostile camp was located twelve miles away.

The command was halted, and as the hostiles were reported camped on a highpoint, well protected and apparently showing great caution on their part, it was decided to make a night march and attack them at daylight. A short halt of about twenty minutes was made. We did not kindle a fire, and about the only food we had was some hard bread and raw bacon. The medical officer, Dr. Davis, was worn out, and the interpreter also unfortunately could go no further. We had already marched continuously for about six hours and were very much worn out and footsore, even the scouts showing the fatigue of the hard service. These night marches, when we followed a trail purposely made over the worst country possible, and crossing and recrossing the turbulent river, which we had to ford, were very trying. But the news of the camp being so close at hand gave us new strength and hope, and we hastened on to cover the ten or twelve miles between us and the hostiles. I cannot easily forget that night's march. All night long we toiled on, feeling our way. It was a dark and moonless night. For much of the distance the way led over solid rock, over mountains, down cañons so dark they seemed bottomless. It was a wonder the scouts could find the trail. Sometimes the descent became so steep that we could not go forward, but would have to wearily climb back and find another way. I marched by poor Captain Crawford, who was badly worn out; often he stopped and leaned heavily on his rifle for support, and again he used it for a cane to assist him. He had, however, an unconquerable will, and kept slowly on. At last, when it was nearly daylight, we could see in the distance the dim outlines of the rocky position occupied by the hostiles. I had a strong feeling of relief, for I certainly was very tired. We had marched continuously eighteen hours over a country so difficult that when we reached their camp Geronimo said he felt that he had no longer a place where the white man would not pursue him.

The command was now quickly disposed for an attack, our first object being to surround the hostile camp. I was sent around to the further side. Noiselessly, scarcely breathing, we crept along. It was still dark. It seemed strange to be going to attack these Indians with a force of their own kindred who but a short time before had been equally as criminal. I had nearly reached the further side, intending to cut off the retreat, when the braying of some burros was heard. These watch dogs of an Indian camp are better than were the geese of Rome. I hurried along. The faint light of the morning was just breaking, and I held my breath for fear the alarm would be given, when all at once the flames bursting from the rifles of some of the hostiles who had gone to investigate the cause of the braying of the burros, and the echoing and reechoing of the rifle reports through the mountains, told me that the camp was in arms. Dim forms could be seen rapidly descending the mountain sides and disappearing below. A large number came my way within easy range,--less than two hundred yards. We fired many shots but I saw no one fall. One Indian attempted to ride by me on a horse; I fired twice at him, when he abandoned the horse and disappeared; the horse was shot, but I never knew what became of the Indian. We pursued for a time, but as few of our Indian scouts could have gone farther, we had to give up the pursuit. The hostiles, like so many quail, had disappeared among the rocks. One by one our scouts returned. We had captured the entire herd, all the camp effects and what little food they had, consisting of some mescal, some fresh pony meat, a small part of a deer and a little dried meat, which the scouts seized and began to devour. I had no desire for food. Every one was worn out and it was cold and damp. In a little while an Indian woman came in and said that Geronimo and Natchez desired to talk. She begged food, and left us bearing word that Captain Crawford would see the chiefs next day. The conference was to be held about a mile away on the river below our position, and he desired me to be present. What would have been the result of this conference will never by known on account of the unfortunate attack of the Mexicans next day. It was fortunate that we occupied the strong position of the hostile camp. Our packs as well as the doctor and interpreter had been sent for, but unfortunately they did not arrive that night.

We built fires and tried to obtain a little rest, but I could not sleep on account of the intense cold, and, besides, we had been without food for many hours; in fact, we had not partaken of cooked food for days. With the continual marching day and night no wonder our Indians were tired out and now threw themselves among the rocks to sleep, failing to maintain their usual vigilance. We had no fear of an attack. At daylight the next morning the camp was aroused by loud cries from some of our scouts. Lieutenant Shipp and I, with a white man named Horn employed as chief-of-scouts for my companies, ran forward to ascertain the cause of alarm. We thought at first that the disturbance must have been occasioned by the scouts of Captain Wirt Davis. A heavy fog hung over the mountains, making the morning light very faint. But by ascending the rocks we could see the outlines of dusky forms moving in the distance. Then all at once there was a crash of musketry and the flames from many rifles lighted up the scene. In that discharge three of our scouts were wounded, one very badly, and we quickly sought cover. The thought that it was our own friends who were attacking us was agonizing and we had not the heart to retaliate, but the scouts kept up a desultory fire until Captain Crawford, whom we had left lying by the camp fire, shouted to us to stop. In about fifteen minutes the firing ceased and it now became known that the attacking party were Mexicans, a detachment of whom, about thirteen, were seen approaching, four of them coming toward the rocks where we were. As I spoke Spanish, I advanced about fifty or seventy-five yards to meet them and was followed by Captain Crawford. I told them who we were and of our fight with the hostiles, that we had just captured their camp, etc. Captain Crawford, who did not speak Spanish, now asked if I had explained all to them. I told him I had. At this time we were all standing within a few feet of each other.

The officer commanding the Mexicans was Major Corredor, a tall, powerful man over six feet high, and he acted as spokesman. Looking to the rocks we could see the heads of many of our Indian scouts with their rifles ready, and could hear the sharp snap of the breechblocks as the cartridges were inserted. I can well recall the expression on the faces of these Mexicans, for they thought our scouts were going to fire; indeed I thought so myself. At the same time I noticed a party of Mexicans marching in a low ravine toward a high point which commanded and enfiladed our position, about four hundred yards distant. I called Captain Crawford's attention to this as well as to the aspect of our own scouts. He said, "For God's sake, don't let them fire!"

244

Major Corredor also said, "*No tiras;*" -- Don't fire. I said to him, "No," and told him not to let his men fire. I then turned toward the scouts saying in Spanish "Don't fire," holding my hand toward them. They nearly all understood Spanish while they did not speak it. I had taken a few steps forward to carry out the Captain's instructions, when one shot rang out distinct and alone; the echoes were such that I could not tell where it came from, but it sounded like a death knell and was followed by volleys from both sides. As we all sought cover, I looked back just in time to see the tall Mexican throw down his rifle and fall, shot through the heart. Another Mexican, Lieutenant Juan de La Cruz, fell as he ran, pierced by thirteen bullets. The other two ran behind a small oak, but it was nearly cut down by bullets and they were both killed. About nine or ten others who were in view rapidly got close to the ground or in hollows behind rocks, which alone saved them as they were near, and formed a portion of the party that advanced. Upon reaching the rocks where I had sought shelter, I found Captain Crawford lying with his head pierced by a ball. His brain was running down his face and some of it lay on the rocks. He must have been shot just as he reached and mounted the rocks. Over his face lay a red handkerchief at which his hand clutched in a spasmodic way. Dutchy stood near him. I thought him dead, and sick at heart I gave my attention to the serious conditions existing. The fall of Captain Crawford was a sad and unfortunate event, greatly to be deplored, and cast a gloom over us which we could not shake off.

Being next in command, I hastened to send scouts to prevent the attack attempted on our right above referred to, and after an interval of about two hours the Mexicans were driven entirely away and the firing gradually ceased. They now occupied a strong line of hills, with excellent shelter, were double our strength, and were armed with calibre 44 Remington rifles, which carried a cartridge similar to our own. Our command was without rations and nearly without ammunition, the one beltful supplied to each scout having in many cases been entirely exhausted in the two fights. It was true that many of them had extra rounds, but I estimated that between four and five thousand rounds had been fired and that some of the men had none left.

The Mexicans now called to us saying they would like to talk, but they were too cautious to advance. When Mr. Horn and I went forward, to talk to them, three or four advanced to meet us about one hundred and fifty yards from our position. The brother of the lieutenant who had been killed was crying bitterly, and the whole party seemed a most forlorn company of men, and sincere in saying that they thought we were the hostiles. All their officers were killed, and I believe others besides, but how many we never knew. The fact that our command was composed almost entirely of Indians was a most unfortunate one. With regular soldiers all would have been clear. Our position at this time, confronted as we were by a hostile Mexican force, while behind us was the entire hostile band of Indians evidently enjoying the situation, is probably unparalleled. We had scarcely any ammunition, no food, and our supplies were with the pack-train almost unprotected -- no one knew where -- while we were many days' march from our own country, which could only be reached through a territory hostile to our Indians. The governor of Sonora had made serious charges against the Indians for depredations committed on the march down, and besides, there was a bitter feeling existing caused by this fight. If the Mexicans had attacked us in the rear, where we were entirely unprotected, our position would have been untenable. Had such an attack been made the result would probably have been the scattering of our command in the mountains, our Chiricahuas joining the hostiles.

It looked very serious, and my future course was governed by the condition. If it were possible I was bound to protect the lives of the white men of the command, the pack-train, and our Indian scouts. Lieutenant Shipp and I were in accord, he appreciating as I did our desperate position. The first attack had been a mistake, and the second had been brought on before the Mexicans could know what had been said to their officers who had been killed. The Mexicans deplored the affair and seemed sincere. I felt a pity for them. They asked me to go with them while they carried their dead away. A small detail took the bodies one by one to their lines, and I went with each body. They then asked me to send our doctor to care for their wounded, and to loan them enough of the captured stock to carry their wounded back. I agreed to do this, but could give them no food, which they also asked. Late in the day the doctor arrived, and after he had attended to our wounded I sent him to look after theirs, some of whom were in a dangerous way. He attended five of them.

The next day I decided to move on, as the surgeon said that the death of Captain Crawford was a matter of but a little time, and our condition made it necessary for us to try and reach our pack-train for supplies and ammunition. I was afraid that the Mexicans might take our pack-train, as it had but a poor escort of the weak and sick. Besides, most of the packers had been armed with calibre 50 carbines (Sharps), while they had been supplied with calibre 45 ammunition. I was in hopes that when away from the Mexicans I might succeed in effecting a conference with the hostile chiefs, and possibly a surrender. This could not be done while the Mexicans were near, and they would not move before we did, as they said they were afraid they might be attacked by the scouts. In order to move Captain Crawford, I had to make a litter and have him carried by hand. As there was no wood in the country, I sent to the river and got canes, which we bound together to make the side rails, using a piece of canvas for the bed.

While busy attending to the making of this, I heard someone calling, and going out a short distance, saw Concepción, the interpreter, standing with some Mexicans about two hundred yards away. He beckoned to me and I went forward to talk to the men, as I was the only one who could speak Spanish, Horn being wounded. I had sent Concepción to drive back some of the captured Indian stock which had wandered off during the fight. As I advanced toward the Mexicans they saluted me very courteously, and in a friendly way said that before they left they wanted to have a talk. It was raining and they asked me to step under a sheltering rock near by; this was the very point from which they had first fired. On stepping under the rock, I found myself confronted with about fifty Mexicans, all armed with Remington rifles, and a hard looking lot. I would here state that I had sent them, according to my promise, six of the captured Indian horses, which, however, they had not received, as they said the horses were no good, being wounded and worn out; but of this I did not know at the time. Old Concepción was detained by them. He was a Mexican who had been stolen by the Apaches when a boy, and was employed as an interpreter, as he knew the Apache language.

The manner of the Mexicans when they found me in their power had undergone a marked change. They became insolent, stating that we had killed their officers and that we were marauders and had no authority in their country. They demanded my papers. I explained that there was a treaty between Mexico and the United States, but that I had no papers, as Captain Crawford had left all our baggage with the pack-train. Their language was insolent and threatening. I now appreciated my position and realized that the consequence of my being away from the command with the interpreter was that there was no one with the scouts who could make himself understood by them. The Mexicans stated that I had promised them animals to take back their wounded, and had not furnished them, as those I had sent were worthless. I told them I would send them other animals on my return, and started to go, when they surrounded me, saying that I must remain until I had sent the mules.

By this time our Indians were yelling and preparing to fight. A few shots would have precipitated matters. The Mexicans called my attention to the action of my scouts, and I told them that the Indians evidently feared treachery and that I could not control them while away. They then said I could go if I would send them six mules, after which they would leave the country. This I promised I would do, but they would not trust my word of honor and held old Concepcion a prisoner till I sent them the mules. I demanded a receipt, which they gave, and afterward Mexico paid our government the full value of the animals.

It was now too late in the day to move, but the next morning I proceeded on the homeward march, carrying Captain Crawford by hand. The Indians, always superstitious, did not want to help, but were persuaded, Lieutenant Shipp and I also assisting. To add to the difficulty, it was the rainy season and the steep mountain sides were climbed most laboriously. It would be difficult to describe this march. With great effort, the first day we only made two or three miles. The wounded Indian was placed on a pony, and although badly hurt, seemed to get along very well. The two other wounded scouts and Mr. Horn were so slightly injured that they moved with no trouble.

An Indian woman came into camp that night and said that Geronimo wanted to talk. I concluded to meet him, and the next morning, after moving about two miles, I left the command and went with the interpreter, Mr. Horn, and five scouts, to a point about a mile or so distant. We went without arms as this was expressly stipulated by Geronimo as a condition. The chiefs did not appear, but I had a talk with two of the men, who promised that the chiefs would meet me the next day. They said I must come without arms. The next day I went to meet them and found Geronimo, Natchez, Nana and Chihuahua with fourteen men. They came fully armed with their belts full of ammunition, and as I had come unarmed according to agreement, this was a breach of faith and I did not think it argued well for their conduct. Apparently suspicious of treachery, every man of them sat with his rifle in an upright position, forming a circle nearly around me with Geronimo in the center. He sat there for fully a minute looking me straight in the eyes and finally said to me:

"Why did you come down here?"

"I came to capture or destroy you and your band," I answered.

He knew perfectly well that this was the only answer I could truthfully make. He then arose, walked to me and shook my hand, saying that he could trust me, and then asked me to report to the department commander what he had to say. He enumerated his grievances at the agency, all of which were purely imaginary or assumed. I advised him to surrender and told him if he did not that neither the United States troops nor the Mexicans would let him rest. Geronimo agreed to surrender to me Nana, one other man, his (Geronimo's) wife, and one of Natchez's wives, with some of their children, nine in all, and promised to meet General Crook near San Bernardino in two moons to talk about surrendering. With this understanding I returned to camp. In a short time he sent the prisoners with the request that I give him a little sugar and flour. This request I complied with, having in the meantime sent some of my scouts for the pack-train, which they had found and brought back. Here, almost at midnight, I was awakened by the scouts who had assembled saying that they had seen the Mexicans approaching to attack us, and that they must have ammunition. I had not intended to use any more just then, as we only had about three thousand rounds left, but they begged so hard that I finally issued one thousand rounds, though I could hardly believe this report. No Mexicans appeared. The hostiles had plenty of money and it was afterward reported that our scouts had sold them ammunition at the rate of one dollar per round.

The next day we continued on our march, which was very difficult on account of our being encumbered with our wounded. On the 17th of January, while sitting with Captain Crawford, he opened his eyes and looked me straight in the face and then pressed my hand. No doubt he was conscious, and I tried to get him to speak or write, but he could not. I assured him I would do all in my power to arrange his affairs, and he put his arm around me and drew me to him, but could only shake his head in answer. This conscious interval only lasted about five minutes, and then the look of intelligence seemed to pass away forever. The next day he died while we were in the march, passing away so quietly that no one knew the exact time of his death. We wrapped the body in canvas and placed it on one of the pack mules. We now moved more rapidly, but when we reached the Satachi River we could not cross it, as it was swollen by the late rains and was deep and turbulent. We were thus forced to go into camp and lose a day. In the meantime the body of Captain Crawford began to decompose, so we hurried on, crossing the river the next day and on the day following reached Nacori. Here we buried Captain Crawford, putting his body in charge of the Presidente of the town and marking well the place of his burial. I could only get four boards (slabs) in the town and used them in making a coffin, the body being wrapped securely in canvas.

The disposition of the people was decidedly unfriendly, and at Baserac and Bavispe about two hundred of the local troops were assembled with hostile intent. To add to the trouble, the scouts obtained mescal and were very unruly. I had to use great care to prevent a conflict at Baserac. I was obliged to pass through the town, as there was a mountain on one side and a river on the other. The officials refused at first to let me pass, but I moved some of the troops through, supported by the remainder, and avoided a conflict. At Bavispe the Indians obtained a large quantity of mescal, and the civil authorities tried to take our captured stock. I sent them out of the camp, and had they not left when they did I am sure the intoxicated Indians would have fired upon them. Here occurred a quarrel between a company of White Mountain Indian scouts and one of Chiricahuas. They loaded their rifles to fire upon each other, while the first sergeants of the two companies fought between the lines, but I finally succeeded in quelling the disturbance. The next day I hurried away, and without further difficulty reached Lang's Ranch, arriving there on the first day of February. Up to that time we had marched over one thousand miles.

I was ordered to return, February 5, to Mexico and look out for the hostiles, who had agreed to signal their return. I camped about ten miles south of the line on the San Bernardino River, and remained there until the 15th of March, when a signal was observed on a high point about twenty miles south. I went out with four or five scouts and met some messengers from Geronimo and Natchez, near the point from which the signal had been made. They informed me that the entire band of hostiles were then about forty miles away, camped in the mountains near Fronteras. I told them to return and bring Geronimo and his band at once, as the Mexicans were in pursuit and liable to attack them at any time. On the nineteenth the entire band came and camped about half a mile from my command. One more warrior with his wife and two children gave themselves up, and I now had thirteen prisoners. I endeavored to persuade Geronimo and his band to go into Fort Bowie, telling them they were liable to be attacked by Mexican troops, but could only induce them to move with me to the Cañon de los Embudos, about twelve miles below the border, where they camped in a strong position among the rocks a half a mile away.

I had notified the department commander upon the arrival of the messengers on the 15th, and on the 29th he arrived at my camp. In the interval, however, before General Crook arrived, Geronimo had almost daily come into my camp to talk to me and ask when the general would get there. On his arrival a conference was held and the hostiles promised they would surrender. General Crook then returned, directing me to bring them in. This I endeavored to do, but this surrender was only an agreement, no arms being taken from them, nor were they any more in my possession than when I had met them in the Sierra Madre Mountains. It was believed, however, that they would come in. Unfortunately, they obtained liquor, and all night on the 27th I could hear firing in their camp a mile or so away. I sent my command on, and accompanied only by the interpreter, waited for the hostiles to move, but they were in a bad humor. They moved their camp at noon that day and I then left. I met Geronimo and a number of warriors gathered together near by on Elias Creek, many of them being drunk, and Geronimo told me they would follow, but that I had better go on or he would not be responsible for my life. I then proceeded to my camp. I had ordered the battalion to camp at a point ten miles on the way back on the San Bernardino. That afternoon the hostiles came up and camped about half a mile above me in a higher position.

I went into their camp and found trouble. Natchez had shot his wife, and they were all drinking heavily. I sent Lieutenant Shipp with a detail to destroy all the mescal at a ranch near by, where they had previously obtained all their liquor. During the day all seemed quiet, but at night a few shots were heard. I sent to find out the cause and found the trouble was over some women; this trouble soon ceased, however, and quiet was restored. I felt anxious about the next day's march, as I would then cross the line and be near troops. The next morning I was awakened and told that the hostiles were gone. I caused a careful search to be made, and ascertained, that Geronimo and Natchez with twenty men, thirteen women and two children had gone during the night, and not a soul as far as I could ascertain, knew anything of the time they had gone, or that they had intended to go. Chihuahua, Ulzahney, Nana, Catley, nine other men, and forty-seven women and children remained. The herd was brought in, and only three of their horses were missing. I directed Lieutenant Faison, with a sufficient detail, to take the remaining hostiles to Fort Bowie; then, with all the available men left, Lieutenant Shipp and I at once started in pursuit.

About six miles from camp we struck the trail going due west over a chain of high mountains. This gave us a full view of the mountains in all directions, but the trail suddenly changed its direction to the south and went down a steep and difficult descent, across a basin so dense with chaparral and cut up with ravines as to make travel very difficult and slow, especially as every bush was full of thorns which tore ourselves and animals. Across this basin, about ten miles, the trail ascended a high mountain, very steep and rocky. The trail of the one horse with the hostiles induced us to think it might be possible to ride; but after reaching the top we found this horse stabbed and abandoned among the rocks; they were unable to take it farther. Beyond, the descent was vertical and of solid rock from fifty to three hundred feet high for miles each way. Here the trail was lost, the Indians having scattered and walked entirely on the rocks. No doubt our pursuit had been discovered from this point when we crossed the mountain on the other side of the basin, ten miles away. These Indians were well supplied with telescopes and glasses, and a watch had doubtless been maintained here according to their usual custom. It is in this way, by selecting their line of march over these high points, that their retreat can always be watched and danger avoided. In the same way they watch the country for miles in advance. These never-failing precautions may serve to show how difficult is the chance of catching these men, who once alarmed are like wild animals, with their sense of sight and of hearing as keenly developed.

We could not descend here, so we were obliged to retrace our steps down the mountain and make a circuit of ten miles to again strike the trail beyond. This we did, but when the stream beyond was reached it was dark, and further pursuit that night was impossible. The next morning we moved down the creek, cutting the trails which had come together about four miles below, and we followed this for about ten miles to the south. The hostiles had not stopped from the time they had left, and now had made about forty-five miles and had a good ten hours start. The trail here split and one part, the larger, crossed over the broken mountains north of Bavispe, into the Sierra Madres, while the other crossed into the mountains north of Fronteras.

The scouts now seemed discouraged. Their moccasins were worn out by the constant hard work of the past five months, and the prospect of returning to the scenes of their last trials was not inviting. Besides, their discharge would take place in about one month. They appealed to me to go no further, telling me that it was useless, etc. This I appreciated and decided to return. We then retraced our way and continued the homeward march. While returning, two of the escaped hostiles joined me and gave themselves up. I arrived at Fort Bowie on the 3rd of April. The results of the expedition were by no means unimportant as we had secured the larger part of the hostiles, seventy-nine in all, of whom fifteen were warriors.

I cannot speak too highly of the noble and soldierly qualities of Captain Crawford, killed by Mexican troops while doing all in his power to help them. He was ever ready, every brave and loyal in the performance of his duty, and his loss was indeed a serious one.

Lieutenant Shipp suffered all the hardships of the campaign, and his services are entitled to high consideration.

Lieutenant Faison showed much ability and energy in supplying the command and in handling the trains. While not with the command during the action with the Indians and Mexicans, his duty was not only a hard one, but full of danger and suffering.

Doctor Davis was very faithful and efficient.

I cannot commend too highly Mr. Horn, my chief of scouts; his gallant services deserve a reward which he has never received.

# A GRIZZLY STRIKES BACK
## (1892)

### George C. Naegle

**Editors' Note:** Pioneers not only had to contend with strange country, inclement weather, and hostile Indians, many feared the wild animals they would encounter in the West. Fierce bears, wolves, panthers, and jaguars had to be reckoned with -- or so they believed. In fact, only one animal -- the grizzly bear -- was a potential threat to human life and limb. But grizzly stories there were aplenty, and the exploits of Grizzly Adams, Bear Moore, the saga of Hugh Glass (first told by George Ruxton in 1847), and other hair-raising adventures with "The Great Bear" have become enshrined in Western legend.

The following is an eyewitness account of one of the few documented human deaths due to a grizzly. The story is unquestionably true; it was reported far and wide immediately after it happened in Mexico in 1892. Edward W. Nelson of the U.S. Biological Survey heard while he was in Chihuahua of a young Morman man being killed by a grizzly near Colonia Pacheco, and wrote of what he had been told about the event. But now, thanks to Tom Whetten and Ron McKinnon of Tucson, the following letter, written by an eye-witness immediately after the young man's death, is available for all to read. The particulars leading up to poor Hyrum Naegle's demise are carefully detailed by his brother, George, who was present during the entire ordeal. Like almost all frontier grizzly "attacks," the bear is closely pressed and wounded by a man with an inadequate weapon. The story first appeared in print as "Encounter with a Bear" in the book *The Last Grizzly and Other Southwestern Bear Stories* published by the University of Arizona Press in 1988.

Neither grizzlies nor the Mormon colonists (who had come to Mexico to escape persecution for practicing polygamy in the U.S.) remained much longer in Chihuahua's Sierra Madre. The Mormons were forced out of Chihuahua by the Mexican Revolution of 1910 and the grizzlies were killed out of the Sierra Madre soon after. Although some of the colonists eventually returned to Chihuahua, the great bear is now considered extinct throughout Mexico. Rumors of grizzlies in the Sierra Madre persist to this day, but they are creatures of campfire talk, not animals of flesh and blood.

~ ~ ~ ~ ~

**My dear brother and sister,** Joseph and Frances, Washington County, Utah:

This letter will surely be a shock and surprise to you and the members of our family in Utah and Arizona, and the pen will but feebly convey to you the sad intelligence of the fate of our dear brother

255

Hyrum, who, from the horrible wounds inflicted by an enraged bear, died last night at 10 o'clock. This news will cause you to feel with us the bitter pangs of grief at his untimely death. I now send you the whole circumstances:

Nearly all winter some of us boys have gone to the valley about fifteen miles from here, west, over the mountain on the Sonora side of the Sierra Madres, to the ranch. There we would stay the week and return home on Saturday night. On account of being so busy, and as father and some other of the boys were over at the new purchase in Sonora, we were usually there only one at a time to look out for the stock, and especially to save the calves and colts from the bears, mountain lions and big grey wolves, which have been very destructive this spring. Already over three hundred dollars worth have been lost. Brother Hyrum came home on Saturday night and said he had encountered a bear but did not get him. He also reported tracks quite thick; so we both went over last Monday; on Tuesday we hunted in different directions, and found several of our best calves gone. Then we decided to go together next day down the river Gabalan [Gavilán], back up North Creek, and gather up all the cows and calves. I believe that was the first day any of us had ridden together, the day through, during the entire spring, and even when two were there we would ride in different directions, so as to get around among the stock and over more country. As we came up North Creek driving a little bunch of cattle, on turning a curve in the canyon and emerging from a the point of a hill, Hyrum exclaimed, "There's a bear!" It was a monster, too. Instantly we jerked our guns and leaped to the ground. Hyrum had a .44-Winchester and I a .45-70 Marlin. We ran a few paces to a clearing where we had a full view and a fair chance at him. As bruin was going along the bottom of the canyon, Hyrum put in the first shot, and I the next, both hitting him. In rapid succession we fired several shots and I think most of them struck the brute. As he climbed the hill on the opposite side, my third shot brought him rolling and bawling down the hill.

Hyrum said, "that's cooked him," but he only lay a second and gathering himself up he scrambled to the top of the hill for about twenty or thirty yards and fell under an oak. Hyrum suggested, "Let's take it a-foot," and started after him, but having only three cartridges in my magazine, in the haste and excitement of trying to put in more, unfortunately, the first one caught fast, and I could neither force it in nor out until I got my pocket knife. By that time Hyrum was across the creek and climbing the hill, following the bear. I looked up and shouted to him not to follow directly after the brute, but to come in below him, take straight up the hill and come out above or on a level with him. He did so, and as soon as he reached the top he fired three shots, bang! bang! bang! as quickly as he could. I think the bear must have been on

256

the run while he was shooting, and with the third shot got out of sight over a little rise. In the hurry to adjust my gun and go there I did not look up again till I got the discharged cartridge out and others in. Both Hyrum and the monster being then out of sight, I jumped on my mule -- a fleet little animal -- and with gun in hand dashed across the canyon. Fortunately I did, for had I taken the journey a-foot, I should have reached there too late, for when I arrived on the top of the hill I could not see nor hear anything of them. I called, "Hyrum, Hyrum, where are you?" -- but received no answer, and sped on a course I thought they had gone but a few rods over a little rise, when I saw the bear above and a little along the hill side, but I could see no Hyrum. Rushing toward the bear, I could see that he had something bloody in his mouth, munching and growling. Not seeing Hyrum anywhere I feared he had him down, and my horror no human tongue can tell when I first saw his blue overall under the bear's body. He was gnawing Hyrum's hand. I shrieked, "My Lord! My Lord! he has got brother Hyrum!" The spurring up of my mule caused the brute to drop the hand and pick up his head. For fear of making an accidental shot and hitting Hyrum, or perchance the shot might not prove fatal to the bear, I jumped off the mule to make sure aim. Being then quite close, my jump to the ground frightened him, or at least instead of touching Hyrum again, or making for me before I could level down and shoot, he started off. Hyrum rolled over on his face and rose on his knees and elbows. Then I could see my brother was not dead, but oh! such a bloody sight I am unable to describe. The bear was then about thirty yards from him. I fired and brought the brute to the ground, but he got up and started again. A second shot, however, brought him tumbling again, this time to get up and turn on me; but as he turned he fell, and grabbed in his mouth a dry pine limb about the size of my arm. That he crunched as though it were a cornstalk, and with it in his mouth he started off again. A third shot brought him writhing to the earth, and as my last cartridge was in the barrel I proceeded within six feet of his head and sent it through the brain of the huge brown bear. I then rushed back to Hyrum. All this was done in half the time it takes to relate.

Now came the trying ordeal for myself. There alone, with Hyrum's mangled body, fifteen miles away from home and help, how I cried and prayed. The poor boy was still resting on his knees and elbows, with the blood entirely covering his head, face and shoulders and still streaming to the ground. The first thing I did was to support his head and administer to him, after which he cried, "Water." I galloped to the creek and brought my hat full of water, and washed his head and face the best I could. Such a mangled head and face you never saw. The skull was laid bare from the top of the fore-head about four inches back, and there was one wound on the left side, three-cornered, about two inches each way and one other wound that we did not discover until just before his death, when some portion of his brain oozed out, two teeth having penetrated the brain. On the back and other side of his head, and just at the corner of his right eye, were seven or eight terribly ugly gashes laying bare the skull. There was a long gash down the right cheek and two under the jaw, which was washed; his upper lip was half torn off. In all, there were twenty wounds on his head, face, and the right hand was chewed through and through; his left was bitten through in several places; there was one fearful bite on the left leg, just above the knee, and one heavy imprint of the bear's paw and claws, though not deep, on the right breast. Of course these wounds on his body were not observable at first, but I could see his critical state, and knowing that God alone could help us in our lonely and helpless condition, I told Hyrum to exercise all faith he had strength to do and I would again administer to him. After this he spoke, and I asked him why he went so near the monster. He said the bear got over a little rise out of sight and was lying down, and he did not see him until within two rods, when the bear sprung up and after him. His gun would not go off, though he kept it leveled on the brute, thinking every second it would act. When the beast was nearly upon him he started backwards, still trying to pull the trigger, but it failed. The bear struck him with his left paw, the right one being disabled, breaking his jaw and knocking him down. The bear then jumped on him, grabbed him by the head with his mouth; and to protect his head and face he put up his hands.

About eight feet from where my bother lay I found his hat and gun. The latter was cocked and contained three cartridges. I think, in the excitement, he failed to press the lever, and that accounted for its not going off.

After tying up his broken jaw and getting him on his horse (which I led), to my astonishment he rode a mile and a half to camp where I laid him upon the bed and washed and dressed his wounds, bandaged them in salt water cloths and give him a little milk and cold water to revive him, as he had swooned a couple of times from loss of blood. He rallied and I asked him what I should do -- go for help or try to get him home alone. He replied, "don't leave me here alone," and the thought to myself of leaving him while I rode fifteen miles over a very rough trail and returned with help could not be entertained. Again, such a thing as Hyrum riding so far in such a condition could not be hoped for nor expected. But to my astonishment he had, by the help of God, ridden one and a half miles, and I told him that same God, and He only, could give him support and strength to reach home, and if he thought he could stand the ride we would make a start at once. So I quickly saddled him a fresh horse, and provided myself with a two-gallon syrup can of water (which I replenished at Bear Spring), and with a cup and spoon. I put my coat and slicker on him, as it was cloudy and threatened rain. Then for the third time I administered to him, helped him in the saddle, made

258

a roll of a pair of blankets and a heavy camp quilt to put in front of him to support him, as I thought I would have to use these for a bed for him before reaching home.  We started at a fast walk, I driving his horse along the trail, he handling the reigns with his left arm.  This went on till dark, then I led the horse through the timber and over the mountain, and by giving him every few moments a little water, which he called for, I arrived with him at his home at 10 o'clock at night, the accident having happened about 3 p.m. on Wednesday, the 22nd.

In passing through our little town I called up Patriarch Henry Lunt to get others to assist in administering to him and dressing his wounds. I sent for Franklin Scott, his father-in-law, who sewed up the worst of the wounds, and also Sister O.C. Moffatt to assist in caring for him, and we continued from that time to apply every remedy within our reach to allay fever and keep out inflammation, etc.  We also sent word to Apostle Thatcher to come and have the doctor from Carolites sent for. We continued our prayers and supplications for Hyrum's recovery.  To all appearance and to the astonishment of every one who saw him, he went on well until yesterday, when about the same time in the p.m. that he was hurt he was taken worse and had quite a bad spell of vomiting. His breathing became heavy and difficult, and the brain began to ooze from two of the gashes in the head.  He gradually sank, until just before his noble spirit fled he made a great effort to throw off the accumulation from his lungs.  With two or three deep gasps he opened his left eye (which was not hurt), and looked as if to say "Good-bye," and died calmly and peacefully.  I think he was conscious to the last, and endured his suffering manfully, patiently and without murmur.

To endure such a ride in his condition was characteristic of his extraordinarily strong constitution.  Not a groan nor a sound did he make while the bear was on him; not one man in one hundred, perhaps not one in five hundred, could have borne what he did without complaint.  The grief of those of the family who surrounded him at his death, and especially the anguish of his young wife was most heart-rending.  Hyrum was only married in January last.  He was 23 and his widow is 19.

I desire to add our gratitude to our Heavenly Father for His tender mercy in bearing him to his home, wife and family; it is a marvel to all how I got home with him.  I tell them nothing but the power of God supported him to reach here.

Poor Hyrum has a record in the Mexican mission that will be a monument of honor to him.  He was president of the Deacons Quorum for a while, and was up to the time of his death, an acting priest and one of my counselors in the M. I. A. [Mutual Improvement Association].

I remain, in sympathy and affection, your Brother,
Geo. C. Naegle,
Colonia Pacheco, Chihuahua, Mexico, June 25, 1892

# DISASTER ON THE DESERT
## (1905)


## J. E. (Jack) Hoffman


**Editors' Note:** Tales of unfortunate explorers succumbing to heat and thirst in the desert are an integral part of the lore of the American Southwest. Even today, the desert sun occasionally claims the life of an inexperienced or ill-prepared traveler stranded in the backcountry.

One of the most curious incidents of death in the desert occurred in 1905 on the coast of Sonora, Mexico. A party of four Americans from Arizona set out to hunt for gold on Tiburon Island in early June -- the hottest and driest time of the year! They were to return in late July but months went by with no word of the explorers. Then, in late October, one of the party's members staggered into a fishing camp near the port of Guaymas, more than a hundred miles south of Tiburon Island. The full story of this ill-fated venture, as told by Jack Hoffman, the sole survivor, was first published in 1983 in the book *Tales from Tiburon*.

Tiburon, the largest island in the Gulf of California, had long been a land of mystery. It was rumored to be laden with gold, but was fiercely guarded by the Seri Indians who lived there beyond the control of Mexican authorities. Separated from the Sonoran mainland by a shallow, narrow channel, one of the many misconceptions surrounding the island was that it could be reached on foot at low tide. While Hoffman and his companions were well armed, they failed to realize the Sonoran coast's true dangers. Waterholes are few and far-between and the desert is a searing inferno during the summer months.

The propecting expedition was conceived and led by Thomas Grindell. A prominent Arizonan, Grindell had been one of Teddy Roosevelt's Rough Riders, clerk of the Arizona Supreme Court, and principal of the normal school at Tempe. At the time of the Tiburon expedition he was thrity-five years old and superintendent of public schools at Douglas, Arizona. Besides Hoffman, the other members of the party were Olan Ralls, recently arrived from Kansas City, and David Ingram, a newcomer from New York.

In September, 1905, Thomas Grindell's younger brother, Edward, a prominent Arizona businessman, launched a rescue expedition to search for the long overdue prospectors. An account of this fruitless but heroic effort was later published in April, 1907, by Edward Grindell in *The Wide World Magazine*, a British adventure journal. It too was reprinted in *Tales from Tiburon*.

Nothing is known about Jack Hoffman other than that he was a resident of Bisbee, Arizona. The origin of the following account by Hoffman is also obscure. The original handwritten manuscript in the files of the Sharlot Hall Museum at Prescott, Arizona, is undated. Much of the narrative reads as if it was taken from a diary, but there is no definite evidence that Hoffman took notes during his ordeal. Grindell's original magazine article also included a brief account by Hoffman which agrees closely with the more detailed version presented here.

The story of the Grindell expedition is a gripping, indeed terrible adventure, proving that truth can be more compelling than fiction.

~ ~ ~ ~ ~

**The Grindell prospecting party** included Prof. Thomas Grindell, Olan Ralls, Dave Ingram (a mining expert), and myself, Jack Hoffman. We started from Bisbee, Arizona, on June 1, 1905, taking four rifles, one shotgun, four six-shooters, 200 rounds of rifle and pistol ammunition per man, 500 rounds for the shotgun, hunting knives, and blankets. We took the El Paso and Southwestern [railroad] to Nogales where we secured such provisions as could not be had on the Mexican side. We rode thence to Santa Ana, Mexico.

From Santa Ana we traveled to Altar by stage where we secured a horse and a burro. About June 12 we went thence to Pitiquito where we secured four more burros and a horse with saddles. We then rode to Caborca where we remained about three days securing more provisions.

We packed the burros and traveled about 50 miles in a southwesterly direction to Rancho Leon. About June 16 we went thence about 75 miles in a southwesterly direction to Rancho de Plumas, where a Papago Indian guide was engaged to direct us to the watering places enroute to the gulf. We packed up about June 19, taking about 23 gallons of water, and traveled south to a mountain range were we arrived in an exhausted condition, having run out of water.

The water the guide directed us to was a greenish color and stank. The burros and horses refused to drink it. The other men tasted it but I refused. Tom Grindell wanted to hurry on so we filled the four five-gallon cans and the canteen (about three more gallons). After all was filled, I prospected up and down the canyon with a shovel and pick and found plenty of fine water about two feet deep in the sand. We all rejoiced at the find and emptied and refilled the cans with good water.

We proceeded south for about three days and reached Coyote Springs, so called. Thousands of dead insects and a dead coyote were found in the water. The stock, although perishing from thirst, refused to drink it. We cleaned out the hole and then the water became good. We remained there about three days.

*June 26.* The country is a beautiful level plain, miles in extent. There was plenty of game -- deer, rabbits, and quail and also mountain lion, which in the night scared our stock so that they all came to where we were sleeping. There are also antelope. Coyote Springs is only about nine miles from the gulf. We visited the gulf, two at a time, the first two days. We were about 80 miles [actually about 30 miles] north of Tiburon Island. A stranded whale was found on the beach, a large amount of the flesh and blubber having been removed by the Seri Indians. Barefooted tracks showed them to be Seris as they always go barefoot.

While prospecting about the mountains close to the gulf, we found two human hands tied to a pole planted in the ground and 12 to 15 feet high. Barefooted tracks about the pole showed it to be the work of Seri Indians. It looked like they had been dancing around the pole. The hands were sun-dried and cured, with light reddish hair -- the hands of a white man.

We packed up and proceeded south about 30 miles, traveling day and night, only stopping to rest the stock. We camped about three miles from the gulf at a low marsh. The mosquitoes were so numerous we could not rest or sleep.

*June 28.* During the night all the stock, except for one burro, broke away, although there was always one man on guard on account of the fresh Indian sign. Dolores, the guide, and Doc (Olan Ralls) headed back toward Coyote Springs, the last watering place, to hunt for the animals. Tom took the remaining burro with the water cans and also went back to the springs, we being almost out of water. He returned the next day about dark as did the guide and Olan with the stock.

*July 1.* We proceeded south and camped about a quarter of a mile from the gulf. We procured plenty of game and were feeling in good spirits, but the stock suffered for the lack of water. There was no grass, only shrubs and a green-barked tree [paloverde] loaded with good edible beans. I filled my pockets with the beans and ate them, knowing that the scurvy was bound to occur for there were no vegetables in camp. The rest of the party refused to eat the tree beans.

*July 2.* We camped close to the gulf and were almost out of water. Two burros and the horses were abandoned as they had played out and could not pack anything. The three remaining burros had to pack everything. The party here agreed to drink but five swallows each at long intervals of the water that yet remained so as to make it last. We were headed for a point opposite the island, about 18 miles farther south, where Tom represented that we could cross over to the island and secure water four miles inland [the guide, Dolores Valenzuela, returned home at this time].

We proceeded about ten miles and camped by the gulf. We were out of water. During the night I was famished for water and drank some gulf water and a cup of coffee made with sea water, with the result that I could not stand on my feet. I later got on my feet and went to the gulf and put my head and arms in the water. The party packed the three burros and proceeded on. I was about a mile in the rear and kept myself drenched with sea water, but drank no more, knowing if I did it would be fatal. I gained in strength and overtook the others about eight miles further south where we made camp on the beach about 2 p.m. The channel here between the island and the mainland is narrow.

*July 4.* Tom and Doc took a burro and water cans and tried for an hour and a half to cross [to Tiburon]. It proved too deep to wade and we were too weak to swim that far. There were plenty of large black sharks in sight -- from one to five could be seen all the time. In the meantime, Dave and I started a fire and fixed up a crude still with a copper pipe two and a half feet long. We finally succeeded in distilling a few cups of water which we divided between us. By the time Doc and Tom returned, there was only about a cupful or less for them. We kept the still working and by five in the evening we had almost enough for all -- a gallon canteen half full.

Doc took the two remaining burros (the other one could not walk), packed them with the five-gallon cans and the remaining water, and headed toward the east where, from information obtained at Altar, there is supposed to be a stock ranch 18 miles inland [Rancho Libertad, a small stock ranch on the Seri frontier, was located about 20 miles inland, but was not always inhabited]. We waited for three days and were barely able to distill water fast enough to keep us. We saved a gallon canteen full and about 5 p.m. on the evening of the third day started inland to where Doc was supposed to be. We traveled all night and the next day until about eleven, only stopping to rest and drinking but three swallows each at long intervals by agreement.

*About July 8.* We were now about 35 miles from the gulf and no ranch. We were almost out of water and agreed to drink one swallow each at long intervals. After sundown, we concluded that we had passed the ranch, if there was any ranch, and started back toward the southwest. After about three miles Dave Ingram and I lay down, unable to walk. There yet remaind about two cups of water, and as Tom could walk, we agreed for Tom to take the water and continue on in hopes he might find the ranch and assistance. We concluded that Doc was somewhere on the desert in a like condition.

*July 9.* In the morning Dave and I felt much refreshed. We concluded to go back toward the gulf. If Tom found assistance he would find us, but he may be in the same condition as ourselves. We chewed cactus, lay in the shade of a giant cactus, and traveled by night on account of the fierce heat.

*July 10.* Early the next morning we chewed more cactus for the sap it contained. We took some to the shade of a large tree cactus to last during the day. On account of extreme thirst, Dave now proposed that we cut each others arms and drink the blood. I objected, saying that if I must perish I will leave my body whole here on the desert, and besides your blood will do more good in your veins than in your stomach. If we did this we would never reach the gulf.

*July 11.*  The sun went down and I urged Dave to get up.  Dave objected and wanted to rest another hour despite the fact that we had lain in the shade all day.  Although we chewed cactus half of the time, our mouths began to swell.  We traveled slowly all night, resting about half of the time.

*July 12.*  We chewed cactus and lay in the shade all day.  We were much emaciated and since Tom left us only about 15 miles had been made toward the gulf.  It was still 20 miles more to the gulf.  Dave now proposed self destruction and I talked him out of the notion, explaining that it was yet possible that Tom might be alive and find relief.

*July 13.*   The sun went down.  I urged Dave to get on his feet, exclaiming that we could yet reach the gulf and that we could save our lives.  Dave refused to get up, saying he could not and at any rate he would have his hours rest after sundown.  I waited about a half hour and again urged him to get up.  Dave threatened to shoot me.  I watched him and waited, asking him again to get up, saying if he did not his bones would lie there for all time.  Dave again grabbed his gun. I waited and watched him, convinced that Dave was insane.  I urged Dave again with the same result.  I said, "Dave, if you cannot get up and come, I'm going.  I can't do you any good to stay with you."  So saying, I looked at the stars for direction and started for the gulf.

*July 16.*  I reached the gulf in about 48 hours.  I lay in the gulf, unconscious half the time.  Then I succeeded in getting four or five sand crabs which I ate raw.  It helped some.  I proceeded north to our last camp.  On the way I managed to get a stingaree fish with my knife in a small lagoon.  It was eaten raw.

I reached camp about 12 noon July 17, and found that extreme high tide had destroyed the larger part of the flour, bacon, and baking powder that yet remained, and all the matches except an empty pepper can full.  The ammunition was wet and full of sand, the shotgun rusty (the only gun left, the rifles having been abandoned in the desert).  The first work done was to dig the 270 rounds of shotgun ammunition out of the wet sand and dry it.  I then took rocks and built a fireplace.  While gathering rocks for the fireplace, I had to stop every 10 to 15 feet and lie in the gulf on account of weakness.  Then wood was secured.  I next took a towel and sewed it around a water bucket.  I put strips of cloth from my shirt around the edge of the bucket.  A hole was cut in a frying pan lid which was put on the bucket and weighed down with rocks.  I used the tea kettle for a boiler (capacity about two gals.).  I built a fire and put about a gallon of sea water in the kettle which I connected to the bucket with a copper pipe 3/8 inch in diameter.  While the steam was going into the bucket, sea water was poured on the outside so it would condense.  In about 30 minutes a tin cupful or more was secured, although the first time the condenser was robbed, less than one half cupful was secured.

I now prepared my first real meal in about six days, consisting of bacon and hotcakes. I felt stronger and took a bucket and secured about 10 or 15 sea crabs. It was about 5:30 p.m. and the tide was out exposing a portion of the gulf bottom about a quarter mile wide and a half mile long. I found that someone, probably Doc, had been here since Tom, Dave, and I had left and had fried bacon and stirred flour in the grease and had eaten part of it and left again. Doc must have taken for granted that he could not save his life for he had the same chance that I took advantage of. I took the shotgun and went inland about a mile for quail, doves, rabbits and secured plenty. I was still weak.

*About July 19.* Providing myself with fried bacon and flapjacks, I took my dagger and canteen of water and went inland to find Dave. The gun was not taken on account of its weight. Before I left I secured Tom's papers, Kodak, and money. I saved water by chewing on cactus. After traveling for about two nights, I reached the locality where Dave was left. The country here is nothing but giant cactus and scrub brush. I looked for Dave for about two hours. The sun came up and it became fiery hot. I remained in the shade of a giant cactus all day.

*July 22.* The sun went down and I was weak and dry and threw away the bacon and cakes. When one is too dry in the desert nothing can be eaten except raw meat and juicy fruit. I started to return without finding Dave, fearing if I lingered too long I would be unable to reach the gulf again. I traveled all night toward the gulf. Early in the morning in an exhausted condition I found five or six ripe petoya fruit [probably *pitahaya dulce* -- organpipe cactus]. This fruit is as large as an apple, juicy, about as soft as ice cream and of a fine flavor.

*July 23.* I reached the gulf about 7 a.m. and remained there until the evening of July 26. Then I packed up my two blankets, frying pan, two buckets, tin teakettle, tin cup, razor, shotgun, ammunition, scabbard, knife, fork, spoon, dagger, raincoat, tin plate, and Tom's book and traveled south along the beach, expecting to reach Guaymas some day if not killed or captured by the Seri Indians. A quantity of flour and bacon was left on account of the weight of the pack. Only about three miles were made by morning. I distilled water all day, shot plenty of pelicans to eat, and allowed myself three spoonfuls of flour per day. I stayed the night to recuperate. The first thing in the morning a tent always had to be made on account of the heat. I secured sticks or poles together with strips of leather cut from the scabbard and covered them with blankets.

*July 27.* At sundown I made two packs, taking in the first the blankets, gun, some ammunition, and the distilling outfit. I traveled about a mile, then doubled back for the other half of the pack, covering about five miles before I camped. I called this camp Petoya Orchard because there were plenty of ripe petoyas here in a large grove several square miles in extent. I remained here about four days on account of the fruit which I hoped would keep down the scurvy. My feet and legs were now bloated up to the knees from an almost entire meat diet.

*July 31.* As the petoya fruit is from six to fifteen feet from the ground, it is secured with a cane pole. Invariably the fruit mashed on striking the ground. Therefore a catch pole is made (one was found made by the Indians) by inserting a sharp stick in the end of a cane pole and fastening another stick beside it to form a V. It is fastened with sinew from a pelican wing and when dry is perfectly tight. The fruit is then secured without mashing and may be eaten with a spoon.

*Aug. 1.* I packed up and traveled over a steep mountain as it appeared that I could not get by along the gulf. While fixing up camp the next morning, I found the remains of the burro ridden by Olan Ralls. I knew the burro by the hide that yet remained. The mountain was so formed that I was misled and followed a canyon on the other side with the gulf in sight. However, it proved lucky for me as I picked up a board there 14 by 14 inches and used it for a lid on my boiler. The tin lid had rusted until it was about to fall to pieces. It was the only suitable board found on the trip. This we may call a lucky find.

*Aug. 2.* About 6 p.m. I proceeded along the gulf. The Indian signs were numerous and fresh. A promontory projected into the gulf so I therefore traveled inland. I reached the gulf again about 9 o'clock in the morning. I made camp amidst plenty of Indian signs. Nearby there were about 20 loggerhead turtle shells, two campfires, broken ollas, and low brush cabins. I remained about two days. The evening of Aug. 4 I returned to Camp Petoya Orchard so as to fill up on the fruit. I returned the morning of Aug. 6 with one half gallon of fruit. No water was taken as the fruit was all that was necessary. I didn't take the gun either, only the dagger and a large baking powder can.

Camp Cave is a natural cave where I remained about two days. Scurvy boils were breaking open above my knees now, although they were not very painful. I had lightened my load by abandoning the leather gun boot, oil coat, tin plate, extra pair of shoes, Tom's book, and the leather cartridge belt, making one pack instead of two.

*Aug. 6.* I reached what I called Camp Market as there is a beautiful butte projecting into the gulf with natural depressions which enabled me to hide so I could secure all the pelicans I needed for food without trouble.

*Aug. 7.* I reached what I called Camp Marsh Entrance about 5 miles from Camp Market. Good beach. I captured a large turtle in the act of digging a hole in the sand above high tide. I secured 48 eggs. Most of the meat spoiled, I having no way to keep it.

*Aug. 11.* Camp Lagoon is a good place where immense boulders, some as large as 14 by 16 feet, have caved from the mountain above. I

267

secured some fish in the shallows. During my stay of three days I also killed plenty of pelicans.

*Aug 14.* Swamp Center. After traveling all night until about 9 o'clock in the morning, I was compelled to travel directly west across a level plain with mud from two inches to ankle deep. Some places had to be avoided as I sank over my knees in black ooze. I reached high ground, an area about ten acres in extent composed entirely of shells about one and a quarter inches long and as thick as your little finger. There were also plenty of mangrove trees at extreme high tide. I was now, from general appearances, on an island about five miles from shore. I remained here three or four days to save up water, for in the distance to the south there was nothing but low marsh as far as the eye could reach. No trees in sight, only desert-like country. In order to get out of the mud between me and the mainland, I made two packs. The first had the gun and about one half bucket of water covered with the usual pelican pouch. In the second was two blankets, buckets, frying pan, copper pipe, etc.

*About Aug. 18.* I traveled all night and all day in the fierce heat. About 4 o'clock I became exhausted. It was about five miles to the gulf. I had about one pint of flour left and some water. I mixed flour and water in a tin cup and ate it to gain strength. I spread my blankets over the brush about 12 to 18 inches high and crawled under. It was a little better than the heat without and I rested about two hours with low white hills in sight in the distance to the west. I said to myself, "If you are sand, I've got you; if you're not sand, you have got me." I knew if it was sand in the distance the gulf was near, otherwise I knew I must perish.

About 6 o'clock I arranged my pack, put my trousers on my shoulders for a pad, and started out barefoot, as was usual when conditions permitted. I covered about two miles when I left part of the pack because I was so weak. I continued on and reached sandy country with many sandburs. I put on my shoes. Sand dunes were reached and on the other side was the gulf. I reached the shore exhausted. There were several hundred pelicans in front of me. I laid my pack down and approached as near as possible, picked out two in line and got both. I was extremely dry and weak so I therefore cut the heads off the pelicans and secured some blood. I lay in the gulf until about one or two in the morning.

I returned for the rest of the pack. I had left about a pint of water on purpose, although being dry, so I would be sure of being able to return to the gulf when I retrieved the pack. I reached the gulf about daylight and built a fire and prepared to distill more water. I was so weak I would have to stop every few minutes and lie in the gulf to gain strength. By about 10 o'clock I succeeded in having some water distilled and I ate some fried pelican. I quickly recovered strength. I distilled water most all day and then slept about 14 hours. The next morning there was nothing to do but distill water, for I never traveled by day except when absolutely necessary on account of the heat.

*About Aug. 20.* I reached an abandoned Seri village on a good beach about 6 p.m. I camped in one of their low brush-covered cabins which was about 4 1/2 feet high and 6 ft. by 6 ft. inside. There was plenty of wood and pelicans!

*Aug. 22.* I packed and traveled along a rough, rocky beach until almost daylight. There were bays also. Traveling is almost always southwest or southeast. I camped on a good beach in the open with no wood. The heat was fierce. There were many sand dunes nearby, and on top some trees and wood. Although badly in need of sleep, I packed and moved south the following night, for without shade to work in I could consume more water in a day than it was possible to distill with my crude apparatus.

*Aug. 23.* The next camp I called Dry Lagoon, it being very sandy and near what appeared to have been a lagoon. There was plenty of dry giant cactus wood, the dry ribs of which made splendid poles for supporting the blankets in making a tent. The wind was blowing 10 or 15 miles per hour, carrying and drifting sand, and it was impossible to keep it out of the frying pan. I was compelled to eat pelican with sand. I found plenty of edible weeds in the dry lagoon and I ate many raw. I did not like them but I had to keep back the scurvy if possible . My legs were badly bloated, my face also. I had a few hundred boils below my knees, white and as small as the head of a pin. I destroyed them with my thumbnail. I also had two or three large flesh boils, out of one of which I squeezed some worms, caused by the sting of a teela fly I believe. I saved some water and stewed some weeds which were more agreeable but full of sand [due to the cactus fruit Hoffman ate, which was rich in vitamin C, it is doubtful if the boils he speaks of were caused by scurvy].

*Aug. 26.* I made camp, naming it Wild Orange as there were some scrubby trees that looked like orange trees with small orange-like fruit. I was unable to eat the fruit [*mangle dulce*].

*Aug. 28.* Camp Plumas. The scenery was beautiful with an immense sand bar dividing a small lagoon from the gulf. The inlet was about 100 yards wide. South of me was a promontory. Every morning the bar was covered with thousands of sea birds of all kinds. When good daylight comes, the minnows or fry leave the lagoon and marsh, and the birds make much noise. It continues for about two hours. I was able to secure some sweet green nuts resembling acorns from scrubby trees [jojoba bushes]. Here is also a small forest of 50 or 60 acres of nothing but giant cactus 15 to 20 feet high and from 18 inches to three feet in diameter. I secured plenty of large sea crabs. They were captured by getting between them and shore in a lagoon where the water is not too deep and grabbing them. They sometimes escaped and the larger ones often drew blood with their claws, but they soon let go without much harm done.

*Aug. 31.* Camp Brook. Here about five to eight brooks or feeders come into a large inland marsh. There were plenty of quail, jacksnipe, curlews, ducks, spoonbills, and a large bird five feet high from bill to feet. It was a wading bird, black and white in color, and not a crane. I secured one by hiding in mangroves. It was very heavily fleshed and better to eat than chicken. They fly in file like pelicans. I don't know its name [probably wood ibis]. I remained here about four or five days to recuperate. Plenty of sea crabs were also captured here.

*Sept. 6.* Camp Cottage. I traveled north again to get around the lagoon, then east three or four miles, then south. I stopped under a large mesquite tree in fine shade. I would have been very much at home here with company. There was no bird life here at this edge of the marsh. I had already provided for such an emergency by having barbecued pelican breast with me. There was nothing to do but distill water.

*Sept. 9.* Camp Aqua, or water. The country is level with plenty of grass and mesquite trees near a shallow body of water about 1000 yards wide. There is fresh water here, but yellow and swampy. It made me sick at first but was very welcome. I had to remain longer at each camping place now and large boils troubled me by appearing close to my knees and ankles. There was also one on the bottom of my left foot and traveling was slightly painful. There were plenty of ducks, like teal, black and white with jet black breasts and fine to eat. I only secured one. They would fly by the hundred before I could get in range. I don't know the scientific appelation. I believe this water to be the upseepage of the Sonora River. It looks like a river but has no current.

*Sept. 14.* Camp Abandon. I reached this camp by crossing the above mentioned body of water. To avoid an accident I took the gun and ammunition over first on my head. About 3 p.m. I began a forced march in the heat of the day. There was no food here. I traveled overland toward the southwest with nothing in sight but rolling country covered with mesquite and cactus trees. I traveled all night and by about 9 o'clock the next morning I was weak and exhausted. I was traveling directly west now to reach the gulf sooner, stopping quite often to rest. I found a land turtle and cut off the bottom shell. I ate six eggs, the liver, and the lights [lungs] merely to gain strength as I was not hungry. I only wanted water. I tied the turtle flesh, together with a rabbit I had shot and eaten the liver of through necessity, to my belt.

About 10 o'clock I came to an abandoned mine inside of a low mountain range. There was some iron oxide copper ore. I was too weak to investigate the workings about 200 feet above me. There was a well about 80 feet deep but I was unable to secure any water.

About 11 o'clock I reached the gulf with my legs and arms striped red from thorn thickets, often 100 yards wide. Under the brush were plenty of rabbits. I lay in the gulf in a drizzling rain, being able to catch with two buckets, frying pan, tin plate, and cup, about two tablespoonfuls of water. At 12 o'clock the fire and still were doing fine and I was feeling all right again. The sores on the bottom of my foot and on my ankle above my heel were open and painful. I filled them with salt to cure them the sooner. I could see sails of a ship too far away to signal.

*About Sept. 18.* Shark Butte. Here the breakers made a continual roaring noise and, as I liked the noise, I came as close as possible to this promontory. I noticed that my ammunition was getting low as I had been living on rabbits, quail, doves, spoonbills, curlews, and snipes in addition to pelicans. I only ate the breast of the pelicans and I decided to kill only the largest birds. About 7 a.m. I killed a pelican about 35 feet out on the water. I jumped in and was bringing the pelican back when within five feet of shore I was pursued by a shark. The shark had likely seen me while I was swimming but when he got to me I was on my feet on account of the breakers. It passed within 18 inches of me and I could have touched it with my hand. I dropped the pelican and the breakers helped to force me to shore. This all occurred in about two or three seconds. The shark was 12 to 15 feet in length. Most sharks here are five to ten feet in length. There are black sharks only.

*About Sept. 22.* Gulf Gallery. An immense rock in the gulf connects with the mainland by a narrow neck about 40 feet wide. There is a natural tunnel through the rock north and south, about 200 feet long, 12 to 15 wide, and 12 to 20 high. There is shelf rock all around 12 to 50 feet wide and beautiful deep water. There were hundreds of pelicans.

*Sept. 28.* Pleasant View Camp was on a promontory, in a cave at sea level caused by erosion. I could look south and count 11 buttes in the distance. I decided that it looked doubtful for me to save my neck, as the buckets were rusting away and, without buckets, no water could be distilled. I had wooden plugs in two or three places already where the rust had formed holes. I gathered about 100 sea snails, spread them on the beach, and covered them four or five inches deep with light wood or cane. After the wood burned up, the snails were done brown. I tried them for future reference and they were good but nothing extra. These snails are eaten by taking two rocks and cracking them like nuts. I ate the entire lot. They are about the size of a walnut and are colored yellow and black. A few green and yellow rock crabs were also captured -- a delicacy.

*Oct. 1.* Black Bay. After traveling along the most uneven, rockiest, and roughest coast, I reached this bay of about 10 or 15 acres under the mountain. This bay extends under the mountains which form the most beautiful natural arch. I could not cross or scale the mountain here. I remained there until I was rested and then returned almost to Camp Pleasant View.

*Oct. 6.* Tunnel. I crossed a tunnel in the mountain -- I couldn't see the other end of it. The water at the mouth of the tunnel was four feet deep. One shoe from my pack fell in and the water took it into the mountain. I waited and the receding water brought it back. I camped nearby. I lived on sea mussels and snails. I had only three or four shotgun shells left. Whenever I got two pelicans in line I used a shell, otherwise I got along without pelican that day, sometimes for two days. In reaching this camp I had to cross a mountain. In crossing some deep chasms, I had to cross over without my pack and then pull it up with a rope. I found two turtle shells here with thick hide yet remaining on the edges. I warmed them in the fire to soften the hide so I could tear it off. I roasted some until dark brown. The remainder I took with me.

*Oct. 10.* Tidal Wave Camp. I camped in a cave -- there are many along here. I had my fire put out three times by tidal waves that came about 25 ft. farther than usual. I would not move for the tide was going out. On my last shot I got two pelicans in line. I picked up one, the other dropped in the water and the current took it north. About 10 o'clock I fried the pelican. After breakfast I went north a ways for the other pelican. I found it on the beach and although just shot, the buzzards had found it and nothing remained for me. At every camp lately there were from 30 to 50 buzzards sitting on the rocks and cactuses and some would come within 20 to 30 feet of me. Every part of pelican has been eaten for some time now. I began to get worried on account of my bloated condition, and feared the loss of my teeth. I killed some rattlers and a few rock crabs and roasted the turtle hide. The turtle hide, being very tough, is roasted and then eaten while traveling as it takes so long to masticate it.

At 5 p.m. I traveled inland because of the rocky coast. There were some caves in the mountains, also some Indian sign. Some deer were seen. Late at night the noise or movement of brush is almost sure to be game of some kind. I continued on, the only proper way. I followed these tactics always since losing the last man.

*Oct 15.* Rocky Cape. I camped in the shelter of an overhanging rock. My cooking utensils were badly rusted and about to go to pieces. It looked uncanny but I would not give up. I went southeast to some shallow water, with a flour sack and the dagger, in search of food. I got a large sting ray in the shallow water. I succeeded in pinning it in the mud with the knife. I got some crabs, one bull snake, and hundreds of sea snails. I fared very well considering these last few days in the desert. There are two kinds of rattlers, the sidewinder being very small was not used for food. Sails were in sight about 15 miles south. I had such a longing for company that I thought of following Indian sign. On considering the matter further, I knew if they did not kill me I could not live as they do. I continued on. I was now within about 25 miles of Guaymas, Mexico, but following the coast meant about 75 miles for me.

*Oct. 20.* This date is correct. Rounding a butte about 8 p.m. I came on somebody's camp. It was a great relief to me. There was no one in sight. There was about 1000 lbs. of salted fish covered with a tarpaulin, 15 gallons of water, and a quantity of turtle blubber. I ransacked the camp looking for flour or vegetables, but nothing doing so I fried blubber. It looked like meat but was nothing but fat. I ate it and drank the fat. Although there was a cave near, I slept on seaweed near camp.

The next morning I prepared to distill sea water, not knowing how far the fishermen had to go to get more. I found turtle flippers about camp and had breakfast on them. I named this place Camp Fisher. About 9 o'clock a boat with three fishermen slowly came into the bay. They saw me and yelled. I replied *bueno* (good). They had been in another bay fishing with spears. I satisfied them that I was not a Seri Indian spy, as I was tanned as black as they. I gave them to understand in Mexican that I had lost my partners and that I was *malo*, or in bad shape. They replied "oh no, you are *mucho gordo*" or fat. I proved to be welcome and had another good breakfast of roasted and seasoned turtle meat, parched corn, and coffee with *panoche* [unrefined sugar]. I ate more than any one of them and they could go some. One was Mexican, two I believed to be Japanese. That night we slept in a cave, the oldest slept about 1000 feet south, still believing me to be a spy and fearing I would betray them. I did not show them the boils on my legs. They told me that they had been there seven days and would go to Guaymas in five days. They remained about four days more and speared about another 1000 lbs. of fish.

*Oct. 24.* We rowed out to the channel and spread sail about 1 a.m. We reached Guaymas at daylight. First I got a shave and haircut. That night I slept in a freight wagon on the dock, being now reduced to $10 Mexican [$5.00 U.S.]. I gave the fishermen my frying pan, dagger, no-good buckets, and $2.60. I did not know how I was to reach Bisbee. A watchman on the wharf found me a place to sleep the next night among a lot of sacked goods.

I was advised to see the president of the railroad, A. G. Nobles. He asked me what I expected him to do. I replied that I belonged in Bisbee and related to him some of the circumstances. I told him I only had about $8 Mexican left. He fitted me out complete. I had no underwear or socks, my shoes were worn out and my coat and trousers as well. Mr. Walter Douglas, president of the Copper Queen Mining Co., telegraphed to furnish me funds and under the circumstances I did accept.

I was well received and was requested to remain for a time. Captain Rynning, Sargent Olds, Ranger Kidder [Arizona Rangers who were sent to Guaymas by Governor Kibbey to assist Hoffman and search for the other members of the party], and Doc Tuesaent from the 'Frisco *Examiner* came to see me. They chartered a launch and we took a seven-day trip up the gulf to the last camping place of the Grindell prospecting party. Conditions were made as pleasant as possible. We even had music on the waves. After I reached Guaymas, Walter Douglas telegraphed $500 to find the remainder of the party. The telegram came while we were on the gulf.

*Nov. 9.* I left for Bisbee. My condition was such I was unable to do anything until the following January. Before I reached Guaymas, E. P. Grindell, Tom's brother, had spent $1,300 searching for the lost party. Dave Ingram's people spent $500.

Several months later, Olan Ralls' remains were found by a party of ranchmen who were in pursuit of some Seri Indians who had tried to make a raid on their stock. I knew them by a piece of cloth.

# PANCHO VILLA RAIDS COLUMBUS, NEW MEXICO
## (1916)

### Colonel Frank Tompkins

**Editors' Note:** Ask any American history buff -- "when was the last time the American mainland suffered an attack by foreign troops?" -- and the respondent's mind will likely wander back to the War of 1812, or even earlier. Yet an American town was attacked, a number of its buildings were burned to the ground, and 18 Americans were killed by foreign troops on a single, oft-forgotten day in 1916. The event marks the last such attack on American soil, and provides as well a final chapter in the history and mythology of the West.

Debate continues as to just why the village of Columbus, New Mexico, and the small American garrison nearby, was attacked by Mexican guerrillas at 4:30 A.M. on March 9, 1916. A brief look at the events preceding the raid indicates that the most obvious explanation is perhaps the best.

Francisco "Pancho" Villa, a career bandit, rustler and horse thief, came out of the Sierra Madre in 1910 to play a significant role in the ultimate success of the Madero revolution in 1911. Upon the overthrow and assasination of Madero by the Huerta regime in 1913, Villa joined forces with Emiliano Zapata, Venustiano Carranza and Alvaro Obregón, a coalition that defeated the Huerta forces in 1914. Peace was short-lived, however, as Villa and Zapata split with Carranza and Obregón. In a series of savage battles early in 1915, Carranza and Obregón defeated Zapata, and then Villa, and chased the Villa forces into northern Mexico. For the next five years, until his truce with the government in 1920, Villa would lead guerrilla forces rather than an army. By the time of the Columbus raid, many of his "followers" were in fact peasant conscripts, poorly armed and trained, poorly mounted, and weakly motivated.

The seeds of the Columbus raid were sown in October of 1915 when the U. S. Government recognized the Carranza regime as the legitimate government of Mexico. Villa, who until that point had had better relations with the United States than had Carranza, was furious at what he regarded as betrayal. His fury was further goaded later that fall when the United States allowed Carranza to transport his troops on American rails to fortify Agua Prieta, on the Sonora-Arizona border, against an attack by Villa's forces. Villa was soundly defeated at Agua Prieta and, not surprisingly, blamed the United States. In *The Border and the Revolution*, Charles H. Harris and Louis R. Sadler reveal a letter that Villa wrote to Zapata in the winter of 1916 calling for a coalition of Mexican forces to attack the United States forces "in their own lairs." No coalition was ever formed, but an attack took place at Columbus, March 9th. "The best evidence," Sadler says, "is that revenge was the primary motivation for Villa's attack on Columbus."

Colonel Frank Tompkins' report, taken from his book *Chasing Villa*, is the best account by a participant in the Columbus fight. Tompkins was a Major in the U.S. Cavalry at the time of the raid and second in command of the U.S. garrison at Columbus, New Mexico. Like the entire book, his narrative on the raid is readable, informed, generally accurate (though Tompkins inflates the number of Mexicans, living and dead, at Columbus) and offers a sense of immediacy that only a participant can provide. There is, however, a defensive tone to the narrative, resulting from the fact that the American garrison at Columbus, despite ample warning, was caught largely asleep at the watch. Yet the American forces clearly turned the tables on the attacking Mexicans. "The best accounting," Sadler says, "shows about 110 Mexicans killed, wounded or captured during the raid and the immediate pursuit." Most of those captured were hanged. Few of the wounded survived. Sadler says, "Villa himself considered the raid a disaster."

It is often asked, "Was Villa even at the raid?" Sadler has the answer: "Mexican documents in our files indicate Villa crossed the border with 485 men and directed the attack from Cootes Hill just west of Columbus." In comparison, 266 American fighting men were stationed at the Columbus garrison.

Within a week of the Columbus raid, General John J. Pershing organized and then led Major Tompkins and a large U. S. "punitive expedition" into Mexico in pursuit of Villa. Some historians harp on the fact that Pershing never caught Villa, and refer to "one or two minor skirmishes" during the expedition. In fact, there were a number of noteworthy fights between Mexican and American troops in Mexico in 1916. At one of them, at Carrizal, thirteen Americans soldiers were killed, eleven wounded, and 23 captured by Mexican *Federales*.

It is evident from a reading of *Chasing Villa* that Colonel Tompkins was much enamored of the accomplishments of the U. S. Cavalry; a reader today can feel his pride in the mounted soldier. Writing the book in 1934 he would comment that the mounted American trooper would have his place, even in modern warfare. It was not to be. The Columbus raid and the subsequent punitive expedition would be the last major campaign of the U.S. Cavalry.

But let us now turn the narrative over to Colonel Tompkins. He was at Columbus early that morning of March 9, 1916. Elsewhere, in Europe, World War I was well underway, and motorized vehicles, artillery, and even air power were rapidly changing the mode of warfare forever. But at Columbus, mounted Mexican and American combatants would give us one last glimpse of the Western Myth.

~ ~ ~ ~ ~

**From the early fall of 1915 to the raid on Columbus, New Mexico,** March 9, 1916, the author was a Major in the 13th Cavalry, commanding the 3rd squadron and acting as executive officer of the

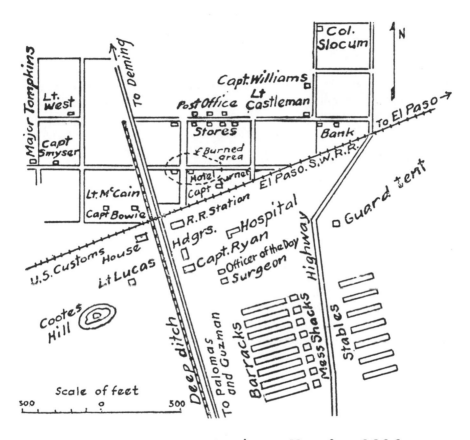

Columbus, New Mexico, March, 1916

regiment (in charge of all tactical training). My duties brought me in close and confidential touch with Colonel Slocum (commander of the American forces at Columbus). I knew of the many reports coming in about Villa; I know of Colonel Slocum's dispostions of troops and approved of all he did. On the afternoon of March 7th I patrolled about 15 miles east of the border gate. Close to midnight of March 7th I accompanied Colonel Slocum to the border gate to interview the commanding officer of the Carranzista troops stationed there. When these soldiers heard our horses approaching, they sprang to arms and took shelter designed to offer protection from attack *from the direction of the United States*. Their conduct showed all the symptoms of a guilty conscience. I believed then and I believe now they were aware of Villa's movements and intentions and I am convinced some of them took part in the attack. In this interview less than 30 hours previous to the attack, this Carranzista officer denied any knowledge of Villa or his movements.

At the time of this attack Columbus was divided into four sections by the El Paso and Southwestern Railway running east and west, and by a wagon road running north and south from Guzman in Mexico to Deming in New Mexico. The town, consisting of scattered houses and stores, was located principally in the northeast section, while the camp lay in the southeast section. The distance from the international boundary to the railroad is about three miles. The camp was bounded on the west by the Deming-Guzman wagon road, and on the north by the railroad. The region consisted of a broad plain covered by mesquite and sloping gently to the south.

The headquarters building, the shack for the officer of the day, a shack occupied by the surgeon, and the quartermaster storehouse were on the west edge of the camp on the Guzman-Deming road; the guard house and stables were located on the east edge of camp, and the barracks and mess shacks lay in between. In addition to the Guzman-Deming road another road meandered through the eastern part of camp. These roads were open to traffic night and day.

The barracks were flimsy wooden structures, the stables were open sheds, but the mess shacks and hospital were bullet proof, made of adobe (mud) bricks. The Guzman-Deming road had a deep ditch paralleling it on its western side. Beyond this ditch to the west was a knoll known at that time as Cootes Hill, named for Captain Cootes of the 13th Cavalry. Between this hill and the ditch was a 'dobe house occupied by two officers. The other officers of the regiment were quartered throughout the village but not more than three or four hundred yards distant from camp. This arrangement had existed for several years.

The Mexicans crossed the international boundary line at a point about three miles west of the border gate. They sifted across in small bands, united at a point safe from observation from our patrols, then marched northeast until within about one half mile of the American camp when they split into two attacking columns. The first column moved to the south of the camp, then east and attacked the stables from a southeasterly direction. The second column crossed the drainage ditch immediately west of the camp at the custom house, where they divided, the first half attacking the camp from the west and the second half moving into the town where they proceeded to loot, murder and burn.

Private Fred Griffen, Troop "K," 13th Cavalry, was the first man killed in the fight. Griffin was a sentinel on post No. 3, around the regimental headquarters, so he was nearest to the first point of attack by the Mexicans. He challenged a Mexican who answered by shooting the sentinel, but Griffin killed this Mexican and two others before he died. Lieutenant James P. Castleman, the officer of the day, hearing the firing, rushed out of his shack and as he turned the corner of the building, collided with a Mexican whom he promptly killed. Sizing up the situation at a glance, he ran to his troop barracks where he found his men formed. Sergeant Michael Fody of this troop ("F") describes what follows:

Just as we cleared the width of the barracks to the lane leading towards headquarters, Lieutenant James Castleman came running to me with his revolver in his hand and took command of the troop. We proceeded towards headquarters and after advancing about two hundred yards we encountered a heavy fire, so close that the flash almost scorched our faces. Instantly every man in the troop dropped to the ground and opened fire. On account of the darkness it was impossible to distinguish anyone, and for the moment I was under the impression that we were being fired on by some of our own regiment, who had preceded us to the scene. The feeling was indescribable, and when I heard the Mexican voices opposite us you can imagine my relief. As soon as there was a lull in the fighting, Lieutenent Castleman ordered the troop on towards the town, where the heaviest firing was concentrated.

To my surprise, at the command "Forward march," every man jumped to his feet without a scratch and advanced. After crossing the railroad track we had our first man hit, Private Jesse P. Taylor, who was shot in the leg. I told him to lie down and be quiet and that we would pick him up on our return. Advancing about ten yards farther Private Revielle tripped over barbed wire, discharging his piece in front of his nose, the concussion of which made his nose bleed. We made about four stands in about 500 yards. Private Thomas Butler was hit during the second stand but would not give up and went with us until he was hit five distinct times, the last one proving fatal.

We advanced and took position on the main street near the town bank, having a clear field of fire. For over an hour we lay in this position but were unable to do effective work on account of the darkness. As soon as it began to get light our ammunition was getting low. I sent Private Dobrowalski to the guard house after some ammunition; he had to get three Mexicans who disputed his way before he could comply with orders.

When the Mexicans set fire to the Commercial Hotel, the blaze illuminated the section. We were then in the dark and had the advantage. The group of which I was a member, numbering 25 men under Lieutenent Castleman, was the largest group under one command during the fight. Our forces were scattered in little bunches throughout the camp and vicinity but did very telling work. As soon as the light was bright enough we made every shot count and soon thoroughly discouraged the invaders. About 6:30 A.M. the Mexican bugler sounded "recall" and it was a welcome sound. The Mexicans began immediately to retreat. Major Tompkins obtained permission from Colonel Slocum to give pursuit.

While the sentinel on post No. 3 was killed at the start of the fight, Private John D. Yarborough, sentinel on post No. 1 at the guard house, was very badly wounded in the right arm when that side of the camp was attacked, but he fought through the entire action with his arm hanging useless.

The part played in this action by the machine gun troop is told by its gallant commander, Lieutenent John P. Lucas.

Lieutenent Lucas reported for duty to the 13th Cavalry in October, 1914, having just arrived from a tour in the Philippines. He describes his first impressions of Columbus as follows:

The town of Columbus, as seen at 4:00 A.M., did not present an attractive appearance. I found out later that it also failed to do so in broad daylight. A cluster of adobe houses, a hotel, a few stores and streets knee deep in sand, combined with the cactus, mesquite and rattlesnakes of the surrounding desert were enough to present a picture horrible to the eyes of one who had just spent three years in contact with the vivid colors and exotic atmosphere of the Phillippines.

I was assigned to troop "A," Captain Alexander H. Davidson. This troop had been sent temporarily to Douglas, Arizona, so I was attached temporarily to Troop "D," which was very ably commanded by Captain Walter C. Babcock. I served, however, very little with either "A" or "D" because in January, 1915, I was assigned to command the Machine Gun Troop of the regiment, and with that troop I remained for over two years.

Life at Columbus was not exciting. There was little to do and plenty of time to do it in. As I look back on it, however, I forget the sand storms, the heat and the monotony of existence in this sun-baked, little desert town. I forget the habit of the rattlers to occupy our houses. I forget also the fact that the nearest tree was in El Paso, 75 miles away. I remember only the pride with which I commanded my troop. Some job, too, because the Machine Gun Troop had been organized by transferring men from other troops, and it requires no unusual deductive powers to determine which ones I got. I loved them all, and the worse they were the more I loved them. They caused me considerable worry, and they were hard to handle, but they were fighting men all of them.

Three exciting events took place during my sojourn at Columbus. First, the "Golden States" passed through every day going east. This occurrence was attended regularly by all those present for duty. Second, the "Golden States" passed through every day going west. This was attended also by all those present for duty. Third, Villa raided the camp and town on March 9, 1916. This, likewise, was attended by all those present for duty.

As to the events preceding the Villa raid I hesitate to give my views. Any statement I should make would be merely hearsay, as I spent the week previous thereto playing polo in El Paso.

I reached camp at 12:00 o'clock midnight, March, 8-9, on the same old "Drunkard Special," going in the other direction this time, and went immediately to my quarters. I lived with Lieutenant Clarence C. Benson in an adobe house about 50 yards west of camp.

I found that Benson had gone to the border, his troop being stationed at the gate, and had taken all the ammunition out of my revolver. In order to reload it I had to open the trunk room, move a lot of boxes, and get some more ammunition out of my trunk. That I did this must have been due to pure "hunch" because ordinarily I wouldn't have taken the trouble; I had seen no one in camp and was not aware that conditions were at all serious. This was the second "hunch" that I had had that evening. The first had caused me to return from El Paso immediately after the last game of the tournament, not waiting until the following day.

About 4:30 A.M. I was awakened by someone riding by the open window of my room. I looked out, and although the night was very dark, I saw a man wearing a black sombrero riding towards camp. From the sounds I heard, it seemed to me he had quite a few companions and that the house was completely surrounded. I knew who they were because Villa's officers affected the type of headgear I had noticed. We heard later that this party was composed of Villa himself and 35 or 40 of his officers. They were the only ones who approached on horseback.

I got hold of my gun and stationed myself in the middle of the room where I could command the door, determined to get a few of them before they got me. I was saved, however, by a member of the guard, and I have always felt that I owed him a great debt of gratitude. Unfortunately he was killed. This soldier was posted at regimental headquarters, which was within sight of my house. He evidently saw the Mexicans approaching because he opened fire on them and they immediately left my house and charged him. They galloped right on through camp and down to the stables which were four or five hundred yards east of the barracks.

When the Mexicans left my house, I was able to get out and follow them on into camp to turn out my men. In the dark I was unable to find my boots so that I was forced to go barefooted for about an hour and a half and had very little skin left on the soles of my feet. It took me over six months to get all of the sand burrs out. The sentinel who had saved my life had gotten one Mexican but had been shot through the belly and was dying when I went by.

I reached my barracks and told the acting first sergeant to turn out the men and follow me down to the guard tent. The guard tent was near the stables and standing order required that we keep the machine guns under lock and key in the guard tent as they could be sold to the Mexicans for five or six hundred dollars apiece. Without waiting for my troop I took two men, a corporal and the horseshoer, and proceeded immediatley to the guard tent. My idea was to get a gun out and in action to keep the Mexicans out of camp. By this time the town was full of them.

So far I had seen no other officers. All those who lived in the town, and a majority of them did, had been surrounded in their houses and had been unable to get out. Two officers, Lieutenant Stringfellow and myself, lived in camp, and were the only ones present in the first phase of the conflict there. The officer of the day was required to sleep in a small adobe house in the center of camp. I had looked into this house as I passed and had seen that it was empty. Lieutenant James Castleman was officer of the day and it developed later that he had turned out his troop -- I have forgotten which one he commanded -- and marched it over to town, where he took station in front of his residence and opposite the bank.

The Mexicans were poor shots and to this fact we certainly owed our light casualty list. One of them fired at me with a rifle while I was on my way to the guard tent. He missed me even though he was so close that I easily killed him with a revolver and I was never noted for my excellence in pistol practice.

We reached the guard tent and got out one of the guns. The sentinel on post No. 1 was lying across the door of the tent. He died later. The three of us set the gun up where we could command one of the crossings over the railroad. It was very dark but we could see the flash of the Mexican rifles. They burned up thousands of rounds of ammunition. As I remember the affair, the corporal acted as gunner while I loaded the piece. The gun was the old Benèt-Mercier, a very complicated weapon, which required perfect conditions in order that it might function. The conditions not being perfect the gun jammed after a few rounds, and we left it in position and went after another. The corporal's remarks were enlightening but not printable. The jam was reduced later and the gun returned to action.

By this time the remainder of the troop had arrived and I stationed the guns in what I considered to be strategic positions to fire on the Mexicans in town. Also about 30 men with rifles had shown up, and these I deployed along the railroad track to fire on the same target. Lieutenant Stringfellow also came up about that time, and, being senior to him, I sent him with some men to protect our left flank from any further invasion from the west.

This may sound like an account of "Alone at Columbus," but, as a matter of fact, none of the officers who were marooned in town were able to get to camp until our fire had cleared up the situation to some extent. About the time I got my "army" nicely deployed the Mexicans set fire to the hotel in town. This lit up the terrain so effectively that we were able to see our tagets very plainly. Also, Castleman's move to town with his troop proved to be strategically correct as it enabled us to bring a cross-fire on the enemy. The Mexicans stood it for a few minutes only, when they commenced to fall back. Captain Hamilton Bowie was the first officer to be released and he immediately came into camp.

I turned over my command to Captain Bowie, and, taking a few men with me, worked around the enemy left into town. My idea was to clear the town and do what I could to protect the families of our officers from the Mexicans. To my surprise I found Castleman and his men there already. I had no idea of his whereabouts before. It was just about daylight when I joned Castleman and a few minutes later the Colonel appeared. I then returned to camp and, after daylight, was sent by the Colonel with 15 or 20 men to relieve Captain Stedje at the gate and allow his troops to pursue the enemy who were, by this time, in full retreat.

I was criticised rather severely in the papers, and even in the halls of Congress, for allowing my guns to jam. As a matter of fact the four guns used up about five thousand rounds *apiece* in the hour and a half they were in action, which was much more efficiency than the most sanguine had ever expected them to display.

The rumor that they had jammed was started by a private of the Hospital Corps who had been sent to El Paso with the wounded. This man could have known nothing about the circumstances because he, in company with some others of equal daring, had barricaded themselves in the hospital, and not only refused to join in the war themselves but also refused to allow some of my men to enter when the latter wished to replace a firing pin in a place where a light could be struck with safety. Needless to say the hospital was of bullet proof construction.

We were also criticised for taking so few prisoners. We did take, I believe, five wounded men and they were, I understand, later tried and hanged for murder. As a matter of fact, no quarter could be shown with safety. I, myself, was fired at by a wounded man, the bullet striking an adobe wall about six inches from my head, and I retaliated. This was not only the natural, but, I am convinced, a necessary thing to do.

I had five men in my troop on the casualty list. One of these men, Sergeant Dobbs, was shot through the liver but refused to leave his gun. He continued firing until he died from loss of blood. I recommended this man for the Medal of Honor, and, later, for the Distinguished Service Cross, but have never heard from either recommendation. One man was shot through the jaw, and three others had minor injuries. Only one man, Dobbs, was killed.

We picked up about 67 dead Mexicans in the camp and town and burned them the following day. It is impossible to say what the Mexican casualties were, but they must have been heavy because the mesquite was full of them. Few of their wounded could have survived.

There were certain incidents of the Columbus fight that were never reported officially, but are nevertheless interesting.

The kitchen shacks of the camp were of adobe construction, erected by the troops and bullet proof. The desert around Columbus was full of rabbits and quail. It was customary for each troop to keep in the kitchen a company shotgun with ammunition. This enabled one of the kitchen crew to go out in the afternoon and bring back a mess of quail or rabbits. When the Mexicans made their attack the unexpected resistance they met broke them up into small groups. The fire of the American soldiers was so hot and accurate that these small groups sought shelter behind the bullet proof kitchen shacks. The kitchen crews could hear them talking outside the kitchen windows -- so they promptly fired into them with the shotguns. Those of the Mexicans who were not killed by this fire took back into Mexico some American shot under their hides.

One group of Mexicans broke in the door of a kitchen shack. The crew were waiting for them: one cook soused them with boiling water while the other cook sailed into them with an axe. When the smoke of battle cleared the only Mexicans left on that particular spot were dead Mexicans.

Another group took shelter against a kitchen wall. They were located by one of the machine guns. The gun crew gave them a burst of fire at short range, firing low to get advantage of ricochets. Few of that party of Mexicans ever saw Mexico again. They were literally cut to pieces by these ricocheting bullets. On my return from the pursuit I took a look at this place and saw several pieces of human skull as large as my hand, with the long hair of the Yaqui Indian attached.

One soldier of the stable crew killed a Mexican with a baseball bat. As a matter of fact the Mexicans were getting it from all sides. In the darkness and confusion some soldiers became separated from their troops. These men carried on a private war of their own, shooting Mexicans whenever they saw one or more. This reception was so totally different from what they had been told to expect that the camp and the town too, was soon cleared of the enemy.

Certain individuals had experiences that are worthy of notice. Captain Thomas F. Ryan, 13th Cavalry, occupied a house on the Guzman-Deming road near the camp headquarters. Behind the house was his adobe garage. At the time of the raid Captain Ryan was on patrol duty at Gibson's line ranch. Mrs. Ryan was in the house alone. As the Mexicans rushed the camp from the west, yelling and shooting, Mrs. Ryan made an effort to get to her bullet proof garage. A Mexican grabbed her by the arm and asked, "*Adonde va?*" (Where are you going?) She answered, "Nowhere." He released her. The usual procedure would have been to kill her on the spot. Mrs Ryan entered the garage and stayed there until the fight was over.

Captain Rudolph E. Smyser, with his wife and two children, occupied a house on the western edge of town across the street from my quarters. The Mexicans battered in their front door as Smyser and his family climbed out of a back window and took refuge in an outhouse. They heard the Mexicans talking of searching the place, so Smyser and family abandoned the outhouse for the mesquite and got pretty well filled with cactus thorns in the process. No wonder Smyser was eager to join the pursuit. His troop caused most of the Mexican casualties in Mexico later that morning.

Lieutenant William A. McCain lived with his wife and little girl in a house near the southwest edge of the town, not far from the railroad track. In the first moments of the attack this house was surrounded by a swarm of Mexicans. In the building at this time, in addition to the family, was a soldier, McCain's orderly. As soon as the first Mexican wave passed, the McCain party evacuated the house, moved south across the railroad tracks, and hid in the mesquite.

When this first wave of Mexicans hit the camp, it acted as all waves act when they bang up against an immoveable mass; it receded. As this wave fell back, it passed all around the bush under which the McCain party were hiding. Captain George Williams, the regimental adjutant, who had been cut off from camp, stumbled into McCain at this moment. McCain and his orderly had between them a pistol and a shotgun. Captain Williams had his pistol. It was still dark. The retreating Mexicans were thinning out; falling back in small groups, in pairs, and singly. They would halt, fire towards the camp and then continue to retreat. Finally, an isolated Mexican discovered the Americans. Before he could give the alarm, Lt. McCain shot him with the shotgun but did not kill him. They pulled him under a bush. He struggled and tried to give the alarm. McCain did not want to shoot him again for fear that the shot might betray their hiding place. Something had to be done to silence the cries of the wounded Mexican. They tried to cut his throat with a pocket knife but the knife was too dull. They finally killed him by hammering in his head with the butt of a pistol. A horrible experience for Mrs. McCain and her young daughter, both of whom were close enough to the Mexican to touch him. Just as the Mexican was killed I rode onto the party with the pursuit column, and it was here that Captain Williams joined me.

It was also at this point that I saw something waving in the brush about 100 yards north. I sent a trooper to investigate. He reported it was a Mrs. Moore, shot through the leg. Her house was in flames a short distance away and her husband had been killed. She had managed to crawl to where I found her. I detached a soldier to look out for her. He managed to get her into camp, and later she was sent to a hospital in El Paso where she finally recovered from her wound, but the memory of her experience of that early dawn will ever be with her.

The reports of the activities of Lucas and Castleman have given a clear picture of the fighting in town and camp. The pursuit of the defeated Mexicans should be described, to complete the picture. The following is taken from the report of the author, Colonel Frank Tompkins, U.S. Cavalry, Retired, who at the time of the Columbus raid was a Major of the 13th Cavalry, stationed at Columbus.

My quarters in Columbus were situated in the western edge of the town and about 300 yards from the Camp Administration Building.

About 4:15 A.M., March 9, 1916, I was awakened by the sound of rifle shots immediately outside my bedroom window, accompanied by shouts of "Viva Mexico" and "Viva Villa." I realized at once that Mexican military forces were attacking Columbus. I dressed and armed myself and intended to join the troops in camp, but this last was impossible, as my house was surrounded by Mexican soldiers, my wife and two other women were in the house, and I could not leave them to the mercy of these bandits.

Just before dawn the Mexican troops were driven back to the west of my house by the fire of our troops, so I considered myself justified in leaving the women alone while I proceeded to camp. I arrived in camp and found Colonel Slocum with the greater part of the command occupying Cootes Hill, immediately west of the Administration building, the troops in the prone position firing on the Mexicans who were south of the railroad with their left flank resting on the railroad track, at a distance of about 500 yards. Colonel Slocum was standing in an erect position, very much exposed to the fire of the Mexican troops, but carefully observing the phases of the fight, in complete command of the situation, and an inspiration to the officers and men of his command.

Realizing that the Mexicans were whipped, I asked Colonel Slocum to allow me to mount up a troop and take the offensive. He authorized me to take Troop "H," commanded by Captain Rudolph Smyser, who had requested that his troop be the one selected to go. In about twenty minutes we managed to mount 32 men and left camp moving in a southwesterly direction. About one half mile out of camp, it not yet being broad daylight, we encountered Captain George Williams, Lieutenant William A. McCain, Mrs. McCain, Miss McCain, and a soldier. These people had been cut off by the Mexican forces and were trying to rejoin camp. They had just killed a Mexican soldier. I dismounted one of my troopers in order that Captain Williams, at his own request, might join my command.

We proceeded southwest, and in the dim light of early morning saw the Mexican column retreating south towards the border. We paralleled their march with the object of cutting off as many as possible as soon as we could get clear of the wire fences. We finally reached the border fence with the loss of one horse killed.

There was an isolated hill about 300 yards south of the fence between the Mexican column and my forces. This hill was occupied by Mexican troops, evidently a covering detachment for their left flank. We cut the fence to the east of this hill, deployed as foragers and advanced, increasing the gait until the command: "Charge!" when our fellows socked in the spurs, let out their charging yell, and swept forward, holding the alignment. The fire of the enemy went high, but they held on until we hit the lower slopes of the hill when they broke and ran. We galloped to the hilltop, returned pistols, dismounted, and opened fire with rifles on the fleeing Mexicans, killing 32 men and many horses.

Realizing that I was in Mexican territory in violation of War Department orders I wrote a note to Colonel Slocum stating that the Mexicans had taken up a postion on a ridge 1500 yards to the south of the international boundary, and asked for permission to take Troop "G," Captain Stedje commanding, in addition to my 29 men of Troop "H" and continue the pursuit. In about 45 minutes I received a reply to use my own judgement. I notified Captain Stedje to come with me. He replied that he heard firing at the border gate and would have to return there. At this moment I saw 27 men of Troop "F" under Lieutenant Castleman following my trail. I sent word to Castleman to come forward at a gallop. I then continued the pursuit and in about 45 minutes struck Villa's rear guard. I had 29 men of Troop "H," 27 men of Troop "F," Captain Smyser, Captain Williams, and Lieutenant Castleman.

We deployed at wide intervals and advanced towards the enemy at a fast trot, the enemy firing all the time but their shots going wild. When we were within 400 yards of them, finding good shelter for the horses, we dismounted, and opened fire, driving the rear guard back on the main body and killing and wounding quite a few. It may be well to state here that the men dismounted while extended, each man linking his horse to his stirrup buckle, thus keeping the animal immobile and allowing every rifle to get on the firing line and get there fast. For this kind of fighting, when the horses were in a fold of the ground but a few yards behind their riders, this method of linking enabled the men to dismount and mount with speed.

We again took up the pursuit, and in about thirty minutes overtook the rear guard. This time we tried to turn their left flank, but became exposed to their fire at close range. I received a slight wound in the knee, a bullet through the rim of my hat, and my horse was wounded slightly in the head. Captain Williams was also wounded slightly in the hand. To avoid this fire we dismounted under cover, advanced to within view of the enemy, and with the men of Troop "H" firing at the Mexican main body at 800 yards, and the men of Troop "H" firing at the Mexican rear guard with battle sights, we soon drove the rear guard back and again took up the pursuit. In advancing from this position we counted twelve dead Mexicans that had been killed from their main body.

Thinking that the Mexicans were going to take up a position on an elevation, I detached Troop "F" to flank this position while I proceeded on the Mexican trail with Troop "H." I again overtook the enemy, but this time on a plain devoid of cover. They soon saw our weakness (but 29 men) and started an attack with at least 300 men, while the remainder of the Mexican forces continued their retreat. We returned their fire until one horse was wounded and one killed when we fell back about 400 yards where our horses had excellent cover. But the Mexicans refused to advance against us in this new position.

After waiting about 45 minutes I returned to Columbus. This was made necessary by the fact that our ammunition was running low, that the men were exhausted from fighting many hours without food or water, and the horses were likewise becoming fagged as they had not been fed or watered for 18 hours and they had travelled very fast over an exceedingly rough country, under a hot sun, for 15 miles and with the same distance to return.

As a result of this pursuit my officers counted between 75 to 100 dead Mexican bandits killed on *Mexican soil*, many killed, wounded or captured horses and mules, the abandonment of two machine guns by the Mexicans, many rifles and pistols, much ammunition, food stuffs and loot which had been taken at Columbus, and most of all we took the fight to the Mexicans, all of which must have had a very depressing effect on the ranks of the *Villistas*.

I returned to Columbus with my little command, reporting to Colonel Slocum at 12:50 P.M., having been gone seven and one half hours, covered 30 miles of rough country, fought four separate rear guard actions without the loss of a single man, and inflicted a loss of from 75 to 100 killed and actually counted.

Villa, "The Lion of the North," was not only defeated at Columbus, but he at once became a fugitive from American justice, and was chased by American troops for over 500 miles through his native country at terrific cost to his prestige and power. The fight at Columbus caused his star to wane, and it so continued until he was assassinated on the outskirts of Parral in 1923.

# BIBLIOGRAPHY

## Sources

Duval, J. C. 1892. *Early times in Texas.* H. P. N. Gammel, Austin.

Earp, W. S. 1896. "How Wyatt Earp routed a gang of Arizona outlaws." *The Examiner* (San Francisco), Aug. 2.

Evans, C. E. 1857. "An authentic narrative of the Crabb massacre." *Daily Alta California* (San Francisco), Aug. 3.

_____. 1858. "Deposition." *In:* J. C. Reid, *Reid's tramp.* John Hardy, Selma, AL.

Garrett, P. F. 1927. *Pat Garrett's authentic life of Billy the Kid.* M. G. Fulton, ed. Macmillan, New York. (Reprint of 1882 edition).

Godfrey, E. S. 1892. "Custer's last battle." *Century Magazine.* Jan.:358-384.

Hoffman, J. E. 1983. "The Grindell prospecting party." *In:* N. B. Carmony and D. E. Brown, eds., *Tales from Tiburon.* Southwest Nat. Hist. Assoc., Phoenix.

Lee, J. D., 1892. "Last confession and statement." *In:* W. W. Bishop, ed., *Mormonism unveiled.* Vandawalker, St. Louis. (Confession first published in 1877).

Maus, M. P. 1896. "A campaign against the Apaches." *In:* N. A. Miles, *Personal recollections.* Werner, New York and Chicago.

McGehee, M. 1891. "Rough times in rough places." *Century Magazine.* March:771-780.

Murphy, V. R. 1891. "Across the plains in the Donner party." *Century Magazine.* July:409-426.

Naegle, G. C. 1988. "Encounter with a bear." *In:* D. E. Brown, and J. A. Murray, eds., *The last grizzly and other southwestern bear stories.* Univ. of Arizona Press, Tucson.

Oatman, L., and O. Oatman. 1858. "Accounts." *In:* R. B. Stratton, *Captivity of the Oatman Girls.* Third ed. R. B. Stratton, New York. (First published in San Francisco in 1857).

Oury, W. S. 1885. "The Camp Grant massacre." Unpublished address in the files of the Arizona Historical Society, Tucson.

Tompkins, F. 1934. *Chasing Villa.* The Military Service Publishing Co., Harrisburg, PA.

White, J. (as told to C. C. Parry and A. R. Calhoun). 1870. "Passage of the great cañon of the Colorado by James White, the Prospector." *In:* W. A. Bell, *New tracks in North America.* Chapman and Hall, London (Reprinted in 1965 by Horn and Wallace).

## References

Acuña R. F. 1974. *Sonoran strongman: Ignacio Pesqueira and his times.* Univ. of Arizona Press, Tucson.

293

Basso, K. H., ed. 1971. *Western Apache raiding and warfare: from the notes of Grenville Goodwin.* Univ. of Arizona Press, Tucson.

Bell, W. A. 1870. *New tracks in North America.* Chapman and Hall, London.

Bishop, W. W., ed. 1892. *Mormonism unveiled.* Vandawalker, St. Louis.

Bourke, J. G. 1891. *On the border with Crook.* Scribner's, New York.

Boyer, G. G., ed. 1976. *I married Wyatt Earp.* Univ. of Arizona Press, Tucson.

Breakenridge, W. M. 1928. *Helldorado.* Houghton Mifflin, Boston.

Brooks, J. 1961. *John D. Lee: zealot -- pioneer builder -- scapegoat.* Arthur H. Clark, Glendale, CA.

_____. 1962. *The Mountain Meadows massacre.* Second ed. Univ. of Oklahoma Press, Norman.

Brooks, J., and R. G. Cleland, eds. 1955. *A Mormon chronicle: the diaries of John D. Lee, 1848-1876.* Two vols. Huntington Library, San Marino, CA.

Brown, D. 1970. *Bury my heart at Wounded Knee.* Holt, Rinehart, and Winston, New York.

Brown, D. E., and J. A. Murray, eds. 1988. *The last grizzly and other southwestern bear stories.* Univ of Arizona Press, Tucson.

Burns, W. N. 1926. *The saga of Billy the Kid.* Doubleday-Page, Garden City, NY.

_____. 1927. *Tombstone, an Illiad of the Southwest.* Doubleday-Page, Garden City, NY.

Carmony, N. B., and D. E. Brown, eds. 1983. *Tales from Tiburon.* Southwest Nat. Hist. Assoc., Phoenix.

Cleland, R. G. 1929. *Pathfinders.* Powell Publ. Col, Los Angeles.

Clum, J. P. 1929. "It all happened in Tombstone." *Arizona Hist. Rev.* Oct.:46-47.

Connell, E. S. 1984. *Son of the Morning Star.* North Point Press, San Francisco.

Crosswhite, F. S. 1984. "John C. Fremont: Explorer, plant collector and politician." *Desert Plants* 6:59-62.

Cunningham, E. 1941. *Triggernometry: a gallery of gunfighters.* Caxton Printers, Caldwell, ID.

Debo, A. 1976. *Geronimo.* Univ. of Oklahoma Press, Norman.

DeVoto, B. 1943. *The year of decision: 1846.* Little, Brown and Co., Boston.

Dobie, J. F. 1939. *John C. Duval: first Texas man of letters.* Southern Methodist Univ. Press, Dallas.

Duval, J. C. 1935. *The adventures of Big-Foot Wallace, the Texas Ranger and hunter.* Steck, Austin. (First printed in 1870).

Egan, F. 1977. *Fremont: explorer for a restless nation.* Doubleday, Garden City, NY.

Faulk, O. B. 1970. *Arizona: A short history.* Univ. of Oklahoma Press, Norman.

Fehrenbach, T. R. 1968. *Lone star: a history of Texas and the Texans.* Macmillan, New York.

Flavell, G. F. 1987. *The log of the Panthon.* N. B. Carmony and D. E. Brown, eds. Pruett Publ. Co., Boulder, CO.

Forbes, R. H. 1952. *Crabb's filibustering expedition into Sonora, 1857.* Arizona Silhouettes, Tucson.

Graham, W. A. 1953. *The Custer myth: a source book of Custeriana.* Stackpole Books, Harrisburg, PA.

Grindell, E. P. 1907. "The lost explorers: the mystery of a vanished expedition." *Wide World Magazine.* April:376-389.

Hafen, L. R., and A. W. Hafen, eds. 1960. *Fremont's fourth expedition.* Arthur H. Clark, Glendale, CA.

Hafen, L. R., and W. E. Hollon, and C. C. Rister. 1970. *Western America.* Third edition. Prentice-Hall, Englewood Cliffs, NJ.

Harris, C. H., and L. R. Sadler. 1990. *The border and the revolution.* Second ed. High-Lonesome Books, Silver City, NM.

Hastings, J. R. 1959. "The tragedy at Camp Grant in 1871." *Arizona and the West.* Spring:146-160.

Kroeber, A. L. 1951. "Olive Oatman's return." *Kroeber Anthropological Papers* 4:1-18.

Lake, S. N. 1931. *Wyatt Earp, frontier marshal.* Houghton Mifflin, Boston.

Lavender, D. 1982. *River runners of the Grand Canyon.* Univ. of Arizona Press and the Grand Canyon Nat. Hist. Assoc., Tucson.

_____. 1982. "James White: first through the Grant Canyon." *American West.* Nov.-Dec.:23-28,30.

Lingenfelter, R. E. 1958. *First through the Grand Canyon.* Glen Dawson, Los Angeles.

Martin, D. D. 1951. *Tombstone's Epitaph.* Univ. of New Mexico Press, Albuquerque.

_____. 1959. *The Earps of Tombstone.* Tombstone Epitaph, Tombstone, AZ.

Miles, N. A. 1896. *Personal recollections.* Werner, New York and Chicago.

Mullin, R. N., ed. 1968. *Maurice Garland Fulton's history of the Lincoln County War.* Univ. of Arizona Press, Tucson.

Nevins, A. 1955. *Fremont: pathmarker of the West.* Longman's Green, New York and London.

Nichols, R. H., ed. 1983. *Reno court of inquiry: official record.* Three vols. R. H. Nichols, Costa Mesa, CA.

North, D. M. T. 1980. *Samuel Peter Heintzelman and the Sonora Exploring and Mining Company.* Univ. of Arizona Press, Tucson.

Page, J. 1991. "Was Billy the Kid a superhero -- or a superscoundrel?" *Smithsonian.* Feb.:137-148.

Potomac Corral of the westerners. 1960. *Great western Indian fights.* Univ. of Nebraska Press, Lincoln.

Powell, J. W. 1895. *Canyons of the Colorado.* Flood and Vincent, Meadville, PA. (Reprinted in 1961 by Dover Books).

Reid, J. C. 1858. *Reid's tramp.* John Hardy, Selma, AL.

Rolle, A. F. 1963. *California: a history.* Thomas Y. Crowell, New York.

Rusho, W. L., and C. G. Crampton. 1975. *Desert river crossing: historic Lee's Ferry on the Colorado River.* Peregrine Smith, Salt Lake City.

Ruxton, G. A. F. 1973. *Adventures in Mexico and the Rocky Mountains.* Rio Grande Press, Glorieta, NM (First published in 1847 by John Murray, London).

Schmitt, M. F., ed. 1960. *General George Crook: his autobiography.* Univ. of Oklahoma Press, Norman.

Siegel, S. 1956. *A political history of the Texas Republic, 1836-1845.* Univ. of Texas Press, Austin.

Stanton, R. B. 1890. "Through the Grand Cañon of the Colorado." *Scribner's Magazine.* Nov.:591-613.

_____. 1932. *Colorado River controversies.* Ed. by J. Chalfant. Dodd-Mead, New York.

Stewart, G. R. 1960. *Ordeal by hunger.* Revised ed. Houghton Mifflin, Boston.

Stratton, R. B. 1958. *Captivity of the Oatman Girls.* Third ed. R. B. Stratton, New York.

Tatum, S. 1982. *Inventing Billy the Kid: visions of the outlaw in America, 1881-1981.* Univ. of New Mexico Press, Albuquerque.

Thrapp, D. L. 1964. *Al Sieber, chief of scouts.* Univ. of Oklahoma Press, Norman.

_____. 1967. *The conquest of Apacheria.* Univ. of Oklahoma Press, Norman.

Tinkle, L. 1958. *Thirteen days to glory.* McGraw-Hill, New York.

Utley, R. M. 1962. *Custer and the great controversy.* Westernlore, Los Angeles.

_____. 1967. *Frontiersmen in blue: the United States Army and the Indian, 1848-1865.* Macmillan, New York.

_____. 1973. *Frontier regulars: the United States Army and the Indian, 1866-1891.* Macmillan, New York.

_____. 1989. *Billy the Kid: a short and violent life.* Univ. of Nebraska Press, Lincoln.

Wagoner, J. J. 1975. *Early Arizona.* Univ. of Arizona Press, Tucson.

Walker, W. 1985. *The War in Nicaragua.* Univ. of Arizona Press, Tucson. (First published in 1860 by S. H. Goetzel and Co., Mobile, AL).

Waters, F. 1960. *The Earp brothers of Tombstone.* C. N. Potter, New York.

Wharton, C. R., 1968. *Remember Goliad.* Rio Grande Press, Glorieta, NM (First published in 1931).